PRICING

Concepts and Methods for Effective Marketing

PRICING

Concepts and Methods for Effective Marketing

ANDRÉ GABOR
Nottingham University Consumer Study Group
Pricing Research Limited London

With Appendices by

John M. Bates
University of Nottingham

Clive W. J. Granger
The University of California, San Diego

Trevor Watkins
Dorset Institute of Higher Education

Gower

First published 1977 by Heinemann Educational Books Ltd as *Pricing: Principles and Practices*

Second edition published by
Gower Publishing Company Limited,
Gower House,
Croft Road,
Aldershot,
Hants GU11 3HR,
England

Reprinted 1990

British Library Cataloguing in Publication Data

Gabor, André
  Pricing: Concepts and Methods for Effective
  Marketing.–2nd ed.
  1. Price policy
  I. Title
  658.8'16   HF5416.5

ISBN 0 566 02703 8

Printed and bound in Great Britain at
The Camelot Press Ltd, Southampton

To my wife

Contents

List of illustrations

Tables

Preface

In this age of shifting costs and practically continuous product development, pricing has become an ongoing activity and often a source of worry to the business executive. This book, the essence of which is based on my experience in the busines world and many years of purposeful research, was written in the hope that, by presenting not only an analysis of the problems involved and detailed descriptions of the existing practices but also the methods developed to help pricing decisions, it will be found useful both in business circles and in courses of marketing studies. I should also like to believe that the chapters which consolidate the findings of my research group will be looked upon by fellow economists as a contribution to our knowledge of actual consumer behaviour.

The core of the text first appeared in book form in 1977. The fundamental views expressed in it as also in the Nottingham papers on pricing from 1955 onwards (the titles of which are listed at the end of this volume) have stood the test of time. In fact they have met with wide recognition and the Nottingham method of buy-response analysis is being successfully used in many countries.

The text of this volume has been carefully revised, improved and further enriched by the addition of new material on the contribution approach, costing and pricing in inflation, transfer pricing and many other issues, plus four detailed case studies from the files of Pricing Research Limited and two new contributions by experts: an appendix on price forecasting (which also embodies the essence of the former chapter on the Bayesian approach) and another on conjoint measurement.

I am greatly indebted to the institutions and companies which have contributed to the cost of the research my colleagues and I have carried out in the course of the last thirty years or so, or have helped by providing facilities for our work. They include the Social

Science Research Council (as it was called until recently), the Nuffield Foundation, the Leverhulme Trust, the Unilever Fundamental Research Fund, the East Midlands Gas Board, the Greater Nottingham Co-operative Society and many others, too numerous to mention individually. I am also particularly grateful to my colleagues and research associates in the University of Nottingham and Pricing Research Limited, London; especially to Professor Clive W. J. Granger, John M. Bates, Trevor Watkins and Richard W. F. Eassie, whose valuable contributions are included in this volume. I also offer my thanks to the University of Nottingham for all the amenities freely provided for our research activities.

Finally, a note about language. It is merely for the sake of brevity that I frequently use the masculine pronoun when referring to manufacturers, buyers and customers: no sex discrimination is intended.

André Gabor
The University of Nottingham
Pricing Research Limited, London

1 Introduction

Generally speaking, a firm is either a price taker or a price maker, that is to say, its attitude to pricing may be passive or active.

Where the ruling price is determined by market forces and the individual sellers and buyers are so small that they cannot expect to influence the price by their actions, each of them still has the choice between acceptance and rejection of the market price. In the short run, rejection on the part of a seller means that he is withholding his goods in the hope of a better price on a later day, either in the same market or elsewhere; in the long run it necessarily means permanent withdrawal from the market.

Situations of this type are characteristic of the markets of primary products, and occur only very seldom in the markets of manufactured goods.[1] Even in the case of many primary products, prices administered by marketing boards or other forms of producers' associations have replaced price determination by the market itself. Very often this means one price for the producers and another for the buyers, and renders individual firms on either side of the market just as powerless as if they were faced by a price determined by market forces.

A firm may be a price taker for other reasons, of which three will be mentioned here. The price may be (1) government controlled,[2]

---

[1] It occasionally happens in highly competitive multi-brand markets that the consumers cease to attach importance to the differences between the various brands and buy the one which happens to be cheapest at the time. In marketing circles this situation is described as the emergence of a 'commodity market'.

[2] The activities of government bodies concerned with price regulation fall outside the scope of this book. The institutions vary considerably from country to country and their practices are subject to frequent and unpredictable changes. They are abundantly described in the specialized literature.

(2) controlled by a price leader or, (3) in the case of a distributor, by resale price maintenance provisions.

There are situations in which a large firm has the choice between exerting an influence on the market and the passive behaviour of the price taker. To mention an example, tobacco manufacturers keep tobacco stocks approximately equal to two years' requirements. The existence of these stocks has a steadying influence on the market: the producers know that the manufacturers can afford to withhold their purchases if they consider the price too high and will buy on any individual day only as much as will not appreciably push up the market price.

This example was mentioned to remind the reader that pricing may be in the hands of the buyer rather than the seller. This aspect of pricing will not, however, be pursued further here and the discussion will be devoted to selling prices only. We shall mainly be concerned with the active price policies of business firms, the scope of which is mostly limited by the actual or expected behaviour of other commercial organizations and the relevant authorities.

In order to be a price maker proper, that is to say, to be able to exercise a truly active price policy which goes beyond the exertion of some upward or downward pressure on the market price by regulating the supply, a firm must be either a monopolist, i.e. the sole seller in the field or, at least, the proprietor of a differentiated product.

A fully-fledged monopoly can exist only if competition is non-existent or so unimportant that it may be entirely disregarded in price/output decisions. Such situations are very rare, and one of the main reasons why pricing can never hope to become an exact science is that so very much depends on the reactions of the competitors, both actual and potential.

A monopoly without competitors and not subject to government regulations is restricted only by the limitations of the market and the fundamental fact that in the last instance all products compete for the same total income. Even though the true monopolist's product has no substitutes in the technical sense, this does not mean that his sales are independent of the price which he decides to charge. Such independence may, however, occasionally apply within certain limits, especially where the product is an essential but relatively inexpensive component of an article the rate of consumption of which is dictated by other factors. Fuse wire is a typical example.

The pricing problems discussed in this book are mainly those concerned with differentiated products sold in competititve markets.

The means by which product differentiation can be achieved include distinctive quality, design, presentation, trade marks, identification with the source of supply and, last but not least, price.[3]

Price is thus only one of the elements of the marketing mix which determine the success or failure of a product, and in any actual marketing situation price exerts its influence in combination with other factors, including the intensity of the competition as it manifests itself in the attitude and behaviour of the customer.[4] Yet, apart from any consequent action on the part of the competition, – an aspect that can seldom be neglected, – price is capable of independent variation and is therefore amenable to analytical and experimental treatment. Owing to the unquestionable importance of price in the marketing mix and the fact that in the present economic situation even the pricing of established products has become a practically continuous task, it is not only possible but essential to apply such treatment.

According to an American business consultant, 'price is the *only* variable in the marketing mix that generates income, all the others, – product development, packaging, advertising and sales promotion, etc. – generate costs'.[5] While this is certainly true in a formal sense, it would seem preferable to paraphrase it, and say instead that the purpose of all the other elements in the marketing mix is to make the product sell in the appropriate quantity at the desired price, and add that if the price is not right, all the merchandising effort might be wasted. It should also be noted that since in this competitive world profit margins tend to be slender, even slight differences in price can greatly affect profitability.

It is generally recognized that what motivates the customer to buy is not so much the product as its *image*, and that apart from previous experience of the user, the image is largely dependent on the effect of the marketing mix. Let us therefore cast a brief glance at each of the main elements of the marketing mix, often referred to as *the four Ps*: *P*roduct, *P*rice, *P*romotion and *P*lace (i.e. distribution).

---

[3] An important aspect of product differentiation is that it makes advertising possible.

[4] 'I once made a list', says Garrit Lydekker of the Thompson company, 'of all the factors that can influence sales. I had forty-five of them written down before I got bored with it, I'm sure there are more.' Martin Mayer, *Madison Avenue USA*, Penguin Books, Harmondsworth, Middlesex, 1958, p. 57.

[5] Daniel Nymer, 'Does Your Pricing Pay?', *Marketing*, April 1970, p. 24.

The supreme importance of the product cannot be doubted. When asked to rank the factors that generate sales, both businessmen and their customers (industrial buyers and consumers alike) will put the product above the other three *P*s. They are quite right to do so, since a product that fails to answer its purpose could not be salvaged by any marketing effort. But even an excellent product might be unprofitable if the price is not right or the rest of the marketing mix is inefficient.

Closely connected with the product quality are *the reliability of supply and the guarantees and after sale services provided*. For industrial customers the services may include the provision of market intelligence and technical information, help towards improving the image of the customer's company, also operator training, either in the supplier's or in the customer's plant. The goodwill of the industrial buyer is a valuable asset; suitable gifts might help to maintain it – as long as they do not amount to bribes and offend legal restrictions. The supplier should do his best to serve the actual decision maker but never try to by-pass the buyer himself.

Product development is a highly relevant factor, but it is also established that very high proportions of new products fail – an aspect that is further discussed in Chapter 12.

As far as promotion is concerned, all sound marketing executives are fully aware of the fallacy of the popular idea according to which powerful companies can manipulate the demand for their products at will, because most people are so stupid that they will keep buying anything that is heavily advertised. Yet advertising can be a highly effective marketing factor in two ways. The first is that it can greatly accelerate the *initial* penetration of a new product, insofar as it can induce potential customers to make trial purchases, but if the product fails to fulfil the promise created by its image, no amount of advertising will lead to repeat purchases. The second effect of advertising comes into play when a brand has to fight for its share in a competitive market. In such situations media advertising and other forms of promotion can contribute to the maintenance of the market share, or even help to increase it. The reason why this is so is that loyalty to the supplier on the part of industrial buyers, as with the brand loyalty of the consumers is absolute only as far as a certain fraction of the customers is concerned; the rest of the sales, which often accounts for the bulk of the market share, comes from those who also purchase competitive products. It has been found that if, in such a situation, the advertising or other regular promotion on the part of an individual supplier is discontinued, his market share will gradually drop to a lower level even if the aggregate sales of the product at large remain unchanged. Motor car fuel is a typical example of such a market.

It is worth noting that another popular belief according to which advertising necessarily leads to prices that are higher than they would be otherwise is not correct either. In fact where successful promotion leads to increased sales, the fall in unit production costs often results in *reduced* prices.[6]

Distribution, that is to say, availability of the product where and when it is needed, is undoubtedly an important factor, but widespread distribution can be achieved only if the product is favoured by the final customer. For obvious reasons the channels of the distribution prefer fast movers to slow movers, even if the margin on the former is significantly lower than on the latter.

Now to *price*. First of all, the outstanding importance of price will immediately be recognized if we consider that the first two *P*s, namely *Product* and *Price*, can result in sales even in the virtual absence of the other elements of the marketing mix. Secondly, contrary to the earlier belief according to which price represents only the cost of acquisition to the customer, it also has two other functions of great importance: *price acts as an indicator of quality at the time of purchase and frequently remains an attribute of the product also after the purchase.* Effective pricing must take into account all the three aspects of price – how this can be achieved is one of the main topics with which this book is concerned. Thirdly, price is of special importance also because, in the inflationary conditions of the present, price revision has become an ongoing activity which calls for a systematic approach.

Credit terms and discounts are closely connected with price and hence deserve full attention. Credit terms have increased significance in difficult times like the present: reduced speed of stock turnover and high interest rates induce industrial customers and distributors to delay payment beyond the agreed date: 'your cheque is in the post' and 'we have mislaid your invoice' have become popular excuses. Offering generous cash discounts is not always an effective remedy: many complaints can be heard about customers who deduct the cash discount even from payments made with considerable delay.

---

[6] In their review of 56 items of the literature, Paul W. Ferris and Mark S. Albion concluded that the effect of advertising on price was an unresolved issue. Cf. 'The Impact of Advertising on the Price of Consumer Products', *Journal of Marketing*, **44**, Summer 1980, pp. 17–35.

What has helped in some instances is the friendly approach: the appeal to the common interest, leading to the acceptance of an interest charge on overdue accounts. Price variation by quantity discounts, trade discounts and cash discounts is discussed in detail in Chapter 6.

Once we have accepted the importance of pricing, the next question is how the issue should be approached. The existing pricing studies are either descriptive or prescriptive. The former are primarily concerned with the recording of the actual behaviour of firms and markets, while the latter are attempts aimed at the discovery of the principles and methods that should be followed in order to optimize the outcome of pricing decisions.

It might be thought that a properly conducted descriptive study would automatically provide the answer to the problem of optimization by revealing the principles which arise from the practices of the most successful firms. In fact, this is seldom, if ever, the case. Descriptive studies are not by any means useless: they can give insight into both the realities of market situations and the internal problems of firms. However, they could lead to universally valid conclusions only if they happened to unearth a method the effective application of which was not unduly dependent on conditions that may never occur again. For instance, the initial success of Woolworth was generally attributed to the 'no article above sixpence' principle, but when during the early stages of the Second World War shortages of its standard products and rising costs forced the company to abandon this rule, the firm flourished better than ever before.[7]

Examples of descriptive studies are listed in the references appended to this chapter. The reader who cares to consult them will find that in most of those the conclusions of which are based on information obtained from one or more of the executives of the firms covered, the information is not systematically compared with actual behaviour as reflected in the records of the companies concerned. Where such checks were applied, considerable discrepancies were found between the declared principles of the executives and the evidence of the records.[8]

---

[7] However, Woolworth suffered serious losses in later years by failing to adapt to the substantial changes in its markets.

[8] Cf. especially I. F. Pearce, 'A Study in Price Policy', *Economica (NS)*, **23**, May 1956, pp. 114–127 and I. F. Pearce and Lloyd R. Amey, 'Price Policy with a Branded Product', *Review of Economic Studies*, **24**, (63), 1956–7, pp.

Some of the investigators used an entirely different approach: they compared the variations in prices derived from available data with some preconceived theoretical model. Impressive as several of these studies are, they have not produced results that could be of interest to the businessman.

What is revealed by the available factual studies is the multiplicity of purposes and a frequent failure to distinguish between the different aspects of pricing. If there is one thing that clearly emerges from them, it is the need for the systematization of the approach, with strong emphasis on the prescriptive principles and methods. The present volume has arisen out of an attempt to fill this gap and is based on over twenty-eight years of research into pricing and the experience of the author both as a company executive and as a consultant.

The central theme of this book is that while pricing has many aspects, it cannot be fully effective unless it is customer-oriented. It differs from previous treatises on the subject insofar as it does not simply enjoin pricing executives to take this tenet to heart, but also shows how the relevant information can be collected and used in the formulation of sound pricing decisions.

The book consists of two parts. Part I is devoted to a critical review of existing pricing practices, with an appendix on price forecasting, and Part II to the methods whereby customer attitudes and behaviour can be explored and the data applied to the pricing of new products and the revision of the prices of established products.

The presentation throughout is as simple as possible. It makes use of some arithmetic but does not call for any knowledge of mathematics, except the appendices to Part I and Part II, which the non-mathematically inclined reader need not study.

49–60. Note also the findings of Bryan Atkin and Richard Skinner as reported in *How British Industry Prices*, Industrial Market Research Limited, London, 1976, pp. 43–4: out of 190 companies whose executives claimed that their selling prices were calculated on cost, 188 admitted when further questioned that these prices were not invariably maintained.

References

A selection of descriptive studies of pricing is listed below. Neither inclusion nor omission should be interpreted as a judgement on the merits of any of the works in this field.

P. W. S. Andrews, *Manufacturing Business*, Macmillan, London, 1949.

Bryan Atkin and Richard Skinner, *How British Industry Prices*, Industrial Market Research Limited, London, 1975.

Jules Backman, *Pricing Practices and Policies*, National Industrial Conference Board, New York, NY, 1961.

R. H. Barback, *The Pricing of Manufactures*, Macmillan, London, 1964.

David M. Barton and Roger Sherman, 'The Price and Profit Effects of Horizontal Mergers: A Case Study', *Journal of Industrial Economics*, **33**, (2), December 1984, pp. 165–78.

Boston Consulting Group, *Perspectives on Experience*, The Boston Consulting Group, Inc., Boston, Mass., 1968.

R. Cassidy Jr, *Price Making and Price Behavior in the Petroleum Industry*, Yale University Press, New Haven, Conn., 1954.

R. Cassidy Jr, *Competition and Price Making in Food Retailing*, Ronald, New York, NY, 1962.

Kenneth Coutts, Wynne Godley and William Nordhaus, *Industrial Pricing in the United Kingdom*, Cambridge University Press, Cambridge, 1978.

R. Dixon, 'Industry Structure and Price Adjustment', *Journal of Industrial Economics*, **32**, (1), September 1983, pp. 25–38.

Stephen C. Farber, 'Cyclical Price Flexibility: A Test of Administered Pricing', *Journal of Industrial Economics*, **32**, (4), June 1984, pp. 465–76.

John V. Farley, J. M. Hulbert and D. Weinstein, 'Price Setting and Volume Planning by Two European Industrial Companies: A Study and Comparison of Decision Processes', *Journal of Marketing*, **44**, (1), Winter 1980, pp. 46–54.

Lawrence A. Gordon *et al.*, *The Pricing Decision*, National Association of Accountants, New York, NY, 1981.

R. M. Grant, 'Pricing Behaviour in the UK Wholesale Market for Petrol 1979–80: A "Structure-Conduct" Analysis', *Journal of Industrial Economics*, **30**, (3), March 1982, pp. 271–92.

D. C. Hague, *Pricing in Business*, Allen & Unwin, London, 1971.

D. C. Hague, W. E. F. Oakeshott and A. A. Strain, *Devaluation and Pricing Decisions: A Case Study Approach*, Allen & Unwin, London, 1974.

W. Warren Haynes, *Pricing Decisions in Small Businesses*, University of Kentucky Press, Lexington, Kentucky, 1962.

Peter, M. Holmes, *Industrial Pricing Behaviour and Devaluation*, Macmillan, London, 1978.

G. Johnson, 'The Pricing of Consumer Goods', *Yorkshire Bulletin of Economic and Social Research*, **14**, (3), 1962, pp. 74–80.

A. D. H. Kaplan, J. B. Dirlam and R. F. Lanzilotti, *Pricing in Big Business*, The Brookings Institute, Washington, DC, 1958.

R. F. Lanzilotti *et al.*, *Pricing, Production and Marketing Policies of Small Manufacturers*, Washington State University Press, Washington, DC, 1964.

Andrew Likierman, 'Pricing Policies in the Texturing Industry, 1958–71', *Journal of Industrial Economics*, **30**, (1), September 1981, pp. 25–38.

R. McFall Lamm, 'Prices and Concentration in the Food Retailing Industry', *Journal of Industrial Economics*, **30**, (1), September 1981, pp. 67–78.

William J. Merrilees, 'Anatomy of a Price Leadership Challenge: An Evaluation of Pricing Strategies in the Australian Newspaper Industry', *Journal of Industrial Economics*, **31**, (3), March 1983, pp. 291–311.

R. C. Skinner, 'The Determination of Selling Prices', *Journal of Industrial Economics*, **18**, (3), July 1970, pp. 201–17.

Aubrey Silberston, 'Price Behaviour of Firms', *The Economic Journal*, **80**, (319), September 1970, pp. 511–76.

J. R. Vernon and C. W. Lamb, Jr, (eds), *The Pricing Function*, D. C. Heath and Company, Lexington, Mass., 1976.

Part I
PRICING THEORIES AND PRACTICES

OVERVIEW

In the first part of this book, we shall start with a brief critical appraisal of the elements of price theory, and then proceed from inside the business firm, discuss its various goals, their policy implications, and the role of price in the choice of investment projects.

Next, we shall survey and compare the main pricing practices: profit-oriented and cost-based pricing, paying special attention to the contribution approach. The chapter on the pricing of industrial goods will also deal with export pricing and other specific issues, including discount structures; with Appendices on transfer pricing, product analysis pricing and value analysis. Price discrimination, as manifested particularly in the practices of public utilities, pricing at the retail level and the pricing of services will be the topics of the last three chapters of this part. The consumers' side will receive little mention since it will be discussed in detail in Part II.

The Appendix to Part I on the problems and methods of price forecasting, contributed by J. M. Bates, also deals with learning and experience curves, product life cycles, pricing under uncertainty and competitive bidding.

2   The theory of price

The purpose of the traditional theory of price is to help us to understand the behaviour of producers, distributors and consumers. Like all theories, including those developed in the physical sciences, it is based on abstractions, but whereas in the field of the physical sciences the accepted theories give good approximations to the quantitative aspects of the phenomena concerned and, owing to their predictive value, can serve as practical guides to action, the same cannot be expected from the economist's traditional theory of price.

The reasons for this are two-fold. First, since economics is concerned with the behaviour of human beings, it can duly be looked upon as a branch of applied psychology, and it is common knowledge that, unlike inanimate matter, people do not invariably react to the same stimulus in the same way. Second, the abstractions on which the traditional theory of price is based are far too restrictive to justify its application, except in some rather rare special cases.

The first difficulty is fundamental to the subject-matter, and hence the economist should not be blamed for it. The assumptions deliberately introduced into the analysis are, however, a different matter; for these the economist is responsible, and since the inadequacies of the basic theory have been recognized, repeated attempts have been made to bring it nearer to reality.[1]

In its basic form, the theory rests on the following four assumptions in respect of the supply side of the market: (1) the businessman has only one aim, and that is the maximization of his total profit, both in the short run and in the long run; (2) his firm

---

[1] For a modern approach to the complexity of the problem cf. B. S. Frey and K. Foppa, 'Human Behaviour: Possibilities Explain Action', *Journal of Economic Psychology*, **7**, (2), June 1986, pp. 137–60, (71 references).

produces (or handles) only one product or, if it has several products, they are invariably produced and sold in the same proportions; (3) the businessman knows exactly what each level of output would cost him; and (4) he also knows how much he could sell at each possible price.

These assumptions immediately lead to the conclusion that the firm will increase its rate of output up to the point where any further increase would add more to its costs than to its sales revenue. This can be demonstrated both by simple algebra and by a diagram, included in any intermediate textbook of what is usually termed the theory of price or micro-economics.

Few, if any, businessmen would accept these assumptions as being sufficiently realistic for the theory built upon them to be of practical use. But before we turn to the more modern versions of the theory of the firm, let us have a quick look at the corresponding theory of demand.

Here we encounter a set of three basic assumptions, the relevance of which to real life is limited: (1) the customers are fully aware of the quality and price of each of the goods and services offered for sale in the market; (2) they take account only of the present situation and hence their behaviour is in no way influenced either by the events of the past or by expectations of the future; and (3) if they are consumers, they will distribute their expenditure so that their purchases should give them the maximum possible satisfaction, but if they are businessmen, they will buy with the maximum amount of profit in mind.

These considerations lead to the concept of what is known as the law of demand, according to which the customer will always buy more at a lower price than at a higher price.[2] Its algebraic expression is the demand function; its diagrammatic representation is the demand curve, illustrated in Figure 2.1.

Price elasticity of demand

A great deal of evidence exists to support the proposition that an individual's reactions to price changes depend on the relative magnitude of the differences concerned rather than on their absolute

---

[2] The exceptions to this rule are discussed in Chapter 11, in connection with the modern view of consumers' choice.

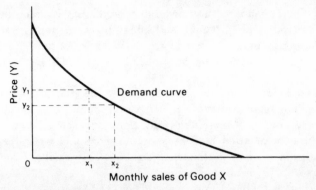

Figure 2.1   Demand curve

value.[3] It is therefore appropriate to record price differences as ratios or percentages, and to measure the resultant variation in the rate of purchases in the same way. This idea is at the bottom of the concept of the *price elasticity of demand*. It can be defined as:

Price elasticity of demand =

$$\frac{\text{Percentage change in the rate of purchases}}{\text{Percentage change in the price}},$$

or, using the terminology of Fig. 2.1:

$$E = \frac{x_2 - x_1}{x_1} \bigg/ \frac{y_2 - y_1}{y_1}.$$

The elasticity concept is useful in discussing certain fundamental relationships. For example, if the individual firm is so small in relation to the market that it can sell at the prevailing price any quantity it is able to produce, this can conveniently be summed up by stating that the elasticity of demand for the firm's product is infinity.

In the case of a monopoly that has no competitors worth speaking

---

[3] In other words, it is the percentage change in price that matters: the significance of a price increase of 5p, say, depends on whether the original price was 10p or £5. This leads to the contention that the individual's subjective price scale is a ratio scale, also called a logarithmic scale. On such a scale equal distances represent equal percentage changes. The proposition is closely related to the Weber-Fechner law of experimental psychology. Cf. R. A. Batchelor, 'The Psychophysics of Inflation', *Journal of Economic Psychology*, **7**, (3), September 1986, pp. 272–3.

of, the consequences of a price change can fully be attributed to its customers' reactions. This means that its demand is less than infinitely elastic and, in the extreme case, it may even be perfectly inelastic over a limited range, meaning that price changes within the limits of that range leave the quantity sold unaffected.

In between these two extreme cases there is a further benchmark by which the significance of elasticity can be judged. This benchmark is unit elasticity, which means that changes in the price are exactly compensated by opposite changes in the number of units sold, so that total gross sales returns remain unaffected when the price is increased or decreased. For example, if the price of the product is reduced from 21p to 20p per unit, and in consequence of this price reduction the quantity sold per week rises from 800 units to 840 units, the weekly sales revenue will remain unchanged at £168.

If elasticity is between 0 and -1,[4] this is equivalent to saying that a price reduction could not possibly be profitable because even though it would increase the quantity sold, there would be a fall in the total sales revenue. It follows that, in the absence of other considerations, wherever elasticity is between 0 and -1, profitability should increase if the price were raised.

If elasticity is numerically greater than unity, (say -1.4), a price reduction would increase total sales revenue and, unless total costs increase by as much or more than the returns, this would also enhance total profits.

Theoretical economists are apt to assert that businessmen ought to be interested in the elasticity of the demand for their product. Any knowledge of the extent to which the market would react to a price change is of course of considerable value to the price setter, but it is easy to show why the elasticity concept has not been found particularly appropriate for this purpose.[5]

Let us assume that large-scale test marketing at various prices has yielded these results:

---

[4] Elasticity is always negative where a *fall* in price results in a *rise* in the quanity sold.

[5] A related concept has, however, proved itself useful for judging the comparative sensitivity of the potential demand as estimated by a highly practical method of modern market research. This application is described below in Chapter 13, pp. 303–4.

Estimated monthly sales of Product X

Price	range	average
pence	units	units
20	380–420	400
19	410–450	430
18	455–505	480
17	550–610	580

Expressing the changes in terms of the elasticity concept, we find that:

Reducing price from 20p by	*should increase average sales by*	*hence the price elasticities are*
1p (5%)	30 units (7.5%)	−1.5
2p (10%)	80 units (20%)	−2.0
3p (15%)	180 units (45%)	−3.0

The example shows that there is no such thing as *the* elasticity of demand for a good, since even if we start from a given price, elasticity will tend to vary with the magnitude of the price change. Even more important is the fact that whereas the figures in the first table contain data of immediate use to the price maker, the elasticities derived from them in the second table conceal rather than reveal the essence of the information, and the accuracy which they imply is, of course, highly spurious. It should further be noted that there also exist several other formulae for computing elasticities which give different values.[6]

One of the accepted formulae is that of point elasticity. It has been used to derive demand functions from sales data, but since it involves two unrealistic assumptions, namely that changes in price and quantity proceed by infinitesimally small steps, and that the elasticity remains constant throughout the observed price range, it is hardly surprising that the results have not been found useful by pricing executives.[7]

---

[6] Cf. André Gabor, 'The Theory of Constant Arc Elasticity Functions', *Bulletin of Economic Research*, **26**, (2), November 1974, pp. 114–27, and 'A Further Note on Arc Elasticity', *op. cit*, **28**, (2), November 1976, p. 127.

[7] The applications of the technique for business purposes as also its limitations are well explained in Roswell H. Whitman of R. H. Macy & Co, 'Demand Functions for Merchandise at Retail' in *Studies in Mathematical Economics and Econometrics*, (Oscar Lange *et al.*, eds.), University of Chicago Press, 1942, pp. 208–21. Cf. also Douglas J. Dalrymple, 'Estimating Price Elasticity', *Journal of Retailing*, Winter 1966–7, pp. 1–4; Henry Theil, *Theory*

Using mass consumption data extending over long series of years, econometricians have attempted with varying success to determine the long-run elasticity of demand for some broad product categories, such as, e.g., wheat, eggs, tea, sugar, butter and beer. In this kind of analysis the effects of changes in income, tastes and the size of the population can be separated, and the results may sometimes be of use to government planning but only seldom, if ever, to businessmen. Apart from the fact that the information is inevitably more related to the past than to the present, the main reason is that the tendencies observed have validity only as far as the product category as a whole is concerned. However, an individual firm may experience shrinking sales in an expanding market and increasing sales when the market as a whole is contracting. The automobile market has provided examples of both phenomena in recent times: the sales of some British producers were shrinking both in their home market and abroad even when the markets themselves were expanding. On the other hand, the growth of the sales of Japanese automobiles went on after the total sales of all makes started to fall.

So much for the basic theories of supply and demand. The more modern theories do recognize the fact that businessmen may not be interested in profit alone but also in the extent and growth of their sales, market share, inventory position, liquidity, prestige, labour relations, etc., and that the customer's choice is influenced by a multiplicity of factors, including his social standing, the opinion of his friends, advertisements, shop displays, etc. Also, according to a popular theory that contains a solid core of realism, businessmen stop in their efforts to reach an improved solution to the problem in hand as soon as they have approximated their aim to a reasonable

and Measurement of Consumer Demand, (2 vols.), North Holland Publishing Company, Amsterdam and New York, 1976; Douglas J. Dalrymple and George H. Haines, Jr, 'A Study of the Predictive Ability of Market Period Demand', *Applied Economics*, **1**, (4), January 1970, pp. 277–85; W. J. Baumol, 'On Empirical Determination of Demand Relationships', *Economic Theory and Operations Analysis*, 3rd ed., Prentice-Hall, Inc., Englewood Cliffs, NJ, 1972, pp. 234–54; J. C. Driver, 'Price Elasticity Estimates by Quasi-Experiment', *Applied Economics*, **11**, (2), June 1979, pp. 147–55; S. A. Neslin and R. W. Shoemaker, 'Using a Natural Experiment to Estimate Price Elasticity: The 1974 Sugar Shortage and the Ready-to-Eat Cereal Market', *Journal of Marketing*, **47**, (1), Winter 1983, pp. 44–56; and M. J. Driscoll, J. L. Ford and A. W. Mullineux, 'The Elasticity of Prices with Regard to Monetary Components: Some Estimates for the UK 1948–79', *Applied Economics*, **17**, (1), April 1985, pp. 95–106.

extent. Their behaviour is said to be 'satisficing' rather than optimizing.[8]

As far as the consumers are concerned, what might, perhaps, be called the counterpart of the 'satisficing' theory of business behaviour is the observation that much of the consumers' purchasing behaviour appears to be simply repetitive rather than consciously striving for maximum satisfaction.[9]

Yet another, somewhat earlier theory, which has given rise to much discussion, suggests that when exposed to a few easily identifiable competitors (a situation called *oligopoly* by economists) prices will be fixed by adding a customary profit margin to the costs, and that once a price has been so arrived at, it will tend to remain unchanged. The reason for this alleged rigidity is said to be the belief that a price cut would immediately be followed by the main competitors, and the market as a whole would not expand sufficiently to make the lower prices worthwhile. Each firm in this situation is also supposed to fear that if it should increase its price, the others would not follow suit and that hence it would lose a high proportion of its customers.[10]

Since the purpose of the proposers of these theories was not to provide guidance either to producers or to consumers but merely to rationalize their behaviour, it is small wonder that the business

---

[8] Herbert A. Simon, 'A Behavioral Model of Rational Choice', *Quarterly Journal of Economics*, **64**, 1955, pp. 99–118; Richard M. Cyert *et al.*, *A Behavioral Theory of the Firm*, Prentice-Hall, Englewood Cliffs, NJ, 1963; *Prices: Issues in Theory, Practice and Public Policy*, (A. Phillips and O. E. Williamson, eds), University of Pennsylvania Press, Philadelphia, Pa., 1967.

[9] G. Katona, 'Repetitiousness and Variability of Consumer Behaviour', *Human Relations*, **12**, 1959, pp. 35–49, and *The Powerful Consumer*, McGraw-Hill, New York, 1960, pp. 139–42, where also much of business behaviour is claimed to be repetitive and not problem solving. For other modifications of the basic theory cf. Frey and Foppa (1986) quoted in note 1 above.

[10] R. L. Hall and C. J. Hitch, 'Price Theory and Business Behaviour', *Oxford Economic Papers*, **2**, May 1939, pp. 12–45; P. W. S. Andrews, *Manufacturing Business*, Macmillan, London, 1949; F. Machlup, 'Marginal Analysis and Empirical Research', *American Economic Review*, **36**, September 1946, pp. 519–54; Austin Robinson, 'The Pricing of Manufactured Products', *Economic Journal*, **60**, December 1950, pp. 771–80; R. S. Edwards, 'The Pricing of Manufactured Products', *Economica, (NS)*, **19**, (75), August 1952, pp. 298–307.

world has not taken much interest in them. As aptly remarked by Monroe and Della Bitta,

> There is an elegant tradition of pricing models in economic theory, but these models do not provide operational rules for management to follow. Moreover, the reality of the economists' pricing models is questionable.[11]

One might have hoped for a rather more practical approach from the contributors to the proceedings of the 1982 Conference on Pricing Strategy, but having seen the papers, it is impossible not to agree with Nagle's comment:

> Economic theory is just that – theory. No economic model captures the full richness of a practical pricing problem or sets out a complete prescription for solving it. Even with an understanding of economic theory, marketers are still left with the problem of how to price products.[12]

Pricing policies have, however, materially benefited from the application of certain modern methods based not on abstractions but on the realities of pricing issues. They and the specific theories to which they have led are described in some of later chapters of this book.

Summary

The brief review of the main concepts and theories of price formation contained in this chapter leads to the conclusion that, valuable as they may be for the understanding of certain fundamental economic relationships, there are weighty reasons why they are not suitable for the solution of practical pricing problems. This applies particularly to the popular concept of the price elasticity of demand. Some elements of economic theory will, however, be discussed further in subsequent chapters, but only to the extent to which they are relevant to our purposes.

The issue has been approached in the context of the market, where supply and demand meet, and exchange takes place. In the

---

[11] Kent B. Monroe and Albert J. Della Bitta, 'Models for Pricing Decisions', *Journal of Marketing Research*, **15**, August 1978, p. 426.

[12] Thomas Nagle, 'Economic Foundations for Pricing', *The Journal of Business*, **57**, (1), Part 2, January 1984, pp. S22–S23. This issue contains all the papers presented at the conference.

next chapters we shall examine the supply side in considerable detail, starting with a scrutiny of the manifold aims of business activity and the observed behaviour of businessmen, without, however, losing sight of the importance of the demand.

3 Business goals and behaviour

Pricing should serve the basic goals of the firm, and it is therefore appropriate to examine them and the ways in which they influence business behaviour in general and pricing in particular.

It is generally agreed that the fundamental purpose of a business enterprise is to make money for its owners, but the idea that businessmen maximize their profits all the time, or even that they constantly strive for the highest attainable profits is certainly an exaggeration. To say that it is proper for a business to prefer larger profits to smaller profits does not mean that all other considerations, such as a reputation for honesty and reliability, the conditions of the workforce, etc., should be altogether neglected. Not even the most abstract theory denies that most, if not all, businessmen act within the law and observe the conventions of the community. Yet it is easy to see that profitability is of overriding importance and that any businessman who neglects it is doing so at grave risk to his own future and that of his firm. In fact, most other aims, such as, for example, increased sales and a favourable inventory position can be identified as the means whereby profitability can be enhanced, while yet others, such as prestige, improving labour relations, etc., are impossible to pursue in the long run if the firm is not working profitably. Looking at it another way, it may safely be said that a firm which has achieved all its objectives except profitability and has no reasonable hope of doing better in the future could hardly be considered successful.[1]

---

[1] It is sometimes naively assumed that profits matter under the conditions of capitalism only. The truth is that very great importance is attached to profitability also in what is known as the socialist camp, that is to say, in the centrally planned economies. The reasons for this are two-fold. First, whereas it is possible to subsidize one economic activity by using the profits of another, it is not possible to run all enterprises at a loss, even if no private capital is involved, (unless, of course, the deficiencies are covered from

There are, of course, situations where profits have to be sacrificed, temporarily or permanently, as, for example, where an expensive innovation is necessary in order to safeguard the future prospects of the enterprise or in a national emergency, but this does not mean that once such a situation arises, profits may safely be forgotten. On the contrary, it then becomes doubly important to watch the profit angle and to be aware of the extent to which profitability is impaired by the change in policy.

The whole of the early theory of the firm and even the bulk of the modern developments of it identify the profit motive as aiming for the maximum attainable amount over any given time period, such as a month, a year or the whole life span of the firm. However, it is not difficult to see that this is neither the only nor the most relevant form of profit maximization. There are at least three others: (a) maximization of the mark-up rate, or, what amounts to the same thing, the percentage of profit included in the total value of sales; (b) maximization of the rate of return on the net worth of the firm, that is to say, on the capital of its owners; and, finally (c) maximization of the rate of return on the total assets of the firm, whether owned or not. These four principles will now be discussed in turn and it will be argued that the last mentioned concept is the most fundamental of all.

Maximization of the total profits over any period irrespective of the size of the capital tied down in the enterprise is a proposition which no sound businessman would entertain as his long-run policy, since it would mean that capital should be poured into the firm until the increase in total profit due to the last increment is equal to the interest charge on it, disregarding any other more favourable investment opportunity.

An exception is the special case where the total capital of the firm is unalterably fixed, but as a matter of fact, capital can generally be increased or reduced at very short notice. Bank loans and trade credit can mostly be raised or repaid as soon as the decision to do so is taken. It is not of course denied that there can be variations both in the liquidity position of a firm and in the ease with which credit can be obtained, but apart from such constraints, decisions to vary the total assets at the disposal of the company should turn on two major considerations: (1) the effect of the transaction on the overall

---

taxes levied on the consumers). Second, profit has been found to be an excellent indicator of efficiency, which cannot be neglected under any economic system if decline is to be avoided.

rate of return on the total asset value of the firm and (2) the best alternative use open to the chunk of capital concerned. It follows that an addition to the capital of a company will promise to be beneficial to its owners only if it can be invested *inside or outside the firm* at a rate that exceeds the expected rate of return on its present asset value. There are, however, situations where investment in the firm appears attractive to the providers of new share capital, even though it is envisaged that the high rate of return so far enjoyed by the original shareholders will thereby suffer some reduction. When such a situation arises, the interest of the original shareholders can be safeguarded by the allocation of bonus shares or by the offer of a rights issue at a preferential price.[2]

As far as pricing is concerned, the principle of total profit maximization demands that price should be set at the level at which a small change in total cost would just equal the change in total revenue. Quite apart from the difficulties of finding the appropriate point, if this precept is followed, the rate of return on capital will generally be lower than the maximum attainable, except in the special case already mentioned where both the capital of the owners and all forms of loan capital are unalterably fixed for the firm.

Maximization of the mark-up rate implicitly presupposes the stipulation of a level below which sales should not fall, otherwise it would mean putting the price so high that only a single unit is sold. Keeping this reservation in mind, it can be said that striving for a high mark-up rate is sound policy for a retail co-operative society that pays dividends to its customers in proportion to their purchases,[3] and for some producers' co-operatives. For any other company the mark-up rate matters only insofar as it is an effective means whereby the profit target can be communicated to the sales personnel – a point of which more will be said later.

We now come to the third principle, that of *maximizing the rate of return on that part of the capital only which belongs to the owners of the firm*. It

---

[2] For a further development of this argument cf. André Gabor and I. F. Pearce, 'A New Approach to the Theory of the Firm', *Oxford Economic Papers*, **4**, (3), October 1952, pp. 252–65, reprinted in *Readings in Industrial Economics*, (C. K. Rowley, ed.), Vol. I, Macmillan, London, 1972, pp. 18–33.

[3] The system, introduced in Britain over a decade ago, which replaced co-operative dividends automatically credited to the members' accounts by dividend stamps, represents no break with the principle: the societies endeavour to increase the rate at which stamps are given per unit value of sales. The difference is only that the stamps are given to members and non-members alike.

has been argued by many economists and even by some management consultants that it is reasonable for a business to borrow money up to the point where the internal rate of return, that is to say, the rate of profit the firm can achieve on the last unit of money borrowed, equals the rate of interest payable to the lender. This argument rests on two fallacies, the first of which is the implicit assumption that the owners' capital, i.e. the net worth of the firm, is unalterably given, whereas it is generally variable. The second fallacy consists in the confusion of the worst alternative use of the loan capital, namely the re-lending of it at the same rate at which it has been borrowed, with its best alternative use which may well be outside the original firm. The extensive diversification of most large companies and their prevailing interest in takeovers, mergers and the acquisition of shares in other firms even without controlling interest clearly indicate that, unlike some backward theoreticians, businessmen are not inclined to entertain these fallacies. No sound businessman would wish to saturate any specific activity of his firm with capital to the point where not an extra penny is added to net profits as long as there are better opportunities available in some other direction. Such opportunities mostly exist in the modern world, even if some short-sighted businessmen fail to recognize them.

There is one rather important exception to this rule. If the controlling interest is not *de facto* vested in the owners of the capital of the enterprise but in a monopoly factor, such as, for example, the freehold of a piece of good building land or the rights in a valuable patent, then it is in the interest of the monopoly to call in capital to the point where its net revenue is maximized. A strong monopoly factor may be able to claim exceptionally high profits, well above the market rate, while the providers of capital have to be satisfied with a rate of return which is equal to or only slightly better than what could be earned outside the monopoly. But where there is competition, it is generally the capital which is in the governing position, and capital will always tend to flow in the direction from which the highest rate of return can be expected, with due regard to the varying risks of different enterprises.[4]

---

[4] It is useful to distinguish between those risks that occur with sufficient statistical regularity to be insurable or covered by an appropriate provision, so that they can be classed as cost factors, and the uncertainties of enterprises which cannot be so covered. Since the future is never fully predictable, the prospective returns of any venture are inevitably linked with some element of uncertainty. The choice of the businessman is

It might seem tempting to exploit even a weak monopoly, the kind which arises where the owners of the share capital (or, more generally, the equity or risk capital) of the firm also possess the rights of, say, an established brand name in a multi-brand market, by taking in loan capital up to a very high point. However, apart from the profits forgone by neglecting other investment opportunities, there is also the limitation on the extent of the loan capital imposed by the dangers of *high gearing*, meaning an unduly high proportion of loan capital to equity capital. Say that the capital of such a firm consists of £5,000 share capital and £95,000 loan capital, borrowed at a fixed rate of 12 per cent, so that the annual interest charge is £11,400. In a year when the firm makes a profit of £15,000 on the whole of the capital then, after the interest on the loan capital is paid, £3,600 or 72 per cent will be the return on the share capital (before tax), but if in any year the overall profit drops to £6,400 or less, the entire share capital will be lost and the firm will be forced into liquidation or bankruptcy. Since the capital market is well aware of this danger, any firm prepared to accept the risk of high gearing would find it difficult if not impossible to obtain the requisite finance. It should be noted, though, that the proportion between share capital and loan capital considered as high gearing varies greatly from country to country and also over time.

In spite of the limitations of the practical relevance of the principle, let us note that in the case of a monopoly or if the owners' capital is fixed but the loan capital is variable, profit maximization (in the absence of better investment opportunities in some other enterprise) would entail the same pricing precept as the maximization of profits over a given time period, namely setting the price as near as possible to the point where the addition to cost by the last unit just equals the resulting increase in revenue. This is what economists call the equation of marginal cost with marginal revenue.[5]

Maximization of the rate of return on the total assets of the firm is the last

---

therefore not simply between the returns of prospective projects but between returns each of which is linked with an estimated uncertainty factor, and the greater this factor, the higher must the reward of success be to attract enterprise – cf. the results of the study of US and Canadian companies by L. A. Gordon *et al.*, *The Pricing Decision*, National Association of Accountants, New York, NY, 1981, pp. 17 and 20. The implications of uncertainty for pricing decisions are discussed in the Appendix to Part I.

[5] It is also the principle behind marginal cost pricing (or, more properly, incremental cost pricing), discussed in Chapter 5 pp. 70–80.

and most important of the four variants of the profit principle listed earlier in this chapter. Its meaning is simple: irrespective of the origin of the funds, every pound of capital should be put to the most profitable use available. It is, however, both customary and in most cases sound practice to deduct from the total assets of the company bills payable and the amounts owed to trade creditors.

The case for it has already been argued in some of the foregoing passages. It is a fact of life that when there are profitable investment possibilities inside a competitive firm or, to be more specific, in one of the enterprises within the firm, there will generally also be other projects competing for the available capital. Once this is recognized, it is not difficult to see that it would be foolish to saturate any single project with capital to the point where a further dose would only just cover its cost. The enterprising businessman who is not afraid of expanding his activities, will be wise to follow the policy which is well exemplified by the development of the first chain stores. Each of the chains started with one small shop and when it was operating successfully, no effort was made to enlarge it to the point where any further addition to it would not have increased profits. Instead, a second shop was opened, then a third and so the process went on. Meanwhile another outlet for further investment was also found: diversification by extending the range of products carried.[6]

There is no simple pricing rule for the maximization of the rate of return on capital. Price does, however, play an important part in deciding which way capital should flow. This aspect is discussed in detail in the next chapter.

Let us now turn to some of the business goals not directly centred on profit maximization.

The first of these is frequently encountered: it is *the profit target*, stated either as a percentage return on capital or as a money amount. Whether or not it represents a deliberate restriction of the profit below the maximum which could in fact be obtained, or simply an attempt to state in advance what the management considers attainable depends on the circumstances. It seems to be right and proper that a publicly owned enterprise enjoying a

---

[6] Needless to say, not every small shop develops in this way. Most of the people who run small businesses, be they retailers, repairers or other tradesmen, look upon their own limited ability as their main asset and, especially if they lack organizational and managerial skills, as is frequently the case, will dread the very idea of expanding the activities of their firm. Their business behaviour tends to be imitative rather than consciously optimizing, and this applies also to most of their pricing practices.

monopoly position should not exploit it to the hilt but satisfy itself with what may be termed a reasonable return on the capital employed in it or, alternatively, that it should be directed to cover its current costs only, with the taxpayers providing the funds for the periodic replacement of its fixed assets. The actual practice tends to be strongly influenced by social and political considerations which are outside the scope of this work.[7] There is, however, a general principle here which is worth noting: just as any loss made by a public enterprise is in effect a subsidy, so any profit made by it is tantamount to a tax. And there is no fundamental reason why the goods or services provided by a public enterprise should be exempt from taxation.

As far as private companies are concerned, the setting of a target rate of return is a corollary of budgetary planning and control and cannot therefore be avoided in the management of any large-scale enterprise. Large companies must plan for the future and the fact that such planning necessitates a profit forecast does not necessarily indicate the deliberate renunciation of higher profits.

There is some evidence to suggest that in the absence of government control the profit targets of private companies are forecasts of what may be termed the norm for the future, that is to say, the benchmark by which actual performance will be judged. If the target is exceeded, the executives of the company will be rewarded rather than reprimanded. In a study of the pricing goals of twenty of the largest American industrial corporations:

> about one-half of the companies explicitly indicated that their pricing policies were based mainly upon the objective of realizing a particular rate of return on investment, in a given year, over the long haul, or both; but in most cases the target was regarded as a long-run objective ... For the nine-year period, the target-return companies earned slightly more to substantially more than their indicated profit objective (International Harvester being the only exception).[8]

Before we leave this topic let us note that however realistic a profit target and the corresponding mark-up may appear to the businessman or even to an independent observer, the actual outcome will always depend on the market.

---

[7] The two-part and block tariffs peculiar to certain public utilities are discussed in Chapter 7.

[8] Robert F. Lanzilotti, 'Pricing Objectives in Large Companies', *American Economic Review*, **48**, (5), December 1958, pp. 921–40; reprinted in *Price Policies and Practices*, (D. F. Mulvihill and S. Paranka, eds), John Wiley & Sons, New York, 1967, pp. 63–83.

The stabilization of prices, margins and market shares is also an objective frequently mentioned by company executives, especially if they are conscious of the influence of their own pricing decisions on the behaviour of their competitors and thereby on the state of the market.

Executives intent on stabilization will avoid price cutting for fear of a price war, and will not raise the prices of their company to a level where competitors could make serious inroads on their sales. What this means is that the sensible businessman will always keep the long-run profitability of his company in sight, and will be prepared to sacrifice possible temporary gains for the prospect of more permanent gains. In some situations it is the *potential* competition that represents the greatest danger: competition from firms not yet active in the specific market concerned. While it is true that, in many branches of industry, the newcomer cannot start in a small way, this provides scant protection for the established firm since the new rival might appear in the form of a giant company at present active in different fields but ready to diversify further if there is promise of good returns to the large capital it can command.

The striving for stability may, however, also manifest itself in another way, since the nearer a firm is to a monopoly position in a given market, the more it is able to stabilize its prices and margins. Some firms aim at a dominant market share which will make them a price leader, others endeavour to enter into some overt or tacit understanding with their main competitors.

According to a view which has gained some popularity in recent years, *the executives of large firms measure their success by the growth of their sales* rather than by the profitability of their activities. It is suggested that the return on capital acts as a mild constraint only: there is a minimum which has to be provided to keep the shareholders quiet, and the principal aim is to expand the company at the highest rate compatible with the profit constraint.

The first point to note here is that his sales figures are always currently available to the businessman whereas profitability is assessed only periodically, some time after the end of each accounting period. It is therefore natural that the primary measure of success should be the sales record.

Even though exceptions are possible, increased sales generally mean improved profitability, that is to say, growth is not so much a rival aim as rather a means by which higher returns can be obtained. Growth which fails to fulfil its promise of profitability can spell disaster and has in fact brought ruin to many a company whose executives were guided by the mistaken belief that growth was its own reward.

The second point is that if we take a long-term view of past experience, we find that the overall tendency is for markets to expand, hence even if a firm is merely intent on keeping its relative position unchanged, it has to increase its sales in the same proportion as the growth of the market.[9]

Where market penetration is incomplete, pricing for growth generally means that the price is kept low or even lowered periodically so as to bring the product within the ambit of the lower income groups. Where market penetration is high, growth tends to necessitate increasing marketing costs, and hence unless the increased turnover also leads to lower unit costs of production, the price must be kept high enough to cover the costs of growth.

We have now surveyed the main *long-term* goals of business firms and have indicated their influence on pricing decisions.[10] The *short-term* objectives can, of course, be very different from them; Fisher's curious list[11] is a good illustration of the variety that arises when the examples include both answers of businessmen to a question about their aims and precepts advocated by textbook writers:

1. To penetrate and pre-empt the market for a product by charging a low price.
2. To cream the market and to obtain early profits and liquidity by charging a high price.
3. To assist in phasing out an obsolescent product by making it unattractively expensive.

---

[9] There are, of course, also contracting markets and the leading firm might then be tempted to consolidate its position by buying up its rivals. An increasing market share in a shrinking market is, however, hardly the sign of sound management. The proper advice to a firm in such a market is to get out of it as fast as it can without incurring disproportionate losses.

[10] For the further discussion of these and some other pricing objectives and policies cf. Robert E. Hampel, 'Pricing Policies and Profitability', *Management Accounting*, **59**, (1), July 1977, pp. 53–6; E. Jerome McCarthy and William D. Perreault, Jr, *Basic Marketing*, Richard D. Irwin, Inc., Homewood, Ill., 1984, pp. 552–79; and particularly the interesting findings of L. A. Gordon, *et al.*, *The Pricing Decision*, National Association of Accountants, New York, NY, 1981, p. 9 and passim.

[11] Lawrence Fisher, *Industrial Marketing*, Business Books, London, 1969, pp. 199–200.

4. To discourage competition from entering the market.
5. To avoid customer and political criticism.
6. To support a company image.
7. To encourage market expansion by a low price/high volume policy.
8. To avoid unduly provocative action which could lead to prices falling to a level inconsistent with long-term profitability.

The list is inevitably incomplete but should suffice to allow us to turn to the next topic: the relationship between price and the choice of investment projects.

Summary

In this chapter we have surveyed the main long-term goals of business firms and have discussed their implications for pricing decisions.

First we dealt with the four principles of profit maximization, centred on (1) total profit, (2) the mark-up rate, (3) the rate of return on the net worth of the firm, and (4) total asset value, and have argued that (4), the maximization of the rate of return on the total asset value of the firm is both the most general and the most appropriate of the profit principles.

It is undeniable that profit maximization is seldom, if ever, the sole aim of a firm, but it seems that most, if not all the other legitimate aims of businessmen are either means towards furthering profitability or can be pursued in the long run only if the firm is working profitably. We discussed a selection of these aims: the profit target, which is generally a realistic forecast rather than a deliberate limit set on the amount of profit to be achieved, and the stabilization of the market and growth, both of which are in fact in the interest of profitability. Finally, we listed some of the short-term aims, since they too might influence the choice of investment projects, to which we shall turn in the next chapter.

4   The role of price in investment decisions

Once a product has been fully developed and is in production, the limits within which its price can be set are severely restricted. Complete freedom in pricing exists only before substantial resources have been tied down by the productive process; at this initial stage the choice may be free between a penny whistle and a grand piano or, to use a rather more realistic example, between producing cheap, throw-away type ballpoint pens or the solid gold variety.

It is therefore appropriate to start the discussion of pricing problems with an examination of the way in which price can affect the choice between different investment propositions.

Discounted cash flow

Some years ago *Discounted Cash Flow*, or *DCF* for short, became the fashionable procedure for investment appraisal both in the business world and in the nationalized industries. Its essence consists in taking account of the time pattern of all payments and receipts from the inception of the project through its entire expected life, and to discount them to present day. If this is done with the application of a test discount rate, the present day values will indicate which of two or more projects would yield the largest surplus, and any project which promises to result in a deficit would automatically be discarded.

Alternatively, DCF can be used to calculate the rate of discount which gives a present-day value of zero. The rate so obtained is the internal rate of return of the investment project under consideration, which may be judged by this criterion.[1]

---

[1] The main features of DCF are demonstrated in the Appendix to this chapter. For a simple introduction to its principles and methods cf. C. J. Hawkins and D. W. Pearce, *Capital Investment Appraisal*, Macmillan Studies in Economics, The Macmillan Press Ltd, London, 1971.

Since the future is invariably uncertain, it is essential to take into account not only the magnitude of the cash flows but also the subjective estimates of the probability of each estimated value over the whole period. The difficulty here is that single figures are not generally satisfactory expressions of expectations. Each person involved in the assessment of a project may have his own ideas both of the magnitude of the cash flows and the probabilities attached to them, and even if the team should reach a compromise agreement, the composite estimate of the net cash flow of the eighth year, say, could well look like Table 4.1.

Table 4.1
Example of estimated cash flows and probabilities

Estimated net cash flow of Year 8 (receipts less payments)	Estimated probability
£100,000 or more	10%
60,000–99,000	20%
30,000–59,000	40%
0–29,000	25%
OUTFLOW 1,000–10,000	5%
	100%

Any compression of Table 4.1 into a single figure would be largely arbitrary, whereas if every one of the projected outcomes for the eighth year is to be combined with each of the estimates for the other years, the result would be almost certainly inconclusive. The expedient in general use consists in making single pessimistic estimates of all the cash flows and to scale receipts down very heavily in respect of the later years.

It would seem therefore that this inevitable complication makes the use of DCF really safe only in those spheres where past experience suggests that predictions of outlays and returns can be made with reasonable certainty for fairly long periods, as for instance in electricity generation. Even there, the outcome of investments made in recent years in the expectation of constant rates of economic growth and steady fuel prices provides clear demonstration of the fallibility of the method.[2]

---

[2] For a thorough and incisive critique of DCF cf. R. M. Adelson, 'Discounted Cash Flow – can we discount it?', *Journal of Business Finance*, **2**, (2), Summer 1970, pp. 50–66.

While it would hardly be right to suggest that the planning of its cash flows can be altogether neglected by any business firm, experience shows that it can effectively be done for relatively short periods only. If the period for which forecasts can be made with fair confidence is not longer than five years or so, and the time which will elapse between the initial outlay and the onset of the income flow is short, it seems that it is perfectly sound to eschew DCF and resort to less-involved methods of investment appraisal. Two simple methods will be used in the demonstration to be presented, and it will subsequently be argued that the same conclusions would emerge also if more sophisticated procedures were employed.

The choice of technology

The example which follows has been selected so as to bring out two main points, both of which tend to be neglected when investment decisions are taken in industry. The first is that the choice of the process by which a given product should be manufactured is not simply a question of technical superiority and cannot be decided merely by reference to the cost of production either. Unfortunately, this choice is traditionally left to the engineers of the firm, whose calculations are usually based on the most efficient rate of utilization of the equipment. What is often being overlooked is a general feature of modern technology: the more appropriate the machinery is for high rates of output, the lower will be its flexibility, that is to say, its ability to produce at different rates of output without much variation in unit cost. The second point is that the expected price and the limits within which it is likely to vary must greatly influence the choice between investment projects, even if variations in the rate of output are not expected. In order to bring out these points in full clarity, the example has been simplified by making the following assumptions:

1. The company has firmly decided that a certain product, the present factory door price of which is £3.20 per unit, should be manufactured at the rate of 10,000 units per annum, and it is confidently expected that the market can absorb this quantity.
2. The issue that has to be decided is, therefore, merely the choice between two methods of manufacturing the product concerned. *Technology A* requires standard machine tools operated by skilled labour, while *Technology B* involves fully automated

equipment and hence leads to a reduced wage bill. As far as price and sales are concerned, it is a matter of indifference which of the two technologies is used.

3. Finally, we shall assume that both types of equipment are obtainable at short notice, and that the capital required by either method of production will have to be provided only when the equipment is fully operational.

The relevant financial details of the two technologies are shown below:

	Technology A	Technology B
Total capital requirement	£16,000	£40,000
Total annual cost	£28,000	£25,000
Total annual sales return	£32,000	£32,000
Total annual profit	£4,000	£7,000
Rate of return on capital	25%	17.5%

In this table *total capital requirement* includes both the capital invested in fixed assets, such as buildings and machinery, and the money required to finance stocks and work in progress; *total annual cost* stands for the outlay on wages, materials, etc., necessitated by the production of 10,000 units, including maintenance of the equipment but no interest charge for the use of capital; the *total annual sales return* is based on the present factory door price of £3.20 per unit; *total annual profit* is the straight difference between annual sales return and cost; and the *rate of return on capital* is the annual profit expressed as a percentage of the total capital requirement. It is therefore analogous to the internal rate of return as obtained by the Discounted Cash Flow method of investment appraisal.

If the choice now turns on the rate of return on capital, Technology A is clearly preferable to Technology B. The same conclusion arises if the simple pay-back period is used as the criterion, since the expected gross profits of the first four years would equal the capital of Technology A, whereas in the case of Technology B it would take about five years and nine months to repay the capital if the proceeds were devoted to this purpose before any distribution of profits could take place.

This method has long been in use in industry, and although it has been severely criticized by the protagonists of DCF for not taking account of the entire life span of the project and the scrap value of the machinery at the end of it, the approach is fully justifiable if we accept the not unreasonable view that beyond five years or so, forecasts of prices and sales become highly uncertain and would figure with very low values, if any, in a DCF computation.

There is also a variant of the method which includes a charge for the use of the capital tied down by each of the projects. It follows from what has been said in Chapter 3 about the maximization of the rate of return on the total assets of the firm that any actual interest charge on the capital concerned is irrelevant, except insofar as projects which do not promise enough disposable revenue to cover the interest payments on borrowed funds plus a generous safety margin must automatically be rejected.[3] It is, however, perfectly in order to include a *test rate* corresponding to the test discount rate of DCF when the present day value of a project is computed. This is often called the *cut-off rate*, and it is reasonable to adopt for this purpose the current (or expected) internal rate of return of the company, since any additional project with a lower rate would reduce the previous (or expected) average. Needless to say, this would be sound practice only at times when the company was doing well.

For the sake of the example, let us set the test rate at 10 per cent and see how it affects the decision process. Its application is shown below:

	Technology A	Technology B
Total capital requirement	£16,000	£40,000
Total annual profit	£4,000	£7,000
Less 10% on capital	−£1,600	−£4,000
Net surplus	£2,400	£3,000

[3] It is a fallacy, unfortunately very widespread, that if a company happens to have idle funds earning little interest, it is in order to finance with them projects of low profitability, unlike other funds, borrowed at a higher rate, which must be put to more profitable uses. The fallacy consists in taking not the best alternative use of the funds concerned into consideration but the worst. Sure enough, if the company is doing well and has large liquid reserves, it can afford to put money even into schemes like a new sports pavilion to promote the welfare of its employees, but there should never be any doubt that the true cost of such a project is the profit forgone by not investing the funds in the most profitable way open to the firm.

On this comparison, Technology B appears to be more profitable than A. It would seem therefore that the real choice is between the two alternative criteria: rate of return or net surplus, and once this choice has been made, the selection of the technology is automatically settled.

It will now be demonstrated that the observed discrepancy between the indications of the two criteria depends on the one hand on the test rate which has been adopted and, on the other hand, on the price forecast.

The relationships involved are illustrated in Figure 4.1. The lines AA' and BB', which represent Technology A and B, respectively, show the dependence of the rate of return on capital on the price of the product. The rate of return criterion, represented by a vertical line at the expected price of £3.20, cuts AA' above BB', and thus indicates the superiority of Technology A, while the horizontal line at the level of the 10 per cent test rate, representing the surplus criterion, cuts BB' to the left of AA' and hence suggests that Technology B should be preferred.[4]

The AA' and BB' lines meet at point P, which corresponds to a price of £3.00 and a rate of return on capital of 12.5 per cent. This means that if either of the two criterion lines should pass through this point, it will indicate indifference between the two technologies, whereas above point P Technology A will be seen as being more profitable, and below P Technology B, *irrespective of which of the two criteria is employed*. If, as in our example, one of the criterion lines passes above P and the other below P, their indications will be discrepant.

---

[4] The same relationships can easily be expressed algebraically. If we denote the price by p and the rate of return by r, with subscripts a and b to identify the technology concerned, the dependence of the rate of return on the price can be written as:

$$r_a = 62.5p - 175$$
$$r_b = 25p - 62.5$$

The two rates are equal if $p = £3.00$, while at $p = £3.20$ we find $r_a = 25$ per cent and $r_b = 17.5$ per cent.

The prices required to obtain a given target rate r_t are determined by

$$p_a = 2.80 + 0.016r_t$$
$$\text{and} \qquad p_b = 2.50 + 0.04r_t$$

It can be seen that a target rate of return of 25 per cent, say, will be reached with Technology A at a price of £3.20, whereas with Technology B it would take a price of £3.50 to achieve the same target rate. But at a test rate of 10 per cent $p_a = £2.96$ and $p_b = £2.90$.

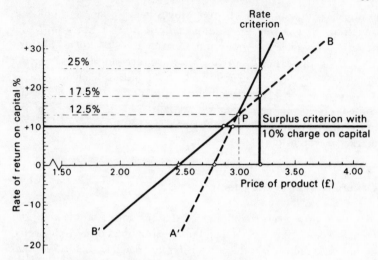

Figure 4.1   Price and rate of return on capital

The question is now how to make the proper choice in such a situation which could arise just as well with other methods of investment appraisal, including DCF. The answer lies in bringing the marketing aspect into play.

If the forecast suggests that although the present price of the product is £3.20, competition is likely to force it soon down to a level below £3.00, Technology B offers better prospects of survival than A because, as can be seen in the diagram, B would cease to be profitable only if the price were to fall to £2.50 or below, whereas A would become unprofitable as soon as the price fell to £2.80.[5]

It could therefore be said that if the forecast is optimistic, in the sense that the present price of £3.20 is expected to hold in the foreseeable future, it is reasonable to prefer Technology A, whereas if the price is likely to drop below £3.00, the choice should fall on Technology B. The 10 per cent test rate criterion may also be interpreted as an expression of the belief that, in the long run, competition (or, perhaps, government interference) will not tolerate a profit rate in excess of 10 per cent which, if costs remain the same, indicates a ceiling price of £3.00.

We can therefore conclude that cost comparisons cannot alone

---

[5] This assumes that the funds tied down by the project consist of equity capital only, that is to say, there are no fixed interest obligations. If, however, the funds were borrowed at 8 per cent, say, the break-even point would be at £2.93 for Technology A and at £2.82 for B.

establish which of two or more investment projects should be preferred. If it is safe to assume that the market can absorb the quantity on which the computations are based, the issue will turn entirely on the expected price of the product, and forecasting the price or, rather, the range within which the price is likely to settle, is a problem which neither the engineers nor the accountants of the company are qualified to tackle. It falls into the province of the marketing division, which may have to conduct or commission market research to provide estimates.

Generalization of the conclusions

Reality is always more complicated than examples of this kind, but the aspects that have been deliberately simplified or even neglected do not materially affect the conclusion just reached. Let us see what happens if we relax the restrictive assumptions.

First of all, we took it for granted that the quantity sold per annum will remain invariant throughout. If it is expected to vary with the price or independently of it, this can easily be brought into the assessment procedure, as can any differences in the capacities of the technologies concerned. For example, if without an appreciable change in direct unit costs Technology A could produce up to 12,000 units per annum while Technology B was capable of increasing output to 15,000, and the market can be expected to expand substantially in response to a price reduction to £3.00 per unit, full utilization of the capacities would render Technology B superior by both criteria.[6]

Next, we assumed that the choice is merely between alternative methods of manufacturing the same product, whereas in reality there may well be other, entirely different, projects competing for the same resources. Since the criteria can be applied in the same way to different investment propositions, this would not raise any new problems, except insofar as it would call for separate diagrams to demonstrate the relationships between prices and rates of return.

Third, it is perfectly legitimate to ask that if the company could command a capital of £40,000, what would it do with the excess of £24,000 if Technology A were adopted. The answer is that it is not

---

[6] For an interesting discussion of the investment life cycle cf. John Sizer, 'Accountants, Product Managers and Selling Price Decisions in Multi-Consumer Product Firms', *Journal of Business Finance*, **4**, Spring 1972, p. 76.

the separate projects but rather the different possible combinations of projects capable of utilizing the total capacity available for additional investment that should be compared. However, it could turn out that it would be reasonable for the company not to exhaust its credit to the full on this occasion.

Fourth, it was stipulated that the time necessary to set up either of the two projects was of no importance since it was short in both cases, and also that no payment would be made for the equipment until the onset of the product flow which would be at the full rate right from the start. If these conditions do not apply, it would be reasonable to assess the capital requirement and cash flows of each technology by the application of DCF. This would not, however, affect the essence of the conclusions.

Fifth, the effects of taxation were disregarded in the example. They should, of course, be given full consideration in any realistic study of profitability. The expedient of using after-tax figures throughout might not alone be sufficient since the timing of the money flows including the tax payments might affect the capital requirements.

Finally, it was tacitly assumed that the unit cost of materials, labour and other current cost factors would remain unchanged over the foreseeable future, whereas they are likely to vary and, in an inflationary age, it is virtually certain that the upward movements will predominate. Here the issue turns very much on the nature of the competition. If it consists only of firms in the home country who have to acquire their resources in the same markets, changes in factor prices would affect all of them in a similar way, and consumers' incomes are also likely to increase in a similar proportion, if not more steeply. It follows that in such a case it is quite legitimate to disregard this aspect at the time when the investment decision is taken. If, however, the competition includes overseas firms or firms in the home country whose production uses largely different resources,[7] the forecasts should take it into consideration that a wage rise at home, say, would not force the foreign competitors to increase their prices.

It appears, therefore, that the conclusions which we have reached are not invalidated by the move from the hypothetical situation towards reality. It has been demonstrated that since the prospects of

---

[7] This would apply to most exporters and, *inter alia*, also to firms whose products are mainly bought as gifts and hence forced to meet competition on a very wide front.

investment projects are directly dependent on the expected prices of the products concerned, the choice cannot be based on cost computations alone, and that it is essential that the marketing division of the company should be consulted even if the choice is merely between the different technologies for manufacturing a given product.[8]

Additional considerations

The point just made concerning the effects of inflation needs supplementation, insofar as attention must be called to some further aspects of the issue. First of all, there is the moot point whether the expectation of inflation should encourage additional investment and early replacement of old machinery or suggest retrenchment rather than expansion. There is no easy answer to this question since experience has shown that the direction in which inflation tends to influence investment depends largely on other circumstances. Up to recent years the records suggested that in developed industrial countries the highest increases in productivity coincided with the inflationary periods, whereas in underdeveloped countries increased rates of inflation were generally accompanied by lower productivity. More recently, several of the highly industrialized Western economies experienced exceptionally high degrees of inflation coupled with declining productivity.

Is it the relation of the rate of interest to the return expected from investment that is the clue to the answer? This belief, which was once very popular, was discounted by the conclusion of the Radcliffe Committee, according to which the investment decisions of enterprises in the private sector turn on the general liquidity position rather than on the rate of interest.[9] While this could not be said to be definitely wrong, it has not stood the test of time well. It now seems that it might qualify for the epithet *ignotum per ignotius*,[10] since all it really says is that businessmen increase investment when

---

[8] The method here discussed was first described in André Gabor, 'Marketing's Role in Investment Decisions', *Marketing*, September 1970, pp. 44–7. For a somewhat different approach cf. James J. Finerty, 'Product Pricing and Investment Analysis', *Management Accounting*, (NAA, USA), **53**, (6), December 1971, pp. 15–18.

[9] *Report of the Committee on the Working of the Monetary System*, HMSO, 1959.

[10] Explanation obscurer than the thing it purports to explain.

they consider the time favourable for such action. It is evident that any proper explanation of the apparent contradictions observed could not ignore political aspects, and for this reason the issue will not be further discussed here. It may, however, be noted that the analysis presented above is fully in line with the view that the rate of interest plays only a minor limiting role in investment decisions.

There is yet another facet of the relationship between inflation and investment that calls for mention. Technology keeps advancing and especially if wages run ahead of prices, there will be strong inducement to reduce the costs of production by installing new equipment.[11] Consider this example; it will illustrate the point and also shed light on the pricing problem associated with it:

Annual sales: 50,000 units at £1.00 each		£50,000
Costs: Labour: 10,000 hours at £2.00	£20,000	
Materials: 10 tons at £1,000	10,000	
Overheads	16,000	46,000
Profit before tax		£4,000

The overheads include all the administrative and marketing expenses, also the depreciation charge on fixed assets as allowed by the tax authorities, but no interest charge on the capital employed. Since the total capital tied down by the division concerned is £25,000, the return on capital is 16 per cent.

Two years later it is found that although sales have increased by 5 per cent in real terms and the price was adjusted in proportion to the rise in unit cost, the profitability of the division had declined from 16 per cent to 14 per cent.

What actually happened was that while hourly wages increased by 12 per cent, the price of materials by 18.5 per cent and overheads by 25 per cent, improvements in labour productivity and more economical use of the materials, *achieved by installing additional fixed equipment*, reduced the rise in unit cost to 10 per cent. The new situation, as reflected in the accounts, is shown in Table 4.2.

On this account the drop in the rate of return on capital appears to be 2 per cent, but if we look at the reality of the situation, we have

---

[11] In most cases the new equipment will be labour-saving, but, in fact, the businessman will be at least as interested in an investment project that will achieve a reduction in total direct costs of, say, 20 per cent by replacing one of the materials by a cheaper kind without any change in the labour content of the product as in another project that could achieve the same saving by making part of the labour force redundant.

Table 4.2
Calculation of the rate of return on capital

Annual sales: 52,500 units at £1.10 each		£57,750
Costs: Labour: 9,500 hours at £2.24	£21,280	
Materials: 10 tons at £1,185	11,850	
Overheads	20,000	53,130
Profit before tax		£4,620
Original capital less two years' depreciation on the fixed assets	£21,000	
New investment less depreciation	12,000	
Total capital employed	£33,000	
Rate of return on capital		14%

to conclude that the true decline in profitability must have been in excess of this figure. Unless the new advances in technology have substantially reduced the value of the old equipment (in which case the standard depreciation allowance should be supplemented by further provision out of taxed profits), inflation must have increased the value of the fixed assets over and above what they were worth two years earlier. Hence the present value of the total capital employed is probably higher than £33,000 and the rate of return on capital less than 14 per cent.

We can conclude that in order to maintain the level of profitability, price should have been increased by more than 11 per cent, provided, of course, that this would not have had such an adverse effect on sales as to wipe out the effect of the higher margin. Alternatively, if permitted by the capacity of the equipment, an appropriately higher number of units sold could also have restored profitability to its previous level without raising price by more than 10 per cent.

Summary

Once the manufacturing facilities for a given product have been installed, the range within which price can profitably be set is severely limited. Complete freedom in pricing exists only before the investment is undertaken, and it was therefore appropriate to examine at this stage the role of price in the choice between investment projects.

Until recent times, the profitability of investment projects was judged by simple methods, generally based on the results expected from the first four or five years of operation only. According to the protagonists of the sophisticated Discounted Cash Flow (DCF) approach, the earlier methods should be regarded as obsolete, but in fact there is little evidence, if any, to substantiate the claim that DCF leads to better decisions. The essence of DCF is demonstrated in the Appendix to Chapter 4, but the simpler methods were sufficient to demonstrate that even the choice between alternative technologies to manufacture a given product cannot properly be exercised by considering the cost angle only. It was shown that it is essential to take also the expected price and the likelihood of its stability into consideration.

In order to bring out the main points with full clarity, an example was used which involved a number of simplifying assumptions, but a subsequent scrutiny revealed that they have not materially affected the substance of the conclusions reached, which could therefore be regarded as possessing general validity. Finally, we demonstrated the effect of inflation on investment decisions and called attention to the fact that since advances in technology generally involve additional capital investment, the return on capital may be adversely affected if, in an inflationary period, prices are adjusted only at the same rate at which costs have increased. The Appendix to Chapter 5 deals with inflation in relation to costing and pricing.

The relation between the rate of return on capital and pricing will be further discussed in Chapter 5; here we must note that its consideration is truly relevant only in connection with investment decisions. Once the investment is made and the product launched pricing must be market-oriented – insistence on a desired return on capital can bring disaster if it requires a price that is too high to enable the requisite volume of sales.

APPENDIX TO CHAPTER 4: DISCOUNTED CASH FLOW

The essential features of the main DCF methods can best be explained by means of an example. Consider a proposed project that is expected to generate the cash flows shown in Column 2 of Table 4.6 below.

The net flow of each year represents all the estimated revenue from sales plus the scrap value at the end of the useful life of the plant, less all the capital outlays and current costs, including those for repairs and maintenance but without any provision for depreciation. Allowance should, however, be made for all the taxes that would have to be met, including the tax on company profits.

The present value PV of an amount A due after n years computed with a rate of interest (or 'test rate') r is given by the formula

$$PV = A/(1 + r)^n$$

For example, the present value of the net flow of the fourth year is

$$PV_4 = 600/1.1^4 = 600/1.4641 = 409.81 \approx £410$$

Applying the formula with values appropriate to each of the amounts concerned and rounding off to the nearest pound we obtain the figures in Column 4 of Table 4.3.

Table 4.3
Calculation of the present value of the net flow of funds

Year	Net flow of funds	Discount factor (10%)	Net present value	
0	− 500	1	− 500	
1	− 600	1/1.1	− 545	− 1,045
2	+ 300	1/1.21	+ 248	
3	+ 450	1/1.331	+ 338	
4	+ 600	1/1.4641	+ 410	
5	+ 400	1/1.61051	+ 248	
6	+ 245	1/1.771561	+ 138	+ 1,382
		Total net present value		+ 337

The total net present value so obtained is the difference between the investment required in year 0 by the project concerned and the amount that would have to put down at the test rate (10 per cent in this case) to generate the same income flow. The demonstration

Table 4.4
The flow of funds with a test rate of ten per cent

Year	£	Description of flow
0	+ 837	Outlay (500 + 337)
	+ 84	Interest
	+ 1,521	
1	+ 921	
	+ 600	Outlay
	+ 1,521	
	+ 152	Interest
2	+ 1,673	
	− 300	Withdrawal
	+ 1,373	
	+ 137	Interest
3	+ 1,510	
	− 450	Withdrawal
	+ 1,060	
	+ 106	Interest
4	+ 1,166	
	− 600	Withdrawal
	+ 566	
	+ 57	Interest
5	+ 623	
	− 400	Withdrawal
	+ 223	
	+ 22	Interest
6	+ 245	
	− 245	Withdrawal
	0	

displayed in Table 4.4 is also a check on the accuracy of the computation.

The internal rate of return is the rate of discount which renders the total net present value of the project zero. That it happens to be 20 per cent in this case is shown in Table 4.5.

Table 4.5
The net flow of funds discounted with the internal rate of return

Year	Net flow of funds	Discount factor (20%)	Net present value	
0	− 500	1	− 500	
1	− 600	1/1.2	− 500	− 1,000
2	+ 300	1/1.44	+ 208	
3	+ 450	1/1.728	+ 260	
4	+ 600	1/2.0736	+ 289	
5	+ 400	1/2.48832	+ 161	
6	+ 245	1/2.985984	+ 82	+ 1,000
		Total net present value	0	

There is no straightforward mathematical formula for determining the internal rate of return of a given project. It can be approximated by trial and error or short-cut methods, but it is best to leave the task to an electronic computer.

When comparing two different projects, the net present value and the internal rate of return criteria do not invariably point in the same direction. For this reason and those discussed in Chapter 4, DCF is similar to all the other methods of investment appraisal, insofar as it is merely a means whereby information is provided for the decision maker, who has to consider very carefully all the explicit and implicit assumptions on which the results rest.

5 Profit-oriented and cost-based pricing

Pricing policies

The term pricing policy is used here in a variety of senses. It would certainly not be inappropriate to speak of a profit-oriented pricing policy or a pricing policy designed to increase the firm's market share, and one could also distinguish between inward-looking, cost-oriented pricing policies and market-oriented pricing, both of which can be further subdivided. Then again, it could be said that it is a question of policy whether the prices of the company are to be declared and adhered to or open to negotiation.

Kotler suggests that the entire marketing policy of a firm – which necessarily includes pricing – is governed by its position in the market.[1] He distinguishes between four situations: that of the *leader*, the company with the largest market share, anxious to retain its position; the *challenger*, generally with the next largest share, aiming for leadership; the *follower* who does not dare to adopt an independent policy; and the *nicher*, operating in a relatively small but secure corner of the market, overlooked by the giants. (Eventually, the successful nicher's firm is likely to be acquired by one of the larger companies – or even ousted if his product or process does not enjoy effective patent protection.) This list is not exhaustive; for example, it does not cover the situation not infrequently encountered where several firms of not very dissimilar size are in competition with one another, and none of them dares to step out of line because of the fear that if he were to cut his price, this would immediately be followed by others, while any increase in his price not justified by a cost increase which also affects the other firms would not be imitated and hence place him in a vulnerable position.

Clearly, there can be no single answer to a problem as complex and varied as that of pricing, and a policy that has proved successful

---

[1] Cf. Philip Kotler, *Marketing Management: Analysis, Planning and Control*, 4th edition, Prentice-Hall., Inc., Englewood Cliffs, NJ, 1980, pp. 272–88.

in one situation may be entirely inappropriate in another. But this does not mean either that all pricing policies are of equal merit or that the choice between them is always clear-cut. In industrial markets a great deal of pricing appears to be based on the work of the cost accountant, the prices are often openly declared in price lists and yet most of the actual bargains are the result of negotiation.

Negotiated prices are generally associated with industrial markets and declared prices with consumer markets, but although this is by and large true, there are some notable exceptions. On the one hand, some manufacturers are in a sufficiently strong position to sell at their declared prices only (generally coupled with a schedule of quantity rebates) even in the industrial field, and, on the other hand, it has to be recognized that where resale price maintenance cannot be enforced, whether because of legal prohibition of the practice or because of the superior market power of the distributors, it is the latter rather than the manufacturer who set the price for the final purchaser.

Yet another important interpretation of the term pricing policy is concerned with the image of the company or its division. Broadly speaking, there is a choice between various ranges, according to whether the price should imply top quality, good value for money or that the firm's products are the cheapest in the field.

This is sometimes described as an aspect of market segmentation, a description which is certainly not incorrect. It is hardly if ever advantageous for a company to be seen to cater simultaneously for the luxury trade, the comfortably off middle class and the masses that constitute the lower socio-economic groups, but an appropriate product line policy can go a long way towards securing footholds in at least two adjacent strata. In the case of luxury or semi-luxury articles, it is a useful selling point to have some very highly-priced items in the range and promote them not so much in order to increase their sale as rather to enhance the quality image of the more modestly priced items in the same line. This policy has been pursued with considerable success by several Swiss watch manufacturers. The alternative policy is to play down the common origin of the items that constitute the product line by giving them different brand names and perhaps also placing their distribution with separate marketing organizations.

It follows from this last definition of pricing policy that the most momentous decisions are those taken when the introduction of new products is under consideration, also that, if at all possible, the pricing decision, in broad terms at least, should precede product development; that is to say, the latter should purposefully be directed towards the selected price range. The term *backward cost pricing* has been suggested to describe this policy where the product must fit into a system of conventional prices, as is the rule in certain trades. It is discussed further in Chapter 8, (in the section on price lining), and in Chapter 12.

While the general elimination of resale price maintenance necessarily means that, with the exception of those manufacturers who sell directly to the public (or work in one of the rare fields where resale price maintenance can still be legally enforced), the producers and importers have little, if any, direct control over the actual prices charged by the retail distributors of consumer goods to the final purchasers (and frequently no precise knowledge of the prices charged either), the price variations that are possible for the retailers can extend over a relatively narrow range only, and will not permit the distributors efficiently to cross the segment boundaries: the price of the premium brand will not fall below that of the run-of-the-mill brands in the same market.[2]

The image of a brand and that of the manufacturer's company (as also its profitability) can seriously be affected if the marketing policy allows unduly great variations in retail prices. Chain stores and other large distributors who cater for the masses buy in bulk and insist on appropriately low wholesale prices, and if these enable them to undercut the speciality trade, the latter are apt to retaliate by refusing to stock the brand concerned. There are well known instances of manufacturers having suffered severe losses by allowing this to happen whereas, if they had thought of it in time, the detrimental consequences could have been avoided by developing separate lines with different brand names for each of the markets.

The ideal pricing policy is simultaneously profit-based, cost-conscious, market-oriented and in conformity with any other aims the businessman may have, as long as they do not lead to contradictions, as for instance the naive desire to sell the largest quantity at the highest price and produce it at the lowest cost.[3] (What one can reasonably aim at is to sell as much as possible at a

---

[2] Cf. Robert S. Guthrie, 'The Relationship Between Wholesale and Consumer Prices', *Southern Economic Journal*, **47**, April 1981, pp. 1046–55.

[3] Commenting on the results of his survey which covered 728 companies, David D. Shipley noted that 'The vast majority of firms in the sample set

selected price, and to produce the quantity required at as low a total cost as is compatible with the specified quality of the product.) Since pricing policies and procedures are intimately connected, they will be discussed together in the remaining part of this chapter.

Pricing procedures

1 Profit-oriented pricing and target rates

The various profit goals listed in Chapter 3 provide criteria rather than explicit precepts for pricing, if only because, apart from the here-today-gone-tomorrow kind of adventurer, no sensible business-man would knowingly endanger the long-run profitability of his firm in favour of some temporary gain. The future being inevitably uncertain, this means that pricing policy should strongly be influenced by the regard for prestige and the desired image of the firm. Exploiting any momentary situation would mean increasing the price whenever demand is keen and lowering price when demand slackens.

There are, however, circumstances in which account can be taken of regular fluctuations in demand by a systematic variation of prices which will enhance rather than spoil long-run prospects. The different high-season – off-season tariffs of seaside hotels, the moderately priced luncheon menus of some restaurants that also cater at higher prices to diners, the reduced price railway tickets valid only outside rush hours are typical examples of these practices. (The seasonal sales of department stores do not quite belong to this category since it has become their regular practice to withdraw from the counters much of the usual merchandise during the period of the sale in order to make room for other assortments of goods, bought specifically for this purpose, which are then offered as bargains.)

Another situation in which adaptation to market fluctuations is appropriate is that of the pure price taker. Deviation from the ruling

---

multiple pricing goals. Indeed, together the respondents cited 2,153 objectives, yielding a mean of 2.9. Only 7.3 per cent of the firms pursue a solitary goal.' Cf. 'Pricing Objectives in British Manufacturing Industry', *Journal of Industrial Economics*, **29**, (4), June 1981, p. 435. Similar tendencies were found to prevail in US and Canadian companies; cf. Lawrence A. Gordon *et al.*, *The Pricing Decision*, National Association of Accountants, New York, NY, 1981, pp. 14–17 and 23.

market price (or controlled price) not being open to him, he can maximize his profits by adjusting his output so that the addition to total cost attributable to the last increment should just equal the corresponding addition to his gross sales returns. It is not a mere coincidence that this is mostly impossible; for instance, the heavy fluctuations in farm prices not subject to authoritative stabilization arise just because farm output cannot immediately be adjusted to take advantage of the momentary state of the market.

Maximization of the mark-up rate which, as it was pointed out in Chapter 3, is the legitimate policy of retail co-operative societies, means that competition with other enterprises is carried out more by the lure of the dividend (or dividend stamps) than by the price, and for those members of the public who prefer a modest nest-egg to a reduction in day-to-day expenditure, this can be a strong attraction.[4]

Maximizing the rate of return on capital provides what is perhaps the most difficult criterion of all, but it has been shown in Chapter 4 how it can be practically applied to investment appraisal. Not even the minimum desired rate of return is in its original form an appropriate indication of pricing policy to the lower echelons in the company in charge of the day-to-day business, but when interpreted in terms of sales, costs and margins, the target rate can serve as an efficient directive. The relationships concerned are displayed in Figure 5.1. The diagram in this figure is shown in its traditional form, excluding all forms of debt owed by the company. In fact, as already mentioned in Chapter 3, p. 28, it is both customary and generally sound practice to deduct from the total asset value bills payable and the amounts owed to trade creditors.

---

[4] In a survey carried out some years ago, high proportions of the customers of British co-operative stores revealed that they considered the prices higher than in other shops, but the majority changed its view when asked to take the dividend into consideration. Cf. *Mrs Housewife and her Grocer*, A. Bird & Son Ltd., Birmingham, 1957; also André Gabor and A. P. Sowter, 'The Customers' Views', *Co-operative Management and Marketing*, **3**, (12), December 1970, pp. 46–50.

In recent years heavy price cutting by the large commercial chains has forced the retail co-operatives to follow suit. The result was that several of them went out of business and, owing to the reduced margins, even the most successful societies had to discontinue dividends on all groceries and certain other fast moving consumer goods.

The relationship between the target rate of return on capital,
the percentage margin and the turnover rate

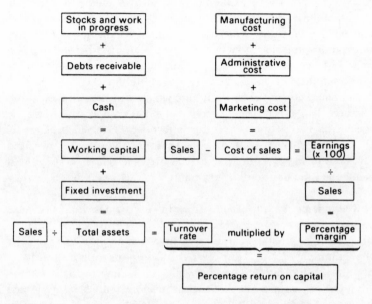

Figure 5.1   Turnover rate, percentage margin and rate of return

As presented in Figure 5.1:

RETURN ON CAPITAL =

100 × (Percentage Margin) × (Turnover rate) per cent,

but as a directive to the sales department it is more appropriate to
state the target as:

RETURN ON CAPITAL =

$$100 \times \frac{(Sales) - (Total\ Costs)}{(Total\ Assets)}\ per\ cent.$$

Put into words, it may be interpreted as 'keep your sales going
and expand them, if possible, but watch the margin'.

The actual profit margin, being the difference between the total
value of sales and all the costs incurred over the year, can be
expressed in various ways. As a percentage of sales we can write it
either as:

PERCENTAGE MARGIN =

$$100 \times \frac{\text{(Sales)} - \text{(Total Costs)}}{\text{(Sales)}} \text{ per cent,}$$

or as:

PERCENTAGE MARGIN =

$$100 \times \frac{\text{(Target Rate)} \times \text{(Total Assets)}}{\text{(Sales)}} \text{ per cent.}$$

The percentage margin is sometimes confused with the mark-up rate. The difference between them is that the former is an expression of the returns as a percentage of sales, whereas the latter relates the returns to the costs. The mark-up can also be stated in two equivalent alternative ways, either as:

MARK-UP RATE =

$$100 \times \frac{\text{(Sales)} - \text{(Total Costs)}}{\text{(Total Costs)}} \text{ per cent,}$$

or as

MARK-UP RATE =

$$\frac{100 \times \text{(Target Rate)} \%}{\text{(Turnover Rate)} - \text{(Target Rate)} \%} \text{ per cent,}$$

where the target rate is the required return on total assets.[5]

The relationship between the mark-up rate and the percentage margin is simply:

MARK-UP RATE =

$$\frac{100 \times \text{(Percentage Margin)}}{1 - \text{(Percentage Margin)}} \text{ per cent;}$$

and

PERCENTAGE MARGIN =

$$\frac{100 \times \text{(Mark-up Rate)} \%}{1 + \text{(Mark-up Rate)} \%} \text{ per cent.}$$

So far we have assumed that the mark-up rate is applied to total cost, that is to say, to the sum of all the manufacturing, administrative and marketing costs, but some firms interpret it as the margin which should provide both for the target rate of profit

---

[5] Note that in the formulae shown here all rates as also the percentage margin figure with their proper values. Thus, for example, a 20 per cent target rate should be entered as 0.2.

and the marketing cost. Though this somewhat complicates the formula, it can be a very useful tool of budgetary control. Since variations in the marketing costs are, at least within certain limits, at the discretion of the sales department, it is as well to make it clear how marketing costs influence the rate of return on capital. The mark-up rate which also covers the marketing costs is defined as the:

GROSS MARK-UP RATE =

$$100 \times \frac{\text{(Target Rate) \% × (Total Assets) + (Total Marketing Costs)}}{\text{(Total Manufacturing Costs) + (Total Administrative Costs)}} \text{ per cent,}$$

and similarly, we have the:

GROSS PERCENTAGE MARGIN =

$$100 \times \frac{\text{(Target Rate) \% × (Total Assets) + (Total Marketing Costs)}}{\text{(Sales)}} \text{ per cent.}$$

A simple numerical example may be used to verify these formulae. Let us assume the following data:

Total Assets	£100,000	Annual Costs:	
Total Annual Sales:		Manufacturing	£125,000
40,000 units at £6.25 each	£250,000	Administrative	45,000
		Marketing	60,000
		Total Annual Costs	£230,000

By applying the formulae, it will be found that:

Turnover Rate	2.5	Return on Capital (Target Rate)	20%
Percentage Margin	8%	Mark-up Rate	8.70%
Gross Percentage Margin	32%	Gross Mark-up Rate	47.06%

If the figures in the example are forecasts, the return on capital is the Target Rate, while the annual sales, costs and margins represent the expected combination which will enable the attainment of the target. It is not, of course, the only such combination; for example, if at the given price total annual sales should rise by 25 per cent without any increase in the capital employed, costs could increase by as much as 27.17 per cent before the rate of return on capital would drop below the original target. And if manufacturing and marketing costs should rise only in the same proportion as sales while administrative costs remain unchanged, the increase in turnover would raise the return on capital to 36.25 per cent. On the other hand, if the output target of 40,000 units could be sold only by lowering the price to £6.00 per unit, this 4 per cent reduction in price would cut the return on capital by half.

So far we have assumed that the firm has a single product only, which is seldom, if ever the case. In most multi-product companies the capital tied down by the different product groups and within them by the individual brands varies between wide limits and is difficult to ascertain with precision. The allocation of costs may not be possible with sufficient accuracy either, and while the average mark-up rate of the firm as a whole can still be of value in judging propositions concerning new products, a single rate of return on capital applying equally to all products becomes unrealistic. For this reason, businessmen often satisfy themselves by setting the target in terms of the average rate of return on capital.

Furthermore, not even a division of a larger company, separate from the rest and devoted entirely to a single uniform product can expect to sell the whole of its output at one and the same price all the way round, especially if it produces both for the home market and for export, and hence the mark-up rate (or the percentage margin) as interpreted above generally arises as the average result of a number of transactions.

To elucidate this point, let us elaborate the above example a bit further by assuming that the sales were distributed over three separate markets with different degrees of competition in each, and that the overall target was achieved by the following pattern of sales:

Market	Annual Sales		Earnings	Percentage Margin	Mark-up
A	14,348 units	£93,750	£11,250	12%	13.4%
B	20,435 units	125,000	7,500	6%	6.38%
C	5,217 units	31,250	1,250	4%	4.17%
Total	40,000 units	£250,000	£20,000	8%	8.70%

Assuming for the moment that the marketing costs per unit are the same throughout, it can be seen that if sales in Market A could be raised so as to yield a gross return of £125,000 without lowering price by as much as 2 per cent, it would be of advantage to abandon Market C altogether, provided this would not leave the division with unused productive capacity. The limiting case is shown here:

Market	Annual Sales		Earnings	Percentage Margin	Mark-up
A	19,565 units	£125,000	£12,500	10%	11.11%
B	20,435 units	125,000	7,500	6%	6.38%
Total	40,000 units	£250,000	£20,000	8%	8.70%

If, however, the goods from C should be transferred to B, and the price in B has to be reduced by more than 0.4 per cent, this would have an unfavourable effect on profits. The limiting position is then:

Market	Annual Sales		Earnings	Percentage Margin	Mark-up
A	14,348 units	£93,750	£11,250	12%	13.64%
B	25,652 units	156,250	8,750	5.6%	5.93%
Total	40,000 units	£250,000	£20,000	8%	8.70%

In general, the marketing costs will not be the same in all the markets, and this will also have to be taken into account in the pricing decision.

The practice of selling the same product or even different products at more than one mark-up rate is described as price discrimination or, in certain situations, as 'dumping', and is often condemned as one of the reprehensible features of monopolistic behaviour. In fact, as demonstrated later in this chapter, its essence is the sensible application of the incremental cost principle and, as shown in Chapters 7 and 8, is the accepted pricing policy of both public utilities and retailing. While it can be misused, it is not basically antagonistic to the interest of the consumers.

2   Cost-based pricing

There can be little doubt that the first aim of any business is survival, that is to say, to avoid closing the year with a loss. This is certainly true in the field of private enterprise, and even the British nationalized corporations were enjoined in the nationalization acts to balance their accounts at least in the long run, taking one year with another. (The fact that several of them are forced to survive on government subsidies year after year does not affect the principle and is not peculiar to public enterprise either – there is hardly a country where no privately owned firm has ever been subsidized.)

There are times when survival alone is justifiably looked upon as a creditable achievement. Such a time was the Great Depression of the nineteen-thirties, and it is small wonder that the device known as the *break-even chart* was born in that period and hailed as a useful guide to businessmen. In spite of its severe limitations, the break-even chart has not lost its relevance and deserves at least brief mention.

Figure 5.2 shows the break-even chart in its original form. B is the break-even point which indicates the minimum annual quantity of output (M) that must be sold to keep the firm out of the red. In a way, this is useful knowledge, but it should be noted that the chart is based on some pretty bold assumptions. Total gross sales returns are shown as strictly proportionate to the quantity of output, which means that prices are supposed to be invariant and also that the product-mix remains the same whatever the quantity sold. The composite price or, rather, the average value appears as the slope of the total gross sales returns line. Furthermore, it assumes that costs can strictly be divided into two categories: fixed costs (F), that is to say, overheads which are entirely independent of the output, and direct costs, such as labour and materials, etc., represented by the slope of the total costs line per unit of output, the total of which varies in strict proportion with the output. In fact, this last assumption is not quite unrealistic, insofar as the type of cost behaviour depicted in the break-even chart has been observed in a

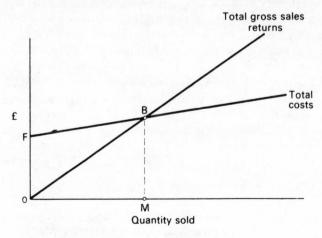

Figure 5.2   Break-even chart: original form

number of instances in manufacturing industry, over a range which extends from some minimum rate of output up to the point where full use is made of normal capacity.

The concept of normal capacity calls for some elucidation. It is not as a rule the same as the maximum technical capacity of the equipment as measured by the throughput when the whole of the machinery is utilized for 24 hours each day, 7 days each week. What is considered 'normal' will vary from firm to firm, from industry to industry and even over time. Normal working may mean, say, an average of 43 hours per week, of which 3 hours are overtime or, in some other trade, it may mean a two-shift or three-shift work schedule, allowing, say, for a 5 per cent safety margin and a day every fortnight for maintenance work. Normal capacity may depend on the traditional customs of the trade, the availability and willingness of the labour force and, last but not least, on the attitude of the chief executive or the board of the company. It has been found in an American enquiry that businessmen tend to look upon capacity as the rate of output at which total unit costs are lower than at any reduced rate of output, and there was also some implication that beyond that point total unit costs were expected to rise.[6]

Since price or, more properly, the average value of the firm's output is represented in the break-even chart by the slope of the gross sales returns line, it follows that if the price so interpreted goes up, the line will swivel upwards with the origin as its fulcrum, and the break-even point will move to the left.

It can be seen that the usefulness of the break-even chart is rather limited. It gives no indication of the level at which the price of any individual product or prices in general should be set, and takes no account whatever of the effect of prices on the quantities sold. It has a variant, however, which does take price changes into consideration. In order to demonstrate it, we have to assume that the demand curve for the company's product is known, for example as displayed in Figure 5.3. (a), which is based on the first two columns of the schedule in Table 5.1.

Figure 5.3 shows (a) the demand curve and (b) the total sales returns in accordance with the third column of Table 5.1, also the fixed cost. taken to be £1,500, and the direct cost at £5.80 per

---

[6] Cf. W. J. Eiteman and G. E. Guthrie, 'The Slope of the Average Cost Curve', *American Economic Review*, **42**, December 1952, pp. 832–38, also its discussion in the same journal, **43**, September 1953, pp. 621–30.

Table 5.1
Selected values of the demand function displayed in Fig. 5.3

In order to sell units of Product T	Price should be £	Total Sales Returns £
100	20.80	2,080
200	17.00	3,400
300	13.88	4,164
400	10.75	4,300
500	8.00	4,000
600	5.75	3,450
700	3.62	2,534
800	1.88	1,504
900	0.62	558
1,000	0	0

unit. The output M_o which would yield the highest profit lies between the two break-even points B_1 and B_2.

	Price £	Quantity sold units	Profit £
B_1	20.80	100	0
Maximum profit point	14.37	280	900
B_2	9.13	450	0

This kind of analysis is more in line with the economist's theory of price and output determination than with the approach of the businessman who can never hope to gain such a complete picture of the behaviour of market demand. It is for this reason that the break-even chart is generally quoted in its original form which takes price as given and indicates the lower break-even point only.

But true success is more than just staying alive. It means also profitability, and we will now turn to the ways in which unit costing endeavours to achieve it.

There are two methods that go under this heading. The first takes the full cost into consideration, including an allowance for all the overheads as calculated by the cost accountant, and adds the profit margin to the total. Full cost, cost-plus and absorption costing are the terms by which this method is known. The second relates the price to the direct cost of the product only, and augments it by what is called *the contribution* to cover both the overheads and the profit margin if sales reach the expected level. There is also a variant of the second method, generally referred to as marginal cost pricing or

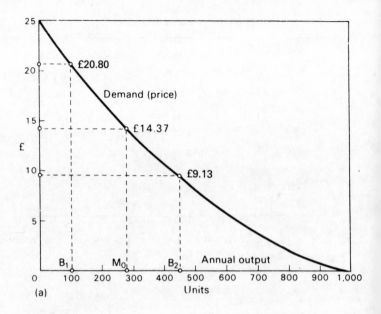

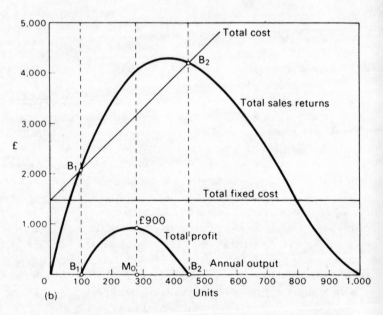

Figure 5.3   Break-even chart with price effect: (a) Demand curve; (b) Total revenue and cost curves

marginal pricing for short, though incremental cost pricing is a more appropriate name for it.[7]

The protagonists of this important variant either take price as something determined outside the firm and look upon the contribution simply as the price less direct costs, or suggest that the mark-up should be applied to the incremental cost, which is not always the same as the direct cost.

The nature of absorption costing and its shortcomings can best be explained with the aid of an example (Table 5.2). Let us consider a company that has three products, X, Y and Z, and plans to operate in the coming year according to the budget shown.

Table 5.2
Example of absorption costing

	Product			
	X	Y	Z	Total
Number of units	9,000	30,000	5,000	Total
Direct labour cost	£ 3,000	£ 7,000	£20,000	£30,000
Direct material cost	18,600	34,400	7,000	60,000
Total direct cost	£21,600	£41,400	£27,000	£90,000

Overhead costs amount to £45,000. This amount could be apportioned to the individual products according to an infinite number of formulae, of which four are displayed in Table 5.3.

The company's profit mark-up on the total absorption cost is 15 per cent. This could be a customary figure or one derived from a profit target of £20,000.

The unit costs of direct labour and materials arise as follows:

	X	Y	Z
Direct labour cost	£0.33	£0.23	£4.00
Direct material cost	2.07	1.15	1.40
Total direct unit cost	£2.40	£1.38	£5.40

[7] According to the economist's definition, marginal cost is the difference in total cost occasioned by increasing output by one unit per period. It is for this reason that the concept is more appropriate to the purposes of theorizing than to practical application. Incremental cost may refer to a batch of any size, (though it is, of course, always possible to calculate its average per unit, i.e. the incremental unit cost).

Table 5.3
Examples of formulae for apportioning overhead costs

		X	Y	Z	Total
(A)	50 per cent on total direct cost	£10,800	£20,700	£13,500	£45,000
(B)	150 per cent on direct labour cost	4,500	10,500	30,000	45,000
(C)	75 per cent on direct material cost	13,950	25,800	5,250	45,000
(D)	100 per cent on direct labour cost and 25 per cent on direct material cost	7,650	15,600	21,750	45,000

The above formulae of absorption cost allocation will then produce the four alternative sets of prices shown in Table 5.4.

Provided the annual output consists exactly of the planned quantities, and further provided that these quantities can in fact be sold at the prices calculated, any of the above formulae will produce the revenue required to cover all the costs and yield profits slightly in excess of £20,000. However, every one of the formulae by which overheads were allocated is arbitrary, as are all the others used by cost accountants. None of them could properly be justified since they are merely expressions of conventions and, as we can see here, they can produce widely differing prices for the same set of products. In this case, the price of X varies from £3.34 to £4.54, the price of Y from £1.99 to £2.58 and the price of Z from £7.42 to £13.11. In view of the fact that absorption cost pricing is frequently applied to get some idea of the prices the competition is likely to quote, it is not difficult to see why trade associations are apt to enjoin their members to adopt standard costing formulae.

When absorption cost pricing is applied in a competitive situation, the likely outcome is that, owing to two important shortcomings of the method, the planned sales pattern will fail to materialize. One of these shortcomings is that the method takes no account of the capital backing the different lines, and hence the more expensive facilities will tend to be kept very active, while the less

Table 5.4
Example of absorption cost prices based on different formulae

		X	Y	Z
(A)	Overheads 50 per cent on total direct cost	1.20	0.69	2.70
	Total unit cost	3.60	2.07	8.10
	15 per cent mark-up	0.54	0.31	1.22
	SELLING PRICE (A)	£4.14	£2.38	£9.32
(B)	Overheads 150 per cent on labour cost	0.50	0.35	6.00
	Total unit cost	2.90	1.73	11.40
	15 per cent mark-up	0.44	0.26	1.71
	SELLING PRICE (B)	£3.34	£1.99	£13.11
(C)	Overheads 75 per cent on material cost	1.55	0.86	1.05
	Total unit cost	3.95	2.24	6.45
	15 per cent mark-up	0.59	0.34	0.97
	SELLING PRICE (C)	£4.54	£2.58	£7.42
(D)	Overheads 100 per cent on labour cost	0.33	0.23	4.00
	plus 25 per cent on material cost	0.52	0.29	0.35
	Total unit cost	3.25	1.90	9.75
	15 per cent mark-up	0.49	0.29	1.46
	SELLING PRICE (D)	£3.74	£2.19	£11.21

expensive facilities will be under-utilized.[8] The other shortcoming is probably even more important: the neglect of the demand.

In order to overcome the first shortcoming, it has been proposed that the cost of capital (which may be identified with the profit

---

[8] It has been suggested that the underpricing of the products requiring expensive facilities may well provide the firm with an impressive volume of orders, which in turn would seem to encourage further investment. When profits begin to wane, the fight for more volume could result in desperation pricing, with disastrous results for the firm and the market. Cf. S. A. Tucker, *Pricing for Higher Profits*, McGraw-Hill, New York, NY, 1966, p. 46.

target) should be allocated to each product according to some indicator, e.g. machine-hours, and it is quite likely that if all the suppliers in a given market would adopt similar procedures, a more balanced situation than that generally encountered at present would develop.[9] While there is some good sense in this suggestion, the solution which it offers is not entirely satisfactory, insofar as it takes only the supply side of the market into consideration.

As far as the demand side is concerned, it is an oft encountered proposition to desist from allocating overheads and look upon the price as the sum of direct costs and a contribution to the fund from which all other costs and profits are to be met. This is the second method of cost-based pricing mentioned above, and we shall use some of the data of the last example to compare it with absorption cost pricing.

Figure 5.4 incorporates certain assumptions similar to those of the break-even chart: up to capacity, the direct costs, clearly separated from the fixed overhead costs, are strictly proportional to the output. However, while the break-even chart displays total costs and returns, in Figure 5.4 unit cost and price are measured on the vertical axis. It should further be noted that whereas the output of the company as a whole is measured along the horizontal axis of the

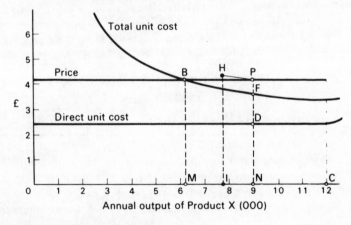

Figure 5.4   Unit costing

---

[9] Cf. H. P. Kelley, 'Cost-price Squeeze: How to establish selling prices', *Cost and Management*, June 1965, pp. 243–51; reprinted in *Pricing Strategy*, (B. Taylor and G. Wills, eds), Staples, London, 1969, pp. 370–80.

break-even chart, in Figure 5.4 the same axis refers to Product X only.

Capacity (C) is assumed to be 12,000 units per annum, and the expected rate of utilization (N) is 75 per cent, that is 9,000 units in the coming year. At this output, direct cost (ND) is £2.40, fixed cost (DF) as allocated by Formula (A) is £1.20 and the 15 per cent mark-up for profit (FP) being £0.54, the resulting price (NP) is £4.14. We can further see that the break-even point where the price equals average cost is at (B), indicating an output (M) of 6,207 units.

Let us now assume that in the following year the market has become more difficult and the expected capacity utilization is down from 75 per cent (N) to 65 per cent (I) for X, as also for all the other products. Pricing formula (A) would then have to be revised accordingly, and the overhead charge on direct cost would become 57.5 per cent, raising the price of Product X from £4.14 to £4.35, denoted by (IH) in Figure 5.4:

Direct costs	£2.40
Overheads £10,800/7,800	1.38
Total unit cost	3.78
15 per cent mark-up	0.57
SELLING PRICE	£4.35

It is obvious that only a very strong monopoly could be expected to act in this way with impunity; any firm exposed to keen competition is more likely to drop its price when sales are falling off. Yet, it is found time and again than when businessmen are questioned about their pricing practices, the majority will say that they use an absorption cost-based pricing method.

One might well ask how it is possible that they survive if they behave in such an irrational way. The answer is that not all of them survive, and those who do will be found to act rather differently from their stated principles.

This discrepancy between avowed behaviour and actual practices should not be ascribed to any intention of the businessman to mislead, but rather to the inability of some researchers not versed in the ways of business to set about the job in an efficient way. If we turn to the reports on the results of enquiries conducted by persons with appropriate business experience, we find evidence that pricing is not in fact carried out by the alleged mechanistic application of cost-based formulae. As Edwards found it, 'the manufacturer has a "hunch" as to the price at which his article can be sold, and makes use of "costing" or "estimating" to justify that price'.[10]

Even more revealing are the studies of Pearce and Amey, who examined the actual pricing practices of the firms studied before they interviewed the executives. In one instance, where the managers of the firm mentioned a profit mark-up of one-twelfth of the cost, a sample of orders confirmed that this was about the average achieved in the year concerned, but the mark-up on the individual orders examined varied between minus 4 per cent and plus 44 per cent. Similarly, Atkin and Skinner found in their enquiry that the main method of pricing appears to be adding a percentage to cost but out of the 190 industrialists who claimed that their prices were based on cost, 188 (99 per cent) subsequently admitted that they did not refrain from modifying their prices on the basis of non-cost-related considerations. The remaining 2 (1 per cent) failed to commit themselves on this issue.[11]

Let us now compare absorption cost pricing with direct cost pricing. As said above, the essence of the latter is to look upon the price as consisting of the direct unit cost and a contribution. Tucker, one of the leading protagonists of this method of pricing, identifies the direct cost with the out-of-pocket expenses necessitated by producing some given batch of a product, while the contribution is simply the difference between the price and all the out-of-pocket

---

[10] Ronald S. Edwards, 'The Pricing of Manufactured Products', *Economica (NS)*, **19**, (75), August 1952, p. 304. According to Fisher, the arguments in favour of absorption cost pricing (also called 'full-cost pricing') are that it reminds the price setter that overheads and profit should be covered, that it is a quick and inexpensive method of approximation where the attitude of the market is unknown, and that there is a feeling that the full-cost price is a 'just price', i.e. that it is generally regarded as a fair means of fixing prices. However, he also suggests that full-cost pricing is 'watered down in practice'. Cf. Lawrence Fisher, *Industrial Marketing*, Business Books, London, 1969, p. 211.

[11] Cf. I. F. Pearce, 'A Study in Price Policy', *Economica (NS)*, **23**, May 1956, pp. 114–27; I. F. Pearce and Lloyd R. Amey, 'Price Policy with a Branded Product', *Review of Economic Studies*, **24**, (63), 1956–7, pp. 49–60; Bryan Atkin and Richard Skinner, *How British Industry Prices*, Industrial Market Research Limited, London, 1975; also G. R. Foxall, 'The Logic of Price Decision Making', *Management Decision*, **18**, (5), 1980, pp. 235–45; and Stewart A. Washburn, 'Establishing Strategy and Determining Costs in the Pricing Decision', *Business Marketing*, **70**, July 1985, pp. 64–78.

expenses.[12] We may, however, look upon the contribution also as the mark-up on direct cost, and use Figure 5.4 to demonstrate how the result differs from that of the absorption cost-based method, even if it yields the same price of £4.14 for Product X. Any individual order of 1,000 units, say, would at this price produce a contribution of £1,740, and an annual output of 9,000 units would contribute a total of £15,660 to the central pool. How much of this would be required to cover fixed costs and how much would be left for profit would depend on the output and sales returns of the company as a whole.

So far there seems to be no difference between the two methods, but whereas absorption cost pricing demanded an increase in price to £4.35 when capacity utilization declined to 65 per cent, direct cost pricing would still accept an order at £4.14, or even at a lower price, provided, of course, that there was no better opportunity available at the moment. For this reason alone, direct cost pricing appears to be both more rational and nearer to actual business practice than absorption cost pricing.

However, the difference between the two methods goes deeper than that. The direct cost plus contribution approach is not so much a method for setting a price as rather for deciding whether the ruling market price or the price of an individual order should be accepted or rejected. It does not therefore entirely disregard the demand for the product, (which is exactly what any rigid absorption cost formula does,) but it still suffers from the limitation that it takes an entirely passive attitude to the market.

A closer examination of the issue reveals that the essence of the direct cost plus contribution approach conforms to the basic definition of economics as a study of the alternative choices open to man faced with an economic problem. The price arrived at by means of absorption costing compared with the price actually attainable purports to indicate (often misleadingly) the apparent profit or loss that would result from acceptance. Not so with the direct cost approach which tells the businessman only whether the price offered is above or below his direct or out-of-pocket cost, but this provides him with a realistic basis for comparing the order in question with the available alternatives.

---

[12] S. A. Tucker, op cit, pp. 80, 121–3 and *passim*. For a systematic exposition of the contribution method see also Albert J. Bergfeld, James S. Earley and William R. Knobloch, *Pricing for Profit and Growth*, Prentice-Hall, Inc., Englewood Cliffs, NJ, 1962.

For example, if the market price of Product Z should fall below £11.40, Formula (B) would indicate that an order for, say, 400 units at £10.00 each would generate sales of £4,000 but involve a net loss of £560, and that the order should therefore be rejected.

The direct cost approach (which may, in this case, well be described as the incremental cost approach) would record a contribution of £1,840, and acceptance should turn on whether or not there is a more desirable utilization of the same facilities available. Let us assume that there exists just one alternative, and that it is an order for 2,000 units of Product X at a price of £3.10. This would lead to sales of £6,200, and according to Formula (B) to a net profit of £400, hence on these counts it looks much more favourable than the first order. However, when we look at the contribution, we find that it amounts only to £1,400. It follows that the first order offers the better opportunity, but there is yet another aspect of the issue to consider before a final decision is taken.

The incremental cost method of appraisal is ideally suited to the purposes of jobbing firms, subsisting on large numbers of relatively small orders, the rejection of any of which would not materially affect the future prospects of the company. But even in this case, if an actual or potential customer should find that Bloggs & Co. invariably put in the highest quotation, he will sooner or later drop Bloggs & Co. from the list of suppliers from whom tenders may be invited.

In the general case, acceptance or rejection should depend on the long-run consequences of the decision. On the one hand, there is the customer to consider. If we reject a particular order of his, he will have to go to one of our competitors who will almost certainly make an effort to oblige him so as to get a foot inside the door. If this order is satisfactorily completed, our customer will be asked for further business and if this is granted, we could lose him altogether. Then, on the other hand, there is the effect on the market as a whole. It was mentioned earlier in this chapter that the image of a company and its profitability can seriously be affected if its marketing policy allows unduly large variations in prices, and reference was made to a remedy consisting of differentiating the brand. Another, oft-used expedient is to undertake sub-contracting when there is empty capacity, yet another is to seek an export market for the cheaper lot.[13]

---

[13] This is frequently described as 'dumping' and resented in both markets.

The knowledge of the incremental cost per unit also enables the estimation of the effect of a price change, applied to all the sales of a given product on its contribution and, thereby, on the total profits of the company. Let us denote the present price by p_0, the number of units sold per annum by n_0, and the new price by p_1. If then the incremental cost per unit is c_i, the break-even level of units to be sold is given by the formula

$$n_1 = n_0 \frac{p_0 - c_i}{p_1 - c_i}.$$

For example, if $n_0 = 12,000$ units, $p_0 = £2.00$, $p_1 = £1.70$ and $c_i = £0.95$, we obtain

$$n_1 = 12,000 \frac{2.00 - 0.95}{1.70 - 0.95} = 16,800 \text{ units;}$$

which means that an increase of 40 per cent of the number of units sold is required to compensate for a 15 per cent reduction in price.

The formula applies whether the new price is higher or lower than the original price, but the incremental cost per unit may depend on the direction of the change. Let us assume that in this case the cost saved per unit not produced is still £0.95, and that an increase of the price to £2.20 is being contemplated. Then

$$n_1 = 12,000 \frac{2.00 - 0.95}{2.20 - 0.95} = 10,080 \text{ units;}$$

a decrease of 16 per cent of the number of units sold would leave the total contribution unaffected.

Both the calculated outputs represent break-even points.[14] If the

---

Customers in the home market ask why they could not be served at the cheaper price, while those who regularly supply similar goods to the export market resent the undercutting of their prices, and lament that if they are ruined, their customers will be at the mercy of the invader. Yet, there are situations where this sort of marketing policy is in the best interest of the consumers all the way round. The issue will be taken up in Chapters 6 and 7, under the heading of price discrimination.

[14] This can be demonstrated with reference to the numerical results:

$$16,800 \times £1.70 = £28,560$$
$$\text{Less} \quad 4,800 \times £0.95 = -4,560$$
$$\overline{}$$
$$£24,000 = 12,000 \times £2.00$$

price reduction is to have a beneficial effect on profits, sales should rise above 16,800 units per year; if the price increase is to pay, it should not reduce sales by as many as 1,920 units.

Table 5.5 contains the break-even points for price changes from -35 to $+35$ per cent and incremental unit cost levels ranging from 0 to 95 per cent of the original price. For example, a 20 per cent reduction in the price of a product the incremental unit cost of which is 30 per cent of the original price will leave the contribution from the product unchanged if the number of units sold rises to 140 per cent of the original level.

The entries in the table are based on the assumption that the incremental cost per unit (taken to be identical with the average direct cost) is not affected by changes in the number of units sold. This is not invariably the case; for example, a retail store may find that by increasing the turnover of a certain product a quantity rebate will reduce the cost per unit from £0.95 to £0.90. Then, if the other figures of the previous example apply, we find that

$$n_1 = 12,000 \, \frac{2.00 - 0.95}{1.70 - 0.90} = 15,750 \text{ units,}$$

hence provided the number of units sold increases by 32 per cent or more, the price reduction will have a beneficial effect on the total contribution, whereas without the quantity rebate this would call for an increase of over 40 per cent.[15]

---

also $10,080 \times £2.20 = £22,176$
            Plus $1,920 \times £0.95 = +1,824$
                                    ———————
                             $£24,000 = 12,000 \times £2.00$

[15] The general formula for the number of units that should be sold per period so as to leave the total contribution unaffected by the consequences of a price increase or decrease when there is also a change in unit cost can be written

$$n_1 = n_0 \times (p_0 - c_0)/(p_1 - c_1),$$

where $n_0 =$ the number of units sold per period before the price change;
$\qquad n_1 =$ the required number of units to be sold after the price change;
$\qquad p_0 =$ the original price; $\qquad p_1 =$ the new price;
$\qquad c_0 =$ the original unit cost; $\qquad c_1 =$ the new unit cost

Alternatively, we can calculate c_1, the new unit cost that would leave the total contribution unchanged when, in response to a price variation, there is a change in the number of units sold per period from

$$c_1 = p_1 - n_0 \times (p_0 - c_0)/n_1,$$

which can also be written

$$c_1 = p_1 - (\text{Required Total Contribution})/n_1.$$

Table 5.5
Break-even points for judging the profitability of price changes

Incremental cost per unit as % of the original price	Percentage difference between the original price and the new price														
	−35	−30	−25	−20	−15	−10	−5	0	+5	+10	+15	+20	+25	+30	+35
0	153.85	142.86	133.33	125.00	117.65	111.11	105.26	100	95.24	90.91	86.96	83.33	80.00	76.92	74.07
5	158.33	146.15	135.71	126.67	118.75	111.76	105.56	100	95.00	90.48	86.36	82.61	79.17	76.00	73.08
10	163.64	150.00	138.46	128.57	120.00	112.50	105.88	100	94.74	90.00	85.71	81.82	78.26	75.00	72.00
15	170.00	154.55	141.67	130.77	121.43	113.33	106.25	100	94.44	89.47	85.00	80.95	77.27	73.91	70.83
20	177.78	160.00	145.46	133.33	123.08	114.29	106.67	100	94.12	88.89	84.21	80.00	76.19	72.73	69.57
25	187.50	166.67	150.00	136.36	125.00	115.38	107.14	100	93.75	88.24	83.33	78.95	75.00	71.43	68.18
30	200.00	175.00	155.56	140.00	127.27	116.67	107.69	100	93.33	87.50	82.35	77.78	73.68	70.00	66.67
35	216.67	185.71	162.50	144.44	130.00	118.18	108.33	100	92.86	86.67	81.25	76.47	72.22	68.42	65.00
40	240.00	200.00	171.43	150.00	133.33	120.00	109.09	100	92.31	85.71	80.00	75.00	70.59	66.67	63.16
45	275.00	220.00	183.33	157.14	137.50	122.22	110.00	100	91.67	84.62	78.57	73.33	68.75	64.71	61.11
50	333.33	250.00	200.00	166.67	142.86	125.00	111.11	100	90.91	83.33	76.92	71.43	66.67	62.50	58.82
55	450.00	300.00	225.00	180.00	150.00	128.57	112.50	100	90.00	81.82	75.00	69.23	64.29	60.00	56.25
60	800.00	400.00	266.67	200.00	160.00	133.33	114.29	100	88.89	80.00	72.73	66.67	61.54	57.14	53.33
65		700.00	350.00	233.33	175.00	140.00	116.67	100	87.50	77.78	70.00	63.64	58.33	53.85	50.00
70			600.00	300.00	200.00	150.00	120.00	100	85.71	75.00	66.67	60.00	54.55	50.00	46.15
75				500.00	250.00	166.67	125.00	100	83.33	71.43	62.50	55.56	50.00	45.45	41.67
80					400.00	200.00	133.33	100	80.00	66.67	57.14	50.00	44.44	40.00	36.37
85						300.00	150.00	100	75.00	60.00	50.00	42.86	37.50	33.33	30.00
90							200.00	100	66.67	50.00	40.00	33.33	28.57	25.00	22.22
95								100	50.00	33.33	25.00	20.00	16.67	14.29	12.50

The entries in this table indicate the break-even levels of the quantities sold after a price change, calculated from the formula n_1 as a percentage of $n_0 = 100(p_0 - c_1)/(p_1 - c_1)$.

Both the break-even chart in Figure 5.2 and the diagram in Figure 5.3 involved the assumption that all the direct costs per unit are the same at any rate of output below the capacity point. While it is recognized that there is a certain minimum rate of output below which this does not apply, it is generally safe to neglect this lower limit since few firms, if any, could survive if their capacities were heavily and permanently under-utilized. More important is the fact that some, if not all, of the direct cost factors (which, in manufacturing, generally include power, lubricating oil, transport, etc., in addition to labour and materials) may be responsible for unit costs which do not remain invariant when the rate of output is changed.

The example last shown has demonstrated how a change in incremental cost can be handled if it applies uniformly to all units. This is not an essential condition of the analysis; it can be relaxed as long as we know how the cost is related to the rate of output. For example, if overtime working is involved, the rule may be that over and above a basic week of 40 hours, say, overtime rates 50 per cent higher than the normal have to be paid. The total variable cost line would then display a kink at the point where the overtime rate begins to operate, and the incremental unit cost would show a step. This is illustrated in Figure 5.5. (a) and (b), for the case of Product W with the following cost structure:

Direct unit costs of Product W:

	Up to 180 units per week	181–200 units per week
Direct labour cost	£14	£21
Direct material cost	3	3
Total direct cost per unit	£17	£24

In Figure 5.5 the capacity (C) includes the possible overtime hours, and (N) denotes the output of 40 hours per week. Up to 180 units per week the average direct cost (not separately displayed in the diagram) would remain constant and identical with the incremental unit cost, then it would gradually increase at a slightly reducing rate, as shown in Table 5.6 for some selected rates of output.

It can be seen that for a single order of 200 units per week the contribution would have to be calculated with a direct unit cost of £17.70, but if two separate orders should have been received in succession, the first for 180 units per week and the second for 20 units per week, the direct unit cost of the former would be £17.00 and of the latter £24.00.

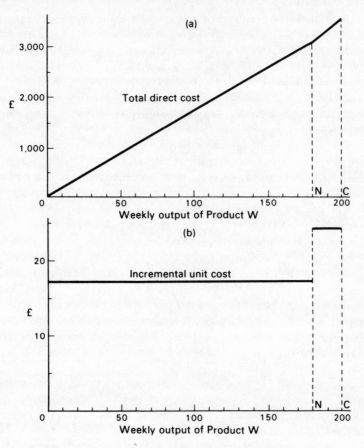

Figure 5.5 Effect of overtime rates (a) on total direct cost; (b) on incremental unit cost

Table 5.6
Average direct unit cost at selected rates of output

Weekly output of Product W	Average direct unit cost	Increase in average direct unit cost
180 units per week or less	£17.00	
185 units per week	17.19	19p
190 units per week	17.37	18p
195 units per week	17.54	17p
200 units per week	17.70	16p

It should further be evident why jobbing firms particularly welcome contracts for recurring work which allows ample time for completion and can hence be carried out over periods when the plant would otherwise be idle. The printing of a quarterly journal provides a typical example: most printers would be prepared to undertake it at a much lower price per issue than they would quote for a brochure of similar size and quantity to be produced at short notice.

If labour is not remunerated by time rates but by some incentive wage system, the analysis will be similar: at every point where a higher piece rate or bonus comes into operation, a break of the kind discussed above will appear on the charts.

Material costs are likely to vary in the opposite direction, mainly owing to quantity rebates or to a reduction in transport costs when the size of the batch reaches a certain magnitude, as for example when the order is large enough to make one or more full wagonloads. But if, in consequence of the urgency of an order, materials have to be obtained in great haste, their cost is likely to increase. The materials may have to be procured from a more expensive source than usual, there could be a need for fast transport (say conveyance by air instead of by rail or boat,) but other reasons for higher material costs are also possible, e.g. the spot price may be higher than the forward price.

There are also step costs of a different kind. If, for example, the work is carried out in separate sheds and only those in use are heated and lit, the average cost per unit of the product will behave as illustrated in Figure 5.6: it will jump a step at each output where another identical shed has to be opened for work, and then gradually decline to the lowest level previously reached.

There are other variable and semi-variable costs which behave in ways different from those here illustrated. Their nature has to be examined individually in each case, and if the item is relatively unimportant, it may be permissible to include an estimate of it in those expenses which are treated as fixed costs.

It should further be realized that neither labour nor material cost is always freely variable. For a variety of reasons labour cannot nowadays be hired and fired at will. Humanitarian considerations are generally present, redundancy payments tend to act as a deterrent to dismissal, and there is also the fact that if dismissed, the best workers will soon find employment elsewhere and thus cease to be available when again needed. For such reasons part or even the whole of the wage bill can become an inescapable cost in the short

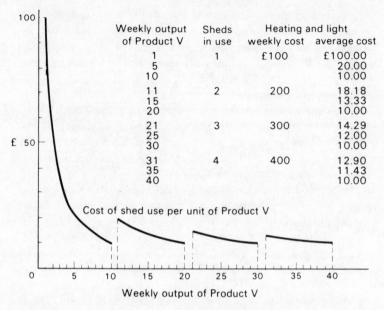

Weekly output of Product V	Sheds in use	Heating and light weekly cost	Heating and light average cost
1	1	£100	£100.00
5			20.00
10			10.00
11	2	200	18.18
15			13.33
20			10.00
21	3	300	14.29
25			12.00
30			10.00
31	4	400	12.90
35			11.43
40			10.00

Figure 5.6 Effect of step cost on unit cost

run and it is then more of the nature of an item of fixed cost than variable cost.

It can also happen with materials: any stock or regular contractual delivery of a perishable substance like milk becomes an inescapable cost, since it will have to be paid for, whether used or not. It is important to realize that true fixed costs are those that arise out of a legal, contractual or moral obligation and are not, as some people mistakenly believe, caused by the depreciation of machinery and other fixed factors. Accountants may have good reasons to charge depreciation regularly but any sensible businessman will know that this does not mean that the amount calculated by the accountant from some conventional formula actually has to be set aside as and when the entry is made in the books. What really matters is whether the item concerned, a machine tool, say, has earned its keep during its active lifetime or not – the actual rhythm of the earnings is largely irrelevant. On the other hand, if the machine should be hired on a royalty basis the amount of which depends on the rate of use, the cost will be a truly variable one, even if not strictly proportional to the output.

Rent is a typical item of fixed cost, but the notional rent of land or buildings owned should be looked upon in much the same way as depreciation charges, simply because, unlike rent paid to a third person, the income forgone by not leasing one's real estate to a tenant does not constitute a charge that has to be met on certain dates. As with machinery, the only thing which matters is that the returns arising out of the use of land or buildings should, in the long run, justify the investment.

It was mentioned above that some authors, including Tucker, identify what we called direct costs with the out-of-pocket expenses necessitated by producing some given batch of a product. The concept of out-of-pocket expenses appears to be self-explanatory, yet it may not always be easy to apply. While the labour force is fully employed, and especially when the order book is so long that any further order accepted must mean another order refused, the true cost of putting available resources to a specific use is the value of the forgone alternative. If, for example, there is some idle capacity in the capital equipment but labour is short, the out-of-pocket costs of labour, (the wage plus bonuses, social security payments, etc.), matter only insofar as they enable us to compare the contributions that are expected to arise from alternative uses of those available factors which put a limit on the extent of the productive activities of the firm; labour in this case.

Table 5.7 demonstrates the application of the contribution method to the assessment of the comparative profitability of three different products of a company in four separate markets by bringing together the relevant data in a comprehensive statement. It is complemented by the detailed definitions of the four main concepts involved.

The basic concepts of the contribution approach

- *Variable costs* are those which depend on output, such as the wages of direct labour, the cost of raw materials, power, etc. In manufacturing industry these costs tend to vary proportionally with output, unless affected by overtime rates, bonuses, quantity discounts or surcharges on material purchases, and such like. They should be apportioned to sales as indicated in Table 5.7.
- *Fixed costs* arise out of legal or moral obligations and can be varied in the long run only. Typical items are rents, interest charges on loan capital, licence fees and the remuneration of the permanent staff. They can arise at various levels, for

Table 5.7
Comparative profitability of products and markets

Product	Market					Less Product Specific Fixed and Programmed Production Costs	Net product contribution
	UK	France	Germany	USA	Total		
ALPHA:							
GC	650,000	300,000	250,000	74,000	1,274,000		
−SPC	180,000	92,000	110,000	8,000	390,000		
=PMC	470,000	208,000	140,000	66,000	884,000	175,000	709,000
BETA:							
GC	475,000	120,000	310,000	150,000	1,055,000		
−SPC	170,000	62,000	57,000	28,000	317,000		
=PMC	305,000	58,000	253,000	122,000	738,000	68,000	670,000
GAMMA:							
GC	189,000	90,000	15,000	63,000	357,000		
−SPC	15,000	18,000	—	21,000	54,000		
=PMC	174,000	72,000	15,000	42,000	303,000	42,000	261,000
TOTAL PMC	949,000	338,000	408,000	230,000	1,925,000	285,000	1,640,000
Less Divisional Fixed and Programmed Costs	280,000	152,000	121,000	75,000	628,000		628,000
NET MARKET CONTRIBUTION	669,000	186,000	287,000	155,000	1,297,000	285,000	1,012,000
					Less Corporate Fixed and Programmed Costs		203,000
					CORPORATE PROFIT BEFORE TAX		£809,000

GC = Gross Contribution (= £ Annual Sales Less Variable Cost)
SPC = Product/Market Specific Fixed and Programmed Costs
PMC = Product/Market Contribution

example, the annual rent of a local warehouse on long lease would be charged to the product for which it is exclusively used, but to the division if used for more than one product, while the rent of the headquarters arise at the corporate level.

- *Programmed costs* are subject to deliberate variation, but once decided upon become inescapable. The cost of advertising, market research, the rent of premises needed for some short period only, as also the salary and expense allowance of a salesman on a short contract fall into this category. Like fixed costs, they can arise at various levels.
- *Corporate profit before tax* is the residual after allowance has been made for all expenses and also for the depreciation of the fixed equipment. The latter is not a true fixed cost, insofar as it does not represent actual outlay over the year, but has to be allowed for in order to arrive at the taxable corporate profit.

In closing, let us emphasize the truth of the old adage, according to which 'cost does not determine price, what it determines is whether the product concerned can be profitably produced or not'. Indeed, as revealed by all properly conducted studies of pricing practices, the businessman has to keep one eye on the market and one on costs;[16] on direct costs and the contribution in the day-to-day conduct of his affairs, but taking all costs into account when making decisions affecting the long-term. The contribution method is best adapted to the former, but there are three cases which explicitly call for absorption costing. The first case is that of the 'cost plus a stipulated profit percentage' contract, much used when a company is commissioned by the government or by another customer to turn out a product with which it has not had any previous experience, as for instance when the order involves development work. The second case arises when a company has to justify its pricing before a regulatory body, and, finally, absorption costing might occasionally be useful in estimating the price a competitor is likely to quote, provided there is some knowledge of his cost accounting practices.

---

[16] Cf. for example, '... 40 of the 44 firms included in this study considered both market conditions and costs in determining the prices of their product lines (i.e. the two procedures were not mutually exclusive)'. L. A. Gordon, *et al.*, *The Pricing Decision*, National Association of Accountants, New York, NY, 1981, p. 23. For an approach recommending the simultaneous consideration of price in relation to internal and external factors cf. Alfred R. Oxenfeldt, 'The Differential Method of Pricing', *European Journal of Marketing*, **13**, (4), 1979, pp. 199–212.

Summary

Having cleared the ground in the foregoing chapters by reviewing the basic theory of price, the main goals of busines enterprises and the principles which should govern investment decisions, we were ready to embark upon the discussion of specific pricing policies and procedures.

Most business firms attempt to pursue more than one goal: they may simultaneously want to achieve profitability, growth, price stability, prestige, etc. Some of the aims may not be compatible with others, but to the extent to which they are, the ideal pricing policy should serve them all and also lead to the appropriate pricing procedure.

The topic of Chapter 5 was profit-oriented and cost-based pricing; the practices most business firms claim to follow in determining their prices. Profit-oriented pricing is generally exercised by setting a target rate for the next accounting period, (usually a year), and the rate decided upon is then translated into terms that can serve as guide-lines to the lower echelons: annual sales, costs and margins. The way in which the target can be achieved is not unique and it has been shown how the out-turn can be affected by changes in the pattern of sales and prices.

Cost-based pricing has two main divisions: absorption cost and direct cost. Absorption cost was used in the original form of the break-even chart and in the variant demonstrated in this chapter. The principal purport of break-even analysis is the emphasis on survival; certainly an important aspect but seldom a sufficient criterion of full success. Absorption costing attempts to determine the unit cost of each product, but since its rules are essentially arbitrary, the results can be dangerously misleading, even if the allocation embraces the cost of capital. The main shortcoming of absorption cost pricing is the neglect of the demand.

Direct cost pricing meets some of the objections to absorption cost pricing but, and this applies especially to the variant known as marginal cost pricing (or, more correctly, incremental cost pricing), it is not so much a method of price determination as rather a guide to the choice between orders competing for the use of the same facilities. The criterion generally used is *the contribution*, meaning the difference between the price and the direct costs. What these costs are has to be determined individually in each case. Wages, for example, are certainly direct costs as long as they are freely variable, but if the alternative to accepting an order is an idle labour force still paid at the same rate, the outlay on wages assumes the character of a fixed cost.

The incremental cost method is well suited to the purposes of the jobbing firm, the long-run prospects of which are not seriously affected by the refusal of an individual order. Most other kinds of firms have to take into consideration the effects of price variations on the market, and may find it preferable to eschew price cutting and resort to sub-contracting or to the production of private label goods for other firms in order to achieve a satisfactory degree of capacity utilization.

Direct costs are often found to vary in strict proportion with the rate of output, but overtime rates, bonuses, etc., which introduce non-proportionality, can be accommodated in the analysis without any great difficulty.

The best known alternative to absorption costing is the contribution approach. Its concepts are defined and their application demonstrated with an example towards the end of the chapter.

There is, however, no alternative to absorption cost pricing where a contract is awarded on the 'cost plus' basis, or if pricing has to be justified to an official body. Absorption costing might also be found useful in estimating the price a competitor is likely to quote.

Attention is called to the example of a check list for price reviews on pp. 296–8. It complements Table 5.7, p. 79.

Costing and pricing in inflation are discussed in the Appendix to this chapter.

APPENDIX TO CHAPTER 5: COSTING AND PRICING IN INFLATION

1 Costing

The fundamental purpose of accounting is to reveal if the company's substance is being preserved and to determine its profitability. However, when costs and prices are not stable over time, historical cost accounting loses its significance and needs adjustments for the changes that have taken place over the accounting period.

There are two main alternatives available for supplementing or replacing historical cost accounting:

1 *Current Purchasing Power Accounting (CPPA)*, which consists in the adjustment of money amounts with the movement of a general price index; and

2 *Current Cost Accounting (CCA)*, the essence of which is the substitution of an up-to-date value for each historical cost item, either by the application of a specific index,[1] or by individual reappraisal. As far as the latter is concerned, there are three different methods available for the revaluation of assets:

   (a) Replacement cost, based on the current purchase price of the item.

   (b) Net realizable value, i.e. sale value.

   (c) Estimate of the present value of the expected future benefit of the asset.

---

[1] In the United Kingdom appropriate index numbers are compiled by the Business Statistics Office and published in the *Monthly Supplement to the Business Monitors: Price Index Numbers for Current Cost Accounting*, MM17, H.M. Stationery Office, London. The Accounting Standards Committee of the accountancy profession has outlined the general principles of CCA in *SSAP 16 – Statement of Standard Accounting Practice No. 16* and *Guidance Notes on SSAP 16*, 1980; both superseded by *Exposure Draft 35 – Accounting for the Effects of Changing Prices*, 1984. This proposed statement of standard accounting practices having been withdrawn in 1985, the profession has no agreed rules of CCA at present. The Accounting Standards Committee has, however, issued *Accounting for the Effects of Changing Prices – A Handbook*, London, 1986. For an expert exposition of the issue see G. A. Lee, *Modern Financial Accounting*, 4th edn, Van Nostrand Reinhold, Wokingham, 1986, Chapter 7, pp. 130–62.

CPPA appears to be well suited for assessing the change in the real value of certain financial assets and liabilities (such as cash, bank balances, debts payable and receivable, the outstanding value of a mortgage, etc.). The index by which the adjustment is made should be selected with a view to the nature of the item; the index of retail prices might be appropriate for some purposes but not for all. If, for example, cash is held in readiness for restocking, its real value is governed by the changes in the prices of the goods on which it will eventually be spent.

CCA is of much wider applicability and there is no reason why any of its three alternative methods should be used exclusively.

Current purchase price, that is, replacement cost, is fully appropriate for materials and bought components of unchanged specifications; it may also apply to items of fixed equipment as long as identical or, at least, similar units are currently available, though in the latter case some adjustment will be required to account for the difference, in addition to the allowance made for the reduction in value due to wear and tear and, possibly, obsolescence. Current wage rates for labour costs of work in progress and of stocks of finished products are also the correct basis for revaluation.

Net realizable value, that is sale value, will only in certain cases equal the replacement cost. It appears to be particularly suitable for estimating the current value of land and some buildings, while in the case of assets that are replaced at relatively frequent intervals, such as fleets of automobiles and trucks, the current trade-in values should provide reliable guidance.

If an item of equipment or a building has no realistic market price but still contributes to the output of the company, the present value of its expected future benefits should be estimated; if necessary, by the judicious application of the Discounted Cash Flow method described in the Appendix to Chapter 4, pp. 46–8.

2   Pricing

There are essentially two methods whereby pricing can effectively deal with continuously changing costs: one of them is to account for the increase (or decrease) whenever prices are revised, while the other consists in the application of escalation clauses to contracts for future deliveries.

It has been forcibly argued by Dean that 'prices must go up faster than costs so as to widen the profit margin enough to compensate invested capital that is made more expensive by inflation'.[2] Dean has, of course, recognized that the ability to increase prices is limited by the behaviour of the competition and recommended rate-of-return pricing for industrial products: the customers should be told: 'To be sure, buying my competitor's product will give you a 25 per cent rate of return and that is better than keeping your old equipment; but buying my product will give you a 30 per cent rate of return'.[3]

It is obvious that if increasing prices ahead of the rate at which costs are rising becomes general practice, this will not just perpetuate but actually accelerate the inflationary tendency. On the other hand, contracts with escalation clauses can be claimed to be of advantage both to the supplier and to the customer, insofar as they provide protection to the supplier against cost increases, while the customer is assured that he will not be charged more than the appropriate value of the goods concerned at the time of delivery.

According to Tatham and Allen, properly constructed escalation clauses should cover the following points:[4]

1 Description of the elements of cost that are subject to escalation;
2 Stipulation of the index to be applied to each cost category;
3 Indication of the frequency with which the contract price will be adjusted; and, in certain cases, also
4 Definition of the limits to which the cost elements concerned may be increased or decreased during specific periods or over the length of the contract.

An interesting example of a very simple escalation clause is the Westinghouse system.[5] It defines the prices of the products of the company as consisting of 55 per cent labour and 35 per cent materials, both of which are escalated, plus 10 per cent profit which is not escalated.

Labour cost is adjusted by the rate of change in the average

---

[2] Joel Dean, 'How to Price During Inflation', *European Journal of Marketing*, Vol. 13, No. 4, 1979, p. 221.

[3] Op cit, p. 219.

[4] Cf. Ronald L. Tatham and Bruce Allen, 'Industrial Pricing Systems and the Changing Role of Buyers and Sellers', *The Pricing Function*, (J. R. Vernon and C. W. Lamb, Jr, eds), D. C. Heath and Company, Lexington, Mass., 1976, pp. 221–31.

[5] Cf. *Electrical World*, September 15, 1974, p. 183.

hourly wage rate at Westinghouse, material cost is escalated by the index of steel prices.

This is how the system might work out in the case of a contract for the supply of switchgear valued at the time of signing at $100,000:

	Base price	Price at delivery	Escalation	Total
	$	$		$
Labour	3.99	4.36	$55,000 \times (4.36 - 3.99)/3.99 =$	5,100
Steel index	169.8	210.0	$35,000 \times (210.0 - 169.8)/169.8 =$	8,286
			Base price of contract	100,000
			TOTAL SALES PRICE	$113,386

The Westinghouse system has the advantage of simplicity and has been claimed to serve its purpose well, yet it seems to call for some critical comments.

1 The above illustration does not show any provision for the case of late delivery. It would appear reasonable to stipulate that, in the case of delayed delivery, escalation should be computed with the index values of the delivery date stipulated in the contract.

2 If the contract is for a large capital item, such as, for example, the building of a bridge or a supertanker, it is customary to arrange for payment at predetermined stages and according to the progress of the work. In all such instances escalation should be computed stage by stage instead of at the time of completion only.

3 It seems unfair to the supplier that his profit should be exempt from escalation. However, the percentage figures of the Westinghouse system reveal that it is based on absorption costing (elements of overhead costs being accounted for in the percentages allotted to labour and materials) and hence some hidden provision for profit escalation might in fact be present in the formula.

The profit element need not necessarily be handled in this way. One possible expedient is to escalate its amount by a general index of wholesale or retail prices, another is to conceal it entirely in the percentages allotted to the other elements. For example, if the Westinghouse formula applied to the same order as above had been 60 per cent labour and 40 per cent materials, the total sales price would have worked out $1,648 higher, since

60,000 (4.36–3.99)/3.99	=	5,564
40,000 (210.0–169.8)/169.8	=	9,470
Base price of contract		100,000

TOTAL SALES PRICE $115,034

Note that the 16.48 per cent by which the (nominal) ten per cent cost element has been adjusted was, in this example, the *straight* average of the percentages by which the labour and material elements have been escalated. The *weighted* average could also have been applied, using the following computation: the 55 per cent labour, 35 per cent materials formula resulted in a price increase of $13,386, which is 14.87 per cent of $90,000. Applying the same percentage to the $10,000 profit element would have added another $1,487 to the total sales price, making it $114,873.

4 It is very important to keep an eye on changes in the capital tied down in consequence of the order concerned. Only in some rare instances (of which the silicon chip is an outstanding example) do advances in technology result in capital saving; otherwise reductions in the variable costs of production generally involve additional investment. This issue is analysed and illustrated with an example in Chapter 4 (pp. 43–4). Here we merely note that the rate of return on the capital of the company could be adversely affected if no proper attention is paid to the financial resources tied down by individual orders.

6 The pricing of industrial goods

General considerations

There are certain goods for which industrial firms are the final customers, but in view of the fact that many of the items purchased by them are eventually resold either to other firms or to the public, it is not possible to draw a clear dividing line between industrial goods and consumers' goods. While the industrial market has certain characteristics that justify a separate discussion, much of the contents of this chapter has general relevance.

It is sometime alleged that, unlike the typical housewife who has no idea of what prices should be since she is not familiar either with the cost of production or with the profit margins necessary for the continued existence of a manufacturer or trader, the industrial buyer is an expert whose judgement cannot be influenced by any of the usual marketing gimmicks. There is some truth in this statement, but it is severely limited.

First of all, most industrial buyers have to purchase such a large variety of products that it would be humanly impossible for them to have full up-to-date knowledge of the lowest manufacturing cost of each. It can occasionally happen that the question is whether the company by which the buyer is employed should manufacture a specific item or purchase it, but even if this is the issue, the decision may well be influenced by factors other than cost alone. If the company is not equipped to make an item, it will hardly be able to determine its true cost, especially since, as has been shown in Chapter 5, the unit cost is so heavily dependent on the rate of production, or, more generally, on the extent to which the capacity used in its manufacture, which might be specialized or versatile, is being utilized. Furthermore, the buyer will not always have a free hand in choosing the supplier since many of the products bought by industrial firms are highly differentiated, and, where this is the case, the department or person requiring them will generally stipulate exactly what should be bought. The buyer's freedom in placing his orders will, however, be less restricted when it comes to non-differentiated products or those produced to the firm's own specification.

Reference is sometimes made to the 'Pareto curve' of industrial purchases, by which is meant the similarity of the size distribution of the orders to the income distribution found in free societies: very small numbers of large items and increasingly large numbers of individually small items. It is an established fact that the larger the expenditure involved, the higher in the hierarchy of the firm will the decision be taken, and hence the more will the buyer's knowledge be supplemented by the expertise or acumen of other executives in the company. But the decision of the latter is also bound to look beyond the price and to take into account also a number of other considerations.

It will be discussed in Chapter 11 how price acts as an indicator of quality to consumers; what we have to note here is that price has this role also in the markets of industrial products. Mistakes are sometimes made, but every sensible industrial buyer will be anxious not to jeopardize the satisfaction of the company's customers with an expensive product by inadvertently incorporating in it some shoddy material or unreliable component. It has been found that even in the case of non-differentiated products, such as basic materials and items produced to standard specifications, a price advantage of up to ten per cent will not induce significant proportions of industrial purchasers to shift from a reliable supplier to a cheaper source.[1]

Since the expertise of an industrial buyer generally consists of acquaintance with the market where he buys rather than of any precise knowledge of the actual cost of production of each item

---

[1] Cf. *Marketing a Non-differentiated Industrial Product*, Industrial Market Research Limited, London, 1972, p. 7; *How British Industry Buys*, Institute of Marketing, Hutchinson, London, 1967; Reed Mayer and Robert J. Boewadt, 'The Pricing of Industrial Goods', *Business Horizons*, June 1971, pp. 27–34; and Ronald H. Barback, 'The Pricing of Industrial Products', *European Journal of Marketing*, **13**, (4), 1979, pp. 160–66.

which he is instructed to buy, industrial markets tend to be looked upon as requiring strictly competition-oriented pricing.[2] While there are some cases where this view may be justified, it should never be forgotten that the actions of the competitors matter only to the extent to which they influence the customers themselves. Even if the market is highly competitive, the buyer will be aware that he has to pay extra for superior quality and reliable supply. He will therefore be justly suspicious if a new firm enters the market with very low quotations, and if an old supplier should suddenly cut prices, the buyer will have to be assured that the quality of the product has not been reduced.

In order to illustrate this point, two instances will be quoted, both personally observed by the author. Some years ago a young engineer from another European country set up in business in England with his invention that made it possible to produce a standard electronic component so cheaply that it could be marketed considerably below the price charged by the established producers. He gave samples to all the leading radio manufacturers who tested the device, confirmed that the result was satisfactory, yet no orders were forthcoming. After six months or so, by which time he had long given up all hope of having his product accepted by one of the largest radio manufacturers, he was surprised to receive a very substantial order from that firm. He remembered the buyer as a pleasant and reasonable person and rang him up to ask why he had suddenly decided to write out the order so firmly refused six months earlier. The answer was 'We liked your product, it was good and cheap, but we also had to see that you can survive on such a low price'. The young engineer, who was at the end of his tether by then, realized that what he considered his strongest selling point had in fact been a deterrent to his potential customers and came very near to causing his downfall.

---

[2] 139 directors, works managers and production engineers were asked in a survey to rank the factors that influence their purchasing decisions. 83 rated past experience as the most important factor and only 21 gave price first rank. Cf. M. T. Cunningham and J. G. White, 'The Determination of Choice of Supplier – A Study of Purchase Behaviour for Capital Goods', *European Journal of Marketing*, Vol. 7, No. 3, 1973, pp. 189–202, also Roger S. Mason, 'Price Competition in Industrial Markets', *Industrial Marketing Management*, October 1974, pp. 275–284; and Benson P. Schapiro and Barbara B. Jackson, 'Industrial Pricing to Meet Customer Needs', *Harvard Business Review*, **56**, (4), November/December 1978, pp. 119–27.

The other instance also involved a British firm, but only indirectly. That firm was operating an oil refinery and had agents in a number of foreign countries, selling its products in the wholesale market. Since the composition of lubricants varies widely with the origin of the crude oil and the processing to which it has been subjected, refined oil is sold by sample and analysis. Long after the firm was well established in the international market, it introduced a new kind of oil. In order to further the sale of this product which had good lubricating properties but a very unusual composition, the firm quoted an exceptionally low price for it, and one of their overseas agents whom I knew went round to his customers, offering it as a genuine bargain. Yet he could not make a single sale, and eventually he realized that the low price made the buyers so suspicious of the quality of the oil that they could not even be persuaded to give it a test.

The agent learned his lesson, he put the sample away and did not touch it for about a year. Then he carried it round again, but this time not with a cheap price as an apology for its composition. On entering a buyer's room, he proudly showed him the analysis, pointed out its novelty and added that the price of this speciality was of course well above the usual level. The response of most of the buyers was favourable, and before long sales were coming in at an increasing rate. The executives of the mother firm, baffled by the success of this agent when none of the others could make more than an occasional small sale of this particular product, soon asked my friend to reveal to them his secret.[3]

It can be seen from these examples that the attitude of the industrial buyer is not always very different from that of the lady who goes for the most expensive cosmetics in the firm belief that only the best is good enough for her, because she knows from experience that 'you get what you pay for'. There are also other features common to industrial and consumer markets, even though they are sometimes considered as being characteristic of the former only. Let us deal with them in turn.

---

[3] It would be wrong to conclude from this that it is always best to leave pricing to the sales personnel. A sample of 108 firms showed that those giving their salespeople the highest degree of pricing authority generated the lowest sales and profit performance. Cf. P. R. Stephenson, W. L. Cron and G. L. Frazier, 'Delegating Pricing Authority to the Sales Force: The Effects on Sales and Profit Performance', *Journal of Marketing*, **43**, (2), Spring 1979, pp. 21–28.

If the item is a small component, the demand will not be sensitive to price changes, since the quantities required will be determined by the sales of the product in which it is incorporated. Reliable suppliers of small but not unimportant components, (like the label of an expensive bottle of perfume or the door handle of a luxury motor car), are in a strong position and can charge profitable prices without fear of being dislodged by intruders. Also, if the user industry is prosperous, it will be less likely to be resistant to a price increase than one that is depressed.

On the other hand, if the item is responsible for a substantial share in the cost of the finished product, a price change might have a considerable effect on the demand for the latter, especially if there is keen competition in the market. In any such case, and quite particularly if the item purchased by the industrial customer is directly or indirectly recognizable in his own product, proof of the preference of the final customer will be a better sales argument in the buyer's room than a lower price. Far-sighted firms selling in industrial markets are aware of this and will carry out consumer surveys for the information of their industrial customers. If they can show that the consumer is willing to pay a higher price for the quality image imparted to the final product by the material or component in question, this should justify an appropriately higher price for the latter. Similarly, if the material or component was a novelty offered at a price below the market, any suspicion on the part of the industrial buyer could best be allayed by providing evidence that its incorporation in the final product would not affect its acceptance by the customers.

Very fierce competition exists in certain industrial markets, especially where the specification is issued by the buyer and the rule is that the contract must be awarded to the lowest bidder. The problem of pricing in such situations is discussed in the Appendix to Part I.[4]

In industrial markets there are generally ways by which returns can be improved without actually increasing the base price. The following recommendations deserve attention:

- Revise the discount structure: if indicated, increase the

---

[4] Cf. also Ronald S. Edwards, 'The Pricing of Manufactured Products', *Economica (NS)*, **19**, (75), August 1952, esp. p. 304; and Michael V. Laric, 'Pricing Strategies in Industrial Markets', *European Journal of Marketing*, **14**, (5/6), 1980, pp. 303–15, (contains 23 references).

minimum acceptable order size or introduce an appropriate surcharge for it.

- Introduce a charge for delivery or, if you already have one, revise it.
- Charge the customers for special services, such as requested modifications of the product, also for overtime working in the case of rush orders.
- Charge interest on overdue accounts.
- In inflationary conditions include an escalation clause in your contracts: cf. the Appendix to Chapter 5.
- Revise your product line: consider dropping the least profitable items; if there is a standard pack, reduce its size.
- Apply Value Analysis: cf. Appendix III to this chapter.

Cost-based pricing of industrial products

In the case of products of a standard nature and with more or less established prices in the market, costing and pricing will often be of the passive character to which reference was made in Chapter 5. The way in which the industrialist consulted by Edwards put it is so apt that it is worth quoting again: 'the manufacturer has a "hunch" as to the price at which his article can be sold, and makes use of "costing" or "estimating" to justify that price'.

This does not mean that no order should be rejected as long as it offers the going price. Direct costing, if properly carried out, will enable the selection of the most profitable (or least unprofitable) orders that can be obtained. The task is then to find out if the available capacity of any of the factors sets a limit on the utilization of the others and to judge the issue by the contributions per factor unit. The scarce factor could be labour hours, machine hours, units of some material in limited supply, etc., while in the absence of any restriction of this kind, when there is idle capacity all the way round and no shortage of any productive factor, the answer to the question will turn either on the absolute amount of the contribution or on the margin. Consider the choice between the orders in Table 6.1.

As we see, Order A gives the largest total contribution, but as a percentage of sales revenue Order C is the most favourable. Order B yields the highest contribution per labour hour, and Order D per machine hour. In such a case the question of acceptance or rejection may turn on the importance attached to each of the four criteria. If, for example, business is brisk and labour easy to hire and fire but the

Table 6.1

The contributions of four alternative orders related to labour hours and machine hours

	Order A	Order B	Order C	Order D
Sales revenue	£21,000	£17,000	£15,000	£12,000
Direct cost	15,000	13,000	10,500	9,000
Contribution	£6,000	£4,000	£4,500	£3,000
Contribution margin	28.6%	23.5%	30.0%	25.0%
Labour hours	8,000	5,000	6,500	4,500
Contribution per labour hour	£0.75	£0.80	£0.69	£0.67
Machine hours	670	500	450	250
Contribution per machine hour	£9	£8	£10	£12

total of the potential calls on machine hours is well in excess of the actual capacity, Order D will be the most advantageous. However, the final decision should also take into account the reactions of the customers and the probable effects on the behaviour of the competition. Consideration of these aspects could well result in the acceptance of that order which looked least attractive by the main formal indicator.

It was mentioned in Chapter 5 that there are situations where costs normally classed as direct or out-of-pocket expenses, such as wages, become fixed costs in the short run and hence any contribution to them should be welcome. Yet the long-term advantages and disadvantages of changing a price must always be kept in mind: the importance of just surviving from one day to the next should not be overestimated – it might be better to look for greener pastures or even to go into liquidation today rather than later, after further large losses have been suffered. It is always dangerous to provoke extensive price-cutting and to let prices drop to a level where no profitable production is possible unless the quality of the product is substantially reduced.

Keeping the above points in mind, let us now consider the pricing problems of a company serving the industrial market by supplying a large number of different products. Last year the company achieved sales of £2,800,000, and a pre-tax return of 18 per cent on its capital of £1,000,000. The coming year promises to be somewhat better: it is expected that sales will be up by about 30 per cent, and hence a target rate of 24 per cent on capital appears to be reasonable to the

company. Since the capacity was not fully utilized last year, a 10 per
cent increase in the capital employed will be sufficient to maintain
the planned output. This is then the budget for the year in question:

Direct costs	£2,060,000
Overheads	1,340,000
Profit	264,000
Total sales	£3,664,000

These figures indicate an overall contribution mark-up on direct
costs of 77.86 per cent, (corresponding to 43.78 per cent on sales,)
but it does not follow that each product should therefore be priced in
this way. Almost certainly, the mark-up will have to vary from
product to product and generally also from one customer to another,
over and above any quantity rebates (of which more will be said
further on), especially if the market is highly competitive. This is
also taken into account in Appendices I and II to this chapter.

It has been argued with some force by Bergfeld that if a company
has a standard mark-up rate, it should not be applied either to the
variable cost or to the absorption cost but only to *the value added* to
arrive at the price.[5] While this method could not be claimed to
conform to the principle of the same return on capital all the way
round and hence might not prove optimal from the long-term point
of view, it could be justified in certain situations as leading to the
best *momentary* uses of the available capacities.

Pricing for export

The differences between catering to the home market and an
overseas market are technical rather than fundamental. Whereas the
manufacturer will generally have a feel of the home market, based
on his own experience and the knowledge of how other suppliers
have fared, this will be of very limited use to him when he enters a
foreign market for the first time.

It is well known that many exporters have come to grief because
they failed to realize that the demand in an export market can be

---

[5] Albert J. Bergfeld *et al.*, *Pricing for Profit and Growth*, Prentice-Hall, Inc.,
Englewood Cliffs, NJ, 1962, Chapter 5, 'Pricing the Fundamental
Function', pp. 44–50.

different from that at home. To mention just two cases, it has been reported that a British manufacturer, learning that there was a demand for egg cups in India, immediately dispatched a substantial consignment to his agent, only to learn that they were by far too large to be of any use with Indian eggs. The other case is that of the Japanase car manufacturers, whose first attempt to gain a foothold in the American market ended in failure. They learnt their lesson and carried out careful market research before their next attempt, the success of which is common knowledge.

As far as pricing is concerned, the first thing to note is that the export market is mostly found to be more competitive than the home market, hence unless one's goods possess features which the customers consider superior to those of the competition, there will be great pressure on the margin, and the second is that the costs involved in exporting will tend to be different for one or more of the following reasons:

- Modifications of the product required by the laws of the importer's country and by the nature of its demand.
- Exemption from or remission of indirect taxes in the producer's home country, including any import duty charged on the materials and components of the product.
- Export bounties or duties in the producer's home country.
- Cost of special packaging.
- Cost of transport, insurance and any non-insurable deterioration of the product in transit.
- Import duties and other taxes payable in the importer's country.
- Special marketing expenses and credit terms.
- Some countries require imports to have certain proportions of 'home content'.
- The extra paperwork involved in arranging transport, insurance, finance, etc., also, in certain cases, obtaining export and/or import licences.

Some of these items may be the responsibility of an export agency or the foreign buyer, but even if this is the case, they will have an influence on the price that can effectively be charged.

Quite apart from the effect of the cost factors, the demand conditions might indicate different prices in each of the markets served, leading to the practice of *price discrimination*.

The mark-up will generally be lower on the goods sold for export than on those destined for the home market,[6] but it would be wrong to conclude from this that the home market price is then necessarily higher than it would be in the absence of exports. This can best be demonstrated by an example.

Consider the case of an engineering product, say a motor car, supplied to two markets. Originally, the ex works price was the same for all sales, but subsequently the export price was reduced to a level considerably below that of the home price. Before we decide whether the home buyer has been harmed by this discrimination, we must take into account both the cost items and the nature of the demand in the two markets.

In the original situation the annual output of the company was 100,000 cars of which 90,000 were sold in the home market and 10,000 exported. The pricing is shown in Table 6.2.

Table 6.2
Example (1) of home and export price differences

Unit cost items	Home market	Export market
Direct manufacturing cost	£2,000	£2,000
Contribution	1,100	1,100
Price ex works	3,100	3,100
Tax in home market 25%	775	–
Freight and insurance	–	600
Import duty 5% on £3,700	–	185
After sales service	195	275
Marketing costs	1,000	1,300
Price to final customer	£5,070	£5,460

It was then found that even a substantial reduction in price would only moderately enhance home sales while the export market promised to respond very favourably to a considerable price cut. It was also expected that the increased output would result in a substantial fall in the unit cost of production, albeit this would

---

[6] This applies mainly to manufactured products. Where the export of primary products is in the hands of a marketing board or other monopolistic institution, the home price is often well below the export price. Typical examples are OPEC oil, Brazilian coffee, West African cocoa and groundnuts.

necessitate further capital investment. The prices were therefore adjusted and after two years sales had expanded to 300,000 cars per year, of which 120,000 were sold at home and 180,000 abroad.

Direct manufacturing cost had fallen to £1,760 per car, but the ex works price was not any longer the same for both markets. The new costing schedule is shown in Table 6.3.

Table 6.3
Example (2) of home and export price differences

Unit cost items	Home market	Export market
Direct manufacturing cost	£1,760	£1,760
Contribution	1,000	460
Price ex works	2,760	£2,220
Tax in home market 25%	690	–
Freight and insurance	–	560
Import duty 5% on £2,780	–	139
After sales service	220	300
Marketing costs	900	1,200
Price to final customer	£4,570	£4,419

Clearly, this is a case of price discrimination in favour of the overseas market: the ex works price of the exported cars is almost 20 per cent below that for the home market. Nevertheless, the home customer has no reason for complaint: he has benefited rather than suffered from the change. If it had not been for the great expansion of exports, the price charged at home could not have been reduced by £500 without a detrimental reduction in the profitability and thereby in the viability of the company.[7]

There is, however, a limit to the extent to which the export price can reasonably be reduced, and this is given by the incremental cost of production compared with the incremental sales revenue.

Say the incremental manufacturing cost of another 10,000 cars would be £16m and that this increase in output would not call for any further investment. If now raising the export sales from 180,000 to 190,000 cars could not be brought about without a reduction of

---

[7] We have assumed here that the increase in the total contribution from £110m to £202.8m was sufficient to provide an acceptable rate of return on the augmented capital of the company.

the average ex works price by £32.64 or more, the total contribution would fall, since

$$190,000 \times £(2,220 - 32.64) = £415,598,400$$
$$\text{Less incremental cost} \qquad 16,000,000$$

$$£399,598,400$$

which is just under

$$180,000 \times £2,220 = £399,600,000.$$

If, however, it should be possible to find a separate market for the 10,000 additional cars where they could be sold at an ex works price as low as £1,700, this would still be well worthwhile since it would produce an additional contribution of £1,000,000.

The case of the Swiss watch industry which, in its heyday, was said to export about 95 per cent of its output, shows how the home market can benefit from the economies of mass production which could not have arisen in the absence of exports.

The practice of price discrimination is not by any means restricted to the export industries. It frequently arises also where no exports are involved and various aspects of it are discussed elsewhere in this book.[8]

Summing up, the main point is that the foreign customer is even less interested in the cost of production than the customer in the home market. It is therefore reasonable to approach the problem of pricing for export from what Root calls the base price, meaning thereby the price the final buyer is willing to pay for the product.[9] Direct market research is more likely to provide reliable information on this point than enquiries through trade channels.

---

[8] Cf. Chapter 7, especially pp. 132–5 where the principle is demonstrated with a different example, and Chapter 5, pp. 57–8, where the problem of varying the mark-up from market to market is analysed. Price discrimination also occurs in retail pricing and is accordingly discussed in Chapter 8, On the problem of justifying price differentials cf. Kent B. Monroe, *Pricing: Making Profitable Decisions*, McGraw-Hill, New York, 1979, pp. 249–67.

[9] Franklin D. Root, *Strategic Planning for Export Marketing*, International Textbook Company, Scranton, Pennsylvania, 1966, esp. the chapter 'Planning Export Pricing Strategy', pp. 55–71. It is reprinted in *International Marketing Management*, (M. J. Thomas, ed.), Houghton Mifflin, Boston, 1969, pp. 380–93. Cf. also Nigel Piercy, 'British Export Market Selection and Pricing', *Industrial Marketing Management*, **10**, October 1981, pp. 287–97.

New product pricing

The pricing of new products aimed directly or indirectly at the consumer market is discussed in Chapter 12. Here we are concerned with products for which the final purchaser is another industrial firm.

It would seem that where the market is highly competitive, cost-based pricing should enable the supplier to quote prices that will be acceptable to the customer. Indeed, there are cases where this is so, especially if one's own costing formula is known to be similar to those used by the main competitors. Absorption costing could then be of help, especially if tenders are invited for a product with an entirely new specification. However, if the competitors formulae are not known, absorption costing will be no better than a shot in the dark.

If the novelty of the item is only partial; for instance if the new specification merely changes some of the measurements or tolerances of the product, the price of the original item should provide the starting point, and the price variation may then be calculated on the basis of the difference in direct costs. This price difference need not, however, be in strict proportion to the cost variation; if the new feature offers an advantage to the purchaser, an appropriate increase in the price would be justified.

If the new product is not closely related to any of those currently produced by the firm, there will be no benchmark in the records on which its price could be based, except the expected average rate of return on capital. The question is then whether taking up the new product would improve this rate or not.

The more safely the novelty is protected by letters patents or other means, the more will it enable departure from cost-based pricing and adoption of a customer-oriented approach. This is where market research can help by exploring the nature and extent of the potential demand.

Should the new product be a piece of equipment the advantage of which consists in the cost saving it confers on its user, it may be possible to persuade the first few customers to have it installed on a trial basis, and to agree on the charge for it in relation to the cost actually saved per annum. Experience has shown that while the patents run the best return can be obtained by retaining ownership of the equipment concerned instead of selling it outright, and making a hire charge for its use, based on the rate of its utilization. Well-known successful applications of this method of pricing are the

Goodyear Welt shoe stitching machines, IBM computers and Xerox office copiers.

If the novelty of the new product cannot be effectively protected, it might not be of advantage to launch it at a price that could easily be undercut by a competitor. The question then may be not so much what price should be charged for the new product but rather whether it will sell at a rate sufficient to make its production worthwhile at a predetermined 'keep out price'. Independent market research is likely to provide a more reliable answer to this question than an enquiry carried out by the company's own sales personnel.

When should a product be abandoned?

The average markup rate can serve as a benchmark against which the performance of any individual product may be judged, and if its contribution appears to be inadequate over the year or other longer period, the next task is to identify the customers who habitually order it.

Whether a particular product should be discontinued or not will then depend on the answers to two questions. First, is discontinuation more likely to lead to the loss of one or several good customers, who place large orders that generally extend also to other, more rewarding products, than to the loss of some less desirable customers only, who place insignificant orders, cause trouble by unjustified complaints and tend to pay reluctantly, if at all? The second question relates to the capacity currently devoted to the product concerned: is there a better alternative use for it, or would it be left idle if the product were discontinued?

Regular scrutinies of the records carried out along these lines are likely to lead to decisions that can considerably enhance the profitability of the company. There is also a computer-aided method available for those who prefer a more formal approach.[10]

Quantity discounts

The granting of quantity discounts or rebates may be necessary to

[10] Paul W. Hamelman and Edward M. Mazze, 'Improving Product Abandonment Decisions', *Journal of Marketing*, **36**, (2), April 1972, pp. 20–26.

meet competition, and may also serve as a means to encourage the customer to increase the size of his orders.

Whether the price differences so introduced are discriminatory or not depends on the relation between the extent of the discounts and the variation of manufacturing and selling costs with the size of the orders. The incremental cost principle applies here: if the additional output would not displace other more valuable work, the incremental cost will indicate the limit of the price variation that can be offered without affecting profitability. This is the economist's criterion; where there is legislation to prohibit price discrimination, as in the United States, the definition will depend on the interpretation developed by the courts of law.

The structure of quantity rebates varies to a great extent between different trades, and even the same manufacturer may offer widely different rates on his various products. Mercer & Russell have found that in the case of a bulky, non-differentiated industrial product the quantity discount granted by the trade first increased at an increasing rate with the logarithm of the quantity, and then at a decreasing rate, as indicated by the curve in Figure 6.1.[11] However, the quantity rebates encountered in practice do not invariably

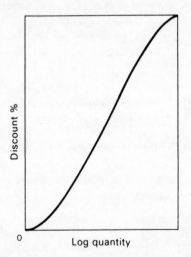

Figure 6.1 Curve of quantity discounts (log scale)

---

[11] A. Mercer and J. I. T. Russell, 'Recurrent Competitive Bidding', *Operational Research Quarterly*, **20**, 1969, pp. 215–6, where the appropriate mathematical formula is also given.

conform to this type. The examples quoted by Dean and Lynn display various patterns, but there is one feature that is common to all of them: the eventual decline in the growth of the rebate as the quantity increases.[12]

Figure 6.2.(a) illustrates the increasing – decreasing type of rebate and Figure 6.2.(b) the case where the individual order involves step-costs, that is fixed-cost elements that are specific to the order in addition to the variable cost. Printing is a typical example: step costs arise with the typesetting, the preparation of the blocks, etc.; they also occur in the manufacture of plastic mouldings and engineering jobs requiring special dies, jigs or templates.

The smooth curves in Figure 6.2(a) and (b) indicate the general character of the rebates; the actual rates are expressed by the horizontal lines.

Quantity discounts should be based on the numbers of units purchased and not on the value of the order, otherwise a price increase might have the consequence of lifting unchanged recurring orders to higher discount brackets. It is also generally preferable to avoid the integrated type of discount, i.e. the kind discussed so far, because it produces situations where a small increase in the number of units ordered will leave unchanged or even actually reduce the total value of the order. This is illustrated in the following example.

List price: £2.00 per unit. Discount: up to 1,000 units nil, over 1,000 up to 5,000 units 5 per cent, over 5,000 units 7 per cent.

Units purchased	Value at list price	Discount	Value after discount
1,000	£2,000	0	£2,000.00
1,052	2,104	£105.20	1,998.80
5,000	10,000	500.00	9,500.00
5,107	10,214	714.98	9,499.02

---

[12] Joel Dean, *Managerial Economics*, Prentice-Hall, Englewood Cliffs, NJ, 1951, pp. 530–536; Robert A. Lynn, Price Policies and Marketing Management. Cf. also J. Crowther, 'Rationale for Quantity Discounts', *Harvard Business Review*, **42**, (2), March/April 1964, pp. 121–127; F. Livesey, *Pricing*, Macmillan, London, 1976, pp. 65–7; and Ashak Rao, 'Quantity Discounts in Today's Markets', *Journal of Marketing*, **44**, (4), 1980, pp. 44–51; James P. Monahan, 'A Quantity Discount Pricing Model to Increase Vendor Profits', *Management Science*, **30**, June 1984, pp. 720–26; and Rajiv Lal and Richard Staelin, 'An Approach for Developing an Optimal Discount Pricing Policy', *Management Science*, **30**, December 1984, pp. 1524–39.

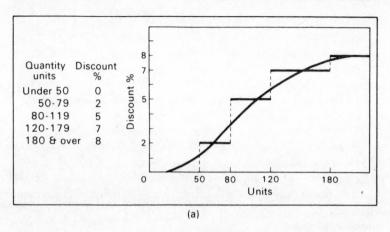

Quantity units	Discount %
Under 50	0
50-79	2
80-119	5
120-179	7
180 & over	8

(a)

Order specific fixed costs: £1,000. Variable cost: £10.00 per unit. The cost savings per unit are the limits of the discounts that can be granted on the listed quantities without reducing the contribution from the order.

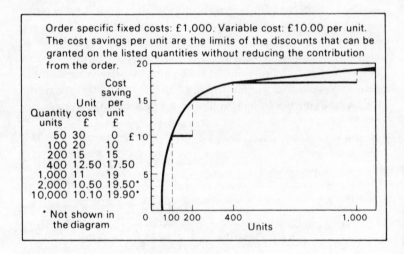

Quantity units	Unit cost £	Cost saving per unit £
50	30	0
100	20	10
200	15	15
400	12.50	17.50
1,000	11	19
2,000	10.50	19.50*
10,000	10.10	19.90*

* Not shown in the diagram

**Figure 6.2   Stepped quantity discounts: (a) ogive type;
(b) diminishing rate type**

Non-integrated discounts with each discount percentage applying only to the quantities between the relevant limits avoid such anomalous situations:

List price: £2.00 per unit. Discount: 1–1,000 units nil, next 4,000 units 5 per cent, all units over 5,000 7 per cent.

Units purchased	Value at list price	Discount	Value after discount
1,000	£2,000	0	£2,000.00
1,052	2,104	£5.20	2,098.80
5,000	10,000	400.00	9,600.00
5,107	10,214	414.98	9,799.02

The argument against integrated discount structures will not hold if there is reason to believe that most if not all of a customer's orders will lift him well above the point where the top discount rate operates, as it might promote sales to make the customer believe that he is getting a special bargain. Similarly, a value-based cumulative discount or loyalty rebate, which applies uniformly to all the purchases of a customer over the year, might be beneficial to the supplier if it effectively encourages the customer to place more orders with him. However, if the variation of the incremental cost with the size of the order is not the same for every one of the supplier's products, a single set of discounts might not be appropriate. In such situations it will be advisable to stipulate separate cumulative discounts based on the units of each product rather than a loyalty discount the size of which depends only on the total value of the purchases of the customer over the year.

Discounts can be expressed in various forms. Percentage rates are common, but they can also be stated in money terms, and the lists may show either the rebates or the reduced prices which arise after the application of the discounts. Yet another variant is the standard price for the medium-sized order, with surcharges for smaller quantities and discounts for orders above the medium range. This last variant is a direct expression of one of the main purposes of quantity discounts: the prevention of losses on small orders.

Several of the electricity tariffs discussed in Chapter 7 incorporate quantity rebates. The step-rate, with the cost per unit falling as consumption per quarter increases is analogous to a list of prices each of which has been reduced by the appropriate quantity discount. The principle of the two-part tariff is seldom used outside the field of public utilities, but some firms make a fixed charge per order to cover handling expenses. The principle of the block tariff is identical with that of the non-integrated type of quantity discount.

Since quantity discounts are partly expressions of cost savings and partly of a promotional nature, it is not possible to lay down any general principles for the determination of their magnitudes. Except where they are dictated from the outside by convention or competitive action, it is up to the individual price setter to find out how large they should be. On the cost side, the savings on production and selling costs provide some guidance, and it should be possible to test the reactions of a sample of customers to variations in quantity discounts and set the rates in harmony with the indications of the results.

Trade discounts

Distributor discounts tend to vary with the nature of the customer's business. Export sales often enjoy a special rate, and manufacturers who sell both through wholesalers and direct to some large retail distributors or other important customers will generally grant the highest discounts to the wholesalers.

There is an important exception to this rule: components that need more or less frequent replacement, such as, for example, motor car tyres, spark plugs, batteries, light bulbs, etc., are supplied at dramatically reduced prices in the industrial market, often less than half the prices charged to wholesalers or retail distributors.

In the case of goods that have a seasonal demand but can be produced at an even rate throughout the year, like coal and fuel oil, for example, seasonal rebates may encourage the customers to stock up during the slack period. The determination of the proper magnitude of these rebates is not easy: if the difference between the two prices is too small, the rebate will be ineffective; if it is too large, it might shift rather than eliminate the peak.

How large should general distributor discounts be? Ideally, they should be sufficient to cover the distributor's costs and provide him with a reasonable profit margin. However, even the costs of distributors in the same category tend to show considerable variations and cannot be determined with any great precision. As with the quantity discounts, convention and competitive pressures are largely responsible for the magnitude of the various distributor discounts in actual use, and only in certain cases can they be directly related to differences in selling costs.

Table 6.4 illustrates the relationship between the price of the product, the distributor's margin, the volume of sales and the total contribution enjoyed by the distributor.[13]

---

[13] Cf. also the break-even table (Table 5.5), p. 73, which deals with the same issue but only when the unit cost of the product remains invariant.

Table 6.4
Relationship between price and distributor's margin

Required annual contribution: £2,000,000
Variable cost per unit: £20.00

| | Distributor's margin on retail price | | | | | |
| | 25% | | 33⅓% | | 40% | |
Retail price	Factory price	Minimum volume	Factory price	Minimum volume	Factory price	Minimum volume
£	£	units	£	units	£	units
100	75.00	36,364	66.67	42,855	60.00	50,000
99	74.25	36,867	66.00	43,479	59.40	50,762
95	71.25	39,025	63.33	46,158	57.00	54,055
90	67.50	42,106	60.00	50,000	54.00	58,824
89	66.75	42,781	59.33	50,852	53.40	59,881
85	63.75	45,715	56.67	54,541	51.00	64,517
70	52.50	61,539	46.67	74,991	42.00	90,910

Experience has shown that while raising the commission of one's own salesmen on selected lines can be very effective in increasing the sales of the products concerned, extra high distributor discounts do not by themselves induce retailers to place large orders for products that are unpopular with their customers. Unduly high discounts are more likely to lead to price cutting, unless resale price maintenance is being strictly enforced.

However, in recent years large distributors in general and supermarket chains in particular have asserted their market power over the manufacturers. They buy direct instead of through wholesalers, and have had considerable success in persuading the manufacturers to grant them even higher rebates than those otherwise reserved for the middleman. Furthermore, the supermarkets keep putting pressure on the manufacturers to reduce their own advertising and contribute instead to the supermarkets' promotion expenses.

It is invariably useful too to consider any problem in marketing from the point of view of the customer – indeed, empathy with him is an essential condition of success. Let us therefore examine how variations in price and unit cost may affect the distributor.

We shall assume that, in the previous year, the sales of the product concerned resulted in a sales revenue of £1,000,000 to the distributor, and since his margin was 20 per cent, it yielded a gross contribution of £200,000.

1 If either because of the lack of responsiveness of demand to price variations or because of competitive action there is no change in the physical volume of sales,

a price cut of	will reduce the contribution by
2%	10%
5%	25%
10%	50%
15%	75%

2 If average unit costs remain the same in spite of variations in output, to maintain the contribution at the level of £200,000 per annum[14]

a price cut of	requires an increase in the physical volume of sales by	to yield a gross sales revenue of
2%	11.1111%	£1,088,889
5%	33.3333%	£1,266,667
10%	100.0000%	£1,800,000
15%	300.0000%	£3,400,000

3 If, as it mostly happens, unit costs can be reduced if sales are increased, the situation may be more favourable:[15]

if a price cut of	increases the physical volume of sales by	the fall in average unit cost required to obtain a total contribution of £200,000 is
2%	4%	1.54%
5%	10%	3.98%
10%	20%	8.33%
15%	30%	12.98%

---

[14] Formulae for calculating the second and third columns of the table:

Required increase in V = 100c/(M−c) per cent, and
Required gross sales revenue = £ S × M(1−c)/(M−c),

where M = original percentage margin; c = percentage cut; V = original physical volume of sales; and S = original gross sales revenue.

Thus, if M = 0.20, c = 0.02 and S = £1,000,000, we obtain

Required increase in V = 100 × 0.02/(0.20−0.02) = 11.1111 per cent, and

Required gross sales revenue = £1,000,000 × 0.20(1−0.02)/(0.20−0.02) = £1,088,889.

[15] Formula for calculating the third column of the table: ·

Required fall in average unit cost = 1 − [(1 + v) (1 − c) − M]/(1 + v) (1 − M) per cent,

where M = original percentage margin; c = percentge cut; and v = percentage increase in physical volume of sales.

Thus if M = 0.20, c = 0.02 and v = 0.04, the required fall in a.u.c. is
1 − [(1 + 0.04)(1 − 0.02) − 0.2]/(1 + 0.04)(1 − 0.2) = 1.54 per cent.

4 The effect of a price reduction may, of course, amount to a very high increase in sales. If, for example, a 15 per cent cut in prices results in the doubling of the physical volume of sales, a fall in average unit costs of 6.25 per cent would be sufficient to maintain the contribution at the level of £200,000, while a 12.5 per cent fall in average unit costs would raise it to £300,000.

5 In the above example, an original contribution margin of 20 per cent was assumed. If it was 8 per cent only, a 15 per cent cut in prices which results in the doubling of the physical volume of sales would require unit costs to fall by 11.96 per cent to maintain the contribution at the £80,000 level. If the increased sales call for additional capital in the distributor's business, mere maintenance of the total annual contribution will result in a decrease in the rate of return on capital.

Cash discounts

Trade discounts are often complemented by an extra allowance in return for prompt payment. Such cash discounts are generally offered as a percentage of the amount of the invoice, that is to say, they apply to the figure that is left after the deduction of the trade discount. For example, the terms may be 35 per cent trade discount, plus 2 per cent cash discount if payment is made within ten days of the date of the invoice, or 30 days net. On goods of a gross value of £100, the trade discount is then £35, and the cash discount, 2 per cent of £65, £1.30.

For the buyer who prefers to pay 30 days after the date of the invoice, the cost of the credit of which he avails himself will be £1.30 for 20 days on £63.70, which is equivalent to an annual rate of interest of 37.245 per cent. If he then makes purchases of similar value on the same terms each month, the amount of the interest he has to pay will rise, while the actual amount of the credit which he enjoys will not increase at all. If his monthly order is for goods priced at £100 less 35 per cent trade discount, his outstanding debt will be £65 for 240 days over the year, and nought for 165 days. The cash discount which he eschewed will amount to £15.60, which is 24.490 per cent of £63.70, but since his *average* outstanding debt over the year was only £41.88½, he has indeed been charged interest at an annual rate of 37.245 per cent. But if the terms are: 2 per cent cash discount provided payment is made within seven days of delivery or 60 days net, the actual annual rate of interest involved is only 14.055 per cent.[16]

This kind of cash discount encourages early payment at a cost to the seller that is equal to the saving by the buyer who pays within the stipulated period. However, especially if the cash discount is granted only if payment is made on or before delivery, the seller will have fewer bad debts and also save on the cost of sending statements and reminders to remiss customers.

Cash discounts may also have the purpose of encouraging early purchasing rather than early payment. If this is the case, the period over which the discount applies should be extended. Gist[17] mentions periods of up to 70 days, and also 'anticipation' discounts, granting an extra allowance, over and above the cash discount, for payments before the end of the basic cash discount period. For example, an 'anticipation' of 6 per cent means that for each day by which the date of the payment precedes the last day of the period, 6%/365 (or 6%/360, if a common accounting convention is adopted,) may be deducted from the amount of the invoice reduced by the basic cash discount.

Variations in the cash discount can of course be used as a competitive weapon, but any seller who suddenly offers an exceptionally large cash discount might expose himself to the suspicion of being overstocked or in difficulties with his cash flow.

Summary

Industrial customers are supposed to be better informed about the costs of producing the items which they buy than the ordinary shopper, and this is certainly true if the choice is between buying a certain component from outside or having it made by the buyer's own company. Otherwise the industrial buyer's expertise will not be

---

[16] Cf. R. M. Grant, 'Transaction Costs to Retailers of Different Methods of Payment: Results of a Pilot Study', *Managerial and Decision Economics*, **4**, (4), 1983, pp. 89–100; also by the same author, 'On Cash Discounts to Retail Customers: Further Evidence', *Journal of Marketing*, **49**, (1), Winter 1985, pp. 145–6 and comments by Charles A. Ingene and Michael Levy, *ibid*, pp. 147–8.

[17] Ronald R. Gist, *Retailing: Concepts and Decisions*, John Wiley & Sons, New York, 1968, pp. 410–13.

all that different from that of the typical housewife: both will have a fair idea of the competitive prices in the market, at least as far as frequently purchased items or those requiring large outlays are concerned, and they will both be reasonably familiar with the quality of the different brands and the reliability of the various suppliers. Like the private customer, the industrial buyer will expect to have to pay more for a superior product than for one of lower quality, and will not readily abandon a reliable supplier for a small price advantage.

Cost-based pricing is much used in the field of industrial products. Absorption costing can be helpful if the formula used is known to be the same as that of the main competitor; otherwise direct costing is to be recommended, even though it is of more help in choosing between different orders at given prices than in determining what prices should be quoted.

Pricing for export involves additional issues but they are technical rather than fundamental. The manufacturer's knowledge of the foreign market is generally incomplete and there are several specific factors that will influence the relevant costs. The price may have to differ between the home market and the foreign market also if the demand conditions are different. This leads to the practice of price discrimination. Contrary to popular belief, it could be to the benefit of the home consumer even if what he pays is above the export price. Market research can be of substantial help in finding the appropriate product for a new market and the price the exporter should charge.

Absorption costing is frequently used for the pricing of new industrial products. This may be of some help if the product is new to the firm but not to the industry, or if its novelty consists in some minor modification only, provided it can be relied upon to give an estimate of the competitor's costs. Where the use of the new product confers a definite cost advantage on the customer, the price or royalty charge can be related to the cost saved.

If the novelty of the product cannot effectively be protected, it is unwise to charge for it a price that is likely to be substantially undercut by the competition. A 'keep out price' is then indicated.

Abandoning products that have outlived their usefulness is an important task that is often neglected. The decision should be based on the likely consequences on the behaviour of the firm's customers and on the alternative use of the productive capacity.

Quantity discounts play an important role in the industrial field; they help to meet competition and to induce customers to place orders of profitable size. They exist in several forms, and both their structures and their magnitudes show considerable variations. The electricity tariffs discussed in Chapter 8 also include examples of quantity rebates.

Some manufacturers quote prices that are subject to quantity discounts only; others list their recommended or maintained resale prices from which distributors can claim rebates. The highest rebates are generally those granted to wholesalers, but there are exceptions to this rule.

Seasonal rebates can be used to relieve slack periods but, as with all the other discounts, the determination of their optimal magnitudes may present problems.

Cash discounts may be used both to encourage prompt payment and to induce early ordering.

Variations in discounts can have a considerable effect on the profitability of the seller. The examples shown demonstrate the relationships between prices, distributors' margins, the volumes of sales required to maintain profitability and the behaviour of unit costs.

There are three appendices to this chapter:

Appendix I is devoted to the discussion of the problems of transfer pricing and suggests that the interest of the corporation may best be served by using more than one transfer price for the same transaction.

Appendix II contains an outline and critical evaluation of product analysis pricing; a method that is market-oriented and therefore commendable for its approach in spite of its shortcomings. Its essence consists in analysing the value of each product into materials, bought components, product properties and special features, of which the first two are valued at replacement cost plus a handling charge, and the other two at the values placed on them by the customer. This is correct in principle, but, regrettably, the only method PAP offers for determining and adjusting these values is to watch how orders are running.

Appendix III presents a brief exposition of value analysis and value engineering.

Price forecasting and competitive bidding are discussed in the Appendix to Part I.

APPENDIX I TO CHAPTER 6:   TRANSFER PRICING

In many large enterprises goods are frequently supplied and services rendered by one division or wholly owned subsidiary to another, and it is in this connection that the problem of transfer pricing arises.[1] Owing to the high degree of concentration which has taken place in the course of recent decades both in manufacturing and in the field of distribution, this issue has very much increased in importance and new aspects of it have arisen with the unprecedented growth of multinational corporations.

The first point which should be kept in mind in this connection is that the only genuine sales are those that are made at the end of the line to customers external to the corporation as a whole, and that therefore any contribution or profit which arises as the result of a mere transfer is purely illusory. Furthermore, even a sale to an external customer is a gift until it is paid for. That much is generally agreed by all the authorities who have contributed to the discussion of this subject, also that the overriding aim should be the profitability of the corporation or group as a whole. However, substantial differences of opinion are expressed when it comes to the principle to be followed in the selection of the optimal transfer price.

Much of the diversity of opinion seems to be rooted in the unwarranted assumption that any single transaction can have one transfer price only, whereas, as argued further below, there are situations which call for two or more different prices for the same transfer. This aspect has unfortunately been overlooked also in an otherwise valuable study of the domestic and international transfer pricing practices of United States and Japanese enterprises,[2] the results of which imply remarkable degrees of conformity between the proportions to which the different methods are used by each of the two sets of companies in the samples. The definition stipulated in that study, according to which the transfer price is 'the unit price assigned to goods and services between the parent company and

---

[1] The case where one of the parties is only partly owned by the other is considered below, in Sections 7, 8, 10 and 11.

[2] Roger Y. W. Tang, C. K. Walter and Robert H. Raymond, 'Transfer Pricing – Japanese vs. American Style', *Management Accounting* (USA), January 1979, pp. 12–16. However, see Sylvain R. F. Plasschaert, 'The Multiple Motivations for Transfer Price Modulations in Multinational Enterprises and Governmental Counter-Measures: An Attempt at Clarification', *Management International Review*, **21**, (1), 1981, pp. 49–63.

subsidiaries or between divisions within the same firm'[3] implies that
the respondents were asked only about the prices which figure on
their transfer invoices, whereas these are not necessarily the same as
those which guide marketing decisions or serve to assess performance.

Let us now look in some detail at each of the different
considerations that should govern the determination of transfer
prices.

1 For promoting the overall profitability of the corporation as a
whole, the actual incremental cost of each transaction as it has
arisen up to the point of transfer appears to be optimal for marketing
decisions. However, it is very difficult if not impossible to determine
this cost, even if it is taken to be practically identical with the
variable cost incurred, as eventually computed by the costing
department of the tranferor. Hence *standard variable cost* (brought
up-to-date as far as possible) arises as the best expedient for
estimating the gross contribution of sales to third parties. If, after
proper allowance for the additional costs which arise in the
transferee's division there is a net annual contribution, this will
provide *prima facie* evidence that its existence is justified.

The case for the use of the standard variable cost in marketing
decisions is convincingly argued and illustrated with three highly
interesting actual case studies by Smallman.[4] He is fully aware of
the prevalence of divergent practices and noted (in an unpublished
paper) that in their endeavour to establish profit centres 'millions of
marketing manhours are wasted in negotiations and argument
between managers of two companies in common ownership on the
magnitude and currency of transfer prices'.

2 The standard variable cost (and even the actual incremental
cost) is not invariably identical with what has been termed the
opportunity cost or alternative cost of a transaction. Consider the
case of a subsidiary distributor organization – situated in the same
country as the manufacturing company or abroad. If it does not
produce at least as large a contribution as could be obtained by
direct sales to third parties, other reasons would be needed to justify
its maintenance, for example, ensured loyalty, reliable response to
central directives, minimization of tax liability or directing the cash

---

[3] *Op cit*, p. 13.

[4] Alan Smallman, 'Transfer Pricing and its Misuse', *European Journal of Marketing*, **13**, 4, 1979, pp. 167–71.

flow where it will be of greatest advantage to the corporation. These last two aspects are further discussed under 5 and 6 below.

The investigation of the alternatives forgone by selling through wholly owned subsidiaries should go further than the mere comparison of the transfer price with the prices quoted to independent distributors. This point is strikingly illustrated by the experience of several of the large manufacturers of electronic computers: they have found that some of their independent distributors have discovered lucrative sub-markets for the standard models, and managed to obtain prices up to more than twice as high as charged by the manufacturer's own organization for direct sales to customers.[5]

3 The market price has been recommended by several authors as the ideal transfer price if the item transferred is of the character of a commodity and dealing with a wholly owned subsidiary does not offer any discernible advantages over buying from or supplying to third parties.[6] Unfortunately, this concept is not invariably free from ambiguity. On the one hand, the nearer the character of the product in question comes to that of the basic commodities (like non-ferrous metals, say), the more volatile will its market price be, which will also differ from place to place. The proper market price appears to be that at which the transferor could have sold the goods in question in the open market. If the transferor also sells directly to third parties, the net price obtained for such sales appears to be appropriate, provided the transferee division also operates in the same market. It can easily be shown that if the transferee's business is situated elsewhere, and the two markets are so effectively separated that they can have different market prices, transfers at the price ruling in the transferor's market might lead to sub-optimal decisions. This assumes that the potential output of the corporation is not so small that its sales could not have any influence on either of the two market prices – otherwise it would sell at the higher of the two prices only.

4 Similar considerations arise if the wholly owned subsidiary is not a distributor but a supplier of raw materials or components. If

---

[5] Cf. Andrew Tessler, 'Price Warfare and How to Win', *Marketing*, April 1980, p. 97. Confidential information obtained from some of the manufacturers concerned reinforces the validity of Tessler's observations.

[6] One of the more recent advocates of this method in the situation concerned is Alexander Young. Cf. his *Pricing Decisions – a Practical Guide to Interdivisional Pricing*, Business Books, London, 1979, esp. Ch. 4.

identical or, at least, similar supplies could be obtained from third parties at a cost not greater than that incurred by the subsidiary, its existence could be justified only if it ensures some such advantages as, say, greater security of supply, more even or superior quality, more even flow of deliveries or, perhaps, (as explained in the next section), a lower overall tax burden. If the supplies are so specific that they could not be obtained from any other source currently available, the transfer price should preferably be set at standard variable cost, while the efficiency of the supplying division must be assessed in the same way as that of any internal department.

5 In certain situations the transfer price may be used, within legal limits, to minimize *total* tax liability. If both transferor and transferee are situated in the same country, an appropriate division of the taxable profit between them could be of advantage if the rate of the profit tax is progressive. It might even pay to acquire the company of a subsidiary supplier or distributor that offers no advantage other than a substantial accumulated loss, provided it is permissible to write it off against current profits. In the case of international transfers, a reduced transfer price will attract less ad valorem import duty and, within the European Economic Community, less Value Added Tax, but might increase profit tax liability and vice versa.

Within the United States, Section 482 of the US Internal Revenue Code limits the use of transfer prices to ensure that profit tax is not avoided, and the US Treasury Department has adopted regulations applicable to all types of intercompany transactions. Similar legislation is also in force in some other countries. The report of the OECD Committee on Fiscal Affairs, *Transfer Pricing and Multinational Enterprises*, Organization for Economic Cooperation and Development, Paris, 1979 (100 pages) recommends all member states to empower their tax authorities to adjust invoiced transfer prices to the level that would have been arrived at by 'arm's length' negotiations, that is between bargaining parties which did not share any common interest.[7] While this document takes the view that only such prices could ensure the just distribution of profits between the transferor's country and that of the transferee, it makes no secret of the substantial difficulties encountered when it comes to the determination of an 'arm's length' price in the absence of factual

---

[7] The problems of arms-length pricing are discussed in David R. Lambert, 'Transfer Pricing and Interdivisional Conflict', *California Management Review*, **21**, Summer 1979, pp. 70–75.

evidence. For further comments on this aspect cf. section 12 below.

6 Where regulations impede the free movement of capital between two countries, it might be possible to use transfer pricing within the legal limits to direct the cash flow to the country where it will best serve the interest of the corporation. However, in addition to any regulations concerning foreign exchange transactions, it must also be kept in mind that the customs authorities of many countries have the right to adjust invoiced transfer prices if they can be shown to be unrealistic.[8]

7 If one of the two companies involved in the transfer is not a wholly owned subsidiary of the other but is partly the property of a third party, negotiation of the transfer price appears to be the only equitable expedient. However, the actual transfer price need not necessarily be arrived at on an 'arm's length' basis; friendly consideration of the common interest might be a better principle to adopt.

8 In the last case considered, transferor and transferee will operate as individual profit centres, and it has been contended that profits are better indicators of efficiency than contributions, and that therefore negotiated transfer prices should be preferred also in cases of common ownership. However, transferor and transferee are seldom if ever of equal bargaining strength and hence the negotiated price is likely to favour one of the parties more than the other, and withholding the knowledge of the variable cost from the transferee could easily lead to sub-optimal marketing decisions.

9 As we have seen, the invoiced price need not be the same as that on which marketing decisions are based, and unless the profit centre contention is accepted, the net sales revenue less the variable cost up to the point of transfer and the specific costs incurred by the transferee represents the contribution on which the performance of the subsidiary distributor and that of individual members of the sale personnel should generally be judged. An exception to this rule would be indicated if the sales division was specifically directed by the central office to cut its usual mark-up in order to increase its market share, even if this policy should result in a temporary fall of the total contribution. In such a case it would be equitable to judge performance as if the standard mark-up had been applied and also when an individual salesman is specifically instructed to get his foot

---

[8] Cf. Seung H. Kim and Stephen W. Miller, 'Constituents of the International Transfer Pricing Decision', *Columbia Journal of World Business*, **14**, Spring 1979, pp. 69–70.

inside the door of a potential customer by offering him a substantial special rebate. Some of the large multinationals have a system of standard bonuses for application in such cases.

10 The pricing of services rendered by one division to another should be handled with great care. If they are performed by permanent staff whose salary would be payable in any case and should therefore be ranked with the fixed costs of the corporation, the incremental cost principle would demand that the performance of their services should not give rise to any transfer price, especially if they claim only relatively small proportions of the time of the personnel concerned. If, however, the service involves *avoidable cost*, (an example of which would be market research carried out by temporary staff hired by the transferor on behalf of the transferee), it would seem logical to charge for it at the rate actually incurred. All the same, there may be some room for negotiation here, especially if transferor or transferee are only partly in common ownership, or if the possibility that the transferee could obtain the same services cheaper than the transferor could not *prima facie* be excluded.

So far we have interpreted the standard variable cost applicable to the point of transfer as an acceptable estimate of the incremental cost; now we have to consider the case where after-sales service is performed by the transferor, such as, for example, repairs under guarantee. If any avoidable cost is incurred thereby, it would be equitable to add to the transfer price of the goods a charge for these subsequent services, assessed by reference to past experience.

11 Where the decision involves investment in a subsidiary, the transfer price becomes irrelevant and only the general principles of investment appraisal apply. These are the main aspects that need to be examined:

- Does the proposed project promise to improve the long-term return on capital of the corporation as a whole?
- How much additional fixed and working capital will be tied down by the project?
- Are the negative and positive cash flows generated by the project acceptable?
- Is it the best investment opportunity available at the time, inside or outside the companies in common ownership?

If the proposed project concerns a subsidiary that is only partly owned by the corporation, both the investment decision and the proportions of capital to be provided by the two parties must be arrived at by negotiation. It is, of course, possible that the subsidiary in joint ownership will have accumulated reserves available or be able to obtain the necessary capital by the issue of new shares or debentures.

12 In a recent publication of the National Association of Accountants[9] the authors suggest a general rule for selecting transfer pricing techniques. According to them the formula is

$$TP = SVC + LCM,$$

where TP stands for Transfer Price, SVC for Standard Variable Cost and LCM for the Lost Contribution Margin. The latter is defined as the difference between the market price of the product concerned and its standard variable cost, and is taken as representing the opportunity cost of the transfer. The value of LCM is zero if the product has no market price and no suitable substitute can be found.

Transfer prices so arrived at would presumably satisfy the provision of Section 482 of the US Internal Revenue Code, but except in the case where the product has no market price could not be said to be suitable for the formulation of marketing decisions.[10]

[9] R. L. Benke, Jr. and J. D. Edwards, *Transfer Pricing: Techniques and Uses*, NAA (USA), 1980. Cf. also the summary in *Management Accounting*, June 1980, pp. 44–6.

[10] For a more detailed discussion of the issues dealt with in this Appendix cf. André Gabor, 'On the Theory and Practice of Transfer Pricing', Chapter 9 in *Demand, Equilibrium and Trade*, (A. Ingham and A. M. Ulph, eds), The Macmillan Press Limited, London, 1984, pp. 149–170. It lists 63 references.

APPENDIX II TO CHAPTER 6: PRODUCT ANALYSIS PRICING

Product Analysis Prjcing (PAP for short) was developed in the Glacier Metal Company, Ruislip, Middlesex, England, and has been in use there since 1960. Outlines of it have been made public some time ago[1] but it has not so far spread to any significant extent. Yet, the method is not without merit and hence deserves consideration.

The Glacier Metal Company is an engineering firm whose products are sold in industrial markets. It sends out several hundred quotations every week and the orders are mostly to the customer's own specification.

The central idea of PAP is that the price which the buyer is prepared to pay is directly determined by those aspects of the product that have significance for him. It claims that these aspects can be quantified and a value schedule attached to each, based on the buyer's judgement rather than on the cost of the product. The appropriateness of the quotations derived from these values, and the extent to which the prices approximate the optimum level can be judged by the percentage of the market captured. This amounts to the recognition of the fact that most of the industrial buyer's expertise consists in being aware of the prices of the effective competitors and of the differences in those characteristics which are not explicitly covered by the specification, such as consistent quality, fair settling of complaints, reliability with regard to delivery dates, etc.

PAP is a system of delegated pricing, in the sense that once its basic principles are developed and approved by the chief pricing executive, it should produce consistent quotations without the need of constant supervision. This is not of course a unique feature of PAP, but it must be admitted that it is often neglected when other pricing systems are used.[2]

---

[1] Wilfred Brown and Elliott Jaques, *Product Analysis Pricing*, Heinemann Educational Books, London, 1964. It contains a detailed but rather cumbersome exposition of PAP. For a shorter and somewhat more readable description cf. Leon Simons, 'Product Analysis Pricing', in *Pricing Strategy*, (B. Taylor and G. Wills, eds), Staples Press, London, 1969, pp. 334–45.

[2] 'It is not always evident that the price makers in the various big companies know there is a policy, even if an inconsistent one.' A. D. H. Kaplan, J. B. Dirlam and R. F. Lanzilotti, *Pricing in Big Business*, The Brookings Institute, Washington, DC, 1958, p. 276.

According to PAP, the essential characteristics of each product can be classified as (1) *materials*, (2) *bought components*, (3) *product properties*, and, finally, (4) *feature properties* (or *special features*), all of which have independent values. Their determination is an important task which must be undertaken at high executive level.

The first step of the procedure consists in the division of the company's actual and potential output into separate *product categories*, these being defined as groups which share the same basic properties. These properties are generally determined by the main function of the product to which they are essential, but the quantity of each product property may vary from order to order.

What the originators of PAP call a product category is often called a product line by others, but the two concepts are not entirely identical. A product line of motor car accessories, for instance, may contain items of widely different character, such as windscreen wipers, floor mats, anti-freeze liquids, etc., whereas PAP's product category could be illustrated by, say, thin wall bearings or bathroom taps. There is room for considerable variation in the materials, in the dimensions, in the finish, but they will all have the same basic properties without which the article could not serve as a bearing or a tap, as the case may be. These basic properties must all be measurable, like weight, length, diameter, etc., and should exclude all the more individual characteristics, as, for instance, chromium or enamel finish and so on, which PAP terms special features or feature properties.

Clearly, the dividing line between product properties and special features is at least to some extent open to judgement, but this is the sort of problem which can be solved more easily in practice than in theory. What product properties and special features have in common is that both are imparted by processing within the company and capable of quantitative expression. The other constituents of the product are the materials and bought components, which pose no problems of measurement.

Once the product categories are defined, a set of samples of items from each category should be selected, so that each set should represent the proper range of each of the relevant product properties and special features. The actual number of the samples in the set will depend on how many different items figured in recent orders and also on the number of significant properties. It was found that with a fairly simple product, like bearings, twenty to thirty samples were sufficient. In order to avoid the necessity of extrapolation, the sample should include items from both ends of the size range.

Each sample should be accompanied by its typical price, meaning the price at which recent orders were secured, and if this appears to be exceptional, it should be adjusted after discussion with the sales manager. Adjustments will certainly be indicated if the actual price took account of a quantity rebate or surcharge; also if the customer was one who generally pays a price which is above or below the average. The adjusted values represent first estimates of the *target prices* and, after allowance for the *market percentage*, which is common to the entire product category, of the *trial standard values*.

The task is then to analyse the trial standard values into the elements of the pricing scheme shown in Figure 6.3.

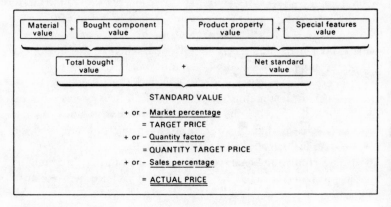

Figure 6.3   Product Analysis Pricing scheme

Material values should not be based on historical cost but rather on replacement cost to which a handling percentage has been added. In the original scheme of PAP the quantity of the material to be valued was the total gross amount; in a modified version the quantity is only what is actually present in the finished product. The argument on which the latter practice is based is that the customer is not interested in the extent of the waste, which may well be true, but of course this modification means that if the *normal* waste (or minimum unavoidable waste) is 25 per cent, say, the unit value of the material actually incorporated in the product must be set one-third higher than it would have been in the original scheme. The magnitude of the handling percentage may depend on such things as transport and storage charges, etc., but not on any cost of processing within the company.

Bought components should also be valued at replacement cost; the principle being that the total charge made for them should not exceed what it would cost to the customer were he to decide to order the product without such components and fit them himself. This indicates also the way in which the relevant handling charges should be determined.

The sum of these two items is the *total bought value* which will be deducted from the *trial standard value* of each sample. What is left is the *net trial standard value*, which is to be analysed into the values imputed to *product properties* and *feature properties* (or *special features*).

At this stage each of these properties has to be given a quantitative measure of the extent to which it is present in each of the samples, and the list is then handed to the analyst, who must be a person familiar both with the technical aspects of the products and with the appropriate mathematical and computational methods.

The analyst will consider the *special features* (or *feature properties*) first and attempt to determine their values by reference to two similar items: one with and the other without the particular feature concerned. This may not be a simple process since some of the features may be variable in extent, (as, for example, tolerances,) and the value function may have to be non-linear.

Once all the special features are valued, their sum will be deducted from the net trial standard value and the residue so obtained will represent the *trial product property value* of each item. These will be listed together with the quantitative measures of each of the product properties, and the analyst should now attempt to derive the value function for each of the product properties with the aid of a computer. If the first round produces no acceptable solution, he will try to identify the item that appears to be out of harmony and may suggest a reassessment of its trial standard value.

The protagonists of PAP recognize that this kind of problem is not capable of a straightforward mathematical solution, but claim that approximation by trial and error (or appropriate short-cut methods) will not encounter any insurmountable difficulties in establishing acceptable relationships between the measurements of the characteristics and the values to be assigned to them.

Once all these relationships are established, the system can be tested by deriving from the quantitative data and the value functions *standard values* for each item. In general, these will not exactly correspond to the trial values from which they were derived, but if the discrepancies between them are such that the new values imply increased consistency of the price structure, the new values will be superior to the trial values.

The *market percentage*, which may be positive or negative, will be the same for each item within the same product category at any given time. This percentage should not be looked upon as representing profit but as the factor which equates *standard value* with the *target price*, the latter being the average price that the company hopes to achieve, after proper allowance for quantity rebates or surcharges and the sales percentage differential, which will be discussed presently. Variation of the market percentage makes it possible to adapt the price level of the company to changes in the market, (for example, aggressive policy by a strong competitor might make it advisable to reduce the market percentage on all the product categories concerned) without any alteration of the method by which the standard values are derived.

The market percentage is shown in Figure 6.3. as a factor applied to the standard value, but according to a more recent suggestion it should be applied to the *net* standard value only, that is to say, to that part of the value which has been imparted to the product by processing within the company. The argument is that changes in the current prices of materials and bought components should not be amplified by the market percentage. Clearly, this is a debatable point.

The *quantity factor* calls for little explanation since it represents the usual rebate for larger quantities and/or surcharge for small lots. It is obvious that it should be in line with what is the usual practice of the competition, (since this is what the customer would expect to see,) unless the company's policy dictates a deliberate departure from it. For example, it may be decided to discourage small orders and encourage large ones by appropriate adjustments of the quantity factor.[3]

The *sales percentage* could more appropriately be called the 'customer percentage', this being an adjustment that may vary from buyer to buyer. It is intended to take account of such things as for example the concession made to an important customer who regularly places orders for several different products and hence expects a price advantage over and above the usual quantity rebates, or it can be an expression of the advantage the company

---

[3] Quantity rebates are discussed in Chapter 6, pp. 101–6.

enjoys when it supplies a reliable product that is itself small and relatively inexpensive but will, for example, eventually form a component of an expensive machine. It is well known that in such cases reliability and dependable supply will count for much more than a low price, and a satisfied customer will be very reluctant to experiment with a new supplier even if he quotes a considerably lower price.

Once all these points are satisfactorily settled, it will be possible to formalize the whole pricing procedure. To start with, a pricing sheet will be prepared for each of the product categories. It will contain the following data:

- Descriptive title and code number.
- Definition of the limits of the products within the category.
- Material handling percentage for each of the materials and component handling percentage for all the listed components.
- Features chart, showing values for all the special features known to appear in the category.
- Formula for obtaining the product property value.
- Market percentage for the product category.
- Quantity rebate and/or surcharge scales.

By reference to the appropriate data sheet, the pricing department should be able to calculate the quantity target price for any specification submitted by the sales department.

The sales percentage will be applied by the sales manager within the limits stipulated. It could be, for example: 'freedom to quote down to 7 per cent below or up to 10 per cent above the quantity target price – any proposed quotation outside these limits to be referred to the chief pricing executive'.

It will be the chief pricing executive's task to keep watch over the way in which orders are running, over the utilization of the capacity of the company and over any deviations of the structure of orders from the desired product mix. Generally, he should be able to make the necessary adjustments by changes in the market percentage. Changes in the prices of materials and bought components will automatically be reflected in the total bought value and should call only exceptionally for a reappraisal of the handling percentages.

PAP is commendable for its clear recognition of the fact that under competitive conditions only a market-oriented pricing policy can be successful. It is undoubtedly capable of further development but in its present state it suffers from certain serious shortcomings which severely restrict its applicability.

First of all, it has no proper method for discovering the actual values which customers attach to the properties of each product, apart from 'watching how orders are running'. This may well be all right for a firm in Glacier's position: picking up trade from hundreds of small orders each week from a very large number of customers providing their own specifications, but could easily be detrimental to a firm that handles small numbers of large orders. (Methods for gauging consumers' valuations are discussed in Part II of this book.)

Second, PAP contains no provision for the adjustment of prices when wages go up or when there is an increase in productivity shared by all the firms in the industry. The advice of the protagonists of PAP is to watch what the competition is doing and act accordingly, which is not so much a principle as rather the negation of one. This particular shortcoming is not, however, difficult to remedy. Even if the day-to-day determination of prices is done by the PAP system, wage costs of the individual products will still be available if a piece-work system of wage payments operates, and if wages are paid by the hours worked, it will anyway be advisable to keep time sheets. The wage records will have to be consulted only when necessitated by a change in wage rates or productivity.

Third, PAP could not replace costing systems which are necessary for the purposes of cost control and can also be used to gauge the limit to which the competition might go. This means that direct costing may have to be retained, but the costs accountants need not trouble themselves with the allocation of the indirect cost elements. A costing exercise will be necessary whenever the company considers the introduction of an entirely new product since PAP provides no guidance whatsoever for this case. It should further be noted that the elimination of costing records would make the application of the techniques of *value analysis* and *value engineering* (see Appendix III to this chapter) very difficult if not impossible. This would be regrettable since they have proved their worth in thousands of instances.

To sum up, what PAP is capable of achieving is *a consistent set of prices for each individual customer*. Repeated adjustments of the market percentages and sales percentages could, however, result in a highly inconsistent price structure for the company itself, even if its original prices were in fair harmony with one another.

APPENDIX III TO CHAPTER 6:   VALUE ANALYSIS AND VALUE ENGINEERING

The terms Value Analysis and Value Engineering are used interchangeably by some authorities. Others have differentiated between them, as for example Mr. D. I. Spears, Director, Mead Carney & Company Limited, who says:

> Value Analysis is an analytical technique designed to examine all the components of cost of an existing product in order to determine whether or not an item of cost can be reduced or eliminated while retaining all functional and quality requirements. Value Engineering is the application of value analysis techniques to new products in the development and prototype stage.

Value analysis has its origin at General Electric (USA) in 1947; the first major article, by L. D. Miles, was published in the *American Machinist* on 14 July 1949. The technique is now so developed and has scored so many successes that application of value analysis is obligatory in many USA government contracts.

It is emphatically claimed by its main originator, Lawrence D. Miles, that:

> Value Analysis is *not* a substitute for conventional cost-reduction work methods. Rather, it is a potent and completely different procedure for accomplishing far greater results. It improves the effectiveness of work that has been conventionally performed over the years, as it fills its blind spots. Quite commonly, 15 to 25 per cent, and often very much more, of manufacturing costs can be removed by effective application of the teachings of value analysis.

The fundamental purpose of value analysis is to maximize the Value/Cost quotient. It distinguishes between four types of value:

- *Cost value*: the sum of all the costs required to produce the article in question. It is particularly relevant if the work is carried out on a cost-plus-fixed-percentage type of contract.
- *Exchange value*: the power to command a certain price.
- *Esteem value*: the value placed upon the properties or attractiveness of the article, which might well exceed the actual price.
- *Use value*: often relative, for example, use value will increase with the life span of a machine or with reduction in fuel

consumption. It is of primary importance if the product concerned is not for sale but for use within the company.

Thus value analysis endeavours to maintain the value of a product while decreasing its cost of production or to increase its value without a proportional increase in cost. It has a wide range of highly developed and specialized techniques for solving specific problems; methods which have proved their worth in practice. Common to all is that the value analyst takes a completely unbiased look at each of the features and components of a product, and starting from its essential function considers all the possible alternatives of achieving the same performance at a lower cost or a different but fully adequate performance which gives a higher Value/Cost quotient. These methods take account of the fact that in order to improve one property, another might have to be sacrificed, (as, for instance, when both lightness and strength are of significance). Application of the appropriate method will enable the analyst to strike the proper balance.

It would be impossible to go further in a brief note. The interested reader is advised to consult the references listed below.

References

L. W. Crum, *Value Engineering – The Organized Search for Value*, Longman, London, 1971.

Carlos Fallon, *Value Analysis*, Wiley-Interscience, New York, 1971.

W. L. Gage, *Value Analysis*, McGraw-Hill, London, 1967.

Lawrence D. Miles, *Techniques of Value Analysis and Engineering*, 2nd edn, McGraw-Hill, New York, 1972.

Warren J. Ridge, *Value Analysis for Better Management*, American Management Association, 1969.

J. C. H. Roberts, *An ABC of Value Analysis*, Modern Management Technique, Southport, 1967.

Value Engineering and Management Digest, (monthly), Tufty Communications Co., 986 National Press Building, Washington DC 2045, USA.

7 Price discrimination and multi-pricing

The topic of this chapter has particular relevance to the pricing of public utilities, especially gas and electricity, the full discussion of which is not the purpose of this book. Since, however, similar problems and practices are also encountered in other fields of business, it would hardly be right to exclude it altogether. The analysis will involve reference to some elements of economic theory, not for their own sake but because they will help the explanation.

With the exception of some retail establishments, very few business firms, if any, have only one set of prices and stick to them rigorously, irrespective of the identity of the customer. The effects of diverse margins have already been illustrated, here we shall examine the fundamentals of these and related practices, both from the point of view of the seller and that of the purchaser.[1]

It is one of the main arguments in favour of a market economy that, in the absence of restrictions imposed by an outside authority or a monopoly, a transaction freely arrived at will generally be beneficial to both of the parties. The producer's gain will manifest itself in his profit; the benefit of the purchaser, be he another producer or a consumer, can be said to consist in the difference between the highest price that could have been extracted from him and the price he actually paid.

The extent of the profit realized by the seller can be assessed; on the purchaser's side the gain is not as a rule measurable but can be real all the same.[2]

---

[1] Price differences due to quantity rebates, trade discounts and cash discounts are discussed in Chapter 6; for the pricing of different pack sizes of the same product see Chapter 8. For differential pricing at the retail level, cf. David M. Armbrose, 'Retail Grocery Pricing: Inner City, Suburban and Rural Comparisons', *Journal of Business*, **52**, (1), 1979, pp. 95–102.

[2] Consider this case: a manufacturer has received an order for a quantity of one of his products with the stipulation that it must be fitted with a special

Whenever a purchaser is induced to pay a price that provides the seller with a profit larger than the miminum necessary to keep the supply flowing, the seller acquires some or all of the purchaser's potential surplus. The extreme case is that of the hypothetical monopolist who tackles his customers one by one, and charges each of them individual prices set so high that if they were only a shade higher, the customers would rather go without the product altogether or, at least, reduce their rate of consumption below that which would be most advantageous to the seller. This extreme case is, of course, a nightmare, though it is sometimes approximated in special circumstances. In a market economy, the existence of actual or potential competitors and measures of monopoly control generally prevent any substantial domination of the field by an individual seller or combination of several sellers.[3] But the time-honoured principle of charging what the traffic will bear is still active in the price policies of public transport and utility enterprises, whether state administered or privately owned. More will be said

---

component. The only known supplier of this component quotes such a high price for it that our manufacturer begins to wonder whether he should accept the order at all. Then he finds another source from which the component concerned can be bought at a much lower price. The difference between the two prices multiplied by the quantity can be identified as the surplus on the purchase of the component. Had the first source quoted the same low price, the surplus would have gone unnoticed.

When the purchaser is a consumer, the surplus becomes even more elusive and is evident only on certain occasions, e.g. when the consumer happens to pick up a bargain. When his shopping list and the prices of his purchases have remained unchanged for a while, the consumer's surplus becomes hidden, since the notional saving on each item is simultaneously being spent on some of the others.

These examples do not by any means cover the full story but should suffice as illustrations. The concept is French in origin, it was popularized by Alfred Marshall (cf. his *Principles of Economics*, Book III, Macmillan, London, 1890); its ramifications are extensively discussed in J. R. Hicks, *A Revision of Demand Theory*, Clarendon Press, Oxford, 1956, Chapter X, pp. 95–106 and *passim*.

[3] Even in the absence of a monopoly, large producers might have the power to control prices, especially if there is heavy concentration in the industry, meaning thta it is dominated by a small number of large companies. It has been found that the higher the concentration, the greater is the stability of the prices also where there is no sign of deliberate collusion. Cf. for example, R. Dixon, 'Industry Structure and the Speed of Price Adjustment', *Journal of Industrial Economics*, **32**, (1), September 1983, pp. 25–37, and Stephen C. Farber, 'Cyclical Price Flexibility: A Test of Administered Pricing', *Journal of Industrial Economics*, **32**, (4), June 1984, pp. 465–76.

about their pricing practices presently, but let us first examine the underlying principles.

At the time when resale price maintenance was still legal in the United Kingdom, it was taken for granted that branded consumer goods should be offered for sale at the same price all over the country, and even these days, when the retail price is to a large extent at the discretion of the distributors and quite considerable differences in the price of any brand can be observed between shops in the same street, the idea that price uniformity should be equitable still lingers. In actual fact, it amounts to price discrimination if, say, a packet of Wills cigarettes manufactured in Bristol sells at the same price in the street next to the factory and at John O'Groats. The transport costs being different, price uniformity means that the smokers of Bristol 'subsidize' those of John O'Groats. In the United States, where the distances are often greater and there are also considerable differences both in local taxation and in the laws concerning resale price maintenance, the public readily accept the fact that the price of any commodity may vary from place to place. However, where this occurs, *spatial discrimination* could be present.

Spatial discrimination has two main forms: (1) zone (or area) pricing, meaning that while the price concerned is the same within any individual zone (or area), it is different from the prices in others; and (2) basing-point pricing, that is to say a price that is the same for all customers at a certain point, (which is not necessarily identical with the place where the good is produced), *plus* a charge depending on the distance of the point of delivery from the basing-point. Discrimination will be present only if the price differences cannot fully be justified by reference to the differences in the cost to the seller.[4]

---

[4] For a further discussion of the principles and practices of these forms of discrimination see Louis Phlips, *The Economics of Price Discrimination*, Cambridge University Press, Cambridge, 1983, esp. pp. 147–50 and 158–73, also the numerous references, pp. 263–77; and David D. Haddock, 'Basing Point Pricing: Competitive vs. Collusive Theories', *American Economic Review*, **72**, (3), June 1982, pp. 289–306. For some recent examples of these practices cf. M. L. Greenhut, 'Spatial Pricing in the United States, West Germany and Japan', *Economica*, **48**, (189), 1981, pp. 79–86; M. H. Ashworth, J. A. Kay and T. A. E. Sharpe, *Differentials between Car Prices in the United Kingdom and Belgium*, The Institute of Fiscal Studies, London, 1982; and Yves Mertens and Victor Ginsburgh, 'Product Differentiation and Price Discrimination in the European Community: The Case of Automobiles', *Journal of Industrial Economics*, **34**, (2), December 1985, pp. 151–66.

Price discrimination: an example

The economist's analysis of price discrimination is based on the assumption that the manufacturer has precise knowledge not only of what each rate of output would cost him, but also of the reactions of the demand to different prices in every one of his markets. Most standard textbooks of the theory of value contain the graphical solution of the problem, while some of them present it in mathematical terms.[5]

The theoretical solution is of scant interest to the businessman who can never hope to have all the necessary data at his disposal. However, just to show how the analysis works, it will be demonstrated here with a numerical example.

This is the incremental cost schedule of a manufacturer who serves two different markets or, two segments of the same market which are so effectively separated that goods sold in one cannot be transferred to the other:

	Incremental cost per unit (£)
Up to 1,000 units p.a.	70
1,001–2,000 units p.a.	60
2,001–3,000 units p.a.	50
3,001–6,000 units p.a.	40

The relevant demand conditions in the two markets are shown in Table 7.1.

Table 7.1
Example of relevant demands in two markets

Market 1		Market 2	
Price (£)	Units bought p.a.	Price (£)	Units bought p.a.
94	2,900	76	1,100
95	2,850		
96	2,800	78	1,050
97	2,750		
98	2,700	80	1,000
99	2,650		
100	2,600	82	950
101	2,550		
102	2,500	84	900
103	2,450		
104	2,400	86	850

[5] Cf. e.g. Fred R. Glahe and Dwight R. Lee, *Microeconomics: Theory and Applications*, Harcourt Brace Jovanovich, New York, 1981, pp. 305–13, and Steven T. Call and William L. Holahan, *Microeconomics*, 2nd edn, Woodworth Publishing Co., Belmont, CA, 1983, pp. 275–86.

Table 7.2
Example of most favourable level and distribution of output

Total output	Price (£)	Market 1 Units sold p.a.	Price (£)	Market 2 Units sold p.a.	Total sales returns (£)	Total cost[6] (£)	Contribution (£)
3,800	95	2,850	82	950	348,650	212,000	136,650
3,800	96	2,800	80	1,000	348,800	212,000	136,800
3,800	97	2,750	78	1,050	348,650	212,000	136,650

Table 7.3
Example of less favourable levels and distributions of output

Total output	Price (£)	Market 1 Units sold p.a.	Price (£)	Market 2 Units sold p.a.	Total sales returns (£)	Total cost (£)	Contribution (£)
3,750	96	2,800	82	950	346,700	210,000	136,700
3,750	97	2,750	80	1,000	346,750	210,000	136,750
3,850	95	2,850	80	1,000	350,750	214,000	136,750
3,850	96	2,800	78	1,050	350,700	214,000	136,700

[6] This is the calculation of the total cost (meaning the total direct cost):

1,000 units at £70 each	£70,000
1,000 units at £60 each	60,000
1,000 units at £50 each	50,000
800 units at £40 each	32,000
3,800	£212,000

The combinations in Table 7.2 show that the output which secures the highest contribution is 3,800 units per annum, of which 2,800 are supplied to Market 1 and 1,000 to Market 2.

That 3,800 units per annum represents the optimum output can be seen if we consider the outcome of the most favourable distributions of outputs slightly smaller or larger than 3,800 as displayed in Table 7.3.

The reader might like to convince himself of the validity of these results by working out the profits of other possible levels and distributions of the total output.

There is also the question whether the customers in Market 1, where the higher of the two prices is charged, would be better off if the supplies to Market 2 were discontinued. In that case the optimum output would be 2,550 units which could be sold at £101 each as shown in Table 7.4:

Table 7.4
Example of optimum output in Market 1

Price (£)	Market 1 Units sold p.a.	Total sales returns (£)	Total cost (£)	Contribution (£)
99	2,650	262,350	162,500	99,850
100	2,600	260,000	160,000	100,000
101	2,550	257,550	157,500	100,050
102	2,500	255,000	155,000	100,000
103	2,450	252,350	152,500	99,850

It can be seen that owing to the fall in incremental cost, the supplies to Market 2 at a lower price have not in fact harmed the customers in Market 1. The latter have actually benefited, since their own price would have been £101 instead of £96 in the absence of the second market.[7]

The crucial postulate of this demonstration is that the manufacturer will strive to maximize the annual contribution from the product (which, if all the overhead costs are fixed, is tantamount to maximizing the annual profit). This is not necessarily so in every instance and, owing to imperfect knowledge, is unlikely to be

---

[7] For an example of the same issue in pricing for the home market and for exports cf. Chapter 6, pp. 97–9.

accomplished even if the intention is there. It follows that the actual outcome could well be different from that shown here.

The practice of price discrimination is widespread. Railways and other public transport enterprises, whether state owned or not, generally vary their freight charges not only according to the weight and bulk of the consignment, but also with regard to the value of the goods carried. They invariably claim that this does not amount to price discrimination as they will make the same charge for the same goods whoever the customer may be. All the same, this practice is a manifestation of the 'charging what the traffic will bear' principle to which reference has been made above.

Similar considerations apply to the practice of electricity and gas suppliers of charging commercial users at a higher rate than private households, even if the levels and patterns of their consumptions happen to be similar. In fact, both the levels and the patterns of consumption tend to vary, and this brings us face to face with what is known as the peak load problem.

Electricity tariffs and the peak load problem

Since electricity cannot efficiently be stored, the rate of generation must follow or, rather, anticipate, any change in the rate of consumption. This means that capacity must be geared to the peak and will not therefore be fully utilized at any other time. Electricity consumption has a daily pattern, a weekly pattern and a seasonal pattern, all overlaid on a secular trend itself disturbed by the booms and slumps of the trade cycle.

The pattern of gas consumption is not dissimilar, and the fact that gas can be stored modifies rather than eliminates the peak load problem. The possibility of storage affects only one of the four cost factors; a point to which we shall return after having surveyed the basic cost structure of electricity supply and the nature of its tariffs.

The first cost element to be considered is that of providing both generating and transmission equipment adequate to cope with the maximum demand. The cost arises out of the depreciation and maintenance of the plant and the wages and salaries of those members of the personnel whose work is independent of the rate of utilization of the capacity. To this a mark-up should be added to cover the return on capital and possibly some overhead charges not allocated to any of the other elements.

The second element is that of the customer costs. They arise out of the amortization and maintenance of that part of the distribution network which is attributable to the individual consumer rather than to the peak load, also the cost of metering, accounting and collecting, etc.

The third element is the energy cost: mainly fuel and that part of the wages and salaries of generating station personnel which varies with the output.

Finally, there may be residual expenses not included in any of the first three categories, such as, for example, overheads not allocated to capacity costs, advertising costs not accounted for by the sale of domestic or other equipment, etc.

The task is then to allocate all these costs to the individual customers (or, at least, to divide the costs between the different classes of customers) in a way that is both satisfactory to the enterprise and acceptable to the customers. (Certain government regulations or directives might also have to be observed, but this is an aspect the discussion of which falls outside the scope of this book.) Most of the writers on the subject endeavour to justify one or another of the possible methods of charging by reference to the cost side, though there are some who also recognize the importance of the reactions of the customers to the different systems of pricing and to variations in the actual level of the charges.[8]

Before we enter on the discussion of the main methods of charging, let us stop for a moment and consider that the peak load

---

[8] A thorough discussion of the subject and a good source of further references can be found in R. K. Davidson, *Price Discrimination in Selling Gas and Electricity*, Johns Hopkins Press, Baltimore, 1955. For the analysis of the demand side see also André Gabor, 'A Note on Block Tariffs', *Review of Economic Studies*, **XXIII**, (1), 1955, pp. 32–41; M. Boiteux, 'La tarification des demandes en pointe', *Revue Générale d'Electricité*, 1949, (English translation in *Journal of Business*, **XXXIII**, April 1960, pp. 157–79 and in *Marginal Cost Pricing in Practice*, (J.F. Nelson, ed.), Prentice-Hall, Englewood Cliffs, NJ, 1964, pp. 59–89); H. S. Houthakker, 'Public Utility Pricing', *Economic Journal*, **LXI**, (1), March 1951, pp. 1–25; P. O. Steiner, 'Peak Loads and Efficient Pricing', *Quarterly Journal of Economics*, **LXXI**, (4), November 1957, pp. 585–610 and the subsequent discussion with contributions from J. Hirschleifer, H. S. Houthakker, J. M. Buchanan and A. Gabor in the same journal, **LXXII**, (3), August 1958, pp. 451–68 and **LXXX**, (3), August 1966, pp. 463–80. See also the list of recent publications, selected from the extensive literature of the subject, appended to the end of this chapter.

problem, that is, the fact that the capacity to be provided and kept in readiness to cope with the peak demand will not be fully utilized all the time, is not as peculiar to public utilities and transport as it might seem at first. Every retail outlet experiences a daily peak, a weekly peak and an annual peak; the same goes for catering establishments, hotels and most of the other service trades. Manufacturers turning out standard products only may be able to provide for the periods of peak demand by storing some or all of their output during the slack periods, (which is what the suppliers of gas and water do); jobbing firms, however, are more or less in the same position as the service trades, (that is, their peak load problem is akin to that of electricity generation). In a few trades differential pricing is conventionally accepted: many restaurants provide luncheons at lower prices than dinners, hotels at holiday resorts have separate high-season and low-season tariffs, and so on, but apart from some expedients, such as for example, holding sales in the off seasons, competition generally prevents retailers and most manufacturers from following the practices of the public utility enterprises, all of which enjoy at least some degree of monopoly power and are also supported by legislation which heavily restricts the resale of electricity, gas and water, so as to prevent the customer with the low tariff from reselling to those who are simultaneously charged at higher rates.

the main methods of pricing the supply of electricity.

1 In the early stages when electricity was used for lighting only and the metering of the individual customer's consumption was not yet economically possible, it was usual to levy a fixed monthly or quarterly charge per lamp socket. This is now superseded (but an analogous method is still being used in connection with the water supply in some countries, including the United Kingdom).

2 The flat rate per unit consumed, perhaps varying with the class of the consumer (for example, industrial, commercial, public authority, domestic, etc.) appears to be a rather imperfect method since it takes no account of the cost structure. Its simplicity commends itself to some consumers but even though it is still available here and there, it has largely lost its popularity.

3 The step rate with the price per unit falling as consumption increases belongs to the promotional type, since it tends to encourage consumption. However, it suffers from a great disadvantage which can best be demonstrated by an example. Consider this

tariff:

100 units or less per quarter	4p per unit
101–200 units per quarter	3p per unit
201 units and over per quarter	2p per unit

With such a system, the consumer who has reached 100 units in any quarter could consume the next 33 units free of charge, and similarly, he would pay only as much for 300 units as for 200. Clearly, the only way to eliminate this shortcoming would be to fashion the tariff so that the charge drops by some small fraction unit-by-unit; not impossible but hardly practical.

4 The two-part tariff, consisting of a fixed quarterly (or monthly) charge and a flat rate per unit has considerable attraction since it appears to be in general harmony with the cost structure. If the fixed charge could be apportioned so that it covered the appropriate fixed costs and the flat rate the energy cost, it would also seem to be equitable. The trouble is that it is extremely difficult if not impossible to determine the appropriate fixed costs since the capacity element depends on the consumer's contribution to the peak load. It has repeatedly been suggested that, like the block tariff (the next method to be discussed), it works in the wrong direction: being promotional by nature, it will encourage consumption in the peak period and thus increase capacity costs without adequately contributing to them. All the same, it is widely used and unpopular only with those consumers who use very little, if any, electricity in some quarters (or months, if this is how they are billed), yet find that they have the fixed charge to pay. Some of the small consumers are inclined to think that they subsidize the larger consumers, whereas it is often found that the fixed charge paid by the small consumer is not even sufficient to cover that part of the consumer cost for which he is responsible, and that owing to his low rate of consumption the contribution from the unit charge is also insufficient.

In a variant of the method the fixed charge permits the free consumption of a certain limited number of units; in another variant the fixed charge is combined with the block tariff.

5 The block tariff is the one most widely used. It is only superficially similar to the step tariff, the difference being that the unit rate applicable to each block does not affect the rate for any lower block. It is therefore analogous to the non-integrated quantity discount, discussed in Chapter 6. For example:

First 100 units per quarter	4p per unit
Next 100 units per quarter	3p per unit
All units in excess of 200 per quarter	2p per unit

With this tariff 100 units cost £4.00, 101 units £4.03 and 133 units £4.99. The consumer enjoys a drop in the marginal cost of electricity each time his consumption exceeds one of the block limits, and, after the first block, a gradually decreasing average cost per unit. It is therefore decidedly promotional.

The main objection to the block tariff is the same as to the two-part tariff, namely that the increased consumption which it encourages is very likely to add to the peak load without any appropriate contribution to the capacity costs. Its popularity is probably due to the fact that it can be made the tool of market-oriented pricing. The first block with the highest price per unit can be so apportioned that it at least roughly equals the quarterly consumption of electricity within the field where it enjoys an almost perfect monopoly position: lighting, television, air conditioning, refrigeration, vacuum cleaners, etc., while the lower rates of the higher blocks are set so as to be competitive with gas, oil and solid fuel when it comes to purposes which could also effectively be served by the latter: mainly cooking, water heating and space heating. The fact that the higher the consumption per quarter, the lower is the average cost per unit has led to the same mostly unfounded objection as that raised to the block tariff, namely that those who use small amounts of electricity per quarter subsidize the larger consumers.

The number of fixed blocks may be as low as one, after which a flat rate applies, and in fact if it were possible to fashion such a block tariff individually to the potential demand of each consumer, it could be made exactly as effective as one with many blocks.[9]

The block tariff is most generally used for the supply of electricity to domestic premises, but modified forms of it may also be offered to customers with industrial or commercial premises, as long as the peak load for which their consumption is responsible does not exceed a certain limit.

6 The typical tariff for large industrial and commercial users is of the 'demand' variety. In this context, the term 'demand' has a very specific meaning: it is a measure by which the individual customer's contribution to capacity costs can be gauged.

'Demand' is measured by special meters so constructed as to indicate the maximum power[10] taken by the customer between one

---

[9] For the proof of this proposition cf. André Gabor, 'A Note on Block Tariffs', *Review of Economic Studies*, **XXIII**, (1), 1955, p. 35.

[10] While electricity consumption is measured by the kilowatthour (kWh), the measure of true power is the kilowatt (kW). In the case of alternating

reading and another (the interval is generally one month). Some of the later types also record the actual time-pattern of 'demand'.

The annual maximum 'demand', which has to be approved in advance, immediately indicates the carrying capacity of the cable required to supply the customer, but the contribution of his consumption to the peak load of generating capacity also depends on the time pattern of its occurrence. Some account is taken of this fact by those tariffs that base the charges on a combination of the monthly maximum 'demand' and the actual consumption, like the one shown below. It was one of the alternative tariffs offered by the East Midlands Electricity Board to industrial customers in an earlier year. The unit of consumption is the kilowatthour (kWh) in Table 7.5.

Table 7.5
Electricity tariff based on maximum demand and consumption

(A) MAXIMUM DEMAND CHARGE PER MONTH:

£1.025 for each kVA of monthly maximum demand

(B) UNIT CHARGE FOR EACH UNIT METERED:

units per month per kVA of monthly maximum demand	per unit
First 200	1.218p
Next 250	1.197p
Over 450	1.120p
Rebate for consumption between the hours 23.00 and 7.00	0.240p
(requires a capital contribution to the cost of the special metering equipment)	

If in a given month the maximum demand of the customer was 40kVA and his consumption 20,000 units, the total charge would be calculated in this way:

(A) 40 kVA at £1.025 each		£41.00
(B) First 8,000 units at 1.218p each		97.44
Next 10,000 units at 1.197p each		119.70
Next 2,000 units at 1.120 each		22.40
TOTAL CHARGE		£280.54

---

current, there is a difference between this and the apparent power, measured by the kilovoltampere (kVA). If the demand charge is apportioned according to the apparent power, due regard is taken of the power factor, that is, the ratio of the true power to the apparent power. (Cf. Stephen Dresner, *Units of Measurement*, Harvey Miller & Medcalf, Aylesbury, 1971, p. 158.)

The size of the first block is the number of units in the tariff (200) multiplied by the maximum demand of the month in kVA (40), and the size of the second block is calculated in an analogous way.

It is clear that even if the actual consumption of a customer is at a reasonably uniform rate over the working hours, that is to say, even if the average load is equal to or only slightly less than the peak, it would take over 200 working hours per month (about 46 hours per week) to get him beyond the first block. However, with continuous working, interrupted only by maintenance (say 5 days per month), a consumption of about 600 units per kVA could be reached, resulting in an average cost of 1.3556p per unit to the consumer, whereas with a 40 hour week (about 173 hours per month), the unit cost would come to 1.8105p. Thus continuous working would result in a 25 per cent saving on the cost of electricity.

A further saving could be obtained by installing the special metering equipment required to take advantage of the night tariff which allows a rebate of 0.240p per unit consumed between the hours 23.00 and 7.00.

All this shows that the 'demand' tariff as here illustrated is aimed at the evening out of the rate of capacity utilization. The incentives are not, however, strong enough to achieve more than a modest reduction of the peak load problem.

The 'demand' tariff is promotional in character, and like all the multi-block tariffs, it implies the assumption that it is not only the average cost of generation and transmission that falls with increased consumption but also the marginal cost, or, at least, that the marginal cost remains constant. This is not, however, invariably the case. The generating stations and their individual equipments are not as a rule of the same type, age and efficiency, and frequently do not use the same fuel either. If there are differences in efficiency, only the most economical generating equipment will be used when demand is at a low ebb, and marginal fuel costs, etc., will tend to rise as less efficient equipment is brought into action.[11]

7 The ideal consumption pattern would be one that is at the same rate throughout the hour, the day, the week and the year, and it would seem that it could be achieved by a tariff that would charge a different rate for every half-hour, say. To mention just a few of the

---

[11] There is yet a further point here: as demand increases towards the peak, where there is a grid, electricity may have to be obtained from power stations geographically more and more distant from the places of consumption and hence the transmission losses could also rise.

reasons why this is hardly a practical possibility, electricity for lighting is of course mainly demanded during the hours of darkness, space heating is required only when the outside temperature is low, and the extra wage costs of shift working are likely to exceed any saving on the cost of electricity. It is, however, generally worthwhile to encourage the consumer to shift his consumption away from the annual peak by such methods as the 'demand' tariff shown above, and other tariffs of the off-peak or day-and-night type are also being used. In the domestic field, water heating and space heating by storage heaters are the typical applications, and there are many processes in industry that can take advantage of the cheaper off-peak or night rates.

Some writers have warned the electricity generating industry to be careful when offering tariffs of this type, since the result could be not so much a lowering of the peak but moving it to a different position.

So much about the electricity tariffs. To the extent to which they fail to allocate charges in precise proportion to the cost, they are all discriminatory, but this does not necessarily mean that they are detrimental to the public interest.

Gas tariffs

Let us now look at that aspect of the gas industry which makes its problems different from those of electricity: the possibility of storage. It means that the capacity needed to deal with the peak load has two components: production capacity and storage capacity. The proportions in which they will be combined are influenced on the one hand by the pattern of the consumption, and on the other hand by the relative incremental costs of the two capacities, and this has, of course, a direct bearing on the pricing of the supply.

Where the gas is produced entirely by the supplier, it will generally be advantageous to work on the principle that the generating capacity should be kept as low as possible with the storage taking care of most of the peak load, but where the supplier is merely a distributor of natural gas, it might be more economical to distribute the increase between the capacity of the feeder pipeline and the storage facilities.

While in the case of electricity the extent of the capacity required depends on the peak load only, and would not therefore be affected by any addition to off-peak consumption, this is not generally so in

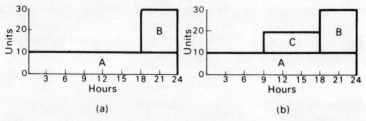

Figure 7.1   Time-patterns of gas consumption: (a) with two customers; (b) with three customers

the case of gas. Figures 7.1 (a) and (b) represent time patterns of gas consumption over a day when consumption is at its annual peak, and let us assume for the sake of simplicity that it would not be economical to store gas during the low seasons. Figure 7.1 (a) shows the consumption of two customers: A takes 10 units per hour throughout the day, and B takes 20 units per hour over 6 hours only. The minimum necessary production (or feeder) capacity will then be 15 units per hour, and the storage capacity $18 \times 5 = 90$ units. Half of the supply of the six hours of the peak will come from current production and the other half will be drawn from storage.

Figure 7.1 (b) shows the time pattern of consumption when a third customer C has entered, requiring 10 units over the 9 hours preceding the daily peak. This increases the minimum necessary production (or feeder) capacity to 18.75 units per hour, but the required storage capacity is thereby *reduced* to 78.75 units; an added complication of the problem of charging each customer according to the actual cost of his consumption. Note also that if production (or feeder) capacity were expanded, say to 20 units per hour (of which only 16.67 units would be utilized during 9 hours each day), storage capacity could further be reduced to 60 units; and storage could be completely eliminated by increasing production (or feeder) capacity to 30 units. It follows that the most cost-effective combination of capacities will depend in each case on the relative costs.[12]

Since the gas tariffs in use are similar to those of the electricity generating industry, expect insofar as there is no precise equivalent of the 'demand' tariffs for gas, they will not be further discussed here.

---

[12] Cf. J. Tzoannos, 'An Empirical Study of Peak-Load Pricing and Investment Policies for the Domestic Market of Gas in Great Britain', *Applied Economics*, **9**, 1977, pp. 133–53.

Electricity, gas and public transport are not by any means the only fields where tariffs of the types shown are used. To mention just one further example: most telephone services use two-part tariffs[13] and discriminate between different classes of customers.

Summary

Price discrimination is generally regarded as the practice of charging different prices for the same commodity, and condemned as being detrimental to the welfare of at least some of the customers. Spatial discrimination is widely practised; its main forms are zone (or area) pricing and basing-point pricing, resulting in a diversity of prices not corresponding to the actual differences in cost; charging different prices in the home market and for export belongs to the former category. That spatial discrimination is not necessarily harmful to those who pay the higher price where there is a difference in the nature of the demand between two areas was demonstrated by an example.

Another form of discrimination is known as discrimination by quantity. It generally means a lower unit price for the large consumer than for the small consumer, but again, this does not necessarily mean that the former is subsidized by the latter.

Discrimination can be practised only where the seller has at least some degree of monopoly power, as in the supply of electricity, gas, water, public transport, etc. These and other public utility enterprises do in fact use both kinds of discrimination and excuse themselves by pointing out that the same class of customer with the same consumption would not be charged differently.

The peak load problem and the resulting specific cost structures of electricity and gas make it virtually impossible to charge strictly according to cost. Even so, the different tariffs of these enterprises which are surveyed in this chapter include some interesting efforts to approximate this principle and thereby mitigate the peak load problem, to take account of the demand conditions in each part of the market served and to promote the use of their supplies. The practical solution is invariably some compromise.

The peak load problem arises also in many other enterprises: all jobbing firms and retailers have to carry excess capacity much of the

---

[13] Cf. Bridger M. Mitchell, 'Optimal Pricing of Local Telephone Service', *American Economic Review*, **68**, (4), September 1978, pp. 517–37.

time, but competition greatly restricts their ability to allot the appropriate costs to their customers on a discriminatory basis.

The general problems of retail pricing are discussed in the next chapter. Subsequent chapters will deal with the methods by which the appropriate prices for individual items can be determined.

A selection of recent studies of electricity pricing

Jan Paul Acton, Bridger M. Mitchell and Ragnhild Sohlberg, 'Estimating Residential Electricity Demand under Declining-block Tariffs: an Econometric Study Using Micro-data', *Applied Economics*, **12**, 1980, pp. 145–62.

C. Garbacz, 'Electricity Demand and the Elasticity of Intra-marginal Price', *Applied Economics*, **15**, 1983, pp. 699–702, also comments by T. P. Roth, ibid, pp. 703–4.

Eitan Gerstner, 'Peak Load Pricing in Competitive Markets', *Economic Inquiry*, **24**, (2), April 1986, pp. 349–61.

Randy A. Nelson, 'An Empirical Test of the Ramsay Theory and the Stigler-Peltzman Theory of Public Utility Pricing', *Economic Inquiry*, **20**, (2), April 1982, pp. 277–90.

Ali M. Parhizgari and Penny S. Davis, 'The Residential Demand for Electricity: a Variant Parameter Approach', *Applied Economics*, **10**, 1978, pp. 331–40.

Louis Phlips, *The Economics of Price Discrimination*, Cambridge University Press, Cambridge, 1983, esp. pp. 134–41 and 158–75.

Catherina M. Price, 'Public Utility Pricing in Britain', *European Journal of Marketing*, **13**, (4), 1979, pp. 247–59.

Timothy P. Roth, 'Average and Marginal Price Changes and the Demand for Electricity: an Econometric Study', *Applied Economics*, **12**, 1980, pp. 377–88.

R. J. Ruffell, 'Measurement of Own-price Effects on the Household Demand for Electricity', *Applied Economics*, **10**, 1978, pp. 21–30.

Peter Schwarz, 'The Estimated Effect on Industry of Time-of-day Demand and Energy Electricity Prices', *Journal of Industrial Economics*, **32**, (4), June 1984, pp. 523–39.

M. D. E. Slater and G. K. Yarrow, 'Distortions in Electricity Pricing in the UK', *Oxford Bulletin of Economics and Statistics*, **45**, (4), November 1983, pp. 317–38.

G. Jan van Helden, 'Measuring the Price Sensitivity of Household Electricity Consumption by Means of Interview Data', *European Journal of Marketing*, **13**, (4), 1979, pp. 183–93.

8 Pricing at the retail level

The primary purpose of this chapter is to survey the pricing problems and practices of retail distributors, but much of it is also relevant to pricing by manufacturers, even if they do not operate retail outlets of their own. The main research methods for the determination of optimal retail prices are outlined at the end of this chapter and more fully explained in Chapters 11–13.

Introduction

Over the last twenty-five years or so the power of the retail trade to determine the prices at which their merchandise is sold to the final consumer has considerably increased at the expense of the manufacturers' freedom in setting retail prices.

In Britain, as also in other industrialized countries where similar developments have taken place, the emergence of this transfer of power can be attributed to three main reasons: (1) the almost complete elimination of resale price maintenance; (2) the unprecedented growth of the multiples which has resulted in high concentration in the field of distribution; and (3) the spread of private brands (also called 'private label' or 'store brands') and, more recently of generic products, such as unbranded packs of flour, sugar, etc.

Over the same period the literature of retail pricing has been enriched by numerous contributions both from the business world and from academic circles. Some of the titles are listed at the end of this chapter, and the reader who consults them will find that they lead to numerous further references. Sound as many of these writings are, the main message of most of them appears to be that setting prices for the enormous number of goods nowadays offered for sale by any large retail outlet, counted in thousands if not in tens of thousands in the case of the gigantic hypermarkets and the largest department stores, is still more an art than a science.[1] It is easy enough to list all the factors to be taken into consideration and to enumerate the difficulties unavoidably encountered when the price of any individual article is to be determined, and this is exactly what most of the authors have done, but there have been also some more positive contributions, suggesting a systematic approach and pointing to certain ways by which pricing can be improved. In this chapter we shall survey the existing practices and comment on the research methods available to the retailer.

Some basic terms and concepts

It seems natural to the retailer to look upon both his outlays and his profit as proportions or percentages of his sales, and to speak of his margin as the *margin on sales*, (or percentage margin on selling price,) thus distinguishing it from the *mark-up on cost*. The relationship between the two is very simple as long as they are related to the same cost concept, say to the *unit cost*, meaning the price that the retailer actually paid for the merchandise concerned. As already stated in Chapter 5:

$$\text{MARK-UP ON COST} = \frac{100 \times (\text{Margin on sales}) \ \%}{1 - (\text{Margin on sales}) \ \%} \text{ per cent,}$$

---

[1] 'There was no element of deliberate falsehood in the description of pricing policies on the part of supermarket operators. The operators really didn't know how they arrived at their prices. As a matter of fact, the operators seemed disturbed when some were made to realize how far their pricing policies deviated from their own beliefs concerning what their pricing policy is.' (Holdren, (1960), p. 73, note 13.)

'The retailer, despite his much-vaunted "closeness" to the consumer, has no particular contribution, above the level of common knowledge and common sense, to make to the study of the consumer market.' (McClelland, (1963), p. 104.)

Both these quotations are over twenty years old but there is no reason to believe that what they say does not apply any longer. Note that McClelland has had substantial experience as chief executive of a successful chain of grocery stores before he returned to the academic fold.

and consequently

$$\text{MARGIN ON SALES} = \frac{100 \times (\text{Mark-up on Cost}) \%}{1 + (\text{Mark-up on Cost}) \%} \text{ per cent.}$$

Thus a 25 per cent mark-up on cost, say, is equivalent to a 20 per cent margin on sales, since $(100 \times 0.25)/1.25 = 20$.

The cost concerned need not be the purchase price of the merchandise only. It may also include other cost elements as prescribed by the pricing system adopted, and 'sales' may mean either the projected *initial* retail price of an article, or the average sales return per unit *actually realized* on a batch of merchandise.

Small traders who have no costing system tend to look upon their margin as the difference between the net wholesale price (i.e. the unit cost) and the retail price of their merchandise. This may be termed the *gross margin*, to distinguish it from the margin that is left after cost items other than the net wholesale price of the merchandise have been deducted from it. Margins may be expressed in money terms as well as in percentages. *Net sales* may be used to describe the proceeds of retail sales actually realized, as against the crude sales figure which takes no account of offsetting items that arise after a sale has been completed, such as, for example, repairs under guarantee and bad debts.[2]

Retail pricing policies and procedures

It was mentioned in Chapter 5 that there is an aspect of pricing policy that is concerned with the choice of the price ranges within which the company or its divisions should operate. This has special relevance to retail establishments, since it can be highly detrimental to the success of a store if its prices do not consistently conform to the range selected, be it that of *top quality* (the 'money no object' principle), *fair value* ('we are never knowingly undersold') or simply *cheapest* ('so you can't expect our goods to be the best'). The actual segmentation may, of course, go a lot further than these three basic categories since each of them has several possible sub-divisions.

---

[2] It should be noted that the terms gross margin and net sales are not invariably used in the same sense by different authors.

Most department stores have managed to straddle wider ranges of customers than speciality shops by judicious price lining (of which more will be said further on in this chapter); also by the policy of keeping a bargain basement, with goods of increasingly better quality at higher prices on the upper floors (a practice particularly prevalent in the United States), but even they cannot effectively cater for all the socio-economic strata of an industrialized society.

The character and attraction of a retail establishment does not of course depend on its prices alone. Location, choice of merchandise, display, service, publicity and a number of other factors also play highly important roles,[3] but it is being increasingly recognized that the dominant influence is that exerted by its prices.

Strictly speaking, it is not so much the actual or relative price level of a store that counts as its *price image*, and experience has shown that this may be very different from what the management thinks it to be. Fortunately, it can be explored by appropriate consumer research and compared with the images of the main competitors. This issue will be further discussed later in this chapter.

Declared versus negotiated prices

Most modern retail establishments state their selling prices by price-marking each article or by displaying the prices separately – the latter is the regular practice where the items are bar-coded and the price printed on the receipt by scanner at the check-out point – and permit no departure from the prices so declared. There are, however, some exceptions to this rule: the service trades provide many non-standard services at negotiated prices; the neighbourhood shop often does not display the prices of all of its goods and, if it so wishes, may not charge the same price to every one of its customers (or, if it sells perishable goods like fruit, fresh vegetables and flowers,

---

[3] Two of these additional factors each of which should be in harmony with the price level selected deserve special mention. One of them is *ambience*, that is to say, the general character of the store: it has to be luxurious for the top level, tidy and attractive for fair value, simple and sensible for cheapest prices. The other additional factor which should vary with the segment indicated by the price level is *the character of the service*: polite and tactful personal service in the luxury store while self-service is acceptable at the two lower levels, preferably supplemented with some well-trained and attentive assistants at the fair value store but at the lowest level competent personnel at the check-out points is all that could be expected by the customers.

can gradually reduce the price as time goes by), and there is considerable scope for bargaining in the field of consumer durables.[4]

A substantial proportion of the more expensive consumer durables is sold on credit terms, and it is frequently found that where this is the case, the declared cash price tends to be set so as to include a part if not the whole of the charges necessitated by the credit terms, the intention being to make the latter look more favourable. Then the cash buyers soon become aware that the price is at least to some extent open to bargaining, and even play one trader against another to obtain the best terms; cf. Gabor and Granger (1973).

In all the advanced industrialized countries the standard consumer durables have either reached saturation point or are very near to it, and this means that most of the acquisitions by households are for replacement, with the old item given in part-exchange. Wherever this is the case, a substantial second-hand

---

[4] According to the classification of the American Management Association, there are three main classes of consumer goods: *convenience goods, shopping goods* and *specialty goods*. Their description, as supplemented by Kaish, is given below. While this classification is certainly not without merit, as far as pricing problems are concerned, both shopping and specialty goods may be treated as consumer durables.

Convenience goods are purchased frequently, immediately and with a minimum of effort; their purchase is not important since their price is low as is their durability. Their acquisition involves a minimum of pre-purchase anxiety that the item bought will not give the satisfaction aimed at.

Shopping goods are those which the consumer characteristically compares on such bases as suitability, quality, price and style. They involve some pre-purchase anxiety which is, however, reducible by shopping behaviour since the goods are available in assortments broad enough to permit the acquisition of the desired qualities without having to accept too many of the undesired.

Specialty goods involve a high purchasing effort. They are in some ways similar to shopping goods but have physical qualities not readily related to performance characteristics. The alternatives are limited and the pre-purchase anxiety of experiencing disappointment after the purchase is not readily reducible by shopping behaviour.

Cf. American Management Association, 'Report of the Definitions Committee', *Journal of Marketing*, **13**, October 1948, pp. 202–17; *Marketing Definitions: A Glossary of Marketing Terms*, (Ralph S. Alexander, Chairman), American Marketing Association, Chicago, 1960; and Stanley Kaish, 'Cognitive Dissonance and the Classification of Consumer Goods', *Journal of Marketing*, **31**, October 1967, pp. 28–31.

market may develop, with prices typically open to negotiation. It follows that even if the price of the new article is rigidly fixed, (as was, for instance, the price of motor cars in Britain before the abolition of resale price maintenance,) the price at which the old item is to be credited leaves considerable scope for bargaining. The rate of purchases of consumer durables fluctuates much more violently with changes in economic conditions than the consumption of non-durables, and downward price flexibility becomes especially noticeable during slump periods.

Finally, a practice now almost defunct may be mentioned before we leave the topic of negotiated prices: price coding. It means that although each article is price marked, the customer is unable to interpret the symbols by which the price is expressed. This method was once generally used by speciality shops; nowadays, if it still exists, it is unlikely to be encountered anywhere except, perhaps, in a high-class shop whose unwritten motto is 'if you have to ask what the price is, you can't afford it'. The code is based on a ten-letter word like

$$I \quad M \quad P \quad O \quad R \quad T \quad A \quad N \quad C \quad E$$
$$0 \quad 1 \quad 2 \quad 3 \quad 4 \quad 5 \quad 6 \quad 7 \quad 8 \quad 9$$

each of the letters of which stands for a different number. Thus £28.50 would be coded PC/TI. Such a system permits the variation of the price from customer to customer, and can even incorporate instructions to this effect. For example, PC/TI/MT could mean that the shop assistant has freedom to vary the price by 15 per cent either way, according to his judgement of the customer's willingness to pay.

The great spread of self-service has probably been the main factor in eliminating negotiated prices, but there may still be some shops about whose personnel occasionally discriminate between customers: are kind to the poor and charge a little more to the well-to-do. An old-fashioned family butcher is in a particularly strong position to do this since few, if any, of his customers are expert meat buyers.

Simple mark-up or naïve cost-plus pricing

The chief pricing executive of a large chain of department stores has rightly described pricing by adding the same percentage margin to the unit cost of each article as 'the antithesis of good retail merchandising' (May, 1959). This practice may not be defunct but is certainly rarely met with these days, even within the individual departments of a store.

On the other hand, goods that are close substitutes for one another, such as different brands of an otherwise identical or almost identical product, do frequently carry the same mark-up. The actual percentage may be traditional, but that does not necessarily mean that it is not justifiable on rational grounds. The degree of competition accounts for the tradition that fast-moving convenience goods, like cigarettes, carry very much lower mark-ups than slow-moving luxury goods, like jewellery.

There is ample evidence that however long the tradition of a mark-up may be, it will not remain invariant if there is an increase in competitive pressure. First the chain stores and then the supermarkets have introduced aggressive pricing policies into formerly rather stagnant markets and have thereby effectively forced even the most unenterprising traders to abandon rigid mark-ups and move nearer to competitive or going-rate pricing.

Where the recommended retail price of the manufacturer is adhered to by the distributors, the margin is simply the rebate the manufacturer allows from his stated retail price. In such a situation retailers aiming for a price change without upsetting the market have been known to approach the manufacturer to adjust his recommended price rather than change the retail price themselves. More will be said about recommended prices further down, in the section on price variation.

Variable mark-up

The main trouble with any rigid cost-based pricing policy is that it is inward-looking, whereas a price cannot be fully effective unless it is market-oriented. If, by dint of good luck rather than empathy, a cost-based price also happens to result in sales of optimum profitability, all is well, but it is much more likely that a price determined in complete disregard of the customers' attitudes and the way in which their behaviour will be influenced by the reactions of the competitors will be very far from the ideal.[5]

---

[5] It has to be admitted, though, that, as evidenced by the local acceptance of widely different price structures in countries with similar living standards, traditional prices, that is to say, those that have not changed significantly in relation to the general price level for many years, have a good chance of being regarded as the just price of the commodity. However, it does not follow that a price accepted as just is also at its optimum level from the point of view of the seller.

The advocates of variable mark-ups often couch their argument in terms of the elasticity of demand, which may be impressive but, for the reasons discussed in Chapter 2, fails to provide a truly practical approach.[6] However, it is true that the responsiveness of the customers to price differences tends to vary from one product category to another.

It was mentioned in Chapter 7 that the peak load problem of the public utilities is also typical of all retail establishments. Both have relatively high fixed costs and must carry capacities geared to the periods of maximum demand, with the result that they are left with excess capacity at all other times. It is not therefore surprising that, like the public utilities, retailers find it essential to practice price discrimination. This argument has been well developed by Holton (1957) and McClelland (1966).

The public utilities can prevent the resale of their products and have therefore much wider scope for price discrimination than the retailer. Seasonal and other sales, promotions, special offers, extra trading stamps and the like can be of some help in livening up the slack periods, but the main means of discrimination available to the retailer is the variable mark-up.

The general principle is that staple commodities, meaning those that are also offered in identical form by the competition, will carry low mark-ups, whereas non-staples, the quality of which the customers cannot directly compare with the similar merchandise of other traders, will be more profitable if priced with higher mark-ups.

In their earliers years, the supermarkets concentrated on staple food and household products, all typical convenience goods, but as price competition increasingly depressed the mark-ups on this kind of merchandise, the range of products was extended to include

---

[6] If it were possible to determine the actual demand curve facing a given product, and if it were found that it had constant point elasticity, then as long as the unit cost of the product is also constant, the mark-up on cost that will maximize total profit can be shown to be $-100/(\text{elasticity} + 1)$ per cent. The earliest source of this formula, (which is, by the way, analogous to the ideal tariff theorem well known to economists,) appears to be Tibor Scitovsky, *Welfare and Competition*, Allen & Unwin, London, 1952, pp. 289–90. This formula, which is, unfortunately, of no practical use, has also found its way into marketing literature. It is given in many text-books, including Philip Kotler, *Marketing Decision Making*, Holt, Rinehart & Winston, New York, 1971, pp. 702–3; D. Needham, *The Economics of Industrial Structure and Performance*, Holt, Rinehart & Winston, London, 1978, p. 58; and James Bates and J. R. Parkinson, *Business Economics*, 3rd edn, Basil Blackwell, Oxford, 1982, p. 141.

kitchenware, crockery, clothing and many other non-staple items to counteract the fall in profitability of the high turnover, low mark-up staples.

The variable mark-up may well be applied to the unit cost of the article, but where absorption costing is practised, both the variable costs of the retailer associated with the purchase, stocking and sale of it and a portion of the fixed costs of the enterprise are added to the unit cost, so that the mark-up applied to the total is merely the projected profit margin.

This form of costing at the retail level has long been shown to be inappropriate, but this does not mean that it is not in use any longer. The idea that it is not worth stocking an article that does not earn something over and above its *full cost*, sounds obvious but, is in fact quite indefensible, for at least three important reasons:

1 What really matters is not the returns on the sale of any individual product but its effect on the overall profitability of the company. It might well pay to sell a 'loss leader' below its unit cost, or even give it away, if thereby the sale of other products is appropriately increased.

2 On what basis should the fixed costs be allocated? The essential arbitrary nature of absorption costing was discussed in Chapter 5; here we may add that it is customary to apportion fixed costs in relation to the net sales or gross margins experienced in the past, and to determine prices for the future accordingly. A shift in demand could then well result in an apparent loss on some products or even on an entire department of a store, while overall profits show an increase. It would appear then that it should be of advantage to eliminate the loss makers, whereas it could well happen that, if this were done, overall profits would decline. The fixed costs can, of course, be reallocated whenever there are changes in sales or margins, but doing so is in fact an admission that absorption costing is not a safe guide for the price setter.

3 Exactly how should the distinction be made between variable costs and fixed costs? In the short run, all the costs of a retail establishment except the cost of the merchandise sold (if it is to be replaced) are fixed, whereas in the long run all costs become variable.

In the 1950s, dissatisfaction with the rigidities of absorption costing led to the advocation of a kind of direct cost plus contribution pricing by several authorities in the United States. It went under the name of Merchandise Management Accounting or MMA for short. It was described as 'a revolutionary approach to retail accounting' by its main protagonists McNair and May (1957). Others described it as pricing based on marginal principles.

In fact, MMA was a heavily formalized pricing and accounting system for department stores. Its essence consisted in the determination of over a dozen different cost items, (not all of which could be classed as truly variable with sales,) for each department of a store, and adding them to the unit cost of each article, some on a percentage basis, others with some fixed amount per unit. It was therefore a rather complicated hybrid costing scheme which gave no indication of the mark-up to be applied to the total. Hence MMA left the choice of the retail price to the price setter, who was expected to base the decision on the sales expected in response to each possible price.

About a decade later MMA was described as a failure by Dickinson (1966), according to whom it overemphasized the short-term and neglected the long-term cost behaviour, as well as the marketing policies and reactions of the competitors. He also alleged that MMA led to lower prices than the old method because, unlike the latter, MMA's cost concept did not include the general overheads of the company.

A less formal approach to incremental costing was suggested by Scotese (1968), who defined the gross margin as the difference between retail net sales and six cost factors:

1 Unit cost less cash discount plus cost of transport from the supplier to the store.
2 Mark-downs: reductions in the original retail price because of buying mistakes, soilage, damage, etc.
3 Inventory shortages due to theft.
4 Employee discounts.
5 Workroom costs after sale: alterations, installation, etc., if not separately charged.
6 Set-up, repair and any other costs incurred before sale, also miscellaneous expenses.

It is obvious that, with the exception of the first cost factor, these are all very difficult if not impossible to predict with confidence, even if some past experience is available, since they tend to vary widely both between products and over time.

The gross margin should cover all the expenses directly attributable to the individual department except those accounted for by the six cost factors, along with an appropriate contribution to the indirect expenses of general management, accounting, etc.; moreover, something should be left over for profits, unless the article is deliberately sold as a loss leader.

Scotese also listed a number of considerations that should influence the pricing decision, and emphasized that the mark-up should vary with the product rather than just from department to department. He suggested a bold approach to the pricing of regular goods without regard to traditional methods, attention to fashion appeal, application of variable mark-ups to different sizes, charging extra for special orders. His final reminder is 'handle multiple pricing intelligently'.

Scotese's pricing scheme was outlined here as rather typical of the approach of many authors who list the factors the price setter should keep in mind, stress the difficulties, warn against certain pitfalls but unfortunately, even those authors who are themselves successful merchandisers seem to be unable to show exactly how the evidence collected should be used in the determination of price, except by indicating the obvious: highly fashionable articles, especially if they are exclusive to the company, can carry generous margins, goods under heavy competitive pressure must be sold at the going price, and such like.

The determination of variable mark-up rates

The incremental approach or contribution method requires the knowledge of all the direct costs of production. Strictly speaking, the retailer's 'product' is the service that he renders by stocking, displaying, selling, packaging and perhaps also delivering the merchandise bought from the wholesaler or importer, or straight from the manufacturer, and it has been suggested that his mark-up should be related to the cost of his service rather than to the unit cost of the product. However, this approach seems to be appropriate only if the retailer acts merely as an agent in the transaction and not if he buys and sells on his own account. After all, his role is not very different from that of those manufacturers whose product incorporates a high proportion of bought components.

The practice of including the cost of the merchandise in the retailer's costs is therefore fully justifiable, and in fact this is the only one of the cost factors that does not present considerable difficulties of determination. In discussing MMA and Scotese's scheme, reference was made to the fact that pricing is necessarily based on prediction, and that even Scotese's list, which is much more modest than that of MMA, may involve quite a lot of guesswork.

It is therefore not surprising that several authors advocate the use of the gross margin, interpreted as the difference between the selling price and the unit cost or purchase price of a product as the most practical measure of the contribution. The question is then what it should be related to in order to give effect to the general principle that staples should carry low mark-ups and non-staples higher mark-ups.

One of the possibilities is to aim at a uniform rate of return on the capital locked up in the stock of each product, as suggested by Sweeney (1973). This can be achieved by varying the mark-up percentage inversely with the stock turnover rate.

If the stocks of merchandise do, in fact, tie down a considerable proportion of the capital of the firm, it would seem reasonable to suggest that in order to obtain the target rate of return on capital, the annual contribution should depend on the relation between the average magnitudes of the stocks and sales.

An example should help to elucidate the principle. Let us assume that the unit cost of product A is £12.50 and of B £2.00; that the stock of A is turned over five times a year and the stock of B eight times; and also that the gross contribution required in respect of each £100 capital invested in stocks is £240 per annum.[7] It follows that the margin on A should then be £6.00 per article (48 per cent mark-up on unit cost), and on B £0.60 per article (30 per cent mark-up on unit cost).[8]

The variety chain stores and department stores developed the method of requiring from each product a given contribution per square foot of selling space or foot run of shelving; later it was also adopted by the supermarkets. The operation of this principle is so

---

[7] If this figure appears to be unduly large to the reader, let him consider that the sum of the contributions is expected to cover all the costs of the firm except the cost of the merchandise, and provide an appropriate return on the entire capital invested in the firm, not just on what is tied down by the stocks.

[8] The calculation is as follows:

Product A: each £100 worth of stocks consists of 8 units as £12.50 each, and is turned round five times a year, hence 40 units should contribute £240, i.e. £6.00 per unit.

Product B: each £100 worth of stocks consists of 50 units at £2.00 each, and is turned round eight times a year, hence 400 units should contribute £240, i.e. £0.60 per unit.

similar to the one just demonstrated that a separate illustration seems to be unnecessary. The specific trouble with this approach is that the units of selling space within a store vary widely in value according to their position in the store, and that their value in promoting sales depends also on what is displayed on either side of them.

The main problem, shared with the stock method, is that neither the effective selling price nor the rate of turnover of a product can be dictated by the amount of capital or space allocated to it, and if the actual contribution is used to determine the optimum stock to be carried or the extent of space to be occupied by a product, its price has to be assumed as given. The saving grace is that the prices of many of the articles stocked by a department store will, as a rule, be dictated by the market and the prices of those products that are exclusively carried can be related to the former.

The quantities to be sold which will leave the contribution from the product unchanged after a price increase or price reduction are listed in Table 5.5 on page 73.

Price lining

The issues which arise in connection with this topic will be discussed both from the point of view of the retailer and that of the manufacturer.

It is the general practice of department stores to adopt a limited number of prices at which their goods are to be sold. These are called price lines or, in some organizations, regulation prices. A similar system, with the additional feature of an upper limit was, in earlier times, also the main characteristic of pricing by the low-price variety stores, like Woolworth, the original '5 and 10 cent store' (3d and 6d in Britain), and Marks and Spencer, whose prices previous to the 1939–45 war were all below 5 shillings. Persistent inflation and the general rise in the standard of living of the consumers have led to the abandonment of such limits, but price lining is still being widely practised.

Price lining is the reverse of the usual pricing procedure: here the buyer of the store starts with a retail price and looks for merchandise he can sell at the price; or he may himself draft the specification of the product to be sold under his own label, and invite tenders from manufacturers for its supply. If the company aims at a margin of, say, 30–35 per cent on a line that sells at £6.00, the task will be to find a product of appropriate quality at a unit cost in the £3.90 to £4.20 range.

The main argument in favour of price lining concerns the selling angle: the customer will find it easier to choose if the items offered for sale fall into a few distinct categories and there is only one kind at each price point. According to Walker, (1950, page 530), who was at the time pricing executive of one of the large New York department stores, a minimum of three basic price points for each type of merchandise is necessary; described as 'the good, better and best plan'.

It stands to reason that the price points, whether their number is two, three or more, should be sufficiently wide apart to imply appropriate quality differences. Dalrymple and Thompson (1969, page 177), quote men's neckties as an example, and state that they were frequently sold at three prices: $2.50, $3.50 and $5.00.

While observing this principle, it is generally possible to select the price points so that they should either conform to customary prices, where these have become established, or coincide with what are held to be 'charm prices' by the trade. These are prices that are supposed to be more attractive to the customers than others in their neighbourhood; their general characteristic being that they are a shade below the nearest round figure, like 49p or £6.95. While no proper evidence exists to support their alleged efficacy, in Britain, the U.S.A. and some other countries they have become firmly established in certain branches of the retail trade, at least since the early years of this century, if not before.[9] It should also be noted that most, though not all, customary prices are located at 'charm price' points.

The first disadvantage of rigid adherence to price lining is the refusal to trade in articles that do not fit neatly into the line adopted, even though they promise to be very acceptable to the customers. The second is that it can cause quite serious difficulties in times of sharply rising or falling costs. Take the example of the men's neckties quoted above, and let us assume that the margin was 50 per cent. If, now, the unit costs, which were around $1.25, $1.75 and $2.50, respectively, should each go up by 25 per cent, the new retail prices would work out at $3.13, $4.38 and $6.25. The choice to the

---

[9] Cf. Dik Warren Twedt, 'Does the "9 Fixation" in Retail Pricing Really Promote Sales?', *Journal of Marketing*, **29**, (4), October 1965, pp. 54–5. More will be said on this point in Chapter 11.

retailer who sticks to the principle of his price line is between reduced margin, lower quality ties for each of his price points, and finding improved quality ties to fit a new line, with price points at $3.50, $5.00 and $7.00.

The retailer can assemble his product line from different sources, while from the point of view of the manufacturer, whether he also operates retail outlets or not, a product line may be defined as that subset of his products which serve essentially the same purpose and are made available simultaneously in the same market.[10] It follows that the items that make up a product line so defined are at least to some extent in competition with one another, and that hence the manufacturer's interest demands that, in the long run, the profitability of the entire line should be pursued, rather than the short-run profitability of any individual item. This applies particularly if the product line concerned constitutes his entire output or is produced by a separate division of his firm – otherwise the profitability of the whole enterprise should be the overriding consideration.

The retailer's position is somewhat different, insofar as he deals in a multiplicity of products; many thousands in the case of the modern large department store or supermarket, and he might deliberately run not just a single product but even a whole line at a very low margin, if not below unit cost, as long as he believes that it will further the profitability of his store as a whole.

For the manufacturer, running a product line instead of a single grade can serve three main purposes:

1 To provide simultaneous appeal to different strata or groups of consumers, that is, to practise a form of market segmentation.
2 To offer choice to the individual customer and enable him to switch while still patronizing the same manufacturer – often not knowing that the different brands come from an identical source.
3 To cater separately for the multiplicity of needs of the same consumer unit; for example, a saloon car for the husband, a mini for the shopping trips of the wife and a sports car for the

---

[10] This excludes heterogeneous lines which consist mainly of complementary products, such as, for example, educational aids or motor car accessories. Such heterogeneous lines may, of course, contain some product lines that conform to the above definition; otherwise the general rule must be that the constituent items should be roughly of the same standard, and that this should also be reflected in the price structure.

son, or, say, one washing powder for fine woollens, another for heavy duty in the washing machine, and so on.

As far as (1) is concerned, it should be noted that unless there are very substantial gaps between the price points, it would be wrong to assume any close relationship between socio-economic strata and choices of price range. The actual segments and the attitudes of their members to variations in price and product characteristics can, however, be identified by appropriate consumer research.[11]

(2) raises an interesting issue: should the different grades bear the same brand name or, at least, be easily identifiable as products of the same manufacturer, or should this fact be concealed? The answer must depend upon the image of the brand or of the manufacturer's firm, and on the main reason why customers switch: to what extent is it dissatisfaction with the last purchase, the search for variety, or a step towards upgrading their content of living? Again, it is well worthwhile to explore the market by commissioning expertly designed and conducted consumer research. The results should be of help also in pricing, insofar as the customer who is after variety will mainly be interested in alternatives within a fairly narrow price range, whereas the dissatisfied consumer, and the person who, though not exactly dissatisfied, feels that he can afford something better, will look towards the higher price brackets.

Pricing for (3) should take account of the relative importance of the purposes concerned. The washing powder for fine woollens may be looked upon as an accessory of a luxury product, and can therefore carry a relatively high price. In fact, it is unlikely to sell well if its price is too low, while the powder for the weekly wash has more chance to be successful if it appeals to the economy instinct.

Table 8.1 demonstrates four main types of price structures for product lines. In (A) the absolute difference between any two price points is constant, and hence the relative difference is declining as we move up the range. Since the consumer's subjective price scale is tuned to relative rather than absolute differences, each step will appear to be less steep than the one below it.[12] He will, therefore, be attracted to move up the line rather than down. (B) gives further

---

[11] More will be said on this point in Chapter 12, in connection with new product pricing.

[12] Subjective price scales are not of course amenable to direct measurement, but a great deal of indirect evidence exists to support the proposition that they have the character of ratio scales. This issue was briefly mentioned in Chapter 2 (cf. page 16, note 3.); it will be pursued further in Chapter 11 and in the Analytical Appendix.

Table 8.1
Examples of different price structures

Brand or Grade	(A)	Diff.	(B)	Diff.	(C)	Diff.	(D)	Diff.
	£	%	£	%	£	%	£	%
K	24		24		24		24	
		50		50		50		25
L	36		36		36		30	
		33⅓		22		50		100
M	48		44		54		60	
		25		14		50		567
N	60		50		81		400	

emphasis to the same inducement, insofar as also the absolute differences are declining in the upward direction. (C) represents the case of constant relative differences, as illustrated above (page 159) by a line of neckties – a typical example of the instinctive recognition of the nature of subjective price scales – whereas the increasing price differences in (D), and quite especially the high price of the top grade impart glamour that extends also to the lower points of the line. As mentioned in Chapter 5 (page 50), this is the policy adopted by some of the Swiss watch manufacturers, and it has become customary to refer to the top grade as the 'flagship brand' of the firm.

Readers interested in the abstract theory of product line pricing might like to consult Oren *et al.* (1984) and Reibstein and Gatignon (1984).

Multi-pack pricing and price-and-size relationships

The pricing of multi-packs and of different sizes of the same brand may be looked upon as special cases of price lining that are sufficiently important to deserve separate consideration.

Multi-packs are occasionally supplied by the manufacturers, with prescribed or suggested promotional prices, and in the absence of such initiatives it is still open to the retailer to offer his customers two or more packs of any brand at a special price. It is well known that some shoppers are so much attracted by such offers that they fall even for deceptive bargains of the '25p each, two for 59p' kind, but they are certainly in the minority, and there can be little doubt that no well established firm would intentionally put its reputation at risk by such practices. The real question is the same as with all price promotions: what will be its effect on the overall profitability of the store?

From the point of view of the purchaser, the multi-pack has certain advantages over the single pack with similar contents. First of all, since the multi-pack is a precise multiple of the single pack, it makes price comparison simple, whereas, in the absence of legal prescribed quantity regulations, manufacturers have a strong tendency to include only odd sizes in their line, with the express intention of making price comparisons more difficult; both between different brands and between different sizes of the same brand. Second, although the long-run trend appears to be towards an increased preference for the larger sizes of most convenience goods, there are some customers who consider them uneconomical, either because they fear that the contents will deteriorate once the pack is opened, or because they believe that abundance leads to waste. The multi-pack meets both these objections.

Hence while it is likely that the multi-pack offer will primarily attract those customers who were already in mind of buying at least one pack of the product anyway, the special price should also lead to some brand-switching by non-intenders and extra purchases by bargain-hunters. Since an increase in the size of the individual sale is generally of advantage to the retailer, and since a multi-pack offer can be arranged at very short notice and low extra cost, it is a form of price promotion that merits special attention.

Processed foods, household products and many other goods serving a variety of purposes are regularly marketed in packs of different sizes of the same brand, and there are several sound reasons why their prices should be so apportioned that the larger the size the consumer buys, the better value he should get for his money. Larger sizes can mean (1) reduced packaging costs per unit weight;[13]

---

[13] As an indication of the savings in packaging materials that can arise if the pack size is increased, consider the relationship between the volumes and surfaces of cubic packages:

Volume of cube		Surface of cube	
ml	%	mm^2	%
1,000	100	60,000	100
2,000	200	95,244	159
3,000	300	124,805	208
4,000	400	151,191	252

Considerably greater savings are possible with packages of certain other shapes.

(2) savings in handling charges; (3) smaller marketing costs per unit quantity sold; and might also lead to (4) higher rate of consumption; and (5) increased brand loyalty. Higher rate of consumption may come about in two ways: the economy offered by the larger size can gain customers who would find the brand too expensive if it were available at the price of the small size only, and existing users, once they bought the larger pack, often tend to be more lavish in using it.

Studies of the actual price structures of different sizes of individual brands currently marketed in Britain suggest that this important issue tends to be handled with insufficient care at all levels. That the retail prices displayed in supermarkets are frequently inconsistent, in the sense that the large size is more expensive per unit quantity than some or all of the smaller packs of the same brand, is well known and generally attributed to unintentional pricing errors at the store level. What is less well known is the fact that, since similar inconsistencies are also widespread in manufacturers' price lists, the blame cannot entirely rest with the distributors.

It is definitely in the interest of both the manufacturer and the retailer to pay full attention to this aspect of pricing because inconsistencies are liable to breed suspicion, and a suspicious customer cannot be expected to be as loyal as one who feels that he can trust in every respect both his favourite brand and the distributor whom he patronizes.

Manufacturers should endeavour to keep both their wholesale price lists and their recommended retail prices fully consistent and, if possible, help their distributors to maintain the consistency of the price structure, even if the latter should decide to depart from the recommended price level. One way of doing this is to follow the example of wine merchants, whose wholesale lists mostly include a ready reckoner for a variety of mark-up rates.

If the inconsistency is clearly presented as a temporary 'special offer' of one particular size, it has a good chance to meet with a favourable reaction on the part of the customers but if, as it quite frequently happens, the apparent bargain turns out to be the most expensive alternative, this is likely to cast aspersion both on the retailer and on the manufacturer.

Reference was made above to the widespread practice of the manufacturers of those convenience goods which are not subject to prescribed size regulations to make up the line of each brand of odd sizes only, so that no pack should be a simple multiple of any of the smaller sizes of the same brand, or be easily comparable in price with competitive brands. While size structures of this kind can quite

Table 8.2
Examples of consistent size and price structures

	Price Structure (A)			Price Structure (B)		
Size	Price of pack	Price per kg	Price of additional kg	Price of pack	Price per kg	Price of additional kg
kgs	£	p	p	£	p	p
1	1.00	100	100	1.00	100	100
2	1.95	97.5	95	1.95	97.5	95
3	2.85	95	90	2.84	94.7	89
4	3.70	92.5	85	3.66	91.5	82
5	4.50	90	80	4.40	88	74

effectively mask inconsistent pricing there is reason to believe that it is a better policy to adopt straightforward size structures and price them consistently so that the larger the pack size, the lower is the price per unit quantity. The findings of Granger and Billson (1972) and McGoldrick and Marks (1985) support this view.

Table 8.2 shows two consistent price-and-size structures: in (A) the additional quantity unit becomes 5p cheaper at each step, and in (B) the price fall is accelerated so as to make the larger sizes increasingly more attractive.

Count lines represent yet another special case. These are small packs of sweets (mainly chocolate bars), and certain other goods, such as boxes of matches, the price of which is kept stable as far as possible, while the contents of the pack are adjusted whenever there are variations in the costs of production. If the rise in costs reaches a level that would necessitate an unattractively small size, the usual practice is to move to a higher price point to enable an increase in size that will once again permit small reductions, should costs rise any further. An actual example of the customers' reactions to such an increase in size is given in Chapter 13. Cf. Figure 13.2 and the comments appended to it.

There are two reasons for this practice. One of them applies to all count lines: their price being low in terms of the money unit, it could not accurately be regulated for small changes in costs. If there is a slight rise, say two per cent, in the cost of a box of fifty matches, the only way to make the necessary adjustment is to reduce the contents to forty-nine. The other reason concerns count lines of sweets, the main consumers of which are small children, and hence the most effective price is that which tallies with the usual amount of the money gifts these children receive from adults.

Countering cost changes by variation of the quantity or quality of the contents of the pack had become very widespread in inflationary Britain, also beyond the field of count lines. Biscuits formerly sold in 1 lb (453.6 grammes) and half-pound (226.8 grammes) packs were subsequently found in 13½ oz (382.7 grammes) and 6¾ oz (191.3 grammes) packs only. Even though the actual weight of the contents is invariably printed on the pack as required by law, there can be little doubt that such practices tend to annoy the customers. The government has taken action: biscuits are now on the list of those products which may be sold in prescribed quantities only.

Store brand and generic brand pricing

Both in the United States and in Britain, store brands (also called own brands and private label) have made considerable incursions into the market for convenience goods, and are also competing with the national brands of consumer durables. Their attraction to the retailer is two-fold: they offer the possibility of higher mark-up rates and increased customer loyalty to the store.

The most widespread practice is to price store brands slightly below the prices of the national brands which they resemble. This can be a successful policy, especially if (1) the national brands are burdened with high marketing costs, (2) the quality of the store brand is not noticeably inferior to that of the national brands, and (3) the store has a favourable image in the eye of the consumer.

(1) might be the case if the national brands are heavily advertised – though advertising can also lead to lower prices, as argued by Reekie (1979);

(2) will be most easily satisfied if the store brand can be obtained from the manufacturer of one of the premium brands. Some of the manufacturers of national brands accept orders for store brands and are prepared to impart the same quality to them as to their advertised brands, using such orders to utilize otherwise idle capacity, and to price them more on an incremental cost than a full cost basis. There are, however, other manufacturers of national brands whose principle is not to allow any of their products to be sold under a different name. It is not possible to pass a general judgement on this issue; it depends on the circumstances which of the two policies is likely to be more profitable in the long run. Some of the larger retail distributors manufacture their own brands themselves.

As far as (3) is concerned, the appearance, quality and price of the private brands have, of course, themselves considerable influence on the image of the store. If this image is of the highest order, and the store brand is of truly superior quality, it may be priced above the market, but this is a policy that has been adopted only by a few department stores and other shops in the luxury class. Store brands of inferior quality priced appreciably below the market, are much more common. This might be just right for a certain segment of the customers, but it is probably a better policy to provide fair quality supplemented by attractive though not necessarily luxurious packaging, and sell a shade below the prices of the premium brands.

An important point which is often neglected is that all the own brands of the store should be of comparable quality; not necessarily in the eye of the expert, but as judged by the customers.

Experience has shown that in the case of fast moving consumer goods housewives are, on the whole, sound judges of quality and do not fail to recognize equality or unequality of the store brand and the national brands. The same could not be expected in the case of items only infrequently purchased by the household.[14]

Store brands have been with us for many years and it is well known that they have made heavy incursions into a number of markets formerly dominated by national brands. *Generic brands* (also called 'plain label brands') are of more recent origin: they were initiated with notable success by the Carrefour chain in France and have also become common in the United States, while their spread in Britain has been somewhat restricted. On occasion, they have been found to encroach more on the sales of premium brands than on those of the store brands; a phenomenon which supports the belief in the ability of consumers to recognize quality without the aid of attractive and heavily promoted brand names. The reasons why generic brands are not resented by the distributors even though their prices are, as reported by Nielsen (1982) around 20 per cent below those of the store brands, (40 per cent below brand leaders), is that they are fast movers, carry the promise of increased traffic in the store and also offer attractive margins which are, in some cases, even higher than those of premium and store brands. However, according to Simmons and Meredith (1984): 'Future demand for generics is

---

[14] Cf. A. P. Sowter and A. Billson, 'The Further Development and Testing of Theories of Choice', (unpublished research report), Department of Economics, The University of Nottingham, 1975.

likely to be static. Generics are generally regarded as very much a product of the recession'.[15]

Unit pricing

Unit pricing is information provided to the customers of the prices of goods sold by weight or volume or pre-packed in various sizes in terms of a common denominator: unit quantity. In Britain, in some of the States of the USA and in a number of other countries it is prescribed by law in respect of certain goods. Where there are such regulations, they must, of course, be observed, but there remains the question whether the extension of unit pricing to goods not covered by the law is in the interest of the retail distributor.

Studies carried out in the United States suggest (1) that the answer depends very much on the way in which unit pricing is applied; (2) that most consumers need some education in the use of unit pricing; and (3) that the lower socio-economic strata, for whom the savings that could be achieved by an intelligent use of unit pricing would matter most, have very great difficulty in understanding it.[16]

---

[15] Cf. also Cunningham et al. (1982) and McEnally and Hawes (1984).

[16] Cf. particularly T. David McCullogh and Daniel I. Padberg, 'Unit Pricing in Supermarkets – Alternatives, Costs and Consumer Reaction', *Search – Agriculture* (Cornell University, USA), **1**, (6), January 1971, pp. 1–27; C. W. Granger and A. Billson, 'Consumers' Attitudes Toward Package Size and Price', *Journal of Marketing Research*, **9**, August 1972, pp. 239–248; L. Lamont, J. Rothe and C. Slater, 'Unit Pricing: A Positive Response to Consumerism', *European Journal of Marketing*, **6**, (4), 1972, pp. 223–233; Gary P. McFadden, 'An Analysis of Unit Pricing', *Business and Economic Dimensions*, July/August 1973, pp. 29–41; H. R. Isakson and A. R. Maurizi, 'The Consumer Economics of Unit Pricing', *Journal of Marketing Research*, **10**, August 1973, pp. 277–285; James E. Carman, 'A Summary of Empirical Research on Unit Pricing in Supermarkets', *Journal of Retailing*, Winter 1972/73, pp. 63–71; J. Edward Russo, Gene Krieser and Sally Miyashita, 'An Effective Display of Unit Price Information', *Journal of Marketing*, **39**, (2), April 1975, pp. 11–19; J. Edward Russo, 'The Value of Unit Price Information', *Journal of Marketing Research*, **14**, (2), May 1977, pp. 193–201; B. F. McElroy and D. A. Aaker, 'Unit Pricing Six Years After Introduction', *Journal of Retailing*, **55**, (3), Fall 1979, pp. 44–57; V. Ziethaml, 'Consumer Response to In-Store Price Information Environments', *Journal of Consumer Research*, **8**, 1981, pp. 357–69; David A. Aaker and Gary T. Ford, 'Unit Pricing Ten Years Later: A Replication', *Journal of Marketing*, **47**, Winter 1983, pp. 118–22.

Unit pricing can most effectively be practised by self-service establishments in general and supermarkets in particular. As a competitive weapon it will be useful only if the retailer is prepared to pursue an active price policy, since price comparisons based on a common quantity unit imply an honest effort to help the consumer in selecting his purchases. If carried out consistently, it has a good chance of being eventually understood and appreciated if not by all of the customers, at least by a high proportion of them. It is also important to note that if it extends only to a small part of the enormous number of items offered for sale in a modern supermarket, it will go largely unnoticed, and that dual-marking of the packs with hardly legible labels is not by itself sufficient to make it effective. One way to make comparison easy is to list the unit prices of competitive brands on small posters attached to the shelf where the goods themselves are displayed.

A frequently heard objection to unit pricing is that since there are quality differences between most brands, (for example, some liquid detergents are more concentrated than others), comparisons based on the quantity alone could be unfair. The answer to this is that it is quite proper to leave it to the consumer to decide whether Brand A, costing, say, 20 per cent more than Brand B per unit quantity, is indeed that much better.

Price variation

Fashion goods and certain products subject to constant advances in technology can seldom be sold at the same price throughout.[17] They have to be ordered and manufactured well ahead of their main seasons, and since it is not possible to foretell with certainty exactly how strong the demand will be, and it is not a good policy to be out of stock during the high season; it is safer to err in the opposite direction, and be prepared to have to sell at least a small proportion of the batch at reduced prices. Scotese's scheme, quoted above, takes account of this and other reasons, (such as soilage, theft and employee discounts), why the initial price of a short-lived article may have to be set well above the expected average return per unit.

---

[17] Cf. Phillip G. Carlson, 'Fashion Retailing: The Sensitivity of Rate of Sale to Markdown', *Journal of Retailing*, **59**, Spring 1983, pp. 67–76; and Robert M. Frazier, 'Reducing Markdowns for Increased Profitability', *Retail Control*, **53**, March 1985, pp. 2–26.

Another kind of price variation is the essence of a fairly widespread policy of supermarket pricing. The main idea is that every day there should be a few bargains prominently displayed in the store, and this is sometimes coupled with a more or less systematic fluctuation of the prices of especially those goods that are also carried by the competitors.

The purpose of the first part of the policy is to attract customers to the store; to create traffic in the shop, to use the terminology of McClelland (1966). Since it is not easy to produce new genuine bargains every few days, it is not unusual to find in the 'bargain basket' goods at their normal prices; a practice that will not go undetected by most customers and is bound to engender suspicion rather than goodwill.

A further point made by McClelland is the distinction between staples, reminder and suggestion articles. As mentioned before in this chapter, the lines to be priced with low mark-ups are primarily the staples; to this McClelland adds the observation that price cuts will not help if they are matched by the competitors.[18] Reminder articles are salt, boot polish and such like: it is useful to remind the customer of them, but a low price will not increase consumption, though it could result in stocking up. The second category of non-staples, suggestion articles, are items that the customer might not think of buying at all unless his or her attention is drawn to them. It could be a novelty like a new toy for the children, or something brought within the reach of the housewife by a low price, for example, some good-quality crockery. Suggestion articles are therefore useful as leading bargains, and may be less susceptible to competitors' reactions than the staples. McClelland further notes that there is no reason why effective traffic-builders should not be sold below unit cost.

The second part of the policy, frequent fluctuations of the prices

---

[18] Some supermarkets temporarily remove from their shelves any brand that is being currently sold at a cut price by a strong competitor. This practice is more likely to reduce than to increase profits. In an extensive survey conducted by the Nielsen organization in February/March 1975, out of the 22,000 shoppers approached just after they have left a store, 2,522, about one in nine, said that at least one of the items they intended to buy was not available. Only 35 per cent made another purchase instead; 39 per cent said that they were going to buy the item elsewhere, and 26 per cent expressed the intention of looking for the item in the same store on a future visit. Cf. 'Out of Stock – Who loses?' *Nielsen Researcher*, No. 3, 1975, and the Nielsen report *Consumer Reactions to Out-of-Stock*, Nielsen, Oxford, 1975.

around some sort of average level, is aimed at the reduction of selective shopping. No systematic research has so far been conducted to determine whether this type of policy is more likely to breed loyalty in the customers than the alternative of no special offers (or just a few genuine temporary price reductions), prices remaining as stable as permitted by inflationary pressure. Both have been pursued with success, and it is quite possible that each draws its customers from a different segment of the market.

Price promotion, or 'dealing', as it is called in America, has been intensively studied by Hinkle.[19] His principal conclusions, together with some observations of the present author, are briefly summarized here:

Dealing is more effective for new than for established brands, and its success depends significantly both on the size of the price reduction and the magnitude of the trade allowance. There is, however, strong evidence that the reductions intended by the manufacturer or the central management of the chain are not always fully passed on to the customers.[20]

Frequent price promotions of the same brand tend to lead to successively smaller gains and have little power to reverse the downward sales curve of a declining brand.

Advertising and appropriate display are important factors in promotional success, and off-season price reductions are generally more profitable than similar reductions during the principal seasons.

Self-financing promotions, favoured by some manufacturers, offer the buyer of a product the opportunity of purchasing some attractive

---

[19] Charles L. Hinkle, *Temporary Price Reductions as an Element of Marketing Strategy*, Marketing Science Institute, USA, 1964, also, by the same author, 'The Strategy of Price Deals', *Harvard Business Review*, July-August 1965, pp. 75–85. The issue has been examined from another angle by William Schlackman, 'Psychological Aspects of Dealing', *Proceedings of the Conference on Research in Marketing*, Market Research Society, London, 1964, reprinted in *Pricing Strategy*, (B. Taylor and G. Wills, eds), Staples Press, London, 1969. Cf. also N. Bukowitz and R. Walton, 'Contextual Influences on Consumer Price Responses: An Experimental Analysis', *Journal of Marketing Research*, **17**, (3), August 1980, pp. 349–58.

[20] 'Bouncing' is the name given to this practice, which is certainly not in the interest of the manufacturer. It is not, however, firmly established how it affects the overall profitability of the store, since high proportions of the sales are the result of stocking up and brand switching. Store brands are particularly vulnerable if the difference between their price and that of an advertised premium brand narrows significantly.

item at what is represented as a bargain price. To quote a recent example: customers who return the labels of three packs of a well-known brand of cooking fat *plus £3* will receive a set of kitchen tools, the implied value of which is higher than the outlay demanded. The promotion is self-financing, insofar as the cost to the manufacturer is not more or, possibly, considerably less than the cash payment involved.

A form of price promotion that has become increasingly popular in recent years is *double pricing*, sometimes called dual pricing. It consists in marking the article with two prices, the higher of which is stated or implied as being the normal price, and the lower as a special temporary offer.

The higher price is frequently represented as the manufacturer's recommended price, but of course there is nothing to prevent a manufacturer from recommending a price that is set deliberately above the one at which the retailer intends to sell the product. However, for many years after the abolition of resale price maintenance, recommended prices tended to be followed by the retail trade, and when the Monopolies Commission investigated the issue, it was unable to decide whether recommended retail prices were in the public interest or not. Subsequently the Price Commission reported on the nature and extent of the practice which, by that time, had given rise to the main form of double pricing, without, however, the expression of any opinion on its desirability or otherwise.[21]

Double pricing is widespread in the field of consumer durables; some stores appear to have perpetual bargain sales, often at prices represented as being not more than half the normal level, and it is also widely practised in the grocery trade, together with variants of which the '20 per cent free' label is a typical example. Several authors have devoted attention to this issue and the extent to which explicit price variations affect the consumers' choices has been examined in a small but very rigorously conducted experiment by Survey Research Associates Limited, under the direction of Professor A. S. C. Ehrenberg and Mr Len England of the Centre for Marketing and Communication at the London Business School.

---

[21] Cf. Monopolies Comission, *Recommended Retail Prices, HMSO, London,* 1969; and Price Commission, *Recommended Retail Prices* (Report 25), HMSO, London, 1977. A table of the latter, showing the observed percentage discounts from recommended retail prices, is reproduced in James Bates and J. R. Parkinson, *Business Economics*, 3rd edn, Basil Blackwell, Oxford, 1982, p. 139.

Packs of tea, etc., marked only with the name of the product, a higher price crossed out and a lower actual price invariably resulted in very considerable shifts in purchases, even though most of the subjects were unable to recall the previous price.[22]

The Consumer Protection Act 1987 makes it an offence to give misleading price indications to consumers and empowers the Secretary of State to approve a Code of Practice to give guidance and promote good practice in relation to price indications. Time will show what change it will bring to the use of double pricing.

Discount store and mail order house pricing

To the extent to which mail order houses are in competition with other retail outlets, their situation is similar to that of the discount houses. Both have to rely on the attraction of their low prices, achieved by reducing the services surrounding a sale well below the level provided by the more traditional retail establishments.

Discount stores do not as a rule have private brands, whereas the larger mail order houses carry wide ranges of them, and if they have a reputation for giving fair value, they should be able to sell their own brands with good margins.

Some of the discount stores either do not advertise at all, or spend only limited amounts on advertising, in their endeavour to keep their costs as much as possible below those of their competitors, and do not issue catalogues either; this enables them to pursue a flexible pricing policy. Mail order houses fall into two broad classes: (1) the large ones, who sell a very great variety of goods and promote their sales mainly by the provision of catalogues; and (2) the small operators who concentrate on novelties and special bargains which

---

[22] Cf. for example J. S. Coyle, 'What Cost Dual Pricing?', *Progressive Grocer*, **49**, November 1970, pp. 78–84; also by the same author 'Dual Pricing Settles In', *ibid.*, **50**, February 1971, pp. 46–59; E. N. Berkowitz and J. R. Walton, 'Contextual Influences on Consumer Price Responses: An Experimental Analysis', *Journal of Marketing Research*, **17**, 1980, pp. 394–58; Edward A. Blair and Laird Landon, Jr., 'The Effect of Reference Prices in Retail Advertisements', *Journal of Marketing*, **45**, (2), Spring 1981, pp. 61–69; and A. A. Ahmed and M. Gulas, 'Consumers' Perceptions of Manufacturer's Suggested List Price', *Psychological Reports*, **50**, 1982, pp. 507–18. For a comprehensive account of a valuable study in which also several other aspects of the effect of price differences and their presentation were covered, see A. S. C. Ehrenberg, 'Pricing and Brand Differentiation', *Singapore Marketing Review*, **1**, 1986, pp. 5–15.

they regularly advertise in the popular newspapers. Attractive novelties, which the interested consumer rightly or wrongly believes not to be available elsewhere, can be sold at very good margins, but bargains of standard merchandise must promise exceptionally good value to be effective.

Mail order houses perform a special service for customers who live in rural areas, far away from any large shopping centre, and for those who, because of some physical or mental disability, cannot undertake shopping trips, even if there are stores in their neighbourhood. People in such circumstances could be charged higher prices than personal shoppers, but are protected by the fact that the mail order houses also compete for the custom of those members of the public who have easy access to other retail outlets.

A special kind of mail order house offers credit terms as a major attraction. They recruit some of their customers as commission agents, equip them with impressive and rather expensive glossy catalogues, and also charge them with the collection of the instalment payments. The costs of these mail order houses are therefore fairly high, and this is generally reflected in their prices. Most, if not all, their customers come from those members of the lower socio-economic strata, to whom payment by small instalments is more attractive than low prices.

Mail order catalogues offer excellent opportunities to test the alleged efficacy of charm prices, that is, prices set just below a round figure. It is regrettable that so far a report on only one such experiment has been published: it was carried out in the distant past by Sears Roebuck in the United States with results which were entirely inconclusive. However, confidential information received by the present author from a British mail order house suggests that charm prices are significantly more effective in promoting sales than prices at or slightly above round figures. It still remains to be established if this is a general characteristic of the purchasing public or a feature specific to the people who are attracted by the facilities offered by mail order houses.

The pricing of consumer durables

Some of the characteristics of the market for consumer durables were mentioned above, in the section on declared and negotiated prices, where it was pointed out that those customers who are prepared to pay cash when they buy one of the more expensive consumer durables do not invariably accept the declared cash price. They demand, and often receive, quite substantial further discounts.[23]

It is an established fact that the purchase of the more expensive consumer durables is generally preceded by considerable search activity, whether the customer is a cash purchaser or intends to take credit terms. The description of the attitude to 'specialty goods' as given in note 3 to this chapter applies here, but it should be noted that only part of the pre-purchase anxiety arises out of the insufficiency of the knowledge of the physical qualities of the item. It is commonly found that after having decided on the brand he intends to buy, the prospective purchaser will continue his search for the source that gives him the most favourable price and/or credit terms.

Customers who habitually pay for larger purchases by instalments are more interested in the minimum amount of the down payment required and the size of the instalments than in either the length of the period over which payments have to be made or the actual price. Few of them are able to work out for themselves the effective rate of interest they are called upon to pay, or are interested if the relevant information is supplied to them. Some people are inclined to call such behaviour irrational, but it appears to be more justified to refer to it as an issue that turns on the strength of two preferences: time preference and the preference for obligatory rather than voluntary saving. This applies even if the customer has sufficient liquid assets to buy for cash, yet decides in favour of credit terms, knowing that he will pay for them by a higher price and an interest rate which is in excess of what he receives in respect of his accumulated savings. The economist explains this by attributing a high degree of liquidity preference to the subject, due to the precautionary motive, meaning the desire to have ample cash handy

---

[23] Cf. André Gabor and C. W. J. Granger, 'Ownership and Acquisition of Consumer Durables', *European Journal of Marketing*, **6**, (4), Winter 1973, pp. 234–48, esp. Table 24 and comments. However, no discount will be expected in the case of the coveted novelty the demand for which exceeds the supply at the current price, so that there is a waiting list for it, and as long as this is so, the second-hand price may be well above the price of the new article. Cf. R. Harrison and F. M. Wilkes, 'A Note on Jaguar's Pricing Policy', *European Journal of Marketing*, **7**, (3), 1973, pp. 242–6, and the comment of André Gabor and J. M. Bates in the same journal, **8**, (2), 1974, pp. 180–82.

should the need for some unforeseen expenditure arise, and/or the speculative motive, that is, the withholding of cash in the hope of investing it later on more favourable terms than available at present.

It follows from what has been said that, with the exception of certain unique items, the pricing of consumer durables has to be largely competition-oriented, but attractive credit terms will be accepted by a proportion of the purchasing public as a fair compensation for a somewhat higher price or interest rate.

Pricing research for the retailer

There are five main avenues along which retailers can pursue or commission pricing research:

1 Competition studies.
2 Record analysis.
3 Store experiments.
4 Simulated shop situation experiments.
5 Consumer attitude and behaviour surveys.
Each of these will now be briefly outlined.

(1) Most retailers pay some attention to what the main competitors are doing, but few of them see that the observations are carried out with the appropriate efficiency. In fact, regular studies of the pricing and promotional practices of the main competitors can be very useful, whether a passive 'going-rate' pricing policy is to be pursued or an aggressive pricing policy.

The data will enable comparisons between one's own price level and those of the competitors. The usual method is to calculate the cost of the average weekly shopping basket as recorded in the Government's Family Expenditure Survey or, alternatively, by using the weights of the Retail Price Index Number. If, however, there is reason to believe that the local pattern of purchases is significantly different from the average for the country as a whole, it should be of advantage to ascertain the former with the research methods described below under (5).

It should be realized that consumers may not judge store price levels simply by the total cost of their shopping baskets; another aspect which can be investigated by a consumer survey. This issue will be discussed further in Chapter 11; here we shall merely note that the price sensitivity of the customers may not vary only with the magnitude of their average weekly expenditure on each item.

(2) Analysis of the records of the store itself can be of some help in pricing, especially if they show all variations in the selling prices in addition to the sales figures, as is the case where scanning is in use.

If the general price level remains stable while the prices of individual articles undergo variations, it may be possible to construct demand curves from the records. It should be noted, however, that even the most sophisticated analytical technique can only produce an estimate of what the demand was over the period concerned, and experience has shown that even though the result might be of interest from the theoretical point of view, it could not be expected to provide reliable guidance to pricing decisions, partly because there can be no guarantee that the conditions of the past will also apply in the future, and partly because the standard methods for deriving demand curves involve the unrealistic assumption that the sensitivity to small price changes is the same throughout the range.[24]

Analysis of past records may be particularly useful for the multiples, since it will enable comparisons between the performances of the individual stores. If it is found that one store is conspicuously more successful or less successful than the others, an enquiry will be indicated to reveal the reasons for the differences, and the answers obtained may well suggest some change in pricing policy.

Studies of the outcome of promotions can be particularly worthwhile. It is important to note, however, that the successful promotion of one particular brand (or, as it frequently occurs, of one size of that brand only) will necessarily depress the simultaneous sales of the competitive products, and that the extra sales will not represent net gains also because of stocking-up by brand-loyal customers. The extent of these factors will not be revealed by the sales records of the promotion itself.

(3) In-store pricing experiments, consisting of deliberate variation of the prices of selected goods according to a predetermined design combined with regular stock audits, will yield reliable data only if carried out with great precision. Experience has shown that they require constant supervision, otherwise deviations from the intended pricing pattern will almost certainly occur. Supervision is further necessary to ensure that the shelves designated for the

---

[24] These points are further discussed in Chapter 2 above. Cf. also the relevant studies listed in note 7, pp. 18–19.

merchandise used in the pricing experiment are properly stocked throughout.

It is advisable to let each price situation run for not less than two weeks, and, if the advice of Nevin is accepted, cooling off periods should be inserted between the treatment periods, in order to reduce the effects of consumer inventory build-up or depletion.[25]

In-store experiments are fairly costly and time-consuming; hardly suitable for the purposes of the small independent retailer. The large multiples can, however, use them to great advantage, both because of the value of the data obtained for pricing decisions, and as occasional checks on the validity of the results of the cheaper and quicker methods, listed under (4) below. The pricing of store brands presents a particularly suitable field for application.

(4) Simulated shop situation experiments can be performed much more quickly than in-store experiments. A further advantage of the former is that they will also yield consumer classification data and can be extended at little extra cost to provide information on consumer attitudes and behaviour, otherwise obtainable by a separate survey only. Two additional advantages of the simulated shop situation are that it can conceal the identity of the store that commissioned it, and that it can also cover consumers who do not patronize the store concerned. For the large store, and even more for the multiple, the cost is generally well justified by the results.

There are three ways in which simulated shop situation experiments can be performed: (a) by inviting a number of willing subjects to come to a 'laboratory' (generally the office of the researcher) at appointed times in order to help in an investigation; (b) by calling at the home of each respondent; or (c) by hiring a hall or other premises somewhere in the main shopping area, and asking passing shoppers to enter and participate in the enquiry.

Of these methods (a) is the cheapest, but the sample of subjects can seldom be made properly representative and the conditions are generally so artificial that the results could not be relied upon to guide pricing decisions. The primary purpose of such laboratory experiments (much favoured by American academic researchers) is

---

[25] Cf. André Gabor, Clive W. J. Granger and Anthony P. Sowter, 'Real and Hypothetical Shop Situations in Market Research', *Journal of Marketing Research*, 7, August 1970, pp. 355–9, and John R. Nevin, 'Laboratory Experiments for Estimating Consumer Demand: A Validation Study', *Journal of Marketing Research*, 11, August 1974, pp. 261–8. The issue is further discussed in Chapter 13.

to examine the validity of some hypothesis of consumer behaviour.

(b) has the advantage that, by employing a random or quasi-random method of selection, the sample can be made representative of the households of an area;[26] its main disadvantages are that, unless the items are few in number and so small that the interviewer can conveniently carry samples of them, flip-cards must be used, which show only the names and prices of the articles (perhaps supplemented by pictures), and that it takes longer to complete and is more expensive than the hall method.

(c) is the method that is best suited for practical purposes, since it is quick and, if properly conducted, will yield results of direct relevance to pricing decisions at reasonable cost. If no suitable hall or shop is available in the selected area, the mock-up of a supermarket shelf can be set up in a van parked in a side street. The questioning of the subjects proceeds while they are faced with the appropriate set of competitive products; they are asked for their choice in several price situations each of which is clearly displayed to them by exchangeable shelf labels, and they can also be questioned about their attitudes to the products, their usual purchase, their rate of consumption, etc., and, if required, about their opinion of the store which commissioned the survey and its competitors. The methods and actual procedures are further explained in Chapters 10 to 13. Like all the other research possibilities, the hall method is being used much more by manufacturers than by retailers, probably because so far few of even the largest distributors have reached the stage in maturity where expenditure on market research becomes a regular item in the budget.

(5) The possibility of including consumer attitude and behaviour questions in simulated shop situation experiments has already been mentioned. Such surveys can, however, also be conducted separately, either by interviewing shoppers in the street, preferably straight after they have left a store, or by visiting them in their homes. Street interviews are necessarily short, but in this way it can be ensured that the sample will consist of the patrons of a particular store only – the first question put to them can separate the casuals from the regulars. As said above, household surveys can embrace more representative samples of the area and they also have the advantage that the interview need not be particularly short.

---

[26] The main statistical aspects are explained in the Analytical Appendix to Part II.

Attitudes can be investigated in several ways. Motivation research encourages the subjects to talk freely, in the hope that they will unwittingly reveal the secret reasons for their attitudes and behaviour. It is obvious that the conclusions drawn from the information obtained will depend heavily on the interviewer's deliberate or unintentional prompting, on what the interviewer takes down in writing, and on the interpretation put on it by the analyst. For these reasons, motivation research tends to be viewed with some suspicion, though it has claimed notable successes in America.[27]

Another approach employs structured interviews, with questions that have to be read out verbatim by the interviewers. Prompting is forbidden, but a list of expected answers may be printed in the questionnaire, so that the interviewer can record most responses by a tick in the appropriate box, and has to write down unusual answers only. In a variant of the method a card with a set of answers on it is handed to the respondent, who then points out one of the alternatives. When it comes to such statements as, for example, 'Brand A is better than any of the others', or 'Store X can be relied upon to give good value', the answer is given by choosing a point on a 5-point scale, the end-points of which are marked 'Strongly agree' and 'Strongly disagree', respectively. Other scales may also be used.

A problem arises when more than one answer is accepted to an open-ended question. For example, if asked why she prefers her favourite store, a woman might say 'Because it is clean, the staff are polite and the prices are low'. Since the order in which these reasons were mentioned cannot be relied upon to indicate their relative importance, it is customary to include all of them in the analysis, with the result that the percentages of the subjects who gave each answer will add up to more than 100. It seems preferable to call for the main reason only, and ask any subject who names more than one, which is the most important of them.

Attitude answers may give some clue to behaviour, but the latter can also be explored more directly. Shopping habits, frequency of purchase of certain goods, average weekly expenditure on food and such like may be explored in this way, or, alternatively, by the 'diary' or the 'dustbin' methods. The diary method consists in recruiting a panel of housewives who are prepared to record all their purchases over a certain period. Experience has shown that if a list of the usual fast moving consumer goods is printed on each page of

---

[27] For an entertaining account cf. Vance Packard, *The Hidden Persuaders*, Longmans Green, London, 1957, pp. 25–37 and *passim*.

the diary, more purchases will be recorded than in diaries with blank pages. The dustbin method is suitble for investigating the purchases of pre-packed branded goods only. The housewife is presented with a plastic dustbin and is asked to put into it the containers or wrappings of any branded good used. The investigators pay periodic visits to the co-operating households and record both the household's stock of the goods concerned and the contents of the special dustbin. It is usual to offer some reward for participation.

Both of these methods suffer from certain disadvantages. It is well known that the panel of housewives recruited for any diary project will not constitute a truly representative sample of the whole of the purchasing public, since certain groups of consumers, the less well educated and the spendthrifts, will generally refuse to co-operate, and the extent to which the bias so introduced can be corrected by the statistical method known as balancing is severely limited. As far as the dustbin method is concerned, the main trouble is that it cannot be relied upon to provide complete information about the prices paid.

A properly conducted attitude and behaviour survey, especially if it is extended to subjects who mainly patronize the stores of the competition, can provide a great deal of useful information to the retailer. It can tell him what his actual and potential customers think of his pricing policy, (which is considerably more relevant to his success than his own opinion), and can help him also in many other ways, for example, in judging the desirability of taking up brands not previously handled.[28]

Summary

Owing to the abolition of resale price maintenance, the growth of the multiples and the increasing spread of private brands, retailers have gained great freedom in the setting of retail prices. Since most of the retailer's costs are fixed in the short run, their allocation to individual products would be very arbitrary, and this explains why the gross margin, that is, the difference between the unit cost and the selling price, is so popular in retail pricing.

---

[28] Cf. John M. Bates and André Gabor, 'Changes in Subjective Welfare and Purchasing Behaviour: Report on an Enquiry', *Journal of the Market Research Society*, **29**, (2), 1987, pp. 183–207; also Henry Assael and C. E. Wilson, 'Integrating Consumer and In-store Research to Evaluate Sales Results', *Journal of Marketing*, **36**, April 1972, pp. 40–45.

While the attraction of a store does not depend on its prices alone, its pricing policy has a great influence on its image. Broadly speaking, it can be that of top quality, fair value or cheapest – each addressing itself to a different segment of the purchasing public. Retail prices are nowadays very largely declared, but in the fields of consumer durables and some of the services there is still scope for negotiation.

Pricing by the application of a rigid mark-up is a simple but rather inefficient way of pricing. Variable mark-ups are the rule, and it is generally found that staples must carry lower mark-ups than non-staples. The incremental or marginal approach has been advocated but does not seem to have made much progress in retailing. Mark-ups may be allocated according to the capital tied down by each product or by the selling space each occupies. Both are workable methods but not free from certain difficulties.

Price lining is a common practice of retailers and manufacturers. However, the price structures of individual lines are not always found to conform to any definite principle, and this applies also to multi-pack pricing and price-and-size relationships. Count lines represent a special case but the practice of varying the quantity or quality of the contents of the pack instead of adjusting the price has also spread into other fields.

With the exception of some high-class stores, retailers generally price their own brands so that they should be cheaper than the national brands. This applies even where there is no difference in quality. Generic brands have been found to cut into the market shares of both store brands and national brands.

Unit pricing has its possibilities. Retailers tend to be averse to it because they fear that the result would not justify the cost, but it has been shown in America that it can be made an effective and profitable means of competition.

Price variation and price promotions are the common practice of most supermarkets, as is double pricing. However, some of the successful multiples do not indulge in them.

Discount store and mail order pricing is largely based on the low cost–low price principle, except where credit terms are the main attraction. In the field of consumer durables, however, the credit terms as well as the prices are generally under competitive pressure.

In the closing section of the chapter the research possibilities open to retailers are enumerated and outlined. Properly applied, they can be of great help to management.

According to the official classification, the service trades belong to the distributive sector. Since, however, not all the services are dispensed at the retail level, the approach to their pricing problems will be discussed in a separate chapter.

Quantity discounts, trade discounts, cash discounts and the effects of price cuts are discussed in Chapter 6; the general relationship between incremental cost and price changes in Chapter 5.

References

The following lists of books and articles include a number of titles in addition to those cited in Chapter 8 but exclude those given fully in the footnotes. They do not claim to be more than a selection of the literature.

Books

R. Cassidy, Jr, *Competition and Price Making in Food Retailing*, Ronald, New York, 1962.

Frank J. Charvat, *Supermarketing*, Macmillan, New York, 1961.

Douglas J. Dalrymple and D. L. Thompson, *Retailing: An Economic View*, The Free Press, New York, 1969.

Delbert J. Duncan, S. C. Hollander and R. Savitt, *Modern Retailing Management*, 10th edn, Richard D. Irwin, Inc., Homewood, IL, 1983.

Alan Fiber, *The Independent Retailer*, Heinemann, London, 1964.

Harold W. Fox, *The Economics of Trading Stamps*, Public Affairs Press, Washington, DC, 1968.

André Gabor, 'Customer Oriented Pricing', Chapter 3 in *Research Into Retailing and Distribution*, (David Thorpe, ed.), Saxon House, Lexington Books, London, 1974, pp. 43–54.

Ronald R. Gist, *Retailing: Concepts and Decisions*, John Wiley & Sons, New York, 1968.

W. Warren Haynes, *Pricing Decisions in Small Businesses*, University of Kentucky Press, Lexington, KY, 1962.

Bob R. Holdren, *The Structure of a Retail Market and the Market Behavior of Retail Units*, Prentice-Hall, Inc., Englewood Cliffs, NJ, 1960.

Carl M. Larson, R. E. Weigand and J. S. Wright, *Basic Retailing*, 2nd edn, Prentice-Hall, Inc., Englewood Cliffs, NJ, 1982.

Patrick McAnally, *The Economics of the Distributive Trades*, Allen & Unwin, London, 1971.

W. G. McClelland, *Studies in Retailing*, Blackwell, Oxford, 1963.

W. G. McClelland, *Costs and Competition in Retailing*, Macmillan, London, 1966.

Raymond A. Marquardt, J. C. Makens and R. G. Roe, *Retail Management*, 3rd edn, Dryden Press, Chicago, 1983.

P. E. Nelson and L. E. Preston, *Price Merchandising in Food Retailing: A Case Study*, Institute of Business and Economic Research, University of California, Berkeley, CA, 1966.

Harry Nyström, *Retail Pricing: An Integrated Economic and Psychological Approach*, Economic Research Institute, Stockholm School of Economics, Stockholm, 1970.

Lee E. Preston, *Profits, Competition and Rules of Thumb in Retail Food Pricing*, Institute of Business and Economic Research, University of California, Berkeley, CA, 1963.

W. Duncan Reekie, *Advertising and Price*, The Advertising Association, London, 1979.

Peter G. Scotese, 'The Retail Level' in *Creative Pricing*, (Elizabeth Marting, ed.), American Management Association, New York, 1968, pp. 104–11.

H. Smith, *Retail Distribution*, Oxford University Press, Oxford, 1948.

Articles

Anon., 'Cuts and Gimmicks: Successful Supermarketing To-day Depends on Your Image – Price Cutting is No Longer the Force It Was', *The Economist*, May 6, 1967, pp. 584–5.

Robert C. Blattberg, and Gary D. Eppen, 'A Theoretical and Empirical Evaluation of Price Deals for Consumer Nondurables', *Journal of Marketing*, **85**, (1), Winter 1981, pp. 116–29.

Robert George Brown, 'Sales Response to Promotions and Advertising', *Journal of Advertising Research*, **14**, (4), August 1974, pp. 33–9.

Keith K. Cox, 'The Responsiveness of Food Sales to Shelf Space Changes in Supermarkets', *Journal of Marketing Research*, **1**, May 1964, pp. 63–7.

Keith K. Cox, 'The Effect of Shelf Space Upon Sales of Branded Products', *Journal of Marketing Research*, **7**, February 1970, pp. 55–8.

Gordon B. Cross, 'A Critical Analysis of Merchandise Management Accounting', *Journal of Retailing*, **34**, Spring 1958, pp. 21–9.

C. M. Cunningham, Andrew P. Hardy and Giovanna Imperia, 'Generic Brand versus National Brands and Store Brands', *Journal of Advertising Research*, **22**, October/November 1982, pp. 25–32.

Ronald R. Curhan, 'The Relationship Between Shelf Space and Unit Sales in Supermarkets', *Journal of Marketing Research*, **9**, November 1972, pp. 406–12; also comments by M. Lynch and reply by Curhan, ibid, **11**, May 1974, pp. 218–22.

R. L. Davies, 'Evaluation of Retail Store Attributes and Sales Performance', *European Journal of Marketing*, **7**, (2), 1973, pp. 89–102.

Roger Dickinson, 'Marginalism in Retailing: the Lesson of a Failure', *The Journal of Business*, **39**, July 1966, pp. 353–58.

Ronald E. Frank and William F. Massy, 'Shelf Position and Space Effects on Sales', *Journal of Marketing Research*, **7**, February 1970, pp. 59–66.

André Gabor, 'Pricing in the Retail Business', *Marketing*, June 1973, pp. 33–5.

André Gabor and C. W. J. Granger, 'Ownership and Acquisition of Consumer Durables', *European Journal of Marketing*, **6**, (4), Winter 1973, pp. 324–48.

André Gabor and A. P. Sowter, 'The Customers' Views', *Co-operative Management and Marketing*, **3**, (12), December 1970, pp. 46–50.

C. W. J. Granger and A. Billson, 'Consumers' Attitudes Towards Package Size and Price', *Journal of Marketing Research*, **9**, August 1972, pp. 229–48.

Peggy Heim, 'Merchandise Management Accounting: A Retail Experiment in Explicit Marginal Calculation', *Quarterly Journal of Economics*, **77**, (4), November 1963, pp. 671–75.

Richard W. Holton, 'Price Discrimination at Retail: The Supermarket Case', *Journal of Industrial Economics*, **6**, October 1957, pp. 13–32.

Oswald Knauth, 'Considerations in the Setting of Retail Prices', *Journal of Marketing*, **14**, July 1949, pp. 1–12.

A. V. Parker Lessig, 'Consumer Store Images and Store Loyalties', *Journal of Marketing*, **37**, (4), October 1973, pp. 72–7; also 'Comments' by J. H. Murphy and Kenneth A. Coney, and 'Reply' by Parker Lessig, ibid, **39**, (3), July 1975, pp. 66–8.

Peter J. McClure and John K. Ryans, Jr, 'Differences Between Retailers' and Consumers' Perceptions', *Journal of Marketing Research*, **5**, February 1968, pp. 35–40.

Martha R. McEnally and John M. Hawes, 'The Market for Generic Brand Grocery Products: A Review and Extension', *Journal of Marketing*, **48**, (1), Winter 1984, pp. 75–83, (37 references).

Peter J. McGoldrick, 'Grocery Retail Pricing in the UK', *Proceedings of the First CESCOM Conference on Economics of the Distributive Trades*, Rome, September 1980, pp. 432–52.

Peter J. McGoldrick and Helen J. Marks, 'Price-Size Relationships and Customer Reactions to a Limited Unit Pricing Programme', *European Journal of Marketing*, **19**, (1), 1985, pp. 47–64. (34 references.)

Malcolm P. McNair and Eleanor G. May, 'Pricing for Profit: A Revolutionary Approach to Retail Accounting', *Harvard Business Review*, **35**, May/June 1957, pp. 105–22.

Paul May, 'Retail Pricing', *Gazette of the John Lewis Partnership*, **41**, (35), October 1959, pp. 791–93.

David Metcalf and Christine Greenhalgh, 'Price Behaviour in a Retail Grocery Submarket', *British Journal of Marketing*, Autumn 1968, pp. 243–51.

A. C. Nielsen Company Limited, 'Generics – A First Look', *Nielsen Researcher*, No. 1, 1982, pp. 2–7.

Shmuel Oren, Stephan Smith and Robert Wilson, 'Pricing a Product Line', *Journal of Business*, **57**, (2), 1984, pp. S73–S99; also 'Comments' by Steven M. Shugan, ibid, pp. S101–S107 and by Milton Harris, ibid, pp. S109–10.

Robert A. Peterson and James W. Cagley, 'The Effect of Shelf Space Upon Sales of Branded Products: An Appraisal', *Journal of Marketing Research*, **10**, February 1973, pp. 103–4

David J. Reibstein and Hubert Gatignon, 'Optimal Product Line Pricing: The Influence of Elasticities and Cross-Elasticities', *Journal of Marketing Research*, **30**, (3), August 1984, pp. 259–67.

Stuart V. Rich and Bernard D. Portis, 'The Imageries of Department Stores', *Journal of Marketing*, **28**, April 1964, pp. 10–15.

David Rogers, 'Market Research in Retailing: Tackling "Problem" Stores', *Retail and Distribution Management*, **13**, January/February 1985, pp. 21–24.

Ronald Savitt, 'The Wheel of Retailing and Retail Product Management', *European Journal of Marketing*, **18**, (6/7), 1984, pp. 43–54.

Martin Simmons and Bill Meredith, 'Own Label Profits and Purpose', *Journal of the Market Research Society*, **26**, (1), January 1984, pp. 8–27.

A. P. Sowter, 'How Competitive is the Co-op?', *Co-operative Management and Marketing*, **4**, (1), January 1971.

Michael T. Steven, 'Methods of Analysing and Improving Store Profitability', *Retail Control*, **53**, March 1985, pp. 49–64.

Daniel J. Sweeney, 'Improving the Profitability of Retail Merchandising Decisions', *Journal of Marketing*, **37**, January 1973, pp. 60–8.

Q. Forrest Walker, 'Some Principles of Department Store Pricing', *Journal of Marketing*, **14**, January 1950, pp. 529–37.

V. Ziethaml, 'Consumer Response to In-Store Information Environment', *Journal of Consumer Research*, **8**, 1981, pp. 357–69.

9 The pricing of services

In Britain, and in the United States as in some other similarly developed economies, more people are employed in the provision of services than in the direct production of material goods; yet the marketing of services in general and their pricing in particular are relatively neglected aspects of management studies. As Wilson notes in his excellent treatise:

> The use of pricing strategies in industrial goods generally lacks even the little sophistication that exists in the consumer goods field, while in services they are virtually non-existent. In part, this stems from the inadequacies of most costing methods for services which still operate by the 'faith, hope, and 50 per cent' method.[1]

Since the catering for material needs almost invariably involves some services, and there are few services entirely without some material content, there exists no sharp division between goods and services. As correctly noted by Rathmell, 'economic products lie along a goods-service continuum, with pure goods at one extreme and pure services at the other, but with most of them falling between these two extremes.'[2] An example of one of the extremes is the

---

[1] Aubrey Wilson, *The Marketing of Professional Services*, McGraw-Hill, London, 1972, p. 132.

[2] John M. Rathmell, 'What Is Meant by Services?', *Journal of Marketing*, **30**, October 1966, pp. 33–4. Other authors have made similar observations, cf. for example, Robert C. Judd, 'The Case for Redefining Services', *Journal of Marketing*, **28**, January 1964, p. 59, also Wilson, op cit, p. 161, and pedantic economists are inclined to assert that even purely material products are desired only for the services they render to us. Indeed it has been found that the most profitable method of marketing certain novelties is not to sell them outright but charge for their services. Cf. the examples quoted in Chapter 6. pp. 100–1.

market garden that lets customers pick their own strawberries, and of the other the performance of a street musician.

As far as the practices of service pricing are concerned, Sibson distinguishes between six categories:[3]

1 Cost pricing.
2 Competitive pay pricing.
3 Contingency-payment pricing.
4 Fixed prices.
5 Contract pricing.
6 Value pricing.

Let us critically examine these categories to see how they differ from one another and to what extent they are mutually exclusive.

Cost pricing is analogous to cost-based pricing discussed in Chapter 5 above; like the costing of material goods, it can be used with a profit objective in view. The difficulty with this method is fundamental: cost does not make a price effective if it is high above the potential customer's own valuation, and the actual cost to the provider of the service may be well below its worth to the customer. There are also two further points: the neglect of the competition and the fact that the cost itself might depend on the price, insofar as the price is likely to have a strong influence on the frequency with which the service is being used.

Competitive pay pricing is defined as a special variant of the cost approach: the price is based on the competitive or average rate of pay of the type of labour employed in the provision of the service. According to Sibson, this is a method for government enterprises and companies engaged to a substantial degree in government work, and he adds that it is fraught with difficulties. Surprisingly, he makes no mention of the fact that the same principle is also in evidence whenever an employer, government or private, stipulates in advance the pay or range of remuneration that will accrue to the successful applicant for the vacancy concerned. It is, in fact, a highly practical method of indicating the level of qualifications, experience and ability expected from the applicants. Advertisements of vacancies often give clear expression to the competitive principle by

---

[3] R. E. Sibson, 'A Service' in *Creative Pricing*, (Elizabeth Marting, ed.), American Marketing Association, New York, 1968, pp. 147–52.

some such statement as for example 'Commencing salary £15– 18,000; persons not currently earning at least £10,000 should not apply'.

Contingency-payment pricing is the equivalent of piece rates in material production. Examples are agents' commissions of all sorts; most employment bureaux charge their clients only if they have found a suitable job for them, estate agents' commission is payable only if they have sold the property concerned, etc. Sibson is hardly right in presenting it as a category comparable to the first two mentioned, since it gives no indication whatsoever of the magnitude of such renumerations. Sure enough, they are generally an agreed percentage of the salary or the value of the property, but how is the percentage itself determined? The answer is that it is generally a competitive rate, though the agent whose reputation is that he can do better for his clients than the average competitor, may also be able to claim a higher percentage rate. If the rate is a fixed one, it overlaps with the next category.

A form of contingency-payment pricing was once fairly common in the practice of management consultants but seems to be only very rarely used today. The consultant, seeing a way in which substantial savings could be effected, quoted a commensurate fee for his services, and if the prospective client considered the amount excessive, the consultant suggested a proportion, say 25 per cent, of the first year's savings instead of a fixed fee. The client who accepted the latter alternative mostly found that in this way he had to pay much more than the fee originally quoted to him, but since the choice was his, he could not complain.

Fixed prices arise when a controlling agency, which may be a government body, a professional or trade association or a plain cartel, stipulates the prices for specific services. The purpose will be either to protect the public from exploitation by setting the price so that it should be only just sufficient to provide services of acceptable quality, or to eliminate competition between the members and thus protect their profitability. Protection of the public is the usual aim of government agencies, whereas professional associations endeavour to restrict entry and thus create monopoly situations which enable the service establishments to charge higher fees than would arise under free competition. A trade association is likely to find it more difficult to restrict entry into the market than a professional body, and might set the level of the approved charges so that it should not appear too attractive to outside competitors.

Experience has shown that it makes little difference whether the charges are actually fixed or just indicate a maximum level – as long as the trade or profession is reasonably protected and the demand is adequate, all the members will charge the maximum. The stipulated price may, however, also be a minimum, (like the minimum wage in the United States and some other countries), and this can also result in uniformity, but only in slump conditions.

Contract pricing is presented by Sibson as a special case of fixed prices.[4] In fact, where there is a legally binding fixed price, it has nothing to do with price determination whether it is put into a written contract or not. Since the award of a service contract is mostly preceded by competitive bidding or some bargaining, it would seem more appropriate to look upon the charges agreed between the contracting parties as negotiated prices – a category missing from Sibson's scheme.

Value pricing is a valid category indeed, and a very important one too. As we noted in connection with cost pricing, the value of the service to the consumer may be very much below or above its cost. In other words, value alone can decide whether a price is too high, too low or just right. However, there may be a considerable difference between the value of a good or service to a consumer and the price he is able and willing to pay for it. Pricing should therefore focus on the latter rather than on the former.

Value pricing often finds its expression in the mark-up on cost, but not necessarily on all the cost categories. For example, a London firm of management consultants calculates the fee for its services by adding to its out-of-pocket expenses a certain figure per man-day of its qualified staff. This amount, which is seldom varied, is based on an estimate of what the clients think the service is worth to them. The justification of this procedure is that it provides the firm with sufficient profitable business to keep its staff occupied and enables a steady expansion of its activities.

---

[4] 'Sometimes the fixed price is not just set by agreement or practice but is put in the form of a written contract... As in the case of fixed pricing generally, the primary reason for a contract pricing system is frequently the protection of the public at large. There may be an equal advantage to the supplier in that pricing is effectively removed from the competitive scene.' Sibson, *op cit*, pp. 150–51.

The conclusion is that Sibson's list contains incongruous categories and that a somewhat different scheme may be preferable, distinguishing in the first instance between the two basic approaches to price determination, each of which can again be subjected to a dichotomy:

1 *Cost-based pricing*:
  (a) Profit oriented – generally aiming at a profit target as the minimum. Prices fixed by a professional or trade association also belong to this category but, especially if entry is severely restricted, the prices will be related less to costs than to the customers' ability and willingness to pay, and should then be classed under 2(b).
  (b) Government controlled prices – aiming at consumer protection by fixing prices on a cost-plus-a-modest-margin basis.

2 *Market-oriented pricing*:
  (a) Competitive – either passive acceptance of the going rate or aiming at maintaining or increasing the market share by an aggressive pricing policy.
  (b) Customer oriented – prices set with regard to the consumers' attitudes and behaviour. The quality of the services and hence their costs may also be varied so as to remain in harmony with the prices.

In conformity with this scheme, a number of general tendencies can be noted:
1 The prices of services may be declared or negotiated. The former category includes both prices fixed outside the individual service enterprise by an authority or an association, and prices determined by the enterprise itself, in which case, however, they may not be entirely inflexible.
2 The greater the material content, the more will pricing be cost-based. Installation, repair and maintenance of both consumer durables and producer's equipment are mostly priced in this way, whereas costs play only a very minor role, if any, in setting the fees for the professional services of doctors, lawyers, management consultants, performing artists, etc. Certain costs, especially travelling expenses, are often charged to the client separately from the fee.

3 The more standardized the service, the more will its pricing be competitive, with costs indicating the lower limit. Car wash, laundering and dry cleaning are typical examples of largely standardized services, as are certain routine tasks performed by professional persons, such as the chemical analysis of common substances, conveyancing, etc. Price competition may, however, be eliminated by a government agency or a strong association prescribing fixed charges.

4 The smaller the material content, that is to say, the more 'pure' the service is, the more will it be customer-oriented and non-standard. However, each service establishment may have its own minimum charge or list of charges. For example, some management consultants have a fixed charge for every first consultation, which is subsequently credited to the client's account if the negotiations lead to an assignment.

5 The more unique a service is, the greater will be the freedom in pricing enjoyed by its provider. Performing artists of great popularity, medical specialists of high repute, computer software experts of outstanding ability, etc., have considerable scope for exploiting their monopoly position. Where the potential customer is not himself familiar with the service concerned, such as the loving father anxious to find the best doctor for his ailing child, the business executive looking for a first-class management consultant, the accused man of property determined to retain the best criminal lawyer, the choice will be largely influenced by two factors. The first is reputation and the second is price, acting as an indicator of quality.

The situation of the potential client in need of a highly specialized service is often analogous to that of the potential customer intending the acquisition of a 'specialty good'.[5] His pre-purchase anxiety is not readily reducible by search activity, and he will generally be right if he acts on the principle of an old adage of the English farming world: 'You can't pay too much for good land or too little for bad land'. Rushton and Carson correctly observe that:

Customers may often perceive a stronger relationship between price and quality for services than for goods. This, together with the difficulties encountered by customers in the evaluation of services, suggest a greater emphasis and reliance on price as an indicator of quality. Hence it becomes crucial that service prices are set appropriately and it makes it

[5] Cf. Chapter 8, note 4 for the definition of specialty goods.

very risky to 'play' with prices, for instance for promotional purposes.[6]

Few professions, if any, could claim to be entirely free from impostors, but a service establishment charging top prices is unlikely to survive for long if the quality of the services which it renders regularly disappoints its clients.

6 On the whole, services are far more easily variable than physical products, hence their quality can more readily be raised or lowered and their very nature adjusted to the requirements of the individual customer. The ability of the provider does not necessarily impose a limit since, if the price enables him to do so, he can generally hire staff with the appropriate qualifications and experience. *The best advice one can offer to the pricing executive of a service establishment is to set his charges high enough to make the provision of an outstandingly satisfactory service possible.*

Should the service be largely standardized, that is to say, non-differentiated, every reasonable effort should be made to differentiate it so that it should give something extra to the customer. For example, an office equipment maintenance service which has references to prove that its well qualified engineers effectively attend to every request within 24 hours should be able to charge a much higher fee than that ruling in a market where competition has led to price cutting and price cutting to inferior service. In the case of certain professional services there is also the psychological factor that an advice given will not be taken seriously or followed with much faith if it is inexpensive.

7 If the service is commissioned in the absence of a binding quotation, pricing becomes more or less discretionary. This applies also where there is an agreed estimate – it is generally accepted that the building trade, motor car repair services, etc., consider their estimates merely as limits below which the actual cost will not fall. Suppliers of services who aim at repeated orders from their customers will of course be careful not to jeopardize their reputation by undue departures from their estimates.

A pricing strategy, interpreted as an expression of the principle adopted in the pursuit of the long-term aim, is incomplete without the appropriate tactics to be followed in the day-to-day conduct of business. Some of the possible tactical steps are implied by the scheme outlined above, others might be dictated by special

---

[6] Angela M. Rushton and David J. Carson, 'The Marketing of Services: Managing the Intangibles', *European Journal of Marketing*, **19**, (3), 1985, p. 31.

circumstances. Wilson distinguishes between seven different tactics: (1) loss leader; (2) offset; (3) diversionary; (4) discrete; (5) discount; (6) guarantee; and (7) price lining.[7]

Loss leader means charging a reduced price for the first order of a new client, in the hope of continuing assignments at better prices. *Offset* pricing applies when a low basic price is quoted, balanced by higher charges on the extras. *Diversionary* tactics are similar: low charges on some parts of the service only, in the hope of creating an overall image of low prices. *Discrete* pricing can be applied only if the prospective client is a large firm. As we noted in Chapter 6, the higher the cost of an order, the higher in the hierarchy of the business will the decision be taken, and discrete pricing means setting the price so that it should come within the competence of that decision making unit which is favourable to the project. *Discount* pricing means offering discounts not unlike the quantity rebates described in Chapter 6. *Guarantee* is essentially the same as Sibson's contingency pricing: no results, no payment. *Price lining* suggests that variations in cost should find expression in the content of the service rather than in its price.

It is clear that the loss leader tactics can work effectively only if it is explicitly recognized as such by the client, otherwise he will expect the same low price on subsequent assignments. Offset and diversionary tactics apply mainly where the estimate is not a binding quotation, and may be classed with the discretionary pricing mentioned above. Discount pricing is often encountered in service trades, for example office cleaners may charge less per room if the office is large and the service is daily than for smaller offices and less frequent cleaning. It is also being used as a means of temporary promotions: two garments cleaned for the price of one, free fitting of carpets, free installation of household durables, etc. There is, however, yet another kind of discount: that offered to certain classes of persons, especially children under a certain age, old age pensioners and members of certain associations. Price lining, in the sense used by Wilson, is not to be recommended as a method of dealing with increases in costs, unless the reduction in the quality or extent of the service is actually preferred by the client to a rise in the price. But price lining, interpreted as having a set of fixed charges for certain standard services, is a widespread and useful practice.

The transfer pricing of services, that is, of those rendered by one

---

[7] Cf. Wilson, *op. cit*, Figure 12.1: Pricing tactics, p. 136.

division of a company to another division, is discussed in Appendix I to Chapter 6, page 118.

For the results of the investigations of specific cases see the contributions of Rogowski and Goetz.[8]

Finally, it should be noted that appropriate market research can be of very effective help in service pricing. The methods outlined in the later chapters of this book are adaptable to most of the special problems likely to be encountered.

Summary

The pricing of services is a relatively neglected field of study but some of the modern writers, especially Judd, Rushton and Carson, Rathmell, Sibson and Wilson, have made valuable contributions to the systematization and understanding of the relevant principles and practices.

Like the pricing of material goods the pricing of services may be cost-based or market-oriented. These basic categories can be subdivided and their analysis leads to a number of relevant observations about the nature of declared and negotiated prices, the effect of the material content on pricing, standardization, and so on.

Unlike material goods, services cannot be inspected before the purchase. The price setter should therefore never forget that, especially in the absence of previous experience, the potential customer is likely to rely on price as an indicator of quality. Another important consideration is that since customers seldom accept a low price as a valid excuse for shoddy work, the price should be high enough to enable the provision of a service of at least the expected standard.

While pricing strategies are essentially the outcome of long-run considerations, they should also indicate the tactical steps for the day-to-day conduct of business. Tactics mean adaptation to the conditions that rule in the short run, and their choice must be influenced both by the behaviour of the competitors and by the attitudes of the clients.

Research can be of effective help in the solution of the pricing problems of service establishments.

---

[8] Robert J. Rogowski, 'Pricing in the Money Market Deposit and Super-NOW Accounts in 1983', *Journal of Bank Research*, **15**, Summer 1984, pp. 72–81; and Joe F. Goetz, Jr., 'The Pricing Decision: A Service Industry's Experience', *Journal of Small Business Management*, **23**, April 1985, pp. 61–7.

Appendix to Part I
Price forecasting

J. M. Bates

Introduction

The forecasting of future prices is a specialized subject that has
received relatively little attention in the literature. As a rule,
standard techniques are used, many of which were originally
developed for forecasting the volume of sales, even though the
appropriateness of some of these techniques for price forecasting
differs greatly from that for sales forecasting. In particular, when
forecasting sales in the near future, it is generally sufficient to obtain
only *the approximate level* of sales: the company can then ascertain
whether its stocks are appropriate or not and plan remedial action, if
necessary.[1] For forecasting prices in the near future the problem is
seldom if ever as simple as this. The buyer of a primary commodity,
say, is not just interested in knowing whether its price is likely to be
higher or lower next week than it is today; if a fall is anticipated, he
will also wish to know whether the fall is likely to continue in
subsequent weeks. In other words, he will be interested both in the
expected extent of the change and in its timing.

Another problem facing buyers is that many prices are set by
individual sellers instead of being determined in the market by the
interplay of demand and supply factors. Because of the additional
costs incurred each time a price is changed, a seller might alter his
price only very occasionally even if basic supply and demand
conditions are changing more or less continuously. Forecasting such
occasional changes requires different approaches from those usually
adopted for sales forecasts.

The seller's task in determining the appropriate price for his
product is also far from trivial. It might be thought that the answer
to the question 'what will the demand for my product be if I raise or
lower its price by X per cent?' could be found by examining the past
behaviour of demand in response to price changes. However,
experience has shown that it is seldom possible to make reliable
predictions by the analysis of past data, because even though the
available statistical methods can take account of changes in a
number of variables, (such as, for example, the number of customers
and their incomes, the prices of some other goods, weather
conditions, etc.), the data will not in general cover *all* the relevant
influences. Yet in some instances even broad indications derived

---

[1] It should be noted that the period in which the sales forecaster is interested
often depends on the time necessary to carry out certain policy options, such
as, for example, the time needed to plan and execute overtime working.

from past experience can be useful: thus it can safely be predicted that an increase in the charge for electricity will increase the total revenue of the electricity supplier, but the long-run effect, depending on the availability and prices of other forms of energy, could well be the opposite. On the other hand, if the product is sold in a heavily competitive market, even the short-run effect of a price increase by an individual supplier will generally turn out to be unfavourable to him.[2]

It follows from what has been said so far that it is necessary to distinguish between *short-term* and *long-term* forecasts. These concepts do not have the same meaning for forecasters and economists. Short-term forecasting may attempt to predict each perturbation of price over some limited time period, whereas long-term forecasting aims merely at the prediction of the *trend* of prices, without attempting to follow possible fluctuations that might occur around the trend. Because of this difference, the methods of long-term forecasting are simpler to describe. It is for this reason that Section A starts with the discussion of long-term forecasting methods, followed by consideration of the proposals made by various writers concerning the nature and use of *learning* and *experience curves*, and an introduction to the analysis of product life cycles. Section A ends with two examples of price forecasting: one is that of a consumer good whose production costs are decreasing as a result of technological change, while the other is concerned with the price of labour or, more specifically, with the problem of forecasting future wage levels within the company.

Short-term forecasting and its applications are discussed in Section B.

A   Long-term forecasting

1 *Methods used*

There are two principal methods in use; one is based on *judgement* and the other on *regression*. Each will be described here, followed by examples of their applications.

(a) Judgement forecasts   The forecaster makes his forecast simply by forming his own opinion of the influence on the price concerned of what he expects to happen.

---

[2] Cf. the comments on the limitations of demand analysis in Chapter 2 and the references listed in note 7, p. 18.

The method is widely used in industry; it is very flexible insofar as changes in all the relevant circumstances (to the extent to which they are known) can be taken into consideration, and it is quick and virtually costless. It is particularly favoured when the factors involved are major in their effects and erratic in their occurrence, as, for example, if commodity purchases are made from a country expected to announce a currency revaluation.

The chief limitations of the method are that its effectiveness is limited to those people who can judge well, and that by its nature it is difficult to learn from past mistakes. Since the relationship is not generally specified, it might not be possible to determine why any forecast error has occurred. The forecaster may, however, be required to accompany his estimate by a reasoned exposition of his line of thought, quoting any relevant previous experience and current information on which he relied. Such discussion of the reasoning behind a forecast is helpful in enabling management to form views of what might happen. Where several forecasts have been made, it is frequently found that an average is more reliable than the forecast of any of the individuals: by this we mean that its errors are, on average, lower than those of any of the single forecasts. If records of previous forecasts are kept, it is possible to improve the reliability of a forecast even further: a composite forecast can be formed by combining the individual forecasts using weights which give greater emphasis to the forecasts of those whose predictions have been found more reliable on previous occasions. Bates and Granger[3] have found that even where a particular forecaster's method performed worse in the past than that of the others, better results can usually be obtained by including it than by ignoring it. The execution of the averaging itself is best carried out by a trained statistician.

In contrast, other forecasting methods which will be discussed presently involve the assumption of definite mathematical relationships, hence when errors are observed, one can attempt to analyse why they have arisen, often with some – at least partial – success.

(b) Regression Regression analysis is the term used to describe the attempt to discover a statistical relationship between two or more variables. For example,

$$P_t - P_{t-1} = a(S_t - S_{t-1})$$

---

[3] J. M. Bates and C. W. J. Granger, 'The Combination of Forecasts', *Operations Research Quarterly*, **20**, 1969, pp. 451–468.

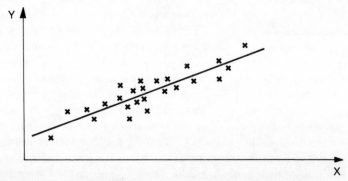

Figure AI.1   Scatter diagram depicting linear relationship

is a formula relating the difference between P_t, the price at time t and P_{t-1}, the price in an earlier period, to the change in stocks between times $t - 1$ and t: $S_t - S_{t-1}$. 'a' is a parameter the value of which can be determined by what is known as a regression method, provided there is a fair amount of data available covering past values of P and S.

Genuine data come in swarms rather than along a single line. This is illustrated in Figure AI.1, with a straight line expressing the central tendency of the swarm or, we might say, the average relationship between X and Y.

Statistical theory offers various techniques for obtaining estimates of such average relationships. The most widely used regression method consists of fitting a straight line to the swarm of points in such a way that the sum of the squares of the vertical differences between the points of the swarm and the line should be the minimum.

This 'least squares' method has three important features. Its main justification is that it yields usable results, another is that it is simple to apply and the method ensures that the sums of the positive and negative differences between the points of the swarm and the line fitted cancel each other out. The method is not restricted to straight lines; it can be adapted to the fitting of curves which follow the shapes of the swarms of points. The appropriate formulae for a number of different relationships and the methods of application are given in most textbooks of statistics, one such being the book by Draper and Smith.[4]

---

[4] Norman R. Draper and H. Smith, *Applied Regression Analysis*, 2nd edn, John Wiley & Sons, New York, 1981, pp. 505–13.

Two of the difficulties encountered when using regression methods for forecasting purposes are:

(i)   Discovering which variables influence the one being examined.
(ii) Predicting the levels of these 'explanatory' variables.

For example, it might be thought that the price of a particular product depends on the rate at which new technology is adopted, and that the rate of adoption will depend on general economic conditions, the measure of which is, say, the variation in the national income. However, much forecasting work is based on simple trends, largely because of the difficulty of predicting such things as general economic conditions.

The forecaster must decide in advance whether a straight line or some particular curve is most likely to express the general character of the trend as indicated by the swarm of points. The formulae most frequently found useful are listed and illustrated here:

(i)   Straight line: $Y = a + bT$, shown in Figure AI.1 above.
(ii) Exponential curve: $Y = a.b^T$, which may also be written $\log Y = \log a + T.\log b$. In this expression, as also in those which follow, Y is the price to be forecast, a and b are constants to be estimated by a statistical procedure and T represents time.

  If $b > 1$, the trend is upward, increasing from period to period by a constant percentage. If $b < 1$, the trend is downward. These cases are shown in Figure AI.2 (a) and (b).

(iii) Modified exponential curve: $Y = c + a.b^T$. The series approaches a certain level called an *asymptote*, the value of which is the constant c. Two of the possible forms are illustrated in Figure AI.3.

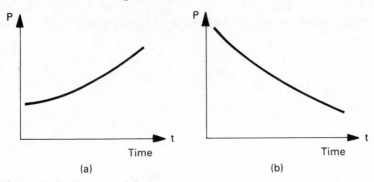

(a)   (b)

Figure AI.2   Exponential curves

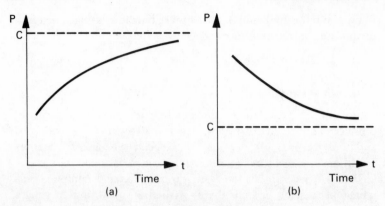

Figure AI.3   Modified exponential curves

If the time series seems to be approaching an upper limit, a formula yielding a curve of the type shown in Figure AI.3 (a) will be appropriate, if it tends towards a lower limit, the formula on which Figure AI.3 (b) is based applies.

(iv) Logistic curve: $\frac{1}{Y} = c + a.b^T$. The reciprocals of the Y values form a modified exponential curve, with asymptotes at zero and c. Two possible forms are shown in Figure I.4 (a) and (b).

(v) Gompertz curve: $Y = c.a.^{b^T}$, which may also be written $log\ Y = log\ c + (log\ a).b^T$. Possible forms are similar to but not identical with those shown in Figures AI.3 and AI.4. As a rule, the Figure AI.3 types are found more useful, with one asymptote at zero and the other at c.

All these curves are discussed in further detail in Draper and Smith, as also in other good textbooks of statistics. As indicated above, the forecaster must choose in advance the type of curve to be

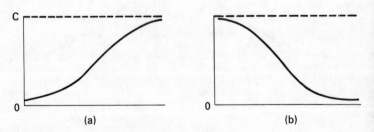

Figure AI.4   Logistic curves

fitted, but if it is then found that another type might give a better fit, this may be substituted. However, unless the relationship expressed by the chosen formula can be supported by other evidence, the users of the result of the analysis should be informed that it was adopted merely because of its closer fit to the data.

2 Learning curves, experience curves and product life cycles

Over the years several writers have observed that the unit costs of production of certain products had decreased over time, and many have suggested specific mathematical forms for the relationship. In much of the early work on *learning curves* it was suggested that direct *unit labour cost* decreased as cumulative output increased.[5] Cumulative output is defined as the aggregate output of a given product since it was first produced. Thus, if the output in each of the first three years of a product's life were 10,000, 15,000 and 30,000 units, respectively, then the cumulative output by the end of years 1, 2 and 3 would be 10,000, 25,000 and 55,000 units. A typical equation expressing the relationship concerned is:

$$C = a.Q^{-b},$$

where C is the direct labour cost per unit of output, Q is the cumulative output and a and b are parameters. The equation may also be written $log\ C = log\ A - b.log\ Q$. If it is true that prices move in line with costs, then price predictions can be made once accumulated output has been predicted. It should be made clear that in this relationship all costs are expressed in 'real' terms, that is to say, after allowance has been made for changes in costs and prices due to inflation. Thus, if money costs remained constant during a year in which inflation was ten per cent, costs in general have gone down relative to prices by approximately 9.1 per cent.

Experience curves are similar to learning curves but go further with their assumptions. The Boston Consulting Group, the protagonists of experience curves, claim that *total unit cost* depends on experience as measured by the accumulated product of the *industry* as a whole. Despite this statement, which is still maintained, it is clear that the Group also believes that the unit costs incurred by

---

[5] See for example W. Z. Hirsch, 'Manufacturing Progress Functions', *Review of Economics and Statistics*, **34**, 1952, pp. 143–155.

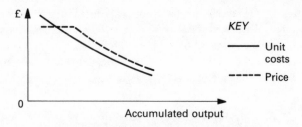

Figure AI.5   Costs, prices and accumulated output

different firms depended on their relative market share, and that some of the economies, for example economies of scale, depend on the level of current output rather than on accumulated output.[6]

Once again the same mathematical relationship is used but it is made more specific: the protagonists of experience curves claim that a doubling of accumulated output invariably leads to total unit cost being reduced by not less than 20 per cent and not more than 30 per cent; also that the reduction continues indefinitely, provided management is efficient.

The price policy suggested by the Boston Consulting Group for the dominant firm of the industry is indicated in Figure AI.5.

Initially, price should be set somewhat below current unit cost and decreased in real terms by about 10 per cent for each doubling of the accumulated output, while costs are decreasing at a rate of 20 to 30 per cent as accumulated output doubles. Subsequently, price reductions should match cost reductions if the firm is to retain its dominance. Other analysts dispute these claims. Abernathy and Wayne agree that higher volumes of production often lead to the lowering of total unit costs but, using the example of Ford's change from their Model T to their Model A, show that experience is *not* wholly transferable when design changes have occurred.[7] Stobaugh and Townsend consider separately the effects of experience and scale on costs and proceed to evaluate differences between costs and prices. More specifically, they reveal that the entrance of new

---

[6] Staff of the Boston Consulting Group, *Perspectives on Experience*, 1968; cf. especially pp. 17 and 18.

[7] W. J. Abernathy and K. Wayne, 'Limits of the Learning Curve', *Harvard Business Review*, **52**, 1974, pp. 109–19.

competitors can also narrow the difference between costs and prices, as can the onset of increased product standardization.[8]

Though the more flamboyant claims of the principal protagonists do not appear to be acceptable, the ideas that they have presented have considerable merit. As learning, or experience, is gained, unit costs frequently tend to decrease, though not necessarily by a steady percentage. However, the unit costs (in real terms) often do follow reasonably closely a mathematical relationship with total accumulated output. Where this is so, the next step is to forecast total accumulated output. Some would choose to forecast this using their own judgement; others would make use of the concept of the *product life cycle*. The basic idea behind this is that the output of most companies has generally to be closely geared to their sales, while variations in sales depend principally on the rate of acceptance of the product by new customers.

The initial acceptance of a new product is generally fairly limited but, as it becomes more widely known, increasing proportions of the public may purchase it and sales rise rapidly. Ultimately, sales approach a maximum as the number of customers purchasing it reaches *saturation level*. Several different mathematical curves have been used to describe this *life cycle*, the logistic curve being one of them. A description and critique of these methods is presented in an article by Polli and Cook.[9] The typical shape of the product life cycle is indicated in Figure AI.6. It is sometimes possible to have a fair idea of the life cycle of fashion articles, many of which are only of one season's duration, but it is not generally easy to estimate the life

---

[8] R. B. Stobaugh and P. L. Townsend, 'Price Forecasting and Strategic Planning: The Case of Petrochemicals', *Journal of Marketing Research*, **12**, (1), February 1975, pp. 19–29; and Robert J. Dolan and Abel P. Jeuland, 'Experience Curves and Dynamic Demand Models: Implications for Optimal Pricing Strategies', *Journal of Marketing*, **45**, (1), 1981, pp. 52–6 (lists 23 references); also George S. Day and David B. Montgomery, 'Diagnosing the Experience Curve', *Journal of Marketing*, **47**, (2), Spring 1983, pp. 44–58.

For a well balanced discussion of the issue see 'Economies of Scale and Learning Effects' by the Department of Prices and Consumer Protection, in *A Review of Monopolies and Mergers Policy*, Appendix C, Cmnd 7198, HMSO, London, May 1978, pp. 77–96; reprinted in *Readings in Applied Microeconomics*, (L. Wagner, ed.), Oxford University Press, 1981, pp. 148–71.

[9] R. Polli and V. Cook, 'Validity of the Product Life Cycle', *Journal of Business*, **42**, (4), October 1969, pp. 385–400. Some further references are listed at the end of this Appendix.

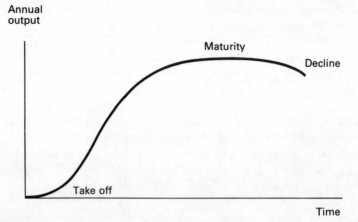

Figure AI.6   Product life cycle

cycle at an early stage, as indicated in Chapter 12 and illustrated by reference to the cases of Dunhill and Corfam.

3 Forecasting consumer product prices and wage levels

Two important problems have been selected in order to illustrate both the methods described above and the problems that are frequently encountered. The first of these is the price of a consumer product, the second is that of wage levels.

(a) Price of a fast moving consumer product   As an example, consider the price of broiler chickens. Before plotting any data, it is worthwhile to ask whether it is money price or 'real' price that is of interest. Since in recent times the price of broilers has increased less than the retail price index, the real price of broilers has in fact decreased: to purchase a broiler chicken, a consumer is now required to forgo less of other commodities than at an earlier time. The forecaster may well be concerned principally with such real prices, particularly if long-term decisions, such as investment, are under consideration; and even if the forecasting is directed at the future money price, the price of the product in relation to the general price level may also be of some importance. Plots of both kinds of price are given in Figures AI.7 and AI.8.

Over the period studied, the general index of retail prices increased by 15 per cent, hence there is some difference between the

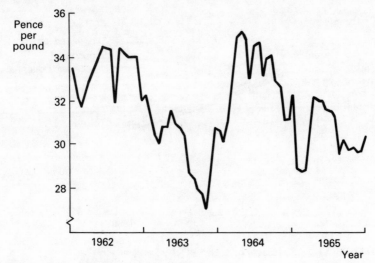

Figure AI.7   Chicken prices, 1962–5

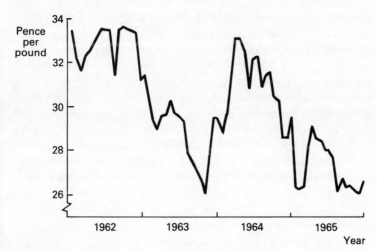

Figure AI.8   Chicken prices deflated by the Retail Price Index after January 1962

two graphs. The impact of changing technology is particularly evident here.

Three different forecasting methods have been applied to the data. The results are shown in Figure AI.9.

Since the accumulated output of chickens was not covered by the available data, we have followed the suggestion of the Boston

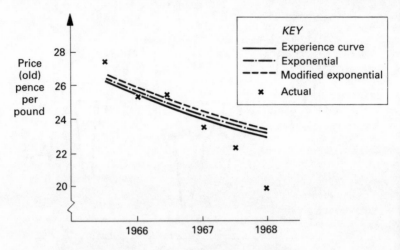

Figure AI.9   Forecasts of trend of chicken prices

Consulting Group in taking the five years 1957–61 as a proxy for the accumulated output in January 1962. The continuous curve expresses the average relationship between log price and the logarithm of accumulated output; the equation suggested by the writers extolling the virtues of experience curves. Strictly speaking, since each of the three curves was calculated by using known figures of output in the years 1966, 1967 and 1968, they are not 'pure' forecasts which would have required the forecaster to base the calculations on *predicted* output levels for the three years concerned.

It was mentioned at the end of Section 1 that the forecaster may change from the type of trend equation originally selected to another if the latter provides a better fit. In this example there would be as yet no reason to replace the initial choice, since the different methods give very similar results.

(b) Wage levels   In forecasting consumer product prices, attention can often be restricted to just two areas: whether time or accumulated output is the more helpful explanatory variable, and which kind of mathematical equation best describes the relationship. Forecasting wage levels presents a more difficult task. One source of difficulty is that there are considerable differences between negotiated wage rates and actual earnings, the two regularly published sets of British wage statistics. The index of wage rates is an expression of changes in the negotiated minimum rates for the basic working week, whereas the earnings index also reflects

overtime payments, bonuses and the so called wage drift, that is to say, the fact that many employers are paying labour at rates above the negotiated minima. Of the two, the earnings index is the more appropriate, even though the inclusion in the index of overtime payments is not always desired. A second source of difficulty is the necessity to assess which of a host of possible factors affect wages significantly and to forecast likely changes in these factors.

Many companies find it necessary to predict wage levels for budgeting reasons, but they rarely have reliable information on overtime payments in the industry, etc., so that series of recent figures may not be available. The usual method adopted is to prepare estimates of total wage payments within the company for the current year and, towards the end of the financial year, these are adjusted in the light of the expected outcome of wage negotiations for the next year.

B Short-term forecasting

There is only one situation in which the pricing decision does not call for the forecasting of one or more other prices. It is that of the *cost-plus contract* which stipulates that the price to be paid for the product will be equal to the actual cost incurred plus an agreed percentage margin. Otherwise, if the price is market-determined, as in the case of metals and other basic commodities, or set by some outside body, it will be essential for future planning to have as reliable an idea as possible of the price to come, whereas if the company is not a follower, that is to say, not a price taker but a price maker, it will have to gauge the future prices of its suppliers and those of its competitors in order to lessen the uncertainty which inevitably faces the price setter.

The call for short-term price forecasting is therefore pretty universal: individual perturbations of prices cannot be estimated from the prevailing trend. In this section a number of suitable forecasting methods will be described and illustrated with examples, followed by the discussion of the pricing problem of competitive bidding.

1 Methods used

Methods commonly employed to derive short-term forecasts are:

- Judgement forecasts.
- Regression analysis.

- Naïve forecasts.
- Exponential smoothing.
- The methods of Box and Jenkins.

There is little to add to what has been said above on the first two methods, but it may be noted that the judgemental method is flexible and can be used for any future period. As regards the regression methods, it is important to remember that causal relationships have a smaller predictive value in the short-term than they do in the long-term. There are several reasons for this; an important one of which is that at any given time there are many temporary factors operating, another is that short-term forecasts require accurate estimates of the timing of the effect of causal factors, and these may be difficult to make.

(a) Naïve forecasts These forecasts are derived from some simple assumptions concerning the continuance in the future of certain past trends. The simplest example is

$$F_{t+1} = P_t, \tag{1}$$

where P_t denotes price at time t and F_{t+1} is the forecast for the next time period $t + 1$. In other words, the forecast for the period ahead equals the latest value of the variable. Another naïve forecasting equation is

$$F_{t+1} = P_t + (P_t - P_{t-1}). \tag{2}$$

Equation (2) is the expression of the belief that the change between the last two periods will continue

The naïve method is quick and simple to operate, requiring little statistical knowledge or analytical understanding of what may affect the variable. It is based on a credible hypothesis: what happened in the past will happen in the future. However, by avoiding any consideration of the factors which may affect the variable, it fails to take into account all the useful information available.

In practice, a naïve forecast is rarely used on its own but to serve as a basis for a more sophisticated forecast: its result being built upon by other techniques. It can also be used as a yardstick against which the performance of another forecast can be evaluated. If the more sophisticated method fails to give a better performance, then it should be modified or abandoned.

(b) Exponential smoothing The purpose of smoothing is to diminish the effect of the random disturbances to which the data are subject. One way of obtaining the current trend would be to take the average

of the last few observations. Exponential smoothing is a form of averaging where the weights given to recent observations are larger than those for more distant observations.

Suppose we have a time series $P_1, P_2, P_3, .. P_t ..$, where P_t denotes the value of variable P (which may be the price of a certain product) at time t. The exponential method for deriving a 'smoothed' time series, Y, from P is to use the equation

$$Y_t = \alpha P_t + (1 - \alpha) Y_{t-1}. \tag{3}$$

The first term of the series is given by $Y_1 = P_1$. Subsequent terms are then obtained by applying the formula; thus the second term becomes

$$Y_2 = \alpha P_2 + (1 - \alpha) Y_1,$$

and the third term $Y_3 = \alpha P_3 + (1 - \alpha) Y_2$, which could be re-written

$$Y_3 = \alpha P_3 + (1 - \alpha)[\alpha P_2 + (1 - \alpha)P_1].$$

Recommended values of α lie usually within the range of 0.1 to 0.4. For series of prices, however, there is generally less need for smoothing than for many other variables and hence values of α above 0.4 may be appropriate even for weekly or daily data; with values of about 0.9 or more for data subject to even less haphazard variations, for example, monthly or quarterly data which are themselves averages of daily observations.

Though this initial step is sufficient for the phrase 'exponential smoothing' to be applied; for forecasting purposes it is customary to use also a second equation for estimating the trend. One possible estimate would be

$$\text{Trend} = Y_t - Y_{t-1},$$

that is to say, the difference between the last two values of the exponentially smoothed series. However, since in practice the values of Y_t are generally found to be subject to some change due to random disturbances in P_t, the original data series, instead of using this simple measure, it is usual to derive an exponentially smoothed trend defined as

$$\textit{New trend} = C(\textit{current trend}) + (1 - C)(\textit{old trend}),$$

where the current trend is $Y_t - Y_{t-1}$ and C is a constant between 0 and 1. If the estimate of the trend at time t is written as T_t, this equation becomes

$$T_t = C(Y_t - Y_{t-1}) + (1 - C)T_{t-1}. \tag{4}$$

Since the latest estimate of the level of the series will now include the trend term, equation (3) is replaced by

$$Y_t = A.P_t + (1 - A)(Y_{t-1} + T_t), \qquad (5)$$

where A is a constant within the range 0 to 1.

It is usual to arrive at the values of A and C by empiricism. The method is this: select a number of possible values for A and C and compare the forecast errors that would have been obtained using these on past data. The values which would have given the best performance in the past are then used for forecasting.

Equations (4) and (5) represent the approach of Holt and Winters to exponential smoothing as specified by an additive trend. They also considered the incorporation of seasonal factors and multiplicative terms have been utilized in forecasts prepared by these methods. For a discussion of these see Chatfield.[10]

(c) The methods of Box and Jenkins Professors Box and Jenkins use *auto-regressive* and *moving average* methods, but because they use these in a very specific way, it is customary to refer to these methods of forecasting by the names of the originators.

An *auto-regressive relationship* is one where the variable is related to past values of *itself*. Such a relationship could be simply

$$P_t = a_1 P_{t-1} + a_2 P_{t-2} + a_3 P_{t-3},$$

where a_1, a_2 and a_3 are coefficients.

Box and Jenkins recognize that there will generally be a difference between the forecast as expressed by the right-hand side of the above equation and the actual value of P_t. One of their basic equations in which this recognition is expressed is

$$P_t - a_1 P_{t-1} - a_2 P_{t-2} - \ldots - a_p P_{t-p} = c_t - b_1 e_{t-1} - b_2 e_{t-2} - \ldots - b_q e_{t-q},$$

$$(6)$$

where the a's and b's are coefficients (to be estimated) and the e_i's are errors (assumed to be normally distributed with mean 0 and variance σ^2 for all t). The left-hand side of equation (6) is the auto-regressive part, and the right-hand side the moving average of past errors. As given in equation (6), the series P_t is the original series (that is, it is not differenced), and in the usual terminology it is said to be of order $(p,0,q)$.

---

[10] C. Chatfield, 'The Holt–Winters Forecasting Procedure', *Applied Statistics*, Volume 27, No. 3, 1978.

For many series Box and Jenkins recommend that they should be differenced, thus

$$p_t = \Delta P_t = P_t - P_{t-1}.$$

If this is done, p_t will replace P_t and p_{t-1} will replace P_{t-1}, and so on in equation (6), and the order of the equation becomes $(p, 1, q)$. If a further differencing is undertaken, we obtain

$$p_t = (P_t - P_{t-1}) - (P_{t-1} - P_{t-2})$$
$$= P_t - 2P_{t-1} + P_{t-2},$$

and the order is then $(p, 2, q)$.

Box and Jenkins suggest differencing d times, making their system of order (p, d, q). This should be general enough for most forecasters!

There are two principal tasks when using this model. The first is to select the order of the system, the second is to estimate the coefficients. In addition, it is advisable to undertake certain diagnostic checks on the results obtained. To learn how these tasks are undertaken, consult Box and Jenkins and Nelson.[11]

2 Examples of forecasting problems

A wider choice of techniques is available for short-term forecasting than for long-term forecasting. The claims made by the protagonists of the various methods are less dogmatic; their general attitude is well illustrated by Professor Barnard's open minded assertion: 'The forecasting methods developed by Box and Jenkins have proved so successful that we are now searching to find alternative methods which forecast better' (1963).

A brief assessment of the methods of Box and Jenkins – which, as we shall see, generally serve quite well – will follow after a few examples of forecasting problems have been considered. The first example, forecasting of retail prices, has been chosen because of its importance to most firms, including those which operate only in industrial markets, because of its influence on wage settlements.

(a) Consumer prices It should be made a rule to plot the available data before any analysis is attempted because a graph can be very informative and may immediately suggest the most appropriate method to be applied.

---

[11] G. E. P. Box and G. M. Jenkins, *Time Series Analysis: Forecasting and Control*, Holden-Day, San Francisco, 1970; C. E. Nelson, *Applied Time Series Analysis for Managerial Forecasting*, Holden-Day, 1973.

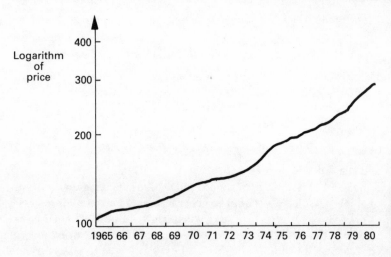

Figure AI.10   US Consumer Price Index

Figure AI.10 shows the US Consumer Price Index over the period 1965 to 1980.

The vertical scale is logarithmic, hence a constant percentage rate of increase of the index would emerge as a straight line. It is apparent from the graph that prices rose faster in the latter half of the period under examination.

Let us now apply some forecasting methods to these statistics. A naïve one-month-ahead forecast is derived by assuming that last year's seasonal pattern will apply for the next month; with a similarly simple method being used to derive a twelve-months-ahead forecast.

For the Holt–Winters version of the exponential smoothing technique it was assumed that the operative components are the level of the index, its trend and seasonal movements. The Box and Jenkins approach suggested a model which employed second differences: no seasonal features were suggested hence the seasonal components were ignored.

To derive forecasts for the January 1978 to August 1980 period, data for 1965–77 were used for the estimation of the parameters[12] of the different methods. Forecasts were made for one-month-ahead

---

[12] The term 'parameter' as used here has the same meaning as 'coefficient' and 'constant' above.

Table AI.1
Optimal parameter values

Method		
Holt-Winters:	Smoothing parameter for level	0.78
	trend	0.21
	seasonal	0.17
Box and Jenkins:	Weight given to moving average error term with lag of one month	0.74

and for one-year-ahead. Certain features of the parameters are given in Table AI.1, and the average squared errors of the forecasts in Table AI.2.

With the Holt–Winters method the optimal parameter relating to the level was found to be 0.78, indicating that much weight is given to the latest forecast error and relatively little to the previous estimate of the level, which means that there is little smoothing done for the level. Once a particular level is reached, it is usually more relevant for prediction than previous levels. In contrasts, the trend and seasonal patterns are more stable and much weight is given to earlier values of both trend and seasonal variations.

For the Box and Jenkins method it is not uncommon to revise a forecast considerably as a result of the errors observed. This particular model is perhaps unusual, also, in not having terms based on errors two or three months previously.

Table AI.2 shows the average forecast errors over the period for which forecasts were made by the three methods: January 1978 to August 1980. Errors were recorded both for the situation where

Table AI.2
Forecasts of the US Consumer Price Index

Method	Characteristics	Average square error	
		1 month ahead	*12 months ahead*
Holt-Winters:	See Table AI.1	0.73	48.6
Box and Jenkins:	See Table AI.1	0.67	72.6
Naïve:	Percentage change in index is estimated to be the same as in previous month	0.69	
	Percentage change in index is estimated to be the same as over the previous year		73.0

forecasts of the index were made one month in advance and where it was forecast twelve months in advance.

Some general comments on these results are appropriate:

(i) Each method has derived its parameters from the period 1965–1977, applying one equation to the whole period. No attempt has been made to take into account such factors as the operation of a government price policy, or movements in currency exchange rates, such as the Smithsonian re-alignments of late 1971. Anyone seriously interested in forecasting retail prices should examine whether factors such as those just mentioned have resulted in discontinuities in the data, for if they were present, the implication is that improved forecasts could be obtained from each of the methods employed.

(ii) The Box and Jenkins method performed best for one month ahead, and the Holt-Winters method for twelve months ahead.

(iii) We have not examined here either regression methods or forecasts based on judgement. Since the power of judgement depends on the individual, a general evaluation of it is not possible. A judgemental forecast made by the author could have been assessed, but since this would not have had any relevance to the reader, it was not attempted. (Anyway, in order to enable a valid assessment, the forecast should have been made in advance, that is to say, before the January 1978 to August 1980 values of the index were known.)

Although a factual assessment of these methods has not been undertaken, some comments are in order here. First of all, modification of a forecast by taking into account the impact of an incomes/prices policy is likely to lead to some improvement, provided it is possible to recognize the 'stages' or 'intensities' of the policy. But note that what is suggested is that forecasts are *modified*, that is to say, that reliance is not placed solely on, say, a regression method. The reason is that the introduction of a prices policy is itself only one factor; it may modify (at least temporally) the movements of the index, but the result could not be entirely independent of other happenings in the economy, many of which may influence price movements. The same comments also apply to judgemental forecasts. The use of judgement is appropriate particularly since no one prices policy is exactly like any previous one! Nevertheless, it is still the right course to start predicting the likely value of the index on the assumption that past (or current) policies are continued, and then examine if the prediction should be modified by taking account of the new (or expected) policy.

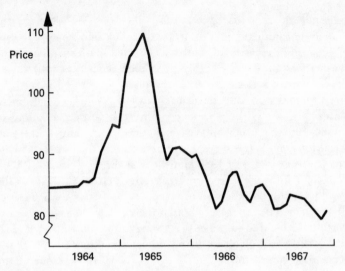

Figure AI.11   Palm oil prices 1964–7

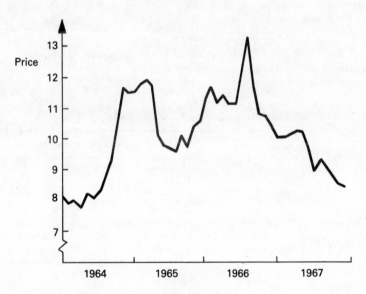

Figure AI.12   Soya oil prices 1964–7

The same conclusion does not necessarily apply to forecasts of other time series: the movements of consumer price indices are subject to so many factors that a first approach is unlikely to produce the best result obtainable.

(b) Forecasting the prices of raw material inputs To illustrate the problems encountered in this field, the price movements of two products will be considered. Both are oils used in making margarine and other food products, but there is a difference between the nature of the two price series, insofar as the price of palm oil is set by a selling organization, while the price of soya oil is market determined.

Table AI.3 shows the parameters derived by fitting equations to the 1964–1967 data as displayed in Figures AI.11 and AI.12, and Table AI.4 records the average square errors of the forecasts made for the twelve months of 1968 and the first three months of 1969.

It is clear from the figures in Table AI.4 that for both series the Box and Jenkins forecasts were considerably better than those of Holt-Winters. The latter were not on the whole even as good as the naïve forecasts – in the absence of a strong trend and with a seasonal pattern that was difficult to discern above a number of apparently haphazard changes this is not altogether surprising. None of the methods applied utilized information on production and consequently they ignored the effect on price of the good harvest of soya in 1968: regression, or judgement, ought to have predicted well for a *few months* towards the end of 1968.

Like Table AI.2, Table AI.4 displays the typical way of comparing forecasts, which is to examine some measure of the average error after the actual values of the predicted variable have become

Table AI.3
Optimal parameter values using 1964–7 data

Method			Optimal parameter values palm oil	soya oil
Holt-Winters:	Smoothing paramaters for:			
		level	1.0	1.0
		trend	0.06	0.07
		seasonal	0.02	0.08
Box and Jenkins:	Weight given to moving average error term with lag of one month		−0.43	−0.28

Table AI.4
Forecasting performance one and two months ahead

Method	Average square error of the last 15 forecasts			
	palm oil		soya oil	
	1 month	2 months	1 month	2 months
Holt-Winters:	11.3	40.9	0.25	1.05
Box and Jenkins:	6.1	30.5	0.11	0.39
Naïve:	12.3	38.3	0.16	0.46

available. But a potential purchaser of palm oil or soya oil would generally want to know also the *direction* of future price changes. The Holt–Winters forecasts frequently failed to 'catch up' with any changes in price, and so were unsuccessful in indicating the direction of future price changes. The Box and Jenkins forecasts correctly predicted the direction of ten out of eleven changes in the palm oil series (in four months there was no change), and correctly predicted ten out of fifteen in the soya oil series. The method was less successful in predicting when an upward price movement would change to a downward movement and *vice versa*. Over the last 27 months of the series, the method correctly predicted *changes in the direction* of the palm oil prices on three occasions in five, but only on two occasions in nine of the soya oil prices. These results are, perhaps, not untypical: many forecasting methods have varying success in predicting a change in direction. Those concerned primarily with predicting changes in direction should consult Granger's book.[13]

(c) Pricing in uncertainty We have hitherto concentrated on the problems of price indices which are aggregates of numerous prices and – with the exception of palm oil – on the prices of products sold in reasonably competitive markets. We shall now consider the case where there are very few producers and each competitor's action needs to be assessed.

For convenience, discussion will be focussed upon the situation where there is just one other rival producer. When forecasting the price of a competitor's product several different considerations are relevant of which the most important is that there is likely to be considerable interaction between yourself and your competitor. He will usually adjust his price if you change yours, but may otherwise alter price only irregularly – either because he is uncertain of your reaction to his price change or because of the cost involved in changing price.

In such circumstances, *conditional* probabilistic forecasts are common. For example, it might be predicted that *if* your price is unaltered, your rival's price will be either v or x (with specified probabilities); *if* you increase price by 10 per cent, his price will be y or z, and *if* you increase price by 20 per cent, his price will be z, again each case with a specific probability attached to it. Judgemental forecasts are the norm and it is advisable to maintain a

---

[13] C. W. J. Granger, *Forecasting in Business and Economics*, Academic Press, New York, 1980.

close liaison between the forecaster and management. The forecast may be based on known movements in costs including the effect of general inflation, estimated stock levels and expected financial liquidity of the competitor – or simply on a guess of your rival's psychology as expressed by his pricing policy.

Whenever the judgemental method is applied, the decision procedure can be formalized by the application of what has become known as *the Bayesian method*.[14] Its operation can best be explained by an example.

Suppose that owing to an increase of wages or the cost of materials the price of your Brand A is under revision, and that there is only one important competitor in the field: Brand B. Say that the new direct cost of manufacturing Brand A is £1.00 per unit and that the choice is between two prices only: £1.50 and £1.95.

The first task is then to consider all the possible reactions of the competitor and assign probabilities to them; remembering that they must add up to unity for each of the two suggested prices of Brand A.[15] The estimates of these probabilities will be essentially subjective, but this does not mean that they must be mere guesses. As hinted above, they should take into consideration – as far as possible – what is known about the past behaviour of the competitor and any other piece of relevant information that can be made available. For example, it might be known to the price setter of Brand A that the manufacturer of Brand B has access to a cheaper source of materials and hence is likely to have lower direct unit costs than Brand A; or, say, that the company manufacturing Brand B was running at a loss last year and could not therefore afford to undercut Brand A as long as its price is not unreasonably high. There will always remain some scope for empathy: the price setter of Brand A should take into account what he would do if he were in the position of the person who is responsible for the pricing of Brand B.

The next point that requires attention is the effect of each of the price situations envisaged on the number of units of Brand A that will be sold over the next accounting period, say a year. Here again the estimate may be based on past experience or on the results of

---

[14] Thomas Bayes (1702–1761) was one of the founders of the science of statistics. The use of his name is customary though not quite appropriate in this case, since the method concerned does not involve the Bayes Theorem of Conditional Probabilities.

[15] Probabilities are customarily expressed as fractions of 1 and not as percentages.

recent test marketing at various prices or on an appropriate consumer survey, taking into account the trend of the economic climate. This last point is particularly important in the case of industrial investment goods and consumer durables, since it is the sale of these categories that tend to fluctuate most with the ups and downs of the economy at large.

Once the forecaster has taken into account the points discussed above, he should have all the entries for columns (1) to (4) of Table AI.5, and they in turn contain all the information necessary to calculate columns (5) to (7). The total sales return is the number of units sold over a year multiplied by the price of Brand A, and the contribution is sales return less direct cost. (The latter is not explicitly included in the table, but as direct cost per unit is £1.00, the number of units sold also indicates the total direct cost.)

Column 7 shows the payoff, defined as the contribution multiplied by the probability, and the totals for each of the contemplated prices of Brand A are the composite payoff amounts. Provided the entries in Columns (1) to (4) are correct, the composite payoff indicates the expected outcome *in the long run*, meaning that if many similar decisions were taken, the average annual contribution will be around £90,000 if the policy is consistently the same which led to a price of £1.50 for Brand A, and £106,400 if the price is £1.95.

However, assuming that the entries are essentially correct, the actual contribution *in any individual year* will be one of the figures in Column (6) and not the payoff shown in Column (7).

It is evident that such a payoff table does not by itself decide which of the proposed prices should be selected. That will be an executive decision, aided rather than replaced by the computation. A bold risk-taker will presumably prefer the higher of the two prices, whereas a more cautious businessman is likely to decide in favour of the lower price – and both will be well advised not to disregard the expected long-run effects of their decision.

In line with the argument presented in Chapter 5, the payoff in Table AI.5 was calculated in terms of the contribution. If, however, Product A should be the only output of the division concerned, its overhead costs, which we shall assume amount to £80,000 per annum, may be deducted from the contribution, and the payoff can then be expressed in terms of the profit so defined. It should be emphasized that only where the product is the only output of the division concered may overheads be included in the calculation of the payoff. The examples quoted in Chapter 5 make it plain that if the division has more than one product, the allocation of overheads

Table AI.5
Payoff for two different price strategies

(1) Price of Brand A £	(2) Probable prices of Brand B £	(3) Probability	(4) Units sold	(5) Total sales returns £	(6) Contribution £	(7) Payoff (3) × (6) £
1.50	1.25	0.2	50,000	75,000	25,000	5,000
	1.50	0.7	200,000	300,000	100,000	70,000
	1.75	0.1	300,000	450,000	150,000	15,000
		1.0			COMPOSITE PAYOFF	£90,000
1.95	1.25	0.1	10,000	19,500	9,500	950
	1.50	0.3	60,000	117,000	57,000	17,100
	1.75	0.5	150,000	292,500	142,500	71,250
	1.95	0.1	180,000	351,000	171,000	17,100
		1.0			COMPOSITE PAYOFF	£106,400

Table AI.6
Payoff after deducting overheads

(3) Probability	(8) Contribution less £80,000 overheads £	(9) Payoff (3) × (8) £
0.2	− 55,000	− 11,000
0.7	+ 20,000	+ 14,000
0.1	+ 70,000	+ 7,000
1.0	COMPOSITE PAYOFF	+ £10,000
0.1	− 70,500	− 7,050
0.3	− 23,000	− 6,900
0.5	+ 62,500	+ 31,250
0.1	+ 91,000	+ 9,100
1.0	COMPOSITE PAYOFF	+ £26,400

by the usual absorption costing method would introduce an arbitrary element into the computation that could easily lead to an unfortunate decision. In our case the deduction of overheads in Table AI.6 has not affected the difference between the two composite payoff figures. It was

$$£106,400 - £90,000 = £16,400$$

in Table AI.5, and in Table AI.6

$$£26,400 - £10,000 = £16,400.$$

Yet it was helpful to bring in the overhead cost because in this way it could be shown that three of the probable outcomes would result in returns below the break-even point.

Outcomes which are expected to yield returns below the break-even point may be of such concern to management as to require a modification of the calculations. Raiffa[16] suggests that where the utility of an outcome differs considerably from the monetary result, the latter should be replaced by an estimate of the utility. For example, a businessman may feel that the outcome of losing £70,500 would create additional future costs, such as borrowing money at very high interest rates or on other adverse terms. Say that he estimates that subsequent losses might amount to a further £10,000, and that the inconvenience caused plus the risk of other unfavourable consequences (for example, the risk of being taken over by a rival company) might amount to the equivalent of a cost of £30,000. Taking all these factors into account would mean a utility of −£110,500 instead of the originally calculated monetary loss of £70,000.

Heavy losses are not the only case where utility may differ from the monetary outcome. A company anxious to acquire a significant share of sales in a particular market may value outcomes with a large market share but only low or even negative profits more highly than outcomes with larger profits but smaller sales. Here, as in many other cases, future prospects are not fully indicated by the short-term monetary outcome.

In the above example the competitive action considered was restricted to the pricing of Product B. Other moves could also have been brought in: the manufacturer of Product B might respond with an advertising campaign, a revamping of Product B, bringing out a

---

[16] H. Raiffa, *Decision Analysis*, Addison-Wesley, Reading, 1968 p. 86 & *passim*.

new product with superior performance, etc. Also, there may have been more than one important competitor in the field whose expected behaviour was not identical with that of the makers of Product B. As long as we can attach any probability significantly larger than zero to such reactions, they can be dealt with in the same way as the different price situations.

Formalizing the decision procedure along the lines indicated offers some very definite advantages over the usual informal approach. The individual estimates of each of the executives involved in the pricing decision will thus be put on record, together with the agreed committee estimates, if any. Apart from the discipline which this will impose on the argumentation, it will help each individual to clarify his own reasoning process and will enable the chief pricing executive to compare the actual outcome with the estimates, and thus determine which members of his staff are most consistent in their predictions. Even the opinion of the person who is consistently unduly optimistic or pessimistic could be of value once it is realized what his bias is, because it can then be rectified by the application of an appropriate correction factor.

(d) Competitive bidding   Closed competitive bidding was very much an intuitive art until about thirty years ago. Since then, it has received considerable help from the application of scientific principles to the solution of its central problem. Elaborate mathematical techniques and computer programmes are now available for locating the price that is most likely to bring success to the bidder, but it must be emphasized that only in rather exceptional cases can the mechanistic process entirely replace human judgement. It should further be noted that the data fed into the various formulae will seldom if ever be completely free from estimates based on the opinion of the pricing executive or his associates.

If nothing is known either about the principles that govern the award of the contract or about the behaviour of the competitors, any bid is merely a shot in the dark, and there is no way in which science could be of help. If, however, it is known that the contract will go to the lowest bidder (which is mostly the case), or, say, that the company whose bid is to be determined enjoys such a favourable reputation that it will almost certainly get the contract as long as its price is not more than 10 per cent above that of its nearest competitor, and there is also appropriate information available about the bidding practices of the competition, the systematic evaluation of the evidence made possible by the modern methods is likely to produce bid prices with considerably higher chances of success than the intuitive estimates of even an experienced executive.

A variety of techniques is available and it takes an expert mathematical statistician well trained in this field to determine which will suit best the circumstances of a given case. The demonstration that follows is intended to indicate the nature and general features of the approach only. It should be kept in mind throughout that variations of the method are possible at practically every point, over and above those explicitly mentioned in the exposition.

The essence of the method is not dissimilar to that of the method discussed in the previous section. It is based on the probability of winning the contract at each of the bid prices under consideration and on the profit (or contribution) that would be earned if the bid were successful. It follows that if we can plot against the mark-up on our cost the probability of winning the contract, we can calculate the payoff by multiplying the expected profit (or contribution) by the probability of getting the contract awarded to us. In the simplest and most rudimentary case this probability arises merely from our own past experience or from the more or less intuitive estimate of the pricing executive. The process is then analogous to that displayed in the first section of this Appendix. If, however, there is further relevant information available, there will be more scope for the application of the mathematical/statistical methods.

We will take the case where tenders are invited for the supply of an undifferentiated industrial product conforming to a strict standard specification. It is known that the contract will go to the lowest bidder, and since this is not a single event but one that has occurred several times in the recent past, there should also be information available about the identity of the firms who have gained previous contracts and the prices they have bid. If, after each event, the prices bid by all of the tenderers are published, all the better, but information about the winners alone might suffice, especially if the number of competitors is small and the bidding is a frequent occurrence.

Before we proceed to the selection of the price to be bid, it is essential to define the immediate aim of the bidder. Even though the long-run objective of the company may be the maximization of the rate of return on capital or, perhaps, the achievement of a certain target rate, once it has been decided to tender for a particular contract, the aim is likely to be to set a price that can be expected to maximize the contribution from this venture, especially if the order would make only a relatively small claim on the capacity of the firm.[17]

If the consequences of not gaining the contract are likely to entail substantial under-utilization of capacity, the minimization of losses may gain prime importance. Then again, the objective could be to prevent the growth of the competitors, in which case attention will be focused on minimizing their profits. Any of these aims as also a number of others can be made central to the analysis and, provided they are not incompatible, it might even be possible to pursue more than one aim at the same time.

The likely long-run consequences of the planned action should always be kept in mind since they may demand departure from the usual short-run objective. Getting a foot inside the door of a potentially important customer might be worthwhile even if the first order would involve a sacrifice. Here we shall assume that the maximization of the total expected contribution is the only objective.

If costs have been reasonably stable over the period to which the information refers, the data can be used at once to establish the bidding patterns of the competitors. If costs have changed, recalculation will be necessary. It may be done either by applying an appropriate cost index to the earlier bid prices, or by noting the percentage difference between one's own price and the simultaneous bid of the competitor on the occasion of each previous tender. The assumption implicit in these methods should be obvious: to throw light on just one of them, the latter procedure can result in misleading figures if one's own mark-up has not been invariant, but this can be remedied by reference to one's direct cost figures instead of the bid prices. It might also be necessary to standardize the bid prices by eliminating the effects of quantity rebates and surcharges.[18]

In this way we shall arrive at the bidding pattern of each of the known competitors. Experience has shown that the patterns are likely to be in a shape such as that indicated in Figure AI.13, which is based on the data in the accompanying table.

---

[17] The contribution concerned should be carefully selected, paying full attention to the variants listed and discussed in Chapter 6, page 94.

[18] As said above, we have assumed that the tenders were invited for the supply of an undifferentiated industrial product. If they had been called in for the execution of some project (such as, for example, construction work), the size of the job would also have to be taken into consideration.

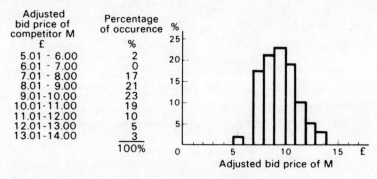

Adjusted bid price of competitor M £	Percentage of occurence %
5.01 - 6.00	2
6.01 - 7.00	0
7.01 - 8.00	17
8.01 - 9.00	21
9.01 -10.00	23
10.01-11.00	19
11.01-12.00	10
12.01-13.00	5
13.01-14.00	3
	100%

Figure AI.13   Distribution of adjusted bid price

A further adjustment may be necessary if there appears a shift in a competitor's bidding policy. For example, it may be found that Company M has been getting increasingly aggressive in recent times.

In the presence of such information and if we also know which of the potential competitors are to submit bids, the probability of winning the contract with a given price can be calculated. Let us assume that M is the only competitor, then on the assumption that the table in Figure AI.13 is a good estimate of his bidding pattern, we can infer that the probability of his bid being higher than £10,000, say, is

$$0.19 + 0.10 + 0.05 + 0.03 = 0.37 \text{ or } 37 \text{ per cent.}$$

Figure AI.14 illustrates the observed relationship between the frequency of M's bid at various prices and our mark-up. The total area under the curve is equal to unity and the shaded area represents the probability of M's bid price being higher than ours and hence the probability of our firm winning the contract at a mark-up of U per cent. The actual shape of the curve may, of course, be different from the one shown in Figure AI.14, both in shape and in symmetry.

The analysis can take account of more than one competitor. What really matters is the lowest bid, and the higher the number of bidders, the greater is the chance of a bid being submitted from the lower part of the range. Statistical procedures can evaluate the probability of any particular mark-up winning the contract, and the general experience is that, provided the data are appropriate, the computer will produce significantly more successful bid prices than

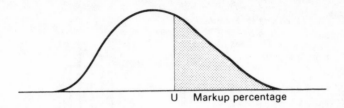

Figure AI.14   Probability of mark-up percentage gaining order

the intuition of the pricing executive. However, it is very important that the pricing executive should have full understanding of any limitations of the data and of the assumptions incorporated in the analysis, and not leave the decision entirely to the computer if he is aware that some important aspect of the situation has been neglected. For example, the mathematical method might correctly indicate the bid price that may be expected to maximize profits, but has not taken any account of the immediate loss that would result if the contract were lost.

Clearly, it will make a great difference to the approach whether the company regularly submits bids for large numbers of individually small contracts or only infrequent bids for large contracts.

Conclusions

A number of forecasting methods has been described. Only a few comparisons have been made, but they should suffice to demonstrate that no one method can be guaranteed to be 'best' for all problems. Indeed, it may be first necessary for the forecaster to decide whether he wants to forecast the *level* of prices as accurately as possible, or whether he wants to forecast the *direction* of price movements or even *when* the present direction will change.

We have indicated how the so-called Bayesian method can be applied to the revision of the price of an existing product, and that the same method may also be used in connection with the pricing of a new brand. It was emphasized that the composite payoff figures should be looked upon as aids to the price setter rather than as indicators of the actual decision to be taken, because however carefully the calculation is carried out, it is unlikely that the results have taken all the facts of the situation into account. All the same, the formalized procedure has general advantages over the informal

approach: it will impose a discipline on the argumentation and lead
to improved decisions.

Finally, this Appendix has also dealt with the problem of closed
competitive bidding. Modern methods of not inconsiderable
complexity are now available to reduce the uncertainty of the
outcome to the individual bidder. It was explained in what way
data arising out of previous experience can be used to find the bid
price that is most likely to be in line with the objectives of the firm.
The method itself is capable of substantial variation and can be
adapted to fit a wide variety of circumstances.

References

R. L. Ackoff and M. W. Sasieni, *Fundamentals of Operations Research*, John
Wiley & Sons, New York, 1968.

G. A. Barnard, 'New Methods of Quality Control', *Journal of the Royal
Statistical Society, Series A*, **126**, (2), 1963, pp. 255–8.

M. J. Beckman, 'A Note on Cost Estimation and the Optimal Bidding
Strategy', *Operations Research*, **22**, May–June 1974, pp. 510–13.

D. Bunn and H. Thomas, 'A Decision Analysis Approach for Unique
Situation Competitive Bidding', *European Journal of Marketing*, **10**, (3),
1976, pp. 169–75.

F. J. Curtis and P. W. Maines, 'Closed Competitive Bidding', *OMEGA, the
International Journal of Management Science*, **1**, (5), 1973, pp. 613–19.

G. Day (guest editor), 'Product Life Cycle' (9 articles), *Journal of Marketing*,
45, (4), Fall 1981, pp. 60–132.

H. Edelman, 'Art and Science of Competitive Bidding', *Harvard Business
Review*, **43**, (4), July/August 1965, pp. 53–66.

Joel R. Evans (ed.), *Product Life Cycles in the Automobile, Food and Proprietary
Drug Industries: Evolution, Description and Analysis*, Hofstra University,
Hempstead, NY, 1983.

J. F. Freund, *Statistics – A First Course*, Prentice-Hall, Englewood Cliffs, NJ,
1970.

L. Friedman, 'A Competitive Bidding Strategy', *Operations Research*, **4**, 1956,
pp. 104–12.

M. Gates, 'Bidding Strategies and Probabilities', *ASCE Construction Division
Journal*, **93**, (CO1), 1967.

P. E. Green, 'Bayesian Decision Theory in Pricing Strategy', *Journal of
Marketing*, **27**, (1), January 1963, pp. 5–14.

F. Haussman and B. H. P. Rivett, 'Competitive Bidding', *Operations Research
Quarterly*, **10**, 1959, pp. 49 & ff.

J. Hirschleifer, 'The Bayesian Approach to Statistical Decision – An
Exposition', *Journal of Business*, **34**, October 1961, pp. 471–89.

G. Lancaster and I. Wesenbund, 'A Product Life Cycle Theory for
International Trade: An Empirical Investigation', *European Journal of
Marketing*, **18**, (6/7), 1984, pp. 72–89.

A. Meenaghan and P. W. Turnbull, 'The Application of Product Life Cycle Theory to Popular Record Marketing', *European Journal of Marketing*, **15**, (5), 1981, pp. 1–50.

A. Mercer and J. I. T. Russell, 'Recurrent Competitive Bidding', *Operations Research Quarterly*, **20**, 1969, pp. 209–21.

K. B. Monroe, *Pricing: Making Profitable Decisions*, McGraw-Hill, New York, 1979, pp. 227–36.

S. Paranka, 'Competitive Bidding Strategy', *Business Horizons*, June 1971, pp. 39–43.

H. Raiffa, *Decision Analysis*, Addison-Wesley, Reading, 1968.

R. Schleifer, *Probability and Statistics for Business Decisions*, McGraw-Hill Book Co., New York, 1959.

R. W. Shoemaker, 'Comment on (H. Simon), "Dynamics of Price Elasticity and Brand Life Cycles: An Empirical Study"', *Journal of Marketing Research*, **23**, (1), February 1986, pp. 78–82.

K. Simmonds and S. Slater, 'The Number of Estimators: A Critical Decision for Marketing Under Competitive Bidding', *Journal of Marketing Research*, **15**, (2), May 1978, pp. 203–13.

H. Simon, 'Dynamics of Price Elasticity and Brand Life Cycles: An Empirical Study', *Journal of Marketing Research*, **16**, (4), November 1979, pp. 439–52.

M. J. Thomas, 'International Product Life Cycles and the International Automobile Industry', *European Journal of Marketing*, **15**, (3), 1981, pp. 41–59.

B. Wernerfelt, 'The Dynamics of Prices and Market Shares over the Product Life Cycle', *Management Science*, **31**, August 1985, pp. 928–39.

J. D. Whitaker, *A Study of Competitive Bidding with Particular Reference to the Construction Industry*, Ph.D. thesis, City University, London, 1970.

L. Winer, 'A Profit-Oriented Decision System', *Journal of Marketing*, **30**, April 1960, pp. 40–42.

D. Wood, 'A Decision System for Competitive Bidding', *European Journal of Marketing*, **5**, (4), 1971, pp. 168–77.

Part II
PRICE AND CONSUMER BEHAVIOUR

OVERVIEW

So far we have approached the problems of pricing by surveying the current practices of business firms and subjecting them to a critical examination. Repeated reference was made to the fact that costs alone cannot justify the price, that whether a price is effective or not depends on the view taken by the final customer, but while it was emphasized that pricing should always be market-oriented and that the activities of the competitors matter only to the extent to which they influence the purchasing behaviour of the consumer, no analysis of his attitude to price and his market behaviour was presented.

These topics will be discussed in the last four chapters of this book and in the Appendices to Part II. We shall start by examining the relevant fundamental features of the consumer's psychology and then proceed to the methods by which it can be explored so as to yield results of direct reference to the effective pricing of both new and established products.

The Analytical Appendix by C. W. J. Granger presents the theory of the buy–response curve, models of multi-brand markets and the statistical aspects of consumer surveys, while the Appendix on Conjoint Measurement, contributed by Trevor Watkins, contains a detailed exposition of a method particularly suited to assist product development.

It seems appropriate to state in advance that contrary to a widespread belief, the available evidence suggests that the consumer's attitude to price and his (or her) market behaviour are essentially rational, in the sense that they are consistent with the striving for the satisfaction of the individual's desires. In the words of one of the founders of modern consumer research:

> The very simple and obvious fact to keep in mind is that products are bought to satisfy human needs, felt or latent. And without a true evaluation of the needs of a given individual (as perceived by the individual himself), it is unfair and inaccurate to describe the purchase of a product or service as 'irrational', 'emotional', or 'impulsive'. Perhaps such a purchase, judged by the critic's standards, might be regarded as imprudent or unwise. But without knowing the buyer's own needs, there is no basis for denigrating him or his buying decision.
> (George Gallup, 'How Advertising Works', *Journal of Advertising Research*, **14**, (3), June 1974, p. 10.)

10   Foundations of customer-oriented pricing

It cannot be too strongly emphasized that the deciding factor in price fixing is the price which the consumer is willing, or can be induced, to pay.

(R. Edwards (quoting the chief accountant of a pottery firm), The Pricing of Manufactured Products', *Economica* (NS), **12**, 1945, p. 304.)

The just price

The idea that there is such a thing as the just price is of very ancient origin. It is many centuries older than the proposition that the proper price of any good or service is that which emerges in a competitive market untrammelled either by monopolies or state regulations.

Until the early years of the nineteenth century the just price was a legal concept in Britain, insofar as the price of bread and the wages of labourers were determined by annual assizes. Subsequently it fell into oblivion until, over a century later, it emerged as the foundation of the rationale of the commissions and other agencies set up by successive governments and charged with the curbing of monopolistic practices.[1] The approach of these bodies to the determination of the just price is pragmatic. Their criteria are inevitably arbitrary

---

[1] Some restrictions on public utility pricing were imposed at earlier dates, but the first general measure was the establishment of the Monopolies Commission in 1948. In the USA, the Sherman Antitrust Act of 1890 marked the beginning of what is popularly described as trust-busting. In both countries the subject has given rise to large numbers of specialized books and articles.

and generally arise in the form of (1) a classification of business expenditure into two categories: those which they allow to be charged as costs and those which they consider unnecessary, (such as, for example, excessive advertising expenditure), and (2) a maximum rate of profit which they deem reasonable. Considerable variations of these criteria can be observed, both between different bodies and over time.

While the concept of the just price eludes precise definition, it is undoubtedly a reality of the psychology of the consumer. How fundamental it is, is well reflected in a passage quoted below in full from 'The Economic Organization of a Prisoner of War Camp', by R. A. Radford:

> There was a strong feeling that everything had its just price in cigarettes. While the assessment of the just price, which incidentally varied between camps, was impossible of explanation, this price was nevertheless pretty closely known. It can best be defined as the price usually fetched by an article in good times when cigarettes are plentiful. The just price changed slowly; it was unaffected by short-term variations in supply, and while opinion might be resigned to departures from the just price, a strong feeling of resentment persisted. A more satisfactory definition of the just price is impossible. Everyone knew what it was, though no one could explain why it should be so.
> (Reprinted with permission from *Economica*, **12**, 1945, pp. 199–200.)

It is worth noting that this clear emergence of the ancient concept of the just price took place in a situation where production costs were completely absent, since all the goods concerned arrived in Red Cross parcels. Historical evidence and experience suggest that the main implication of this remarkable instance remains true also under more normal conditions, in the sense that, though seldom discussed, the concept of a just level of prices, that is, what things *ought to cost*, is permanently present in the minds of most consumers. It is largely independent of the cost of production, which is generally unknown to the consumer, and may vary considerably from place to place and with the passage of time.

Prices which have not changed for some years are more likely to be accepted as just than those which have recently undergone a rise or a fall, but stability alone does not seem to be sufficient to place a price in this category, especially if it is known that the same article is less expensive elsewhere. It can, of course, be the other way round, for example, a British traveller may well feel moral indignation at the sight of cheap liquor in a country where drunkenness is rife.

The concept becomes most definite when it is effectively imposed from above: during World War Two nobody in Britain doubted that the controlled prices of all the rationed foods were *the* just prices.

Confirmation of the presence of the just price in the consumer's mind is also provided by the work of Cooper.[2] His results help us to understand the role played by the just price in purchasing decisions: the consumer judges the prices of different goods and services by comparing them, more or less subconsciously, with some standard which may not, of course, be the same for all persons. The attitudes of people living in the same community do, however, tend to be similar.

Even though Cooper expressed his findings in somewhat different terms, it is clear that the price below which a purchase would be considered a bargain is identical with the individual's subjective idea of the just price.

This brings us to an important point: a price need not be 'just' to be effective from the seller's point of view. People will spend their money both on goods and services which they consider a bargain, and on those which they believe to be overpriced, although, as will be shown in Chapter 11, potential customers may be repelled by prices that are too low in their estimation.

Price consciousness

The assumption that underlies every expression of the behaviour of market demand is that, all other things being equal, price plays a decisive role in the determination of the rate of purchases of the customers.

For this to be true, the customers must have an appropriate degree of price consciousness, the first condition of which is familiarity with the current prices of the goods and services which compete for their expenditure.

The actual knowledge of the relevant prices may not, however, be permanent even in the case of a highly price-conscious individual. For example, the decision to acquire a major consumer durable is generally preceded by some search activity, in the course of which the potential customer will endeavour to gather information about the relevant properties of the various brands and about the prices

---

[2] Peter Cooper, 'Subjective Economics: Factors in the Psychology of Spending', *Research in Marketing*, 1964, pp. 120–33; reprinted in *Pricing Strategy*, (B. Taylor and G. Wills, eds), Staples, London, 1969, pp. 112–21.

quoted by the sellers. While price may play an important part in the actual choice, unless the item acquired turns out to be unsatisfactory, the customer's concern with the price will tend to vanish soon after the purchase and revive only when the time comes round to look for another similar item, either as a replacement or as an addition to his stock. In most cases the price last paid, even if well remembered, will have little, if any, relevance to the purchasing decision concerning a consumer durable because, even if inflation has not meanwhile affected the general level of prices, fashion and technical progress have almost certainly resulted in considerable alterations in the properties of the available types. And there is also the point that the customer himself only exceptionally wants the new item to be identical with the one to be replaced or supplemented.

Hence in the case of durables and certain other transactions involving substantial expenditure, as for example, package holidays, familiarity with the prices concerned will be of a temporary or intermittent character, and must be expected to vary between individuals even around the time of a purchase. The experience of sales organizations operating hire purchase and other instalment schemes also implies that many of their prospective customers fix their attention on the required down payment and on the amount which they have to surrender periodically rather than on the number of instalments, and to an even lesser extent on the total cost of the acquisition which, in the case of a rented appliance, will anyway be indefinite.

The instances mentioned are not the only ones where prices may fade into the background. Some individuals find it difficult to resist a bargain; if they see something attractive at a price which implies to them a genuine reduction, they are strongly tempted to buy it without full regard to the actual cost (and, it is alleged, sometimes without any knowledge of the article purchased). Then, there are certain situations in which most people feel that it would be inelegant if not invidious to reveal that money is a consideration with them; consequently they will not ask for the price until after they have declared that they will buy the article in question. Even if kind is not necessarily irrational, it must be conceded that there are certain transactions in respect of which the cost of acquistion is not an important determinant of the consumer's decision.
certain transactions in respects of which the cost of acquistion is not an important determinant of the consumer's decision.

Permanent price consciousness may, however, be expected to be present in the case of regularly recurrent purchases, especially those which the housewife makes at brief intervals. Food and certain other necessities like soap are the main items in this category.

Knowledge of the extent of the price consciousness of his actual and potential customers should be of considerable interest to the price setter, since it is obvious that the more attention they pay to price, the greater will be its importance in the marketing mix. Furthermore, price consciousness can also reveal the identity of the competition – it has been found in seveal enquiries that it is not by any means invariably the brand with physical properties and price nearest to one's own product.

While it is not possible to measure price consciousness directly, *price recall*, that is to say, the extent to which the price of the last purchase of the good is remembered, is a legitimate first measure of it.

The measurement of price recall

The report on the 1958 Nottingham survey is both the earliest and the most detailed source of data obtained by a systematic enquiry into price recall.[3] In this study, 428 housewives were visited in their homes and answered questions on a total of 5,276 purchases of 15 commodities. They were asked in respect of each if they had bought it within the last week, and, if the answer was in the affirmative, they were further questioned about the brand or type of the commodity, the quantity bought and the price paid. Table 10.1 shows the analysis of the results by socio-economic group.

Price consciousness, measured by the percentages of prices named irrespective of whether they were correct or not, is shown here to be inversely correlated with social status. And, since family income and social status are certainly directly correlated, we may say that as income falls, concern with prices rises. This was not, of course, an unexpected result, except insofar as the rule appears to be valid only if the poor are excluded. They seem to be less concerned with prices than those in Group D, perhaps because they look upon their small purchases as necessities without any near substitutes. It is, however, also possible that the relatively low rate of recall of Group E was due to the fact that it consisted largely of old people, whose memory is often rather poor.

---

[3] André Gabor and C. W. J. Granger, 'On the Price Consciousness of Consumers', *Applied Statistics*, **10**, (3), 1961, pp. 170–88.

Table 10.1
Results of price recall study by socio-economic group

Socio-economic group	%	Number of purchases	Per cent of prices named
A: The well-to-do	2	120	63.3
B: The professional middle class	7	363	66.4
C: The lower middle class	27	1,523	80.8
D: The working class	55	2,895	85.5
E: The poor	9	375	80.3
All groups	100	5,276	82.0

Table 10.2 shows the distribution of price consciousness by commodity. They are listed in descending order of the percentages of prices named.

There are several interesting features about this distribution. The first is the wide dispersion of the percentages of prices named,

Table 10.2
Distribution of price recall by commodity

Commodity	Number of purchases	Per cent of prices named
Tea	376	94.7
Eggs	407	93.4
Sausages	281	90.7
Margarine	264	89.0
Potatoes	379	88.7
Coffee	170	88.2
Bacon	360	84.2
Butter	406	83.7
Jam and marmalade	248	82.3
Cheese	361	80.1
Washing powders and detergents	522	78.9
Sugar	425	78.1
Soap	329	72.6
Breakfast cereal	343	70.0
Flour	405	62.7
All commodities	5,276	82.0

ranging from almost 95 per cent for tea down to under 63 per cent for flour. One would expect to find some direct correlation between the frequency of purchase and price recall, but there is no evidence of it in these data.

The second point to note is the relatively high concentration of branded goods in the lower part of the range, while tea is at the very top. This may well have been due to the fact that, at the time, tea was almost invariably pre-packed in quarter-pound packs, (tea bags were hardly known), and there is also the relatively high brand loyalty of the tea drinkers. In the case of most of the other branded goods in the list, brand loyalty tends to be replaced by brand acceptance, extended to more than one brand, pack sizes tend to vary considerably and are also much less likely to be identified by the price than tea.

Price recall with regard to tea, coffee, sugar and flour was investigated by the author and his research associates also in 1971 and 1984.[4] The results are compared with the 1958 figures in Table 10.3.

Multiple purchases of the same commodity returned by some of the subjects in 1958 are included in Table 10.2 but not in Table 10.3. The elimination of the additional purchases has resulted in a slight upward bias.

The striking features of Table 10.3 are the high values and the similarity of the figures at the three dates, with flour in 1958 as the only exception. There is positive support here for the proposition that the first condition of price-conscious behaviour remains satisfied in the case of frequently purchased items in respect of the majority of shoppers despite variations in the annual rate of inflation which was in the twelve months preceding each survey about 2 per cent in 1958, 8 per cent in 1971 and 4 per cent in 1984, as calculated from grocery prices.

Reports which appear from time to time in the daily press to the effect that most people are not aware of the prices of fast moving consumer goods should be treated with caution. It generally turns

---

[4] Nottingham University Consumer Study Group, *Decimalisation and the Consumer*, Social Science Research Council and University of Nottingham, 1972; John M. Bates and André Gabor, 'Price Perception in Creeping Inflation: Report on an Enquiry', *Journal of Economic Psychology*, **7**, (3), September 1986, pp. 291–314.

Table 10.3
Comparison of the percentages of prices named by shoppers in 1958, 1971 and 1984.

The 1971 figures are the averages of two surveys, held in January and February of that year.

Year	1958	1971	1984
Number of subjects	428	over 2,000	505
Commodity:	%	%	%
Tea	95.0	91.0	90.9
Coffee	90.0	88.4	94.0
Sugar	80.4	86.2	86.8
Flour	64.8	83.4	85.4

out that the people questioned were not asked if they were regular purchasers of the products concerned.

Knowledge of the correct price may serve as a second measure of price consciousness. In 1958 the resale prices set by the manufacturers and largely adhered to by the retailers were used in the checking; a criterion that was probably too strict, yet the percentages of correct prices so obtained were remarkably high, as can be seen in Table 10.4.

By 1984 there was no restriction on pricing at the retail level (except in the case of books). Price competition was widespread, tea and coffee prices which had undergone considerable increases earlier in 1984 were still rising, hence a truly accurate checking was not possible. Prices in the various stores were recorded on one occasion only, and it is highly probable that the tolerances applied should have been wider. Anyway, *prices remembered that are not absolutely accurate can still serve to apportion family expenditure in a way that is at least reasonably near to the optimum.*

As shown in Table 10.1 the 1958 data revealed a marked tendency for the lower classes to name higher proportions of the prices paid. The 1984 results reflected the same tendency. It was also found that at both dates the lower classes tended to recall the prices paid more accurately.

Of the published studies of price recall, those conducted on behalf of an American trade journal in 1963, 1974, 1977 and 1980 deserve

Table 10.4

'Correct' percentages of checked prices in 1958 and 1984

Commodity	1958			1984		
	Number of checked prices	Percentage 'correct'	Tolerance	Number of checked prices	Percentage 'correct'	Tolerance
Tea	339	83.5	Nil	270	52.6	± 10p
Coffee	144	75.7	Nil	215	54.4	± 10p
Sugar	319	83.4	Nil	373	50.4	± 1p
Flour	182	54.9	Nil	234	46.2	± 1p on 0.5 kilo ± 2p on 1.5 kilo

special attention.[5] In the first study, carried out in Colonial Stores, sixty frequently advertised and highly price-competitive branded goods were displayed on tables, and several thousand shoppers were asked to state the price of each item, *irrespective of whether or not they had recently bought it*. The scope of the second study was somewhat smaller but the method was similar: 560 shoppers were questioned about the prices of 44 items in four Fernandes supermarkets in the Boston-Providence area.

Since in all the Nottingham surveys the question about the price of each good was put only to those subjects who said that they had recently purchased it, the results are not truly comparable with those of the American studies. The results of the 1963 and 1974 American surveys can, however, legitimately be compared in respect of the accuracy of the prices of 36 items that were included in both of them.

Table 10.5
'Correct' percentages of checked prices in 1963 and 1974

	Colonial 1963	Fernandes 1974
Percentage of exact prices named of 36 items	20	8
Percentage of prices deviating from the correct price but not by more than 5 per cent	12	16
Total within ± 5 per cent	32	24
Range of prices named	12–91%	7–49%

Some variations in the accuracy of price recall may have been expected, partly because not every item was absolutely identical in the two surveys, (for example, Coca-Cola 6 pk and Camel cigarettes in 1963 were replaced by Coca-Cola 8 pk and Marlboro cigarettes in 1974), and partly because the stores were not the same, but both these factors might have worked either way. Variations in the rate at

---

[5] Anon., 'How Much Do Customers Know About Retail Prices?', *Progressive Grocer*, **43**, February 1964, pp. c104–c106; Walter Heller, 'What Shoppers Know – and Don't Know – About Prices', *ibid*, **53**, November 1974, pp. 39–41; and Jo-Ann Zbytniewski, 'Shoppers Cry "Remember the Price" – But Do They Practice What They Screech?', *ibid*, **59**, November 1980, pp. 119–22. Cf. also Arid Goldman, 'Consumer Knowledge of Food Prices as an Indicator of Shopping Effectiveness', *Journal of Marketing*, **41**, (4), October 1977, pp. 67–75.

Table 10.6
'Correct' price estimates of buyers on eight items covered in both surveys[6]

| | 1977 | 1980 |
	%	%
Domino Sugar	33	31
Del Monte Fruit Cocktail	31	31
Scott Paper Towels	38	29
Campbell's Tomato Soup	27	25
Coca-Cola (Multi-pack)	39	25
Tide XK Detergent	34	25
Clorox Bleach	26	22
Average	31	27

which retail prices were rising appeared to have a marked effect on the accuracy of price recall, and it is possible that the main reason for the decline in price awareness between 1963 and 1974 was the fact that in 1963 consumer prices were rising in the United States at an annual rate of 1.5 per cent only, while the rate was 12.4 per cent by 1974.[7]

As shown in Table 10.6, the 1977 and 1980 *Progressive Grocer* studies permit partial comparison with each other, but not directly with the results of the two earlier enquiries.

A remarkable feature which arises from the results of the British and American studies is the persistence of the ability to recall prices. That the rates of the accurate prices returned were not higher and tended to decline over time is hardly surprising in view of the fact that where the prices are subject to irregular variations overlaid on

---

[6] *Progressive Grocer*, 59, November 1980, p. 122. The percentages are those which were within ± 5 per cent of the actual price at the time of the survey. Note that the subjects were 'buyers' but not necessarily recent purchasers as in the Nottingham studies. 'Overall shoppers are best at remembering prices for ... items that normally don't show wild price fluctuations. The worst levels of price awareness are exhibited for ... products ... frequently on "special" or heavily promoted as loss leaders', ibid, page 120.

[7] The possibility of a contributing factor is implied by the evidence of Table 10.1 on page 239: with the exception of the lowest socio-economic group, price recall appears to be inversely correlated with social status and hence with income. Despite the increase in inflation, there was a rise in the average American household's real income in the eleven years between the two surveys and this might have affected the outcome.

an inflationary trend and are seldom the same between different stores, fully accurate checking is not really possible. It should also be noted that it was found in several enquiries that while the prices of certain fast moving consumer goods could not be recalled by significant proportions of shoppers even if questioned immediately after leaving the store where they purchased them, the price differences simultaneously introduced in the same stores resulted in systematic variations in the sales of the brands concerned. What this implies is that in these instances the role of the reference price was taken over by the price differences between competitive brands.

It is important to realize that *whether the price the potential purchaser recalls is absolutely correct or not, it represents the current price image of the good concerned, and it can be of great importance to the price setter to know how it compares with the actual price, since this is an indicator of the market's response to a price adjustment.*[8]

Whereas, especially at times when prices are rising fast, the price image might lag behind the current price, causing resentment of the price increase, it has also been found in the case of certain brands that the price image of high proportions of the purchasers was *above* the price they had actually paid. The indication then is that, in the eyes of the customers, the current price is below their conception of the just price, that is, it is considered a bargain. It follows that, at least up to a certain limit, a price increase would be unlikely to have an adverse effect on sales.

Since these issues will be further developed in Chapter 11, here we shall only remind the reader that these observations relate to the regular purchasers of the goods concerned. The phenomenon should not therefore be confused with the distorted price images which can arise out of ignorance; thus, for example, a person who has never bought vintage champagne might considerably overestimate its price.

The price image can also play a highly significant role in the choice of the store where a housewife will make the bulk of her regular purchases. It was noted in Chapter 8 (page 176) that the customers may not judge price levels simply by the total cost of their shopping baskets. As we have demonstrated above, their price consciousness, as measured by price recall, varies considerably from one product to another and this variation cannot simply be

---

[8] Cf. Venkatakrishna V. Bellur, 'Consumers' Awareness and Attitude Towards Repricing', *Journal of the Academy of Marketing Science*, **10**, 1982, pp. 125–39.

explained by reference to the frequency of purchase. It is therefore well worth finding out by means of a well designed consumer survey, which are the items by which the price level of a store is in fact being judged by its actual and potential customers.[9] The general principles of retail pricing may be perfectly sound but not by themselves sufficient to enable effective competition to be combined with optimal profitability.

Both the results of an American enquiry and those of an investigation carried out by the Nottingham University Consumer Study Group give strong support to this proposition.[10] The American project covered 27 supermarkets in five cities, over a thousand interviews with housewives and also estimates of the 'real' price level of each store by a weighted index of 80 items. In each city, the subjects were asked to rank the stores, which were at about equal distance from their homes, by their prices. It was found that the validity of the price perceptions, as assessed by comparing the housewives' rankings with the market basket indices, showed extreme variation from almost perfect perception in one community to grossly invalid perceptions in others. This is all the more remarkable as in the United States stores regularly advertise the prices of large numbers of their goods in the local newspapers. The results also showed that housewives can heavily over-estimate the price level of those stores which they do not patronize because of their upper-class image.

The Nottingham enquiry, though conducted in a different way, led to similar conclusions. Both the American and the British studies also embraced other aspects of store preference, but the importance of the price image was evident throughout.

The inference is that store managers who judge the relative price level of their stores in the usual way, by weighting the prices of the

---

[9] The elimination of price labels on individual items where scanners are in use at the check-out points as also unit pricing may well influence the extent of price recall and thereby the price image of the store. Cf. V. Ziethaml, 'Consumer Response to In-Store Information Environment', *Journal of Consumer Research*, **8**, 1981, pp. 357–69; and Brian F. Harris and Michael Mills, 'The Impact of Item Price Removal in Scanner Supermarkets', *Journal of Consumer Affairs*, **16**, Winter 1982, pp. 362–83; also other references listed in note 16, p. 168.

[10] F. E. Brown, 'Price Image Versus Price Reality', *Journal of Marketing Research*, **6**, May 1969, pp. 185–91; and André Gabor and A. P. Sowter, 'The Customers' Views' and 'How Competitive is the Co-op?', *Co-operative Management and Marketing*, December 1970 and January 1971.

main items either by their sales or by some estimate of the normal shopping basket might greatly misjudge the price image of their stores in the eyes of their actual and potential customers.

Summary

Fundamental to the consumer's attitude to price is the ancient concept of the just price, since it serves as a benchmark by which actual prices are judged. However, a price need not be 'just' to be effective from the seller's point of view.

Price consciousness will tend to be intermittent in the case of infrequent items of expenditure, such as, for example, the purchase of consumer durables; also there are certain instances where price generally fades into the background. More permanent price consciousness is found in respect of those items which regularly figure on the consumer's weekly shopping list.

Knowledge of the extent of the price consciousnes of his actual and potential customers can be of great value to the price setter. On the one hand, the degree of awareness of the public of the price of his product will indicate to him what emphasis he should put on price in his marketing mix, and, on the other hand, differences in the degree of awareness of the prices of other brands can reveal which of them are considered by the consumers to be close substitutes for his own product.

Price consciousness cannot be directly measured, but the ability to name the price of the last purchase may legitimately be regarded as its first measure, and the accuracy of the prices named its second measure.

Price recall appears to be inversely correlated with social status, and shows great variations between different commodities. The same applies to the ability to name the correct price.

When prices are stable or rise only very slowly, price recall will be very much higher than in heavily inflationary situations. However, price competition between items which can readily be substituted for one another may remain very keen too in inflationary periods, price consciousness manifesting itself by comparing prices at the point of purchase. The price paid might then be soon forgotten since it has little relevance to the next purchase, but a price image may still be present. Its study can reveal whether the current price is resented by the customers or considered a bargain.

The study of the price image may also be of great importance to pricing at the retail level, since the available evidence shows that the management's view may not be shared by the majority of the actual and potential customers. The reason for such discrepancies is that there appears to be no close correlation between the rates of purchase and the significance attached by the customers to the prices of different products.

References

Peter E. Bennett and Howell H. Kassarjian, *Consumer Behavior*, Prentice-Hall, Inc., Englewood Cliffs, NJ, 1972.

F. E. Brown, 'Price Perception and Store Patronage', *Proceedings of AMA Conference, Fall 1976*, American Management Association, New York, 1976.

Donald F. Cox, 'The Sorting Rule Model of the Consumer's Product Evaluation Process', *Risk Taking and Information Handling in Consumer Behavior*, (Donald F. Cox, ed), Harvard University, Boston, Mass., 1967, pp. 324–369.

Ben M. Enis and James E. Stafford, 'Consumers' Perceptions of Product Quality as a Function of Various Informational Inputs', *Proceedings of AMA Conference, Fall 1976*, American Management Association, New York, 1976.

John A. Howard and Jagdish N. Sheth, *The Theory of Buyer Behavior*, John Wiley & Sons Inc., New York, 1969.

K. B. Monroe, 'The Information Content on Prices: A Preliminary Model for Estimating Buyer Response', *Mangement Science*, **17**, No. 8, April 1971, p. B519 & ff.

Thomas S. Robertson, Joan Zielinski and Scott Ward, *Consumer Behavior*, Scott, Foreman & Co., Glenview, IL, 1984.

E. A. Smith and C. L. Broome, 'Experimental Determination of Effect of Price and Market Standing Information on Consumers' Brand Preferences', *Proceedings of AMA Conference, Fall 1966*, American Management Association, New York, 1966.

L. F. Stephens and R. L. Monroe, 'Price Accuracy as a Consumer Skill', *Journal of Advertising Research*, August 1975, pp. 27–34.

I. Visco, *Price Expectations in Rising Inflation*, North Holland, Amsterdam, 1984.

William D. Wells and Harold H. Kassarjian, *Consumer Behavior*, Prentice-Hall, Inc., Englewood Cliffs, NJ, 1972.

11   Price as a quality indicator

Manufacturers have long been aware of the fact that it is only exceptionally possible to improve the quality of a product without a concurrent increase in its cost of production, and several odd instances have been reported where an increase in price had a definite promotional effect on sales. There was, for example, the case of the car wax which met with strong consumer resistance as long as its price was 69 cents, but started to sell well as soon as it was raised to $1.69. Another case was that of the fountain pen ink, the price of which was successfully increased from 15 cents to 25 cents per bottle after the results of marketing experiments indicated that the higher price was likely to lead to an expansion of the volume of sales, both absolutely and relatively to competitors.

Note that in both cases the article concerned was a relatively inexpensive complement bought for use in conjunction with a comparatively expensive device. In such instances the cost of the complement (or component) has little if any effect on the rate of consumption which is determined by other considerations, and introspection suggests that when the consumer cannot himself judge the quality, he will often prefer the brand with the higher price. The reasons for such an attitude need not be the same in every case, and any formulation of them elicited by straightforward questioning or motivational research may merely be the *ex post* rationalization of an attitude taken without conscious deliberation. But whether the preference for the higher priced brand arose because of a feeling that it would be foolish to risk the performance or condition of the expensive device for a relatively small monetary saving or, perhaps, because of some such thought as 'my fountain pen may not be the best, but I can afford the luxury of the finest ink', there is a common factor which is simply the conviction that higher price means superior quality.[1]

The recorded instances of the promotional effect of the higher price are not all of this type. What we have in mind here is not so much the old anecdote about the man who won his wager because nobody was prepared to buy from him golden sovereigns at half a crown apiece, since the circumstances in which the offer was made were calculated to arouse suspicion, as rather the case of gin, which was not considered a gentlemanly drink and even less a ladylike one until successive increases of the excise duty brought its price closer to that of whisky and other, formerly more expensive, alcoholic beverages.[2] However, the clear recognition that the role of price as a quality indicator can systematically be used as a guide to pricing decisions is of relatively recent origin.

Before we go any further, let us note that the quality image of a product is, of course, also influenced by other elements of the marketing mix. The reputation of the manufacturer and/or the seller, brand name, package, advertising, persuasion by a salesperson, (to say nothing of personal experience and the opinion of friends), can all affect the quality image. (Cf. Huber et al., 1986.) These factors will not be discussed further; what will be shown in this chapter and the next two is how the relationship between price and quality perception can be explored and put to use in marketing.

A historical note

It is of some interest to trace the transformation of the traditional lore, which assumed that the price of an article had no meaning to

---

[1] This belief may not be held by every potential customer, and even if it is, the restraint imposed by income limitation could prevent significant proportions of individuals from acting in accordance with it. The marketing policy designed to deal with this kind of situation has long been practised by certain manufacturers, who sell what is the same product with regard to testable performance under different brand names (or partly unbranded) at different prices.

[2] A similar development has taken place in the soft drink market, originally dominated by Coca-Cola. Pepsi-Cola was launched in 1898, only twelve years later than Coca-Cola, but Pepsi remained a distant second to Coke for nearly half a century. Not until the 1950s, when Pepsi switched its ad campaign from stressing price ('twice as much for a nickel') to emphasizing life-style ('The Sociables'), did it becomes a real contender. (Time, **125**, (18), 6 May, 1985, p. 31.)

the purchaser other than the cost of acquisition, to the modern view of consumer behaviour. The latter is by far the more realistic of the two, insofar as *it takes full account of the fact that price can act as a powerful indicator of quality and may remain an important attribute of the article also after the purchase.*

The traditional view was based on the proposition that, for any given good, a low price must be more attractive to the consumer than a high price, and that any exception to this so-called law of normal demand must be due either to certain anomalous circumstances that can arise only at the two extremes of the social scale, or simply to ignorance on the part of the consumer.[3]

The classical examples of these anomalies are known as the Giffen case and Veblen's 'conspicuous consumption'.

About a century ago Sir Robert Giffen observed that when the cheapest staple food of the very poor increased in price, they were apt to buy more of it. The explanation is that when, owing to the high price, the quantity which poor people consider indispensable claims the bulk of their income, the little that is left over could not be more beneficially spent on anything else.[4]

Somewhat later the highly original American economist and social philosopher Thorstein Veblen (1899) argued that the purpose of considerable proportions of the expenditure of the idle rich is to impress others rather than to satisfy their own needs, and that for this reason the rich will show preference for goods that are known to be expensive.

Subsequently, the case of diamonds, the attractiveness of which as a store of value derives from their high price, became yet another stock example of the allegedly rare exceptions to the law of demand. The promotional effect of a high price remained to be treated as a more or less anomalous phenomenon also in marketing literature as late as 1951 when Joel Dean reported on the experience of some far-sighted manufacturers who, realizing the inadequacies of both cost-based pricing and the policy of matching their nearest competitor's price, turned to experimental marketing in their quest for the most advantageous price. Even though Dean noted that the

---

[3] This view is still embodied in all the currently used text-books of price theory, even though it has been shown that it can be appropriately extended, albeit at the expense of simplicity. Cf. Kalman (1968).

[4] Recorded in Alfred Marshall, *Principles of Economics*, Macmillan, London, 1890, p. 32. The original source of Giffen's observation has never been discovered.

right price was not invariably found to be the lowest one used in the experiment, and, in another chapter, advocated market-oriented pricing for new products,[5] there is no explicit recognition in his otherwise excellent book of the role of price as a quality indicator. This is hardly surprising as, writing a few years later, H. J. Leavitt, Professor of Psychology in the University of Chicago, was fully justified in stating that 'there has been no published research *directly* concerned with the consumer's interpretation of price' (1954, p. 37). He himself conducted a few small-scale experiments with thirty Air Force officers and an equal number of graduate students by facing them with hypothetical choice situations. The products concerned were not luxury articles but ordinary household items, with prices not exceeding one dollar. The results suggested to Leavitt – quite correctly, as we now know – that price has more than one meaning to the consumer, and that a high price may increase rather than decrease the sales of ordinary repeat purchase or convenience goods.

Neither Leavitt's minute experiment nor its slightly modified repetition by Tull (1964) has led to any practical developments as far as pricing is concerned. Meanwhile, working along similar lines but independently of Leavitt and Tull, Pessemier (1960, 1963) used simulated shopping trips to study consumer behaviour, including brand switching in response to price changes. He effectively demonstrated the fact that, in a multi-brand market, the price elasticity of demand depends heavily on the size and direction of the price change, and thus his results support the point made above in Chapter 2, page 18 concerning the nugatory practical significance of the elasticity concept. An application of one of the techniques advocated by him has been reported by Jones (1975), albeit without any reference to Pessemier's work.

Some observations of the effect of price on the perception of quality have been recorded here and there, for example:

> Shortly after World War II one radio manufacturer reduced the price of a new model which had not sold well – probably because the price had been set too high. Contrary to expectations, sales declined even more after the price reduction ... it was found that one type of lamp was sold more readily at a medium price than at a low price ... In other words, we have the possibility of a backward sloping individual demand curve ... This curve has frequently been described for products in respect to which the

---

[5] Joel Dean, *Managerial Economics*, Prentice-Hall, Englewood Cliffs, NJ, 1951, pp. 180–82 and 418–27.

consumers have difficulty in judging the quality. Dresses, wine, detergents, cosmetics and pharmaceutical products are examples of such products.
(B. Fog, *Industrial Pricing Policies*, North Holland Publishing Company, Amsterdam, 1960, pp. 45–6.)

The most important development came from an unexpected quarter, and this must be the reason why it escaped the attention of so many marketing experts and research workers. It was Jean Stoetzel, Professor of Social Psychology at the Sorbonne (1954), who initiated the most original and fruitful approach to the study of price and consumer behaviour. His work was further developed in France by Adam (1958) and Fouilhé (1960), and in Britain by the Nottingham University Consumer Study Group. (Cf. Gabor and Granger 1964, 1965, 1966, 1967; Gabor 1973; also Nottingham 1972.)

Stoetzel's idea represents a radical departure from the traditional theory of demand, which is based on the assumption of complete knowledge on the part of the consumer. It also avoids the other extreme view, according to which the consumer will use price as a quality indicator only if he is completely ignorant of the properties of the items offered to him. He will then plump for the most expensive alternative, whereas he might be better advised to choose the cheapest.[6]

The reason why the customer may eschew a low-priced item in favour of a more expensive alternative can be the Veblen principle, that is to say the desire to impress others, but it could hardly be described as the motive most frequently found behind such behaviour. In most cases the rejection of the cheaper item will be the result of risk avoidance, the risk being that the cheaper item will not give appropriate satisfaction. Especially in the case of frequently purchased convenience goods, the perception of this risk will be an expression of the customer's experience rather than of his ignorance. The recent advertisement of a Belgian lager sold in Britain was clearly based on this relationship: it stressed that Stella Artois was 'reassuringly expensive'.

It could not be denied that there are certain cases where the quality differences perceived by the consumers do not tally with

---

[6] An earlier writer, sensing danger in price as a quality indicator to the public, forcibly argued that the layman will be safely guided by the price only if he is buying in a market dominated by experts. Cf. Scitovszky, (1944–5).

those of the experts. This applies particularly to pharmaceuticals: for example, Maynes and Assum (1982, p. 71) observed that aspirin was on sale in an American town at a variety of prices, the highest of which was 408 per cent of that of the lowest, and Lall (1978, p. 19) noted that tetracycline was available at a price 30 to 50 per cent less than those of the brands of some major firms and 90 per cent below the price of Pfizer's oxytetracycline. However, having bought the most expensive brand will not only give the purchaser the satisfaction of having obtained 'the best that money could buy', but may also well produce a better result than a cheaper variety. It is an established fact that the belief in the power of a medicine can considerably enhance its effect. A similar case is that of cosmetics: the confidence an expensive product gives to the user may well help to make her (or him) more attractive to the opposite sex.

In most other fields the consumers are good judges of quality. The findings of de Buijzer and Stapel (1978, p. 58) are typical: they report that 'price difference attitudes are closely related to quality evaluations', also that 'only 5 per cent of all respondents actually meant what they said when they claimed that quality should not cause price differences'.

Foundations of the limit concept

The new approach is based on the proposition, now firmly established, that each potential purchaser of a given product enters the market with two price limits in mind: an upper limit beyond which he would find the item too expensive, and a lower limit below which he would suspect the quality. Thus outside these limits price acts as a primary barrier to purchase. This does not necessarily mean that items with prices above the upper limit would have no utility for the consumer: he might well prefer a tailor-made suit to the cheaper ready-to-wear article, yet decide to buy the latter, simply because he feels that the difference between the two prices could be better devoted to some other purpose. He might also accept as a gift and make good use of an item the price of which is known to him to fall below his own lower limit, but if he were to purchase one himself, he would rather pay more in order to obtain what he believes to be better value for money.

It is not suggested that the potential customer will buy any item as long as its price falls between his limits, but only that within this range price will not act as an absolute barrier to purchase. It will still act as a quality indicator, especially in the case of a brand with which the customer had no previous experience but, as will be shown presently, it also affects his judgement of known brands.[7]

The existence of these limits is supported by introspection and has been firmly established by the results of a number of large-scale investigations. They can be determined by questioning a representative sample of subjects, all of whom should be regular or occasional purchasers of the good concerned.

The principal questions are of this type:

- 'If you wanted to buy a tin of soup sufficient for two helpings, and saw what you were looking for, which is the highest price you would be prepared to pay?'
- 'Which is the lowest price at which you would still buy – I mean the price below which you would not trust the quality?'

If the group is reasonably homogeneous, such as, for example, housewives in the same broad area, the price limits named by them will be similar but not identical. A certain scatter must be expected, owing to differences in socio-economic status, income, age, education, taste, habit, etc., each of which may cause deviations from the average in either direction.

From the two limits stated by each subject we can derive the proportions of the sample who are potential customers at each price. The actual procedure, which will be demonstrated by a numerical example, is easily performed with the aid of a computer.

Let us assume, for simplicity, that all the prices named by the subjects as upper or lower limits are covered by the price range 10p to 16p, and that the data are as listed in Table 11.1.

The last column of the table, showing the percentage of potential customers, was obtained by subtracting from the (L) percentage the (H) percentage of the price *below it*. Thus, taking the price of 14p as an example, the percentage of those for whom neither this price nor any of those above it was too low is 99, the percentage of those for whom this price or some price below it was too high is 38, and $99 - 38 = 61$. The reason why this procedure had to be followed is that questions of the type illustrated above elicit the limits at which the subjects would still buy. While it would not be inconceivable to formulate the questions so that the answers should yield the lowest price that is already too high and the highest price still considered

---

[7] An effective method by which brand preference and brand loyalty can be determined is described in Chapter 13.

Table 11.1
Calculation of the percentages of potential customers

Price	Percentage who named it as upper limit	(H) Cumulative percentage	Percentage who named it as lower limit	(L) Cumulative percentage	Percentage of potential customers
9p	0	0	0	0	0
10p	0	0	5	5	5
11p	0	0	18	23	23
12p	7	7	43	66	66
13p	31	38	21	87	80
14p	44	82	12	99	61
15p	16	98	1	100	18
16p	2	100	0	100	2
17p	0	100	0	100	0

Table 11.2
Frequency distribution of the price-last-paid percentages

Price	Percentage reporting price-last-paid
9p	0
10p	0
11p	18
12p	14
13p	37
14p	25
15p	5
16p	1
17p	0
	100%

too low, this is not recommended since it would make the questions rather cumbersome and difficult to understand.

After the questions about the limits, the subjects may also be asked to state the price paid for the last purchase of the good concerned. Eliminating those who were unable to answer this question,[8] we shall obtain a distribution like the one shown in Table 11.2.

The related significance of the results can best be appreciated by looking at the diagram in Figure 11.1 which shows the percentages of potential customers and the price-last-paid distribution in juxtaposition.

The curve of potential customers is not a demand curve, but may be interpreted as indicating the probability of purchase by the average customer and, in combination with the price-last-paid curve, it reveals the existence of any discrepancy between the present state of the market and the immediate possibilities which it offers.

The diagram enables the individual manufacturer to locate the position of his own brand and to identify his competition. For example, the diagram in Figure 11.1 shows that the brand or brands marketed at 12p do not enjoy their potential share, and if one's own brand falls into this category, the next logical step is to determine

---

[8] Cf. Chapter 10 for the general significance of the extent of price awareness.

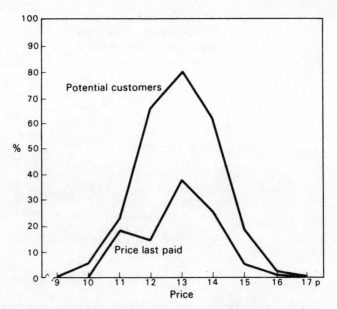

Figure 11.1   Potential customers and price-last-paid curves

the reason for the relative unpopularity of the brand. It will be of help if the price-last-paid question is supplemented by asking for other relevant information, including the name of the brand last bought, that of any other brand of the same product purchased regularly or occasionally, the frequency of purchase, etc.

An application of the new approach

In the above example hypothetical data were used to demonstrate the method of derivation; let us now consider the result of an actual investigation carried out with this method. It was conducted in England before the decimalization of the currency; hence the shilling divisions of the price scale in Figure 11.2.

There are two striking features about this diagram. The first is the general conformity of the potential customers curve with the expected shape: the percentages fall off from the peak in both directions. The decline is somewhat steeper to the left than to the right, which implies that as far as nylon stockings are concerned, a price that is too low is an even more effective curb on purchasing intentions than a high price.

The second point arises out of the appearance of the turrets, each

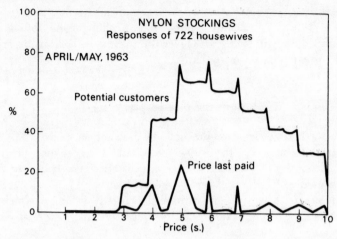

Figure 11.2   Nylon stockings: potential customers and price-last-paid curves

of which is at a price just one penny below the round figure. The pattern is in conformity with what were then the price lining practices of the trade: in the range covered by the diagram stockings were invariably priced at 2s.11d, 3s.11d., etc., up to 9s.11d. As we see, this price structure has become imprinted on the customers' minds and has found clear expression in their responses.

While it is firmly established that price sensitivity varies over the range, and that, in the case of certain goods, there are price points at which there is a sudden change in demand, *such conspicuous preference for the odd price has never been encountered in markets where this sort of rigid price lining was not traditional,*[9] and no investigation reported by other researchers has produced any convincing evidence of the efficacy of what has been described in America as 'the 9 fixation'.[10] It is

---

[9] 'Perhaps surprisingly, the price value of 100 did not provoke much of a "threshold" fall in demand.' Ian Tinn, 'Some Problems with Pricing Research', *Journal of the Market Research Society*, **24**, (4), October 1982, p. 323. Cf. also André Gabor and C. W. J. Granger, 'Price Sensitivity of the Consumer', *Journal of Advertising Research*, **4**, (4), December 1964, pp. 40–44.

[10] Dik Warren Twedt, 'Does the "9-Fixation" in Retail Pricing Really Promote Sales?', *Journal of Marketing*, **29**, (4), October 1965, pp. 54–5. However, there is some weak support in the findings of Douglas J. Dalrymple and George H. Haines, Jr, 'A Study of the Predictive Ability of Market Period Demand–Supply Relations for a Firm Selling Fashion Products', *Applied Economics*, **1**, (4), January 1970, pp. 227–85. Cf. also Zarrel V. Lambert, 'Perceived Prices as Related to Odd and Even Price Endings', *Journal of Retailing*, Fall 1975, pp. 13–22.

therefore questionable whether there are any advantages in pricing a shade below the nearest round figure, though the individual manufacturer will have little choice if the retail distributors insist on the perpetuation of this practice.

The practical solution: the buy-response method

The method of deriving the potential customers curve from the limits returned by the subjects is useful in confirming the foundations of the relevant theory of consumer behaviour and has been used with success also in commercial surveys. It has, however, been superseded by the more realistic *buy-response method*, which is not open to the objection that the questions put to the subjects suggest to them the existence of the price limits.

The buy-response method is much nearer to the normal shop-situation where the prospective purchaser is informed about the price of the article in which he is interested, either by means of a price label or verbally by an assistant, and all he has to decide is whether he should buy at that price or not. It has also been established that the answers given to buy-response questions are in harmony with actual behaviour.[11]

If the method is used to explore the consumers' reactions to the contemplated price change of an established brand, it is sufficient to name the product and then ask the subject to say if he would buy at each of the prices called out. Experience has shown that up to ten prices may be asked from each subject and that it is essential to call out the prices in a random order. The purpose of this is to neutralize the anchoring effect, which could distort the results if the prices were called out in order of magnitude.[12] It is also advisable to start with the prevailing price or one near to it.

---

[11] Cf. André Gabor, C. W. J. Granger and A. P. Sowter, 'Real and Hypothetical Shop Situations in Market Research', *Journal of Marketing Research*, **7**, August 1970, pp. 355–59; John R. Nevin, 'Laboratory Experiments for Estimating Consumer Demand: A Validation Study', *Journal of Marketing Research*, **11**, August 1974, pp. 261–8; also A. P. Sowter and A. Billson, 'The Further Development and Testing of Theories of Choice', (research report), Department of Economics, The University of Nottingham, 1975.

[12] Using a somewhat different method, the manifestation of this effect has been well demonstrated by Monroe (August 1973).

If the number of prices to be investigated exceeds ten, the sample has to be divided into two or more sub-groups of similar composition. The prices to be called out to each group should be selected from the full range.

There are three basic methods of conducting the interviews: calling at the home of each subject, stopping people in the street, preferably as they leave a store and, last but not least, there is the hall-method, which has been found to be the most practical of the three.[13]

Since there might be differences in the attitude and behaviour of the purchasing public between one part of the country and another, it is advisable to set up halls in more than one town. As far as England is concerned, halls in two or three towns have been found sufficient; in a larger country, with greater variations in climate, socio-economic structure, etc., more sample centres are necessary.

If the purpose of the survey is to collect data that will be of help in the re-pricing of a given brand, samples of it and of the competitive brands normally offered for sale should be displayed in the halls, with easily changeable price labels. With such an arrangement it will not be necessary to call out the different prices; it will be sufficient to direct the subject's attention to the new price labels.

The interviewer will approach shoppers in the street, and those who say that they are regular or occasional purchasers of any of the goods under investigation will be invited to enter the hall. Experience has shown that the majority of shoppers is willing to co-operate, and that it is well possible to raise in this way a sample that answers the requirements of the enquiry.

The percentage of the buy-responses, that is, the affirmative answers to the question 'Would you buy X (the product or the brand) at this price?' give the buy-response curve.

Figure 11.3 shows the buy-response and price-last-paid curves of the product group butter; Figures 11.4(a) and (b) display the responses to questions both about the product group baked beans in general and about a specific brand. (These results were obtained in a study commissioned by the Social Science Research Council. Cf. Nottingham University Consumer Study Group (1972), pp. 44 and 47.)

---

[13] Cf. pp. 178–9 for the description of the hall method. The principles of sampling and the statistical problems encountered in such enquiries are discussed in the Analytical Appendix.

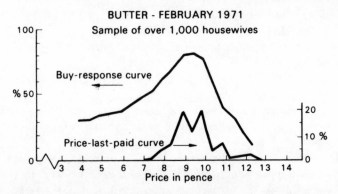

Figure 11.3   Butter: buy-responses and price-last-paid

The formal theory of the buy-response curve is presented in the Analytical Appendix; here we shall concentrate on those aspects which are of practical relevance to pricing problems.

The generic shape of the buy-response curve clearly emerges in Figures 11.3 and 11.4; it is essentially the same as that of the potential customers curve and thus indirectly confirms the existence of the limits. Furthermore, if the subjects are asked to state after each negative answer whether they consider the price too high or too low, we can directly calculate the respective percentages. This extension of the method has in fact been applied in several large-scale studies aimed at the clarification of the basic features,[14] but there is no need for it if the survey is conducted for commercial purposes.

Two aspects are of specific importance: (1) the tendency of buy-response curves to conform to their generic shape and to their normal relation with the price-last-paid curves, and (2) the specific deviations from the norm in individual cases.

In a multi-brand market, overall symmetry of the two curves signifies general satisfaction on the part of the customers, that is to say, the acceptance of price as a correct indicator of value for money. Figure 11.3, showing the curves for butter, provides an appropriate example. Buy-response curves do not, however, drop off as steeply in the region of lower prices than potential customers curves since if, instead of asking for the subjects' lower limit, a price slightly below

---

[14] Cf. especially Gabor and Granger (1966 and 1967), also Nottingham University Consumer Study Group, (1972).

what they usually pay is quoted to them, a certain proportion will interpret it as a 'special offer' rather than a permanent reduction.[15]

There are two reasons why Figures 11.4(a) and (b) are particularly interesting:

1 The diagrams show that while the premium brand is throughout valued more highly than just 'any brand of baked beans', the Heinz name is not alone sufficient fully to counteract the suspicion engendered by the lower prices.

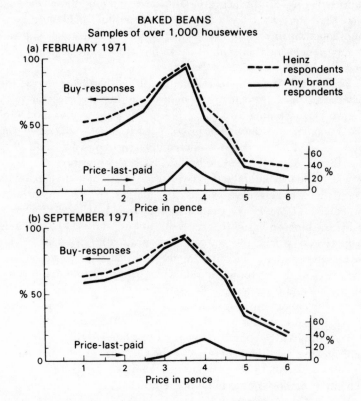

Figure 11.4 Baked beans: buy-responses and price-last-paid: (a) February 1971; (b) September 1971

---

[15] This point is demonstrated with the data of simultaneous enquiries with the two methods in Gabor and Granger, (1966), pp. 62–5.

2 In February 1971 the peaks of the price-last-paid and buy-response curves were both at the 3½p level, and the general symmetry displayed implies that the price structure was considered just by the customers. Seven months later the modal price moved up but the peak of the buy-response curve remained in its previous position, implying that the customers had not yet adjusted to the new price level and resented it.

The same point emerged with even greater clarity in the results of an earlier enquiry, where the products investigated included toilet soap and washing-up liquid. Comparable samples of about 2,000 housewives were approached in both cases and only those who said that they were actual purchasers of the product concerned were questioned further. The response rates showed that toilet soap was in fact bought by almost all of them, but at the time only about 55 per cent bought washing-up liquid.

Figure 11.5 (toilet soap) reflects a satisfied market, whereas the downward displacement of the bulk of the buy-response curve in Figure 11.6 (washing-up liquid), placing its peak well to the left of the range of the dominant prices, clearly shows that even the purchasers of the product considered it overpriced.[16] The indication was that if one of the leading brands, having established its quality image, could substantially reduce its price, it would both increase its market share and also extend the market by gaining a high proportion of the 45 per cent of the households who were not yet using washing-up liquid. In the event, none of the premium brands reduced its price, the market was gradually invaded by an increasing number of private brands, and this acted as a brake on the prices of the premium brands when persistent inflation pushed up the general price level.

So much about the basic features of the buy-response approach. It has led to the recognition that, at least in the case of the usual repeat-purchase or convenience goods, the role of price as a quality indicator rests on the experience of the customer rather than on his ignorance. Furthermore, it allows for the fact that price may also remain an important attribute of the article after the purchase.

---

[16] It may be asked why those who resented the prices of the premium brands did not buy the cheaper ones instead. The answer is that at the time the latter were of rather obviously inferior quality and available in some of the stores only.

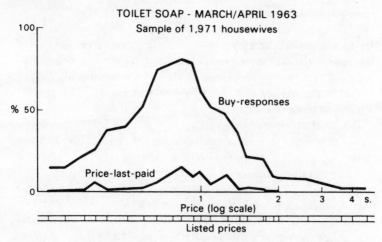

Figure 11.5   Toilet soap: buy-responses and price-last-paid (log scale)[17]

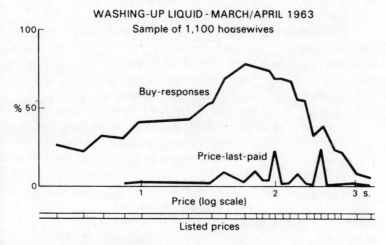

Figure 11.6   Washing-up liquid: buy-responses and price-last-paid (log scale)[17]

---

[17] In accordance with what has been said in Chapter 2 about the nature of the subjective price scale of consumers (a point further explained in the Analytical Appendix), the price scales in Figures 11.5 and 11.6 are ratio or logarithmic scales, along which equal distances represent equal percentage changes. Thus, for example, the distance between 2 and 4 is the same as between 1 and 2. The listed prices, 24 in each case, are those about which the subjects were questioned.

Summary

In the traditional theory the only role allotted to price was that of a measure of the cost of acquistion, and although it has long been an accepted fact that an improved quality almost invariably entails a higher price, the use of price as a quality indicator was generally attributed to ignorance on the part of the customer.

The modern approach, which has led to the development of highly practical methods of market research, accepts the fact that, apart from serving as a measure of the cost of purchase, price also acts as a quality indicator to the customer, and that this role of the price is based more on his experience than on his ignorance. Furthermore, in opposition to the puritanical view, according to which the consumer should derive satisfaction only from certain physical properties of a product, it recognizes that, taking a tablet of soap as an example, the consumer's satisfaction will be greatly influenced by such factors as the brand image, the wrapping, the perfume, *and the price* – none of which has anything to do with the detergent property of the tablet.

The central concept of the new approach is that the customer bent on a purchase will approach the market with two price limits in mind: an upper limit beyond which he would consider the item too expensive for his purposes, and a lower limit below which he could not trust the quality. The potential purchasers at any given price are then those for whom this price is neither too high nor too low.

These limits can be determined, but while the limit concepts are important from the point of view of consumer psychology, the percentages of potential customers can be obtained without direct reference to them by what is known as the buy-response method.

The buy-response curve is based on the responses of a representative sample of customers to various prices. While the curve has a strong tendency to conform to the generic shape, the deviations from it in each individual case are of the greatest importance for the purposes of optimal pricing. Buy-response analysis reveals both the present state and the potentialities of the market; it shows whether the customers are satisfied with the prevailing prices or consider the product overpriced, and has established the fact that the effect of price as a quality indicator is so strong that it can override even that of a well known brand name.

The application of the buy-response method to specific pricing problems and its extension to competitive pricing are demonstrated

in Chapters 12 and 13. The formal exposition of the relevant theory
of consumer behaviour is presented in the Analytical Appendix.

References

The following list contains also a number of titles not cited in
Chapter 11 but excludes those given in full detail in the footnotes.
The interested reader will find many further references in several of
the items.

In this list *PS* means that the item (or its English translation) is
reprinted in *Pricing Strategy*, (B. Taylor and G. Wills, eds), Staples
Press, London, 1969.

Daniel Adam, *Les réactions du consommateur devant le prix*, SEDES, Paris, 1958.

I. R. Andrews and E. R. Valenzi, 'The Relationship between Price and
Blind-rated Quality for Margarines and Butters', *Journal of Marketing
Research*, **7**, August 1970, pp. 393–5.

Anon., 'The Pricing of Consumer Goods', *Retail Business*, September 1971,
pp. 34–42.

Arthur G. Bedeian, 'Consumer Perception of Price as an Indicator of
Product Quality', *MSU Business Topics*, **19**, Summer 1971, pp. 59–65.

James R. Bettman, 'Perceived Price and Product Perceptual Variables',
Journal of Marketing Research, **10**, February 1973, pp. 100–102.

C. Blamires, 'Pricing Research Techniques: a Review and a New
Approach', *Journal of the Market Research Society*, **23**, (3), July 1981, pp.
103–126.

F. E. Brown, 'Who Perceived Supermarket Prices Most Validly?', *Journal of
Marketing Research*, **8**, 1971, pp. 100–102.

P. Charlton and A. S. C. Ehrenberg, 'McConnell's Experimental Brand
Choice Data', *Journal of Marketing Research*, **10**, 1973, pp. 302–7.

P. Charlton and A. S. C. Ehrenberg, 'An Experiment in Brand Choice',
Journal of Marketing Research, **13**, 1976, pp. 152–60.

Peter Cooper, 'Subjective Economics: Factors in a Psychology of Spending',
Research in Marketing, 1964, pp. 120–33. (*PS*, pp. 112–121.)

Peter Cooper, 'The Begrudging Index and the Subjective Value of Money',
Scientific Business, **2**, (7), November 1964. (*PS*, pp. 122–131.)

W. Bradford Cornell, 'Price as a Quality Signal: Some Additional
Experimental Results', *Economic Inquiry*, **16**, (2), April 1978, pp. 302–9.

Steven M. Cox, 'The Relationship Between Price and Quality in Situations
of Repeated Trials', *University of Michigan Business Review*, **31**, May 1979,
pp. 24–9.

David J. Curry, 'Measuring Price and Quality Competition', *Journal of
Marketing*, **49**, (2), Spring 1985, pp. 106–117.

Fred de Buijzer and Jan Stapel, 'Quality Perceptions and Brand Pricing', *European Research*, **6**, (2), March 1978, pp. 57–61.

Fred Emery, 'Some Psychological Aspects of Price', Tavistock Doc. No. 664, March 1962. (*PS*, pp. 98–111.)

Pierre Fouilhé, 'Évaluation subjective des prix', *Revue Française de Sociologie*, 1960, pp. 163–72. (*PS*, pp. 89–97.)

André Gabor, 'Price and Consumer Behaviour – A Review', *Omega*, **1**, (3), 1973, pp. 279–96.

André Gabor and C. W. J. Granger, 'Price Sensitivity of the Consumer', *Journal of Advertising Research*, **4**, (4), December 1964, pp. 40–44.

André Gabor and C. W. J. Granger, 'The Pricing of New Products', *Scientific Business*, August 1965, pp. 3–12.

André Gabor and C. W. J. Granger, 'Price as an Indicator of Quality: Report on an Enquiry', *Economica*, February 1966, pp. 43–70.

André Gabor and C. W. J. Granger, 'The Attitude of the Consumer to Prices', paper presented to the International Business School Symposium, 'New Developments in Pricing Strategy', Bradford, January 1967. (*PS*, pp. 132–51.)

David Gardner, 'An Experimental Investigation of the Price-Quality Relationship', *Journal of Retailing*, **46**, Fall 1970, pp. 25–41.

David Gardner, 'Is there a Generalized Price-Quality Relationship?', *Journal of Marketing Research*, **8**, May 1971, pp. 241–43.

Joel Huber, Morris B, Hollbrook and Barbara Kahn, 'Effects of Competitive Context and of Additional Information on Price Sensitivity', *Journal of Marketing Research*, **23**, (3), August 1986, pp. 250–260.

Jacob Jacoby, Jerry C. Olson and Raphael A. Haddock, 'Price, Brand Name, and Product Composition Characteristics as Determinants of Perceived Quality', *Journal of Applied Psychology*, **55**, December 1971, pp. 570–79.

Jacob Jacoby and Jerry C. Olson, 'Consumer Response to Price: An Attitudinal Information-Processing Perspective', *Purdue Papers in Consumer Psychology*, No. 157, Purdue University, Lafayette, Ind., 1976.

J. Morgan Jones and Fred S. Zufryden, 'An Approach for Assessing Demographic and Price Influences on Brand Purchase Behavior', *Journal of Marketing*, **46**, (1) Winter 1982, pp. 36–46.

Peter Jason Kalman, 'Theory of Consumer Behavior when Prices Enter the Utility Function', *Econometrica*, **36**, July/October 1968, pp. 497–510.

Joseph Kamen and Robert Toman, 'Psychophysics of Prices', *Journal of Marketing Research*', **7**, February 1970, pp. 27–35; discussion by Kent Monroe, André Gabor *et al.* and Kamen and Toman, *op. cit*, **8**, May 1971, pp. 248–57; also Jan Stapel '"Fair" or "Psychological" Pricing?', *op. cit*, **9**, February 1972, pp. 109–10.

Lakshman Krishnamurthi and S. P. Raj, 'The Effect of Advertising on Consumer Price Sensitivity', *Journal of Marketing Research*, **22**, (2), May 1985, pp. 119–129.

Sanjana Lall, 'Price Competition and the International Pharmaceutical Industry', *Oxford Bulletin of Economics and Statistics*, **40**, (1), February 1978, pp. 9–21.

David R. Lambert, 'Price as a Quality Signal: The Tip of the Iceberg', *Economic Inquiry*, **18**, (1), January 1980, pp. 144–150.

Zarrel V. Lambert, 'Product Perception: An Important Variable in Price Strategy', *Journal of Marketing*, **34**, October 1970, pp. 68–71.

Zarrel V. Lambert, 'Price and Choice Behavior', *Journal of Marketing Research*, **9**, February 1972, pp. 35–40.

Martin Lauth Lauridsen, 'The Relationship Between Price and Perceived Quality: An Experimental Study', *Markedskommunikasjon*, **10**, (2) 1973, pp. 1–12.

Martin Lauth Lauridsen, 'The Relationship Between Price and Perceived Quality: A Brief Review', *Markedskommunikasjon*, **11**, (1), 1974, pp. 1–17.

Harold Leavitt, 'A Note on Some Experimental Findings About the Meaning of Price', *Journal of Business*, **27**, July 1954, pp. 205–10.

J. Douglas McConnell, 'Effect of Pricing on Perception of Product Quality', *Journal of Applied Psychology*, **52**, August 1968, pp. 313–4.

J. Douglas McConnell, 'The Price-Quality Relationship in an Experimental Setting', *Journal of Marketing Research*, **5**, August 1968, pp. 300–3.

J. Douglas McConnell, 'An Experimental Examination of the Price-Quality Relationship', *Journal of Business*, **41**, October 1968, pp. 439–44.

J. Douglas McConnell, 'The Development of Brand Loyalty', *Journal of Marketing Research*, **5**, 1968, pp. 13–19.

J. Douglas McConnell, 'Comment on "A Major Price-Perceived Quality Study Reexamined"', *Journal of Marketing Research*, **17**, May 1980, pp. 263–64.

R. S. Mason, 'Price and Product Quality Assessment', *European Journal of Marketing*, **8**, (1), Spring 1974, pp. 29–41.

E. Scott Maynes and Terje Assum, 'Informationally Imperfect Consumer Markets: Empirical Findings and Policy Implications', *The Journal of Consumer Affairs*, Summer 1982, pp. 62–87.

Kent B. Monroe, 'Measuring Price Thresholds by Psychophysics and Latitudes of Acceptance', *Journal of Marketing Research*, **8**, November 1971, pp. 460–64.

Kent B. Monroe, 'The Information Content of Prices: 'A Preliminary Model for Estimating Buyer Response', *Management Science*, **17**, (8), April 1971, pp. B–519–32.

Kent B. Monroe, 'Psychophysics of Prices: A Reappraisal', *Journal of Marketing Research*, **8**, 1971, pp. 248–250.

Kent B. Monroe, 'Buyers' Subjective Perceptions of Price', *Journal of Marketing Research*, **10**, February 1973, pp. 70–80.

Kent B. Monroe, 'The Influence of Adaptation Levels on Subjective Price Perceptions', *Advances in Consumer Research*, (Scott Ward & Peter Wright, eds), Vol. **I**, Association for Consumer Research, Urbana, Ill., 1973, pp. 359–69.

Kent B. Monroe, 'The Influence of Price Differences and Brand Familiarity on Brand Preferences', *Journal of Consumer Research*, **3**, June 1976, pp. 42–9.

Nottingham University Consumer Study Group, *Decimalisation and the Consumer*, Social Science Research Council and University of Nottingham, October 1972.

Folke Ölander, 'The Influence of Price on the Consumer's Evaluation of Products and Purchases', paper presented to the International Business School Symposium 'New Developments in Pricing Strategy', Bradford, January 1967. (*PS*, pp. 50–69.)

Edgar A. Pessemier, 'An Experimental Method for Estimating Demand', *Journal of Business*, **33**, October 1960, pp. 373–83.

Edgar A. Pessemier, *Experimental Methods of Analyzing Demand for Branded Consumer Goods with Applications to Problems in Marketing Strategy*, Washington State University Press, Pullman, Wa., 1963.

Edgar A. Pessemier and Richard D. Teach, 'Pricing Experiments, Scaling Consumer Preferences and Predicting Purchase Behavior', *Science, Technology and Marketing*, (R. M. Haas, ed.), American Marketing Association, Chicago, Ill., 1966.

Robert Peterson, 'The Price-Perceived Quality Relationship: Experimental Evidence', *Journal of Marketing Research*, **7**, November 1970, pp. 525–8.

Peter C. Riesz, 'Price versus Quality in the Marketplace', *Journal of Retailing*, **54**, Winter 1978, pp. 15–28.

Peter C. Riesz, 'A Major Price-Perceived Quality Study Reexamined', *Journal of Marketing Research*, **17**, May 1980, pp. 259–262.

P. S. Raju, 'Product Familiarity, Brand Name and Price Influences on Product Evaluation', Working Paper No. 38, College of Business Administration, State College, Pa., 1976.

W. Schlackman, 'Psychological Aspects of Dealing', *Proceedings of the Conference on Research in Marketing*, Market Research Society, London, 1964. (*PS*, pp. 163–177.)

Tibor Scitovszky, 'Some Consequences of the Habit of Judging Quality by the Price', *Review of Economic Studies*, **12**, (2), 1944/45, pp. 100–105.

Benson Shapiro, 'The Psychology of Pricing', *Harvard Business Review*, **46**, July/August 1968, pp. 14–8, 20, 22, 24–5 and 160.

Benson Shapiro, 'Price Reliance: Existence and Sources', *Journal of Marketing Research*, **10**, August 1973, pp. 286–94.

Donald Shawyer and Norman French, 'The Effect of Price Cues on Perceived Product Quality in a Grocery Shopping Situation', *European Journal of Marketing*, **6**, (4), 1972, pp. 217–22.

H. K. Shrivdasani, 'Price-Perceived Quality Relations', *Indian Management*, January 1972, pp. 1–3.

James E. Stafford and Ben M. Enis, 'The Price-Quality Relationship: An Extension, *Journal of Marketing Research*, **6**, November 1969, pp. 456–58.

Jean Stoetzel, 'Le prix comme limite', in *La psychologie économique*, (P. L. Reynaud, ed.), Librairie, Marcel Rivière et Cie., Paris, 1954, pp. 183–8. (*PS*, pp. 70–74.)

Rex S. Toh and Donald J. Berard, Jr, 'The Differential Effect of Price on the Perceived Quality of Convenience, Shopping and Specialty Goods: A Demographic Analysis', *Acron Business and Economic* Review, **15**, Summer 1984, pp. 38–46.

Donald Tull, R. A. Boring and M. H. Gonsior, 'A Note on the Relationship of Price and Imputed Quality', *Journal of Business*, **37**, April 1964, pp. 186–91.

E. R. Valenzi and I. R. Andrews, 'Effect of Price Information on Product Quality Ratings', *Journal of Applied Psychology*, **55**, (1), 1971, pp. 87–91.

Thorstein Veblen, *The Theory of the Leisure Class*, Macmillan, New York, 1899.

Eugene Webb, 'Weber's Law and Consumer Prices', *American Psychologist*, **16**, July 1961, p. 450.

J. J. Wheatley and J. S. Y. Chiu, 'The Effect of Price, Store Image and Product and Respondent Characteristics on Perceptions of Quality', *Journal of Marketing Research*, **14**, May 1977, pp. 181–6.

12 New product pricing

In most of the product fields of material goods and services growth and profitability depend heavily on the extent to which the firm is a successful innovator. For better or worse, the modern world is dynamic; it welcomes and rewards change, and although there is still room in some trades for the traditionally minded businessman whose guiding principle is to carry on in the way of his forefathers, the numbers of old-fashioned firms are dwindling all the time. Lack of effective innovation can undermine even the position of firmly established monopolies – *vide* the fate of the railways all over the Western world.

New products can be the key to success but, as shown by the results of several recent studies carried out in Britain and the United States, they can also bring failure. The failure rates actually observed varied both from one market to another and with the criterion applied: thus Jenkins reported 98 per cent failure in the American grocery trade, Kraushar found that up to 60 per cent of new products disappeared from the British market within five years of their introduction; according to Nielsen 54 per cent of new fast moving consumer goods were withdrawn after test marketing, while the results of an American investigation, though based on the experience of thriving major companies, still showed an average failure rate of 40 per cent.[1]

---

[1] John R. G. Jenkins, *Marketing and Consumer Behaviour*, Pergamon Press, Oxford, 1972, p. 13; Kraushar, Andrews and Eassie, *New Products in the Grocery Trade*, KAE, London, 1971 and *New Products in Grocers*, KAE, London, 1976; A. C. Nielsen Company Limited, *How to strengthen your product plan*, Oxford, 1966; and *The Conference Board Record*, New York, 1973. Cf. also J. Hugh Davidson, 'Why Most New Consumer Brands Fail', *Harvard Business Review*, **54**, March/April 1976, pp. 117–122; P. M. Kraushar, *New Products and Diversification*, (2nd ed.), Business Books, London, 1977, pp. 19–20; C. Merle Crawford, 'Marketing Research and the New Product

The reasons why new products fail are numerous[2] but there is one feature that is common to all failures: the neglect of the customers' requirements. While it is seldom if ever of much use to ask potential customers what *entirely new* product they would not only welcome but actually purchase, market research is certainly capable of revealing which particular features of existing products are particularly liked or disliked by the consumers. However, it is a fact that even in our days a great deal of new product development relies entirely on opinion inside the company, even in cases where market exploration could considerably reduce the risk of failure.

What is a new product?

A new product may be defined as one that has no near substitute at the time when it is placed on the market. This definition is useful, insofar as it points at the difference between what is a genuine novelty, offering features radically different from those possessed by any other product, and what is merely a new brand (or a re-vamped old brand) that has to compete with one or more others in an established market.[3]

Substitutability being a matter of degree, the distinction can be carried further. New products may be (1) *functionally identical* with those already in the field, like, say, a new brand of toilet soap; (2) *functionally similar*, like a new textile fibre; or (3) *functionally unique*, that is to say, dissimilar to anything seen heretofore, like the first electric bulb.[4]

Failure Rate', *Journal of Marketing*, **41**, (2), April 1977, pp. 51–61 (contains a list of 17 references); and W. Ramsay, 'The New Product Dilemma', *Marketing Trends*, (published by A. C. Nielsen, Oxford in six languages), **1**, 1982, pp. 4–6.

[2] See Garrit Lydecker's comment, Chapter 1, note 4, p. 3.

[3] It has become such a widespread practice to promote the sales of established products exposed to strong competition by adding the prefix 'new' to the brand name that the term is on the way to changing its meaning to the consumer, especially since at the same time the launching of genuine novelties is frequently supported by publicity which emphasizes that in certain other markets the product has long been established in the favour of the discerning customer.

[4] Cf. Richard J. Steele, 'Pricing and the Level of Newness', in *Creative Pricing*, (Elizabeth Marting, ed.), American Marketing Association, New York, 1968, p. 157.

Should the price of a new product be based on cost?

The literature of new product pricing includes contributions from a number of eminent authors. Their approach shows considerable variety, but there is one proposition that none of them disputes. In fact, they all seem to agree that it is the antithesis of a sensible policy to arrive at the price of a new product by taking its unit cost and adding to it some preconceived percentage to cover a contribution to development costs, marketing expenses and profits.

The arguments presented in Chapters 5 and 6 apply here with full force: unit cost is inevitably an ambiguous concept and the principal role of costing a new product is to check the acceptability or otherwise of the price that appears to be appropriate for the market in view. However, if the new product belongs to the functionally similar variety and, if supplied to industrial users at the same price as the product it aims to replace would result in a cost saving to the user without reducing the quality of his final product, it would seem reasonable to ascertain the cost difference and add at least half of it to the price.

New products are characterized by a protected distinctiveness which is doomed to progressive deterioration from competitive inroads, says Dean, the author of several valuable contributions to the art of pricing.[5]

Both the distinctiveness and the protection are strongest in the case of functionally unique products and minimal when it comes to what is merely a new brand, or, if the product belongs to the non-differentiated variety, a new source of supply. Where there is

---

[5] Joel Dean, 'Pricing Pioneering Products', *Journal of Industrial Economics*, **17**, (2), July 1969, p. 165; 'Pricing Policies for New Products', *Harvard Business Review*, **28**, November/December 1950, pp. 45–53; *Managerial Economics*, Prentice-Hall, Inc., Englewood Cliffs, N.J., 1951, esp. Chapter 7, pp. 395–467; 'Pricing a New Product', *The Controller*, April 1955, pp. 163–5, (reprinted in *Pricing Strategy*, (B. Taylor and G. Wills, eds), Staples Press, London, 1969, pp. 534–40) 'Pricing Policies for New Products' was reprinted with a 'Retrospective Commentary' in *Harvard Business Review*, **54**, November/December 1976, pp. 141–53. Cf. also A. O. Oxenfeldt, *Establishing a New Product Program*, American Management Association, New York, 1958, pp. 17–18; George Haines, 'A Study Why People Purchase New Products', in *Science, Technology and Marketing*, (R. M. Haas, ed.), American Marketing Association, Chicago, 1966, pp. 665–685; Kent B. Monroe and Albert J. Della Bitta, 'Models for Pricing Decisions', *Journal of Marketing Research*, **15**, (3), August 1978, pp. 413–428; and Helmut Schmalen, 'Optimal Price and Advertising Policy for New Products', *Journal of Business Research*, **10**, March 1982, pp. 17–30.

neither an appreciable degree of distinctiveness nor effective protection, the margin between the direct unit cost and the net selling price may well be dictated by the market, and in such a case costing can be of positive use in pricing. However, even in such a situation *there will be a better chance of success if the selected price is allowed to determine the permissible cost rather than the other way round.*

The point to keep in mind is that if a new product does not meet with the approval of the potential customers, it will not sell properly even if its price is well below the direct cost of production, whereas if the new product does happen to satisfy a hitherto latent demand, a relatively high price will not generally be a deterrent to purchase, and may even help marketing by enhancing the image of the novelty – note the case of the Belgian lager advertised as 'reassuringly expensive', quoted on page 253 above. As long as there is effective protection, be it due to a letters patent, a registered design, a manufacturing secret or just to the time required to set up the production line, competition will be kept at bay.

Two basic pricing policies

Dean was the first to point out that there are two essentially different pricing policies for new products. One of them results in a *skimming price* and the other in a *penetration price*.[6]

The former stands for a launching price set high above manufacturing cost that skims the cream of demand; a policy that has proved successful for many products. Since the rate of output of a new product tends to be low in the early stages, a relatively high initial price may be considered appropriate for this reason alone. It is attractive since it allows for heavy promotional expenditure and early recoupment of the development costs; also, as said above, it may help in the creation of a high quality image.

A high initial price has two further advantages. First, it ensures that – apart from any price increases necessitated by inevitable rises in unit cost – all subsequent price adjustments will be downward, tapping increasingly wider strata of consumers and fighting back against emerging competition. Second, it provides the foundations for the segmentation of the market: it enables sales to be expanded

---

[6] Cf. Dean, *op. cit*, 1950, pp. 49–50. For examples of skimming price policies cf. Louis Phlips, *The Economics of Price Discrimination*, Cambridge University Press, Cambridge, 1983, pp. 76–8.

without any heavy cuts in the price of the original brand or model by introducing lower priced variants. (One or more of the latter could be used as 'fighting brands', aimed at undercutting the competitors' prices without affecting the market of the premium brand.)

An initial penetration price aims at large sales very early in the life of a product. It is for this reason that it has also been given the name of *volume pricing*. Its application will be indicated if the demand is highly responsive to price and quite especially if the product is of the kind that, to use an American phrase, either goes over big or not at all. It is supposed to be most likely to succeed if it does not call for any bizarre change in the expenditure pattern of the consumer.[7] Finally, a penetration price may act as a deterrent to potential competitors.

The development of sales over time with each of these two pricing policies is illustrated in Figure 12.1. The shapes of the curves are of the types generally encountered, but of course there is no fundamental reason why the eventual penetration of a product

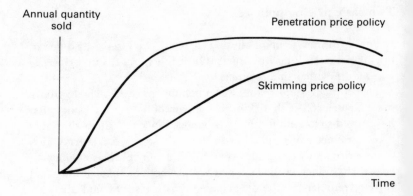

Figure 12.1   Life cycle curves

[7] This also is a point made by Dean, (op cit, 1950, p. 51). It is certainly not a rule without exceptions: for example, the sales of colour television sets and package holidays abroad responded generously to penetration pricing. While Dean may be right as far as bizarre *products* are concerned, it is worth noting that according to the results of J. Hugh Davidson's investigation, the more different a new consumer brand is from those previously available, the more likely is it to succeed. ('Why Most New Consumer Brands Fail', *Harvard Business Review*, **54**, (2), February/March 1976, p. 120.)

initially launched with a skimming price policy should not reach or
even exceed the saturation level that could have been attained had a
penetration price policy been pursued from the start.

It should further be noted that the life cycle of an individual brand
is mostly very much shorter than that of the product category to
which it belongs; also that while it is fairly safe to assume that,
disregarding short-term fluctuations, the characteristic shape of the
product life cycle curve will assert itself in the long run – and,
perhaps, even in the medium run – the actual timing of each phase is
difficult to predict. However, Polli and Cook who investigated the
issue by empirical tests and with the help of a theoretical model,
concluded that the life cycle concept can be useful for the purposes of
marketing planning and intermediate-term sales forecasting, even
though their data showed not inconsiderable year-to-year fluctuations and also displayed some deviations from the basic theory.[8]

The pricing of functionally similar and identical products

The majority of new products launched belongs to the functionally
identical class, and also a high proportion of those that are claimed
to be functionally similar but superior to their competitors tend to be
regarded by the customers as just another brand, in spite of any new
'wonder ingredient' they are said to contain.

It is a well known saying that a new product has no price, but
strictly speaking this refers only to those that are functionally
unique. For such products the pricing decision has to be made
almost in a vacuum, whereas the price of a fundamentally identical
or similar product will be more or less determined by the price
structure ruling in its market. Yet, it is the latter that presents the
more intricate pricing problem, since the call is for a penetration
price, and that will be fully effective only if located precisely at the
right point within a range that has quite a wide span in the case of
the typical multi-brand market.

---

[8] Cf. Rolando Polli and Victor Cook, 'Validity of the Product Life Cycle',
The Journal of Business, **42**, (4), October 1969, pp. 345–400; also the excellent
report of David R. Rink and John E. Swan, 'Product Life Cycle Research: A
Literary Review', *Journal of Business Research*, September 1979, pp. 219–242,
which lists 71 references, and George Day (guest editor), 'Product Life
Cycle' (a set of eight articles by various authors), *Journal of Marketing*, **45**,
(4), 1981, pp. 60–132. Cf. also the Appendix to Part I: 'Price Forecasting',
esp. pp. 203–6.

The most valuable capability the developer of a new product can have is empathy, that is to say, the ability to identify with the prospective customers, to have an instinctive feeling of their tastes, their purchasing habits and of the price at which they would welcome the new product.

Where the market is relatively restricted, as in the case of some industrial products and also certain shopping goods and specialty goods[9] sold through a small number of large distributors, empathy can be cultivated by personal contact with the buyers. Certain fashion goods of short life expectation, the sales of which depend mainly on the orders placed by the trade well before the beginning of the season, belong to this category.

An example from the text-book of a Belgian professor of economics provides a suitable illustration.[10] He describes how the manufacturer would find the appropriate price for a new kind of yarn experimentally produced by his firm. This yarn appears to be superior to what his competitors can offer, and hence the manufacturer expects it to provide a margin or, more properly, a contribution that will be well above the average. He would start by showing the sample to the buyer of one of his largest customers and watch his reaction. If the sample meets with the buyer's approval, the manufacturer will name the highest price he thinks possible, and might add that it is merely an estimate since the costing is still in progress. Should the buyer consider that price too high, the manufacturer will promise to watch his costing and then go on to another potential customer, trying out on him the same price or perhaps one slightly lower. And so on, till after he has seen half a dozen or so of his main customers, he will have a fair idea of the price at which he should launch his new product, and possibly even of the size of the opening orders he may expect to obtain. If, after sales have started, the rate at which the orders are coming in exceeds the productive capacity of his works, he might increase the price, and alternatively, if he finds that the new yarn is not selling well, he could try to stimulate sales by a price reduction. De Bodt notes that since price increases tend to be resented, it is generally better to start

---

[9] Cf. Chapter 8, page 150, note 4 for the definitions of convenience goods, shopping goods and specialty goods.

[10] What follows is a somewhat elaborated account of the case presented by Jean Pierre de Bodt, *La Formation des Prix*, Les Éditions de Visscher, Bruxelles, 1956, p. 58.

with a price so high that any subsequent adjustment of it will be in the downward direction.

Both the cultivation of empathy and the experimental approach to pricing are considerably more difficult in the case of the typical convenience good. Its potential customers are numerous, they are further removed from the manufacturer and do not invariably react favourably to price adjustments.

Test marketing provides only a partial answer to the problem. It cannot be undertaken until the novelty is in actual production, if only in a pilot plant, by which time heavy expenditure might have been incurred. Massy has claimed that reasonably close predictions of the sales over the first three years after launch can be produced after the first six months, but according to the experience of a leading international market research organization, forecasts made at the end of the first six months have less than an even chance of being correct, and it takes up to eighteen months to bring testing to the point where either success or failure becomes a virtual certainty.[11] The reason why it takes such a long time to arrive at a reliable prediction is that it is not the initial sales, easily enhanced by advertising and other forms of promotion, that matter but the *eventual* re-purchase rate.

An example of a functionally identical product that failed after a spectacular initial success is the cigarette launched some years ago by Carreras with the prestigious Dunhill name at the same price as that of the brands catering to the mass market, whereas until then all the Dunhill cigarettes were priced well above the market. Soon after the new product was launched sales rose at such an impressive rate that the results of the first few months, which exceeded even the most optimistic forecasts, were quoted by the advertising agency holding the Dunhill account in its own advertisements. However, soon afterwards sales began to dip; before long they dropped to a critical level and the brand had to be discontinued. Cigarettes belong to the category of goods that either 'go over big' or not at all, since if the turnover is slow, the retailers working on a very slender margin cannot afford to stock it.

---

[11] Cf. William F. Massy, 'Forecasting the Demand for New Convenience Products', *Journal of Marketing Research*, **6**, November 1969, pp. 405–12; 'Test marketing reduces risks', *Nielsen Researcher*, Oxford, January/February 1973, p. 6; also Edward M. Tauber, 'Why Concept and Product Tests Fail to Predict New Product Results', *Journal of Marketing*, **39**, (4) October 1975, pp. 69–71.

Functionally similar products may meet with the same fate. Dupont, the great American combine, developed Corfam, the first synthetic material that not only resembled leather but also had some porosity. It was launched at a skimming price in the footwear trade: Corfam shoes retailed at $25.00, when shoes of comparable finish but with leather uppers were selling around $10.00 a pair. The product was well received, its high quality image appeared to be established, and after manufacturing facilities were expanded, the price was substantially reduced but the mass market failed to materialize. The sales of Corfam were so disappointing that Dupont decided to discontinue the product, but by that time it was in the red to the tune of $80 million according to the reports which appeared in the newspapers. The process was sold and is still in use but the product itself has captured only a very modest share of the market. It is nowadays used for cheap footwear only.

The risks of new product development can never be completely eliminated but they can be substantially reduced by a systematic approach. The originator of one such approach, the nature of which implies that it was meant for functionally identical or similar products, is Oxenfeldt.[12] He is justifiedly critical of those authors who merely list the factors to be taken into account when the price is set for a new product and then suggest that judgement should help in reaching the correct decision. Oxenfeldt holds that to make the problem manageable, it should be tackled in six stages, in this order:

1 Selecting market targets.
2 Choosing a brand image.
3 Composing a marketing mix.
4 Selecting a pricing policy.
5 Determining a pricing strategy.
6 Arriving at a specific price.

Since these steps are to be taken before the actual development of the product, it may be said that what Oxenfeldt advocates is the sound policy of deriving the cost that can be allowed for the development, production and marketing of a new product from the price which has been decided upon with the potential demand in view. However, it seems fair to point out that while his approach is commendably *methodological*, he has not suggested any actual *method*

---

[12] Alfred R. Oxenfeldt, 'Multistage Approach to Pricing', *Harvard Business Review*, July/August 1960.

either for the collection of the various kinds of evidence or for their evaluation.

The use of consumer research in pricing a new brand

The practice of fitting the product to the price rather than the other way round has already been mentioned under the name of backward cost pricing and price lining;[13] here we shall show how consumer research can help in finding the most promising price point for a new brand.

When the launching of a new brand is being considered, the first step generally consists of the determination of the price structure ruling in the market concerned. This is a relatively easy task, also; in the case of certain products, regular agency reports are available concerning the market shares of at least the main brands. Some people would consider these two kinds of information sufficient, whereas all they reveal is the existing situation in the market rather than its potentialities. We have to go one step further and collect quantitative data of a third kind, in order to obtain information on the attitudes of the consumers to the relevant prices.

The information concerned can be elicited from the purchasers of the commodity by a survey conducted with either of the two methods outlined in Chapter 11, and if the product is to be shaped to the price, it follows that the investigation should be commissioned before product development is started.

If the price range is wide and the merchandiser has not yet decided whether the new product should be a relatively expensive brand or a cheaper item, it will be advisable to start by obtaining the potential customers curve, supplemented by information about the price and brand of the last purchase and the approximate frequency of purchase.

To make sure that the subjects are actual purchasers of the product, the first question should always be: 'Do you buy tinned soup (or whatever the name of the product group concerned is)?'. The number of those whose answer to this question is in the negative should be recorded since it will provide the proportion of persons or households who are not at the time regular or occasional purchasers of the commodity, but they should not be questioned any further. In

---

[13] Cf. pp. 51 and 158–62.

the case of consumer durables the reliability of the results will be greatly enhanced if the sample is restricted to subjects who have either recently bought an item belonging to the product category concerned or are seriously considering such a purchase. It might be possible to obtain from the retailers or from guarantee records the names and addresses of recent purchasers, but if they cannot be made available, the only expedient is that of an appropriate filter question applied to a random sample of householders.

The next two questions are about the upper and lower price limits of the subject, followed by the details of the last purchase and the usual classification questions, such as occupation of the subject or the head of the household, age, and, if required, also size of family, educational level, etc.[14]

The data will yield the potential customers and price-last-paid curves, as illustrated by a hypothetical case in Figure 11.1, and an actual example in Figure 11.2. The diagram will show the range of prices, indicate points of special price sensitivity and also reveal whether the customers consider the existing price structure equitable or not.

This first survey may be followed by a second, conducted by the buy-response method and restricted to that part of the range which a preliminary decision has selected for the price of the new product.

How should this part of the price range be chosen? Consider Figure 11.1; the first point to note is that no price below 12p or above 14p is likely to be favourably received by the market, since none of them promises to interest more than about one-fifth of the total of potential customers. In fact, only three prices appear to be worthy of consideration in this simplified example: 12p, 13p and 14p, all of which were found acceptable by over 60 per cent of the subjects. (This does not of course mean that any new product launched at 13p, say, would automatically attract 80 per cent of the customers. The potentialities indicated by the curve should be interpreted in a relative rather than in an absolute sense, taking into account that only 37 per cent actually bought their last tin of soup at

---

[14] If the product group happens to be one about which reliable agency reports based on the retail audit method are available, the data relating to the brand last bought and the frequency of purchase can be used to check the representativeness of the sample. It should be noted, however, that, for the purpose in hand, the proportions of customers associated with each price, irrespective of brand, contain more relevant information than the market shares of the different brands.

that price, and even this proportion might have been shared by several brands.)

The sales manager might be tempted to suggest 12p as the price most likely to be successful, because it would undercut 13p which registered the highest percentage both in the price-last-paid and the potential customers distributions, but the marketing expert should prefer to launch a new brand with a claim to higher quality at a price of 14p, since this promises the sale of about the same number of tins as 12p, with the possibility of a considerably higher contribution. In other words, this appears to be one of the cases where promotion might successfully be based on the *why pay less* principle rather than on the *save 1p* idea. All the same, an introductory offer with, say, 2p off the regular price would not necessarily be out of place, but since such a policy could easily start a price war, it seems safer to eschew it and concentrate on other methods of promotion, calculated to enhance the belief in price as a trustworthy indicator of quality.[15]

The data used in this demonstration were hypothetical but not entirely arbitrary; similar results have been obtained with a number of different products, examples of which can be seen in Figures 11.3, 11.4 and 11.5. However, each case has its own characteristics; they arose with peculiar clarity in the investigation of the market for nylon stockings, as shown in Figure 11.2. The potential customers curve displays only very rough symmetry around the peak, and the established price points are indicated by the positions of the turrets. Here again, the upper part of the range is the more attractive: the relative position of the potential customers and price-last-paid curves implies that certain proportions of those whose last purchase was at a fairly low price would not necessarily consider a higher price a deterrent. If the new product is to be launched in this range, it would seem advisable to fall in line with the prevailing practice and

---

[15] The data of a series of field experiments carried out by a team at Stanford University implies that a low introductory price promotes sales, but when subsequently price is raised to the normal level, sales fall below those of the control experiment with normal prices throughout. Though most of the results were statistically significant, there are several reasons why the evidence presented is not altogether convincing. For example, the report does not say whether the lower introductory price was presented as a special offer or not; the duration of some of the experiments was too short to justify the conclusions, etc. Cf. Anthony N. Doob *et al.*, 'Effect of Initial Selling Price on Subsequent Sales', *Journal of Personality and Social Psychology*, **11**, (4), 1969, pp. 345–50.

adopt a penny-below-the-round-figure price; if only because the retailers might not like it otherwise.

However, it should not be thought that it is invariably the upper part of the price range that holds the better promise. If the picture obtained by the first survey is like that depicted in Figure 11.6, with the peak of the potential customers curve very much to the left of the most popular prices, the indication is that a new brand would have the best chance of success at a price well below those of the premium brands.

Once it has been decided in which part of the range the price of the new brand should be located, the next task is to choose the most appropriate price point, and this raises the question whether the available information about the possibilities of the market is adequate for this purpose.

The reason why it was suggested that it might be advisable to hold the first survey with the method whereby the potential customers curve is derived from the price limits returned by the subjects, even though the buy-response method is undoubtedly more realistic, was that the former can be applied without any previous knowledge of the range and structure of the prices ruling in the market. The results of such a survey, if appropriately conducted,[16] will be sufficient for locating a promising price point, *provided the decision is in favour of the upper part of the price range*, since experience has shown that above the peak the potential customers and buy-response curves have a strong tendency to coincide. However, for prices below the peak the buy-responses indicate higher proportions,[17] hence if this should be the region selected after the first survey, it would be reasonable to hold a second enquiry with the buy-response method, with only those prices called out to the subjects that are still of potential interest at this stage.

If the price structure is known at the outset and the number of prices under consideration does not exceed ten, only one survey will be required, and since up to this number of prices the buy-response method is not more costly than the limit approach, the former should be preferred. Where ten prices are not sufficient to cover the full range, only part of the buy-response curve will be obtained, but it will be the relevant part.

---

[16] Cf. the Analytical Appendix, Section A.3 pp. 333–6, for an exposition of the main statistical aspects of the issue.

[17] Cf. p. 262–3 for the explanation of this phenomenon.

The price to which the new product should be fitted will be suggested by the shape of the buy-response curve and its relation to the price-last-paid curve; it is advisable to place it off the peak of the former but not so far away as to fall into that part where the curve declines very steeply. It is, of course, possible that there will be more than one price that will look attractive, and the firm intent on entering the market might decide to do so with a product line rather than with a single brand.

Once a price has been selected, estimates should be made of the volume of sales to be expected, of the direct unit cost that can be allowed to the product, and of the capital it will tie down. The investment aspect might, however, be negligible if the product is not to be manufactured by the firm itself but ordered from outside.

The new product will be in direct competition with those of the existing brands that are currently selling at or around the selected price. They can be identified from the survey results, and it will then be possible to prepare experimental samples with similar or preferably superior characteristics, without exceeding the stipulated cost limit. Properly packed, these samples can then be subjected to a consumer pre-test: a representative panel consisting of present users of the competitive brands should be asked to compare the samples with those they are actually using, and to rate each by those attributes which they consider relevant. The price of each of the brands, including the experimental packs, should clearly be marked in the test.

In such a test more than one experimental product, also several brand names and forms of packing may simultaneously be examined.[18]

While it is not humanly possible to predict the performance of a new brand throughout its life cycle, the systematic approach described above can go a long way towards reducing the risks of product development. The buy-response curve is not, however, a magic circle; the market profile, as the diagram is sometimes called, provides a clear picture of the existing situation, but it is not always impossible to succeed by stepping outside its limits by the introduction of an appropriate functionally similar product. For example, the market for writing instruments in general and fountain pens in particular was in a pretty stationary state when the price

---

[18] Cf. Peter Kraushar, 'How to Research', *Management Today*, January 1982, pp. 50–53. Conjoint analysis described in Appendix II to Part II offers another approach to the same issue.

range was suddenly extended upwards by the successful introduction of fashion into the field, first by Parker and subsequently by Sheaffer. Later the cheap ballpoint pens broke out of the price range in the downward direction; and in fact what was once a fairly homogeneous market has become distinctly segmented. The throw-away plastic ballpoint pens and the stainless-steel to gold-plated luxury items cater to separate demands: within each of the segments there is keen competition, but none between them.

Going to the upper limit of the existing price range or even beyond it is especially indicated if the dominant aim of introducing the new brand is to impart glamour to the manufacturer's image. It was mentioned above that such a 'flagship brand', to use the current jargon, might serve its purpose even if it does not itself sell at a significant rate,[19] but there are in fact several instances to show that, if properly managed, it can also develop into a money spinner.

The pricing of functionally unique products

As far as pioneering products, that is to say, genuine novelties are concerned, market research can give only limited assistance and may even produce highly misleading information at an early stage. The results of a large survey commissioned before the Xerox process was fully developed led to the prediction that not more than some 8,000 units of the new copiers could be placed in the first year. The actual number turned out to be about ten times as large. To quote another, less well-known instance: one of the leading American corporations which developed cassette-television had the market researched for it twice before any of the systems were commercially available. The first survey led to the conclusion that there was a large market for it, while the second survey indicated that the product would fail. Since that particular system was subsequently abandoned by the developers, it is not possible to say which of the two predictions was nearer the truth, as far as that particular product was concerned.

The point is that the invention, the development and also the pricing of a functionally unique product are creative acts based on intuition. Experience has shown that the opinion of the potential customers is not a reliable guide either to the sales to be expected at

---

[19] Cf. pp. 50 and 162.

various prices or to the price at which the product could most profitably be marketed. This is largely true even if the novelty is an industrial product, since the buyers' expertise cannot be expected to extend beyond their actual experience.

However, very few of the new products coming to the market are truly functionally unique, and if the novelty consists only in some individual feature not possessed by any of the products previously available, there is a basis for comparison and hence scope for consumer research. Concept testing, carried out by noting the reactions of a representative sample of potential customers can be of considerable help in product development and pricing, but only if an effective visualization of the new feature can be provided, preferably by letting the subjects use actual samples.

The fact that intuition inevitably plays an important role in the creation of any genuine novelty does not mean that the problems involved cannot be approached in a systematic fashion. According to Dean, 'Pricing a new product should begin long before its birth. Prospective prices, coupled with forecasted costs, should play a decisive role in product birth control.'[20] The context of this dictum implies that it refers to pioneering innovations, whereas it is, in fact, easier to follow if the product, though new to the firm, is not new to the industry. As said above, a new brand can readily be developed so as to fit into a predetermined cost and price category, but neither the cost of genuine research nor the market value of a product that is entirely new can be predicted with any certainty.

It is therefore all the more important to take stock at the outset and again subsequently whenever it appears that the actual cost of the research and development of the novelty might substantially exceed the amount budgeted for this purpose, also if it seems that the direct cost of manufacture of the finished article or the capital its production and marketing will tie down will be significantly higher than originally envisaged.

As far as the demand side is concerned, no such precise calculations are possible. However, while the actual behaviour of the market is difficult to predict, its limitations can objectively be determined, often without any field research, since there is a great deal of relevant information available in published official statistics, trade directories and other reference books. The size of the market as a whole should be ascertained at an early stage since it might

---

[20] Joel Dean, *op. cit*, 1969, p. 178.

indicate that there is no reasonable chance of making any profit on the new product even if it were to achieve quick acceptance by a large proportion of the potential customers. This is not of course possible without an estimate of the price at which the product should be marketed.[21]

How should the launching price be determined? The basic choice is between a low penetration price, intended to remain at its initial level for a considerable time since it precludes any substantial adjustment in either direction, and a high skimming price, which may be reduced later on, if indicated. High and low are, of course, relative terms and should be interpreted as referring to the percentage mark-up on direct cost rather than to the price itself.

In order to have any market appeal, a functionally unique product must promise some benefit to the purchaser which was not previously within his reach. It could be an addition to his enjoyment of life, either directly or by reducing inconvenience or pain, an enhancement of his prestige, a cost saving or higher profits. It would seem therefore that the application of a skimming price is indicated, unless the distinctiveness of the product is insignificant or not properly protected. For example, should it be known that a similar novelty is being developed by a strong potential competitor and that it is expected to reach the market soon after the launching of one's own product, it might be best to start with a price that is unlikely to be heavily undercut by the competitor, or even with a price so low that it will discourage entry.

Distant benchmarks are best avoided in the search for an appropriate skimming price. It would have been a mistake to price the first domestic vacuum cleaner in relation to the savings on brooms, brushes and dustpans, or the first electric shaver in terms of the razor blades displaced.

It has been suggested that the price maker should establish the utility of the new product to the potential user and set the price accordingly.[22] There is, however, no direct way by which the utility

---

[21] More than one price may be necessary if the product is to be sold simultaneously in two or more markets, for example, in the home market and for export, or if the market is segmented; for example if the novelty is a component, it will be sold at a lower price to the manufacturer who incorporates it in his own product than to the retail outlets which supply it as a replacement.

[22] Cf. e.g. Robert Ferber, 'Contribution of Economics to the Study of Consumer Market Behaviour', *Applied Economics*, **1**, (2), May 1969, page 133.

of a genuine novelty, that is to say, its subjective value to the user, could be established, except in those rare cases where the inducement to buy is in fact restricted to calculable cost savings; a situation that is more likely to arise in the industrial field than in the market for consumer goods.

Attempts have been made to explore how consumers would value a novelty by the 'barter equivalent method'. It consists of showing potential customers a sample of the new product together with a wide variety of totally unlike consumer products. The subjects are then asked which of the well known products they would swap for the novelty, and their answers are supposed to give the pricing executive a rough idea of what price range would appear reasonable to the market.[23] The application of this method seems to be most justified if the novelty is of the kind that people are likely to buy as presents. This is quite frequently the case since a novelty has the general advantage that the person for whom it is intended is most unlikely to possess one already, and it should further be realized that, when buying for their own use an item which is of the nature of a luxury to them, many people tend to look upon it as a present for themselves. It follows that if the barter equivalent method is used in such a case, the products with which the novelty is to be compared should be of the kind that people tend to buy as presents, and it seems advisable to frame the question accordingly, asking the subjects which item, if bought as a present, could be displaced by the new product. In order to emphasize the intended image of the novelty, the display should include at least one of its advertisements. However, the unrealistic nature of the experimental situation and the established fact that few, if any, consumers are able to predict even their initial market behaviour in advance of the introduction of a genuine novelty speak against placing much reliance on the results of such experiments.

The upshot is that, when setting a skimming price, consideration should be given both to the demand to be expected and the likely reactions of the competition, but the absence of obvious benchmarks should be looked upon as an advantage rather than a detriment, since it means freedom to exercise creative pricing.

A skimming price should be approached from above rather than from the bottom as determined by the direct cost. It should not be set so high as to restrict sales below the planned rate of output, but even if this happens to be the outcome of the first pricing decision,

---

[23] Cf. Joel Dean, *op. cit*, 1950, p. 415.

the remedy is easy: after having established a quality image, of which a high price is an important component, a price reduction will be welcomed by the market, whereas a low starting price followed by a price increase would certainly be resented.

It is important to form an estimate of the probable life cycle of the product and to make sure that it is revised from time to time. Forecasts of future sales can never be precise, but it should be possible to say whether the popularity of the product is expected to last one season only or several years; also whether it is more likely to be affected by a change in the attitude of the consumers, (the fate of the typical fashion product), or by an invasion of its market by the competition. Even though the result of both is a fall in sales, the reaction should vary according to its cause. This is what is meant by a pricing strategy: planning the price policy for more than a short time period.

No strategy is complete without its tactics. An example of a tactical decision tree is shown in Figure 12.2; it is a modified version of the diagram Kotler borrowed from an unpublished paper by R. J. Trapp.[24] It should not be looked upon as a prescription but merely as an illustration of the lines along which tactics should be developed.

Based on techniques used in experimental psychology, the method of conjoint analysis was developed which might be of some use in pricing new products, especially when a brand is being introduced whose novelty consists in combining the most attractive features of existing brands with the appropriate price. It is described in detail in Appendix II to Part II.

Summary

Business success is closely tied up with the ability to innovate but at least half of the new products brought to the market result in losses. The risk of failure can, however, considerably be reduced by a systematic approach to product development in general and pricing in particular. The nature of the approach to be adopted depends on whether the new product is functionally unique or merely a new brand that is functionally identical with or similar to those already in the field.

---

[24] Cf. Philip Kotler, *Marketing Management*, 2nd edn, Prentice-Hall, Inc., Englewood Cliffs, NJ, 1969, p. 541.

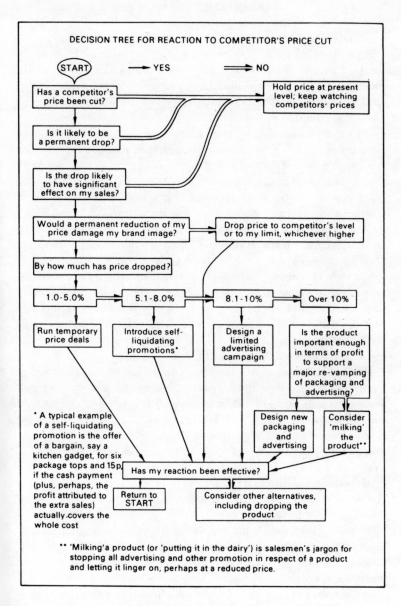

Figure 12.2 Decision tree for reaction to competitor's price cut

Cost plays only a limited role in new product pricing. In fact, it may be said that what cost determines is not so much the price of a product but whether it should be produced at all.

There are two basic pricing policies for new products: the skimming price policy, meaning a launching price high above the current direct cost of production which skims the cream off the market and may be reduced later on, and the penetration price policy, aiming at a high volume of sales and intended to deter potential competitors.

Most of the functionally similar and identical products call for a penetration price. Empathy is a great help in product development and pricing, and if the number of potential customers is small, it can be cultivated by personal contact with them. If, as is the case with most consumer goods, the number of potential customers is large, market research can be used to supplement empathy.

The proper process with a new brand is to choose the price first, and derive from it the appropriate limit for the cost of production. The location of the most promising price point can be greatly facilitated by the application of the consumer research methods described in Chapter 11, since they can reveal both the structure and the potentialities of any multi-brand market. The results will indicate whether the most promising price point is in the upper or lower half of the price range, also if there is any gap into which the price of the new product could fit.

The survey results will show which brands are being marketed at and around the selected price, and which segments of the potential customers will primarily be interested in the new brand. Samples can then be developed and submitted to a consumer panel for comparison with the competitive brands until one is found that both satisfies the potential customers and can be produced at or below the cost allowed to it.

Knowledge of the market profile should also be useful if it is intended to introduce a functionally similar product with a price that is outside the present range.

The invention, development and pricing of a functionally unique product are creative acts that must largely be based on intuition. Market research can give only limited assistance at an early stage since the potential customers cannot, as a rule, predict their own purchasing behaviour when faced with a product that is entirely new to them. The barter equivalent method might, however, give a rough indication, especially if the product is of the kind that people are likely to buy as a present.

The proper price policy for most genuine novelties is that of the skimming price. If the attraction of the novelty is a cost advantage, the price of the product can be based on a sharing of the cost saved. Otherwise there will be no obvious benchmarks available and the price should be approached from above, since a launching price that is too high can easily be remedied by a price reduction, whereas if the initial price is too low, it will be difficult if not impossible to increase it later on.

The probable life cycle of the product should be estimated and a strategy developed that includes the tactical steps to be taken in response to the actions of competitors. Since the future can never be predicted with certainty, the strategy must be revised from time to time. It will be shown in the next chapter how market research can help by finding out in advance how the customers would react to any proposed price change.

Finally, it should be noted that this chapter concentrated on the practical approach to the problems of new product pricing. Readers interested in the theoretical approach will find typical examples in the relevant writings of Kotler, Thomas and Chabris and in Rao's review of the modern literature of the subject.[25]

Conjoint analysis, a technique aimed at the determination of the optimal combination of the characteristics of a proposed new product is described in Appendix II to Part II.

[25] Philip Kotler, 'Marketing Mix Decisions for New Products', *Journal of Marketing Research*, **1**, February 1964, pp. 43–9, and 'Competitive Strategies for New Product Marketing Over the Life Cycle', *Operations Research*, **12**, December 1965, pp. B104–119; Joseph Thomas, 'Price-Production Decisions with Deterministic Demand', *Management Science*, **16**, (11), July 1970, pp. 747–50, and 'Price and Production Decisions with Random Demand', *Operations Research*, **11**, May/June 1974, pp. 513–18; Joseph Thomas and Prem Chabria, 'Bayesian Models for New Product Pricing', *Decision Sciences*, January 1975, pp. 51–64; also Vithala R. Rao, 'Pricing Research in Marketing: The State of the Art', *Journal of Business*, **57**, (1 – Part 2), January 1984, pp. S39–60, (lists 100 references).

13   The pricing of established products

In times of general price stability the initial price of a manufactured product may remain unchanged for a considerable period, especially if, as for example in the case of count lines,[1] variations in the quantity of the contents of the pack or of the quality of the good are not prohibited by the authorities and tolerated by the purchasers.[2]

There are, of course, limits to the extent to which the quantity of any count line or kindred product can be reduced, and when such a limit is reached, the general practice is to put up the price quite sharply and increase the contents of the pack at the same time.

It must be said that the variation of the quantity and/or the quality of the product is not necessarily the best policy to follow even where it is permissible, and there are many products besides those subject to prescribed quantity regulations or other legal limitations,

---

[1] Cf. p. 165 for the definition of count lines.

[2] A policy of product variation was followed by the major British cigarette manufacturers after 1939. For a number of years, the price of the standard brands rose only by the amounts of successive increases in the tobacco duty. Increases in the cost of materials and labour were countered by eliminating cigarette cards and bonus coupons, by reducing both the length and the diameter of the cigarettes and by filling them with cheaper tobacco packed less closely. Further savings were effected by dropping the tinfoil lining and the cellophane wrapping of the cartons. (It was said at the time that the efficiency of the production process was also improved, but this does not seem to have been the major factor in keeping costs down.) The changes in quantity and quality were introduced gradually, hence it was possible that they went unnoticed by some of the smokers – quite certainly by the younger people who had no experience with the pre-war products of the industry. However, this policy, which was partly forced upon the manufacturers by wartime regulations, has probably played an important role in the gradual decline of the popularity of the old brands.

in respect of which such variations are not practicable at all, so that whenever there is an increase in costs, the question arises, what would serve the interest of the firm better: to raise the price, and if so, by how much, or to absorb the cost difference by accepting a reduction in the contribution from the product. Similarly, when there is a fall in the cost of production, a decision has to be taken whether the cost saving (or any part of it) should be taken off the price.

The first task is then to determine whether cost change was specific to the firm or must be expected to affect all the competitors in a similar way. Generally speaking, if only one's own costs have changed, no price adjustment is called for, but if the whole industry is affected, it is not unreasonable to expect that the competitors will pass the cost difference on to the customers, and hence to feel no hesitation in following the same course.

However, this line of thought is based on two implicit assumptions, neither of which will invariably apply. The first is that the original price of the product was optimal, and the second that the reactions of the customers to price changes may be neglected as long as all the prices in the industry move in harmony.

Even if the initial price was fully appropriate at the time of launching, (which cannot in general be taken for granted,) and in the absence of an inflationary or deflationary tendency in the economy, it is highly advisable to reconsider at frequent intervals the prices at which the products of one's firm are being marketed.[3]

Dean suggests that pricing over the life cycle of a product is affected by three different aspects of maturity, which usually move in approximately parallel time paths: (1) technical-maturity, indicated by a declining rate of product development; (2) market-maturity, indicated by consumer acceptance of the basic idea and familiarity with the available brands; and (3) rivalry-maturity, indicated by the increasing stability of market shares and price structures.[4]

Ingenious as Dean's analysis is, its practical relevance is somewhat questionable. Product development can flare up again

---

[3] The revision should, of course, also extend to all the other aspects of marketing policy. Since their detailed discussion falls outside the scope of this book, only brief reference will be made to them here.

[4] Cf. Joel Dean, 'Pricing Pioneering Products', *Journal of Industrial Economics*, **17**, (3), July 1969, pp. 165–6.

after a period of decline; consumer acceptance has its ups and downs, and neither market shares nor price structures do invariably tend towards stability in the modern world. And even if all of them move parallel and in the same direction, there is not much in these concepts to indicate at what level the appropriate price should be set.

It is sometimes thought that when inflation holds sway, as has been largely the case in Britain and a number of other countries over the last forty-five years or so, all the pricing executive has to do is to keep increasing the price of the firm's products *pari passu* with the rate of cost inflation[5] or, at least, to the extent tolerated by any price control regulations. However, prices seldom move in perfect harmony and experience has shown that even if the members of the purchasing public do not voice any loud protests against rising prices, they may remain highly sensitive to price differences, especially to those between competing brands. Inflation does not therefore solve the pricing problem, but it is a fact that when all prices are moving in the same direction, it is easier to correct pricing mistakes than at times of general price stability.

The practical approach to price revision

The revision of the price of an established product may become necessary either because of a change in production costs or because sales fail to reach the expected level. It is reasonable to have an established procedure for examining the problem in the form of a check list, an example of which is given here.

Check lists for price reviews

Check lists are useful (1) for systematizing the approach to pricing problems and (2) for ensuring that no important aspect of the issue will escape attention.

The relevant aspects are not generally the same for each enterprise. The list below should be looked upon merely as an example of the framework which needs adaptation to the circumstances of the company it is to serve.

---

[5] Cf. pp. 43–4 and 83–7 for further discussion of this issue.

The order in which the specimen questions in the list are arranged is not invariant. It would be logical to consider them in the order as listed if the reason for the price review is some change on the production or cost side, and in the inverse order if it has been initiated by an actual or expected change in the market.

1 Production and cost factors

- What is the current cost structure of the product? Has there been any departure from the planned (or standard) cost?
- Have any of the unit factor costs (labour, materials, etc.) changed and to what extent?
- What is the present additional cost of overtime and/or shift-work?
- Have all possibilities of compensating for the increased cost of any factor been fully explored?
- What are the product-specific programmed costs – is there any reason why they should be changed?
- Have the cost changes we have experienced also affected our competitors?
- What are the present limits of productive capacity? To what extent is the capacity currently utilized? If the plant is operating at or near capacity, could extra capital be found to increase capacity and at what cost?
- Are any promising product modifications or extensions of the product line possible? What extra capital would be needed for these purposes and at what cost could it be obtained?

2 Profit and contribution factors

- To what extent is the profit target of the company being attained?
- To what extent do the current contributions differ from their planned levels?
- Where are the break-even points?
- Is there any reason why the contributions should be related to some limiting factor?

3 Marketing factors

- What channels of distribution are being used?
- What is our market share in each of the areas served? Is it increasing, steady or declining?

- How do channels of distribution, areas and current product variants compare in terms of (1) gross contribution over variable cost, (2) specific programmed costs and (3) other marketing costs?
- Are there any other channels of distribution and potential areas available, whether or not already used by the competitors?

4 Price relationships and trends

- Have prices changed recently? If so, what effect on the volume of sales could be attributed to the price changes?
- Is there a noticeable long-run trend in prices, and if so, what is it?
- What is the current price of our product (1) to the distributor and (2) to the final customer? Are our list prices and declared rebates being adhered to? If not, by how much and for what reason do they deviate from the planned levels?
- What types and amounts of discounts are in operation?
- To what extent do our prices, discounts and terms of sale differ from those of our competitors? Is there any price leadership in operation?
- What volume changes would compensate for any price change?
- What information is available or could be obtained to show the reactions to price changes of our actual and potential competitors?

If the reason for the price revision is on the sales side, the first task will be to make sure that the competition has been accurately identified. This is generally a straightforward task in the case of industrial products, though sudden invasion of the market by home-based or foreign competitors cannot always be foreseen.

As far as the consumer market is concerned, the problem is rather more difficult. It is an old adage that all the products a consumer buys are a charge on his income or capital, and are therefore in competition with one another, and this is of course true insofar as the money spent on one item cannot be spent on another. Competition is, however, a matter of degree, and what the price setter should determine is the extent to which price differences between the product in question and others affect his market share.

In the case of most normal convenience goods, that is to say, those consumer goods that are frequently purchased, the nearest substitutes are mostly found within the same product group; for example, the market share of a brand of butter will depend on its price relative to that of other brands. However, the total sales of butter are well known to be highly sensitive to changes in the level of margarine prices and *vice versa*.

It is a common mistake to assume that the consumers will invariably regard those brands within a given product field as being the nearest substitutes for one another that are nearest in price or show the greatest similarity as regards their physical characteristics. The results of several very thorough investigations of this issue have revealed that the standards by which the consumers judge substitutability may be substantially different from those of the marketing experts.[6] A manufacturer with more than one brand in the same product field might find that, unknown to themselves, his brand managers are competing with one another, or that the closest competitor of his premium brand is not another premium brand but the considerably cheaper store brands and generic brands.

It is therefore essential to establish the true competitive relationships before any other action is taken, and this can be done in two ways.

One of them is to hold a controlled shop experiment, carried out simultaneously in a set of supermarkets. Keeping all the other marketing factors constant, the prices of the brands investigated should be varied according to a pre-arranged design, with each individual price situation held for at least a week but preferably for a fortnight. The actual sales should be determined by shop audit, and from these the resultant market share of each of the brands can be calculated. The use of the market share instead of the actual sales figures eliminates the effect of the heavy week-to-week variations in the volume of sales experienced by all retail establishments.

The factors to be kept constant include whatever might temporarily influence the shoppers' choice between the different brands, apart from their prices. The brands concerned must be displayed with equal prominence: same number of facings, same shelf level, same kind of price marking on the items and the shelf labels, and the shelves must be restocked as soon as depletion occurs. There should be no special displays, no special offers of any kind, and the period should be one during which none of the manufacturers of the brands concerned conducts a promotion

---

[6] Cf., for example, André Gabor, Clive W. J. Granger and Anthony P. Sowter, 'Real and Hypothetical Shop Situations in Market Research', *Journal of Marketing Research*, **7**, August 1970, pp. 357–8, and André Gabor, 'Price and Consumer Behaviour – A Review', *Omega*, **1**, (3), 1973, pp. 287–8.

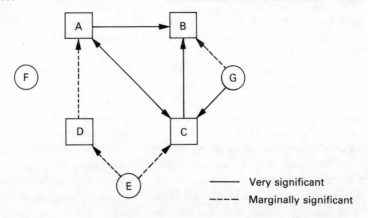

Figure 13.1   Competitive relationships in a multi-brand market

campaign, be it by heavy media advertising, free samples through the letter-box or any other means.

The results of a controlled shop experiment, carried out simultaneously in six supermarkets, is displayed in Figure 13.1. The letters A to G denote seven brands of washing powders; the solid lines indicate that price changes of one of the brands significantly affected the sales of the other, the arrows showing the direction of the relationship. Broken lines denote that the relationship found was only marginally significant.

Brands A and B were premium brands of similar composition but, as the arrow shows, the competitive relationship between them was one-sided, whereas A and C, which were very different according to the experts, were mutually competitive, in the sense that a price change of either significantly affected the sales of the other.

It might well be asked how the non-reciprocal relationship between A and B could have arisen. The answer lies in the market shares: A's share was large, B's relatively small. In order to simplify the demonstration, we shall use round figures and say that A's share was of the order of 50 per cent and B's 5 per cent. If a reduction in the price of A resulted in an increase of A's share to 55 per cent, then even if only a small fraction of this, say one fifth, was at the expense of B, its share dropped to 80 per cent of its previous level: a significant change. But when B's share rose as a result of a price cut in a proportion similar to what A experienced, and even if a large fraction of that cut into A's share, the effect was relatively small and not significant.

The reason why E, F and G are displayed differently is that the competitive relationships were investigated in one direction only.

The buy-response survey

Shop experiments are not free from disadvantages. They require the voluntary co-operation of a set of supermarkets representative of the market as a whole, which is often difficult to obtain, they are time-consuming and can be quite expensive.

Fortunately, there exists a well-tried alternative in the form of the hypothetical shop situation survey, preferably conducted with the hall method, as described on pp. 178–9. It can be carried out much more quickly and at a lower cost than the comparable shop experiment, and it has been established in a number of extensive fundamental research projects and commercial enquiries that, if properly conducted, the hypothetical shop situation method yields reliable results which can be of considerable help to the price setter in deciding whether a proposed price change promises to be advantageous to the firm or not.[7]

The central concept of the enquiry is the buy-response curve, but for the purpose in hand the prices called out or shown to the subjects should refer to the brand and not to the product in general. If the brand in question is available in different sizes, care must be taken to specify the pack size.

Figure 11.4 on page 263 illustrates the fact that the brand-specific buy-response curve has the same shape as the curve for the product group as a whole, except that, in the case of a popular premium brand, the former will be at a higher level than the latter and will not tail off so fast in the region of the lower prices. For a brand that is considered inferior by the consumers, the brand-specific buy-response curve will be at a lower level throughout.

Since the enquiry under discussion need not extend to prices that are outside the range of the contemplated price adjustments, it will

---

[7] Evidence is available in the reference listed in note 11, p. 260. However, the most important proof of the reliability of the buy-response method is the fact that it has been in successful practical use for about twenty years; cf. Peter Kraushar, 'How to Research', *Management Today*, January 1982, pp. 50–53. Such adverse criticism as has been raised against buy-response can be traced to misapplication of the method and/or misinterpretation of the results.

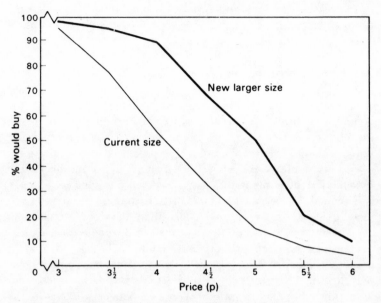

Figure 13.2   Buy-response curves of a count line

generally be sufficient to test not more than six to ten prices. The brand-specific buy-response curve is invariably found to be falling to the right in the region of the current price, hence the shape obtained will always be as illustrated in Figure 13.2. One of the curves refers to the current size of a count line, and the other to the larger size, proposed to be introduced at a higher price as a replacement. The enquiry was conducted shortly before the halfpenny ceased to be legal tender.

The current small size of this count line was the result of several reductions of the quantity, introduced at various dates in the past to counter cost increases while keeping the price at 4p. The fact that it was resented by the consumers is clearly seen by the relatively low acceptance of its price of 4p: only 54 per cent, which is well below the average for the type of product concerned. On the other hand, the larger size could count on a more favourable reception: the buy-responses reached 64 per cent at 4½p, an increase of over 18 per cent in the proportion of potential purchasers. Even if offered at 5p, the new size could count on almost the same proportion of potential purchasers as the old size at 4p.

Conducting the enquiry in the way just illustrated involves one of two assumptions: either that there is no effective competition to the

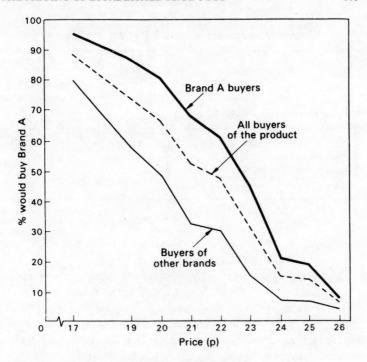

Figure 13.3   Buy-response curves of competitive brands

brand in question, or that the prices of the competitive brands will
remain unchanged.

Figure 13.3 illustrates one of the ways in which a competitive
market can be analysed: the uppermost curve shows the buy-
responses of the purchasers of Brand A, the next curve refers to all
the buyers of the product and the lowest curve displays the reactions
of those who patronize one or more of the other brands. The
similarity between the shapes of the three curves is striking: what is
particularly interesting is the relatively sharp rise in the percentage
of potential purchasers if the price is reduced by 1p from the current
level of 21p, and the relatively less steep decline if the price is
increased by 1p, while an increase by 2p would threaten quite
serious consequences.

The main results are summarized in Table 13.1. The bracketed
percentages are the deviations from the values with Brand A priced
at 21p. For example, when the price was reduced from 21p to 20p,
that is to say, by approximately 5 per cent, the increase in the

Table 13.1
Potential customers of Brand A at various prices

	Potential purchasers of Brand A		
Price of Brand A	Brand A buyers	All buyers of the product	Buyers of other brands
20p (− 5%)	80% (+18%)	66% (+27%)	48% (+50%)
21p	68%	52%	32%
22p (+ 5%)	61% (−10%)	47% (−10%)	30% (− 6%)
23p (+10%)	44% (−35%)	31% (−40%)	15% (−53%)

buy-responses of those who habitually buy Brand A was $100(80 − 68)/68 = 18$ per cent.

The proper significance of these figures can be appreciated only in comparison with the results of other enquiries in the same product field. It should further be noted that buy-responses invariably represent a momentary situation and hence the continued validity of their indications depends on the absence of any substantial change in the product field concerned and in the general economic situation.

Pricing executives who have explored the market for the products of their firm on previous occasions and have noted the effect of the price changes subsequently introduced, increasingly appreciate the practical value of the survey results and find them very helpful in reaching the appropriate pricing decisions.

Competitive situations can further be explored:

- By obtaining buy-response curves also for the products of the main competitors and comparing the reactions of the subjects to the prices of each brand.
- By collecting buy-responses against displays of the competitive brands at various price levels.
- By allowing the subjects multi-brand choices in several price situations.

When comparing the buy-response curves of different brands, the important aspects are price sensitivity and brand preference. Clearly, the steeper the buy-response curve is in the region of the current price, the more sensitive are sales to price changes, and high price sensitivity means low brand loyalty. On the other hand, if when plotted on the same diagram one buy-response curve is in a

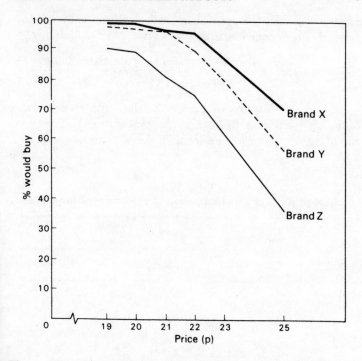

Figure 13.4   Buy-response curves of three non-food brands

higher position than another, this means that if the prices of the two brands are equal, a larger proportion of the purchasers will prefer the former to the latter.

Figure 13.4 shows the relevant parts of the buy-response curves of three competitive brands in the same non-food product field. It is immediately seen that Brand X is the one most highly esteemed by the potential customers, its popularity is approached by Brand Y at low prices only, and that Brand Z is considered decidedly inferior to both of them. The buy-response curves of Brand Y and Brand Z are almost parallel in the 23 to 25p range, but in fact the drop in the potential customers of Brand Y is $100 \times (80 - 57)/80 = 29$ per cent, and of Brand Z $100 \times (63 - 37)/63 = 41$ per cent.

In the above case the prices concerned were the same for all the three brands, and hence the comparison could be effected simply by reference to the percentage change in potential customers in response to a price change from 23p to 25p. Where such identity of price and price changes does not apply, the relative slopes can be used as comparative measures of the price sensitivity of the products concerned. The formula is analogous to that of price elasticity:[8]

$$\text{Relative slope: } = \frac{\text{Percentage change in potential customers}}{\text{Percentage change in price}}.$$

To illustrate its use, let us assume the data displayed in Table 13.2: the present price of Brand K is 25p, that of Brand L 30p and of Brand M 32p. A 1p rise is considered for Brand K and a 2p rise for L and M.

Table 13.2
The effect of price changes on potential customers of three brands

	Potential Customers		
Price	Brand K	Brand L	Brand M
p	%	%	%
25	87		
26	75		
30		72	
32		51	65
34			58
Relative slope	$\dfrac{12/87}{-1/25} = -3.4$	$\dfrac{21/72}{-2/30} = -4.4$	$\dfrac{7/65}{-2/32} = -1.7$

The effect of a price change does of course very much depend on whether or not the competition follows suit. The experienced pricing executive should be able to attach fairly definite probabilities to the possible reactions of the main competitors and use these probabilities in the evaluation of the situation.[9] In order to be able to judge the outcome of each of the probable alternative reactions, when buy-responses for one's own brand are elicited, the display should also include the competitive brands, with the appropriate prices clearly marked.

Similar displays can be used for recording multi-brand choices by asking the subjects not whether they would buy Brand A at the price

---

[8] Cf. Chapter 2, page 16.

[9] Cf. the Appendix to Part I, pp. 219–24 for the appropriate procedure.

called out (or, preferably, displayed), but rather which of the brands they would choose.

The design of any multi-brand experiment needs great care and good judgement, otherwise the results might become unwieldy. For example, if there are four brands and three different prices allotted to each, there will be 81 possible price situations, but it is most unlikely that they should all be of equal importance, and the investigation can be restricted to those few which, in the light of past experience, appear to be most probable.

The pricing executive who has the results of previous market research projects at his disposal will generally be able to keep any further pricing survey within manageable proportions by drastically reducing the number of brands to be covered. For example, a product field might consist of a large number of brands, yet it may be found that most of the retail outlets stock only two brands, and hence the survey can be broken up so that each part deals with the relationship between pairs of brands only. In some other instances it turned out that the market was distinctly segmented, insofar as the potential customers of the premium brands had no interest at all in the cheaper brands, while the purchasers of the latter were inclined to consider the premium brands only if their prices could be reduced to an unrealistically low level.

Competitive situations

The simplest case is that of the two-brand market, for which a fully developed analytical approach is available,[10] well tested in several large-scale enquiries in which hypothetical shop situation surveys were combined with simultaneous shop experiments.

The essence of the method is an adaptation and extension of the buy-response theory. The potential customer faced with a two-brand market will have three choices open to him: he will either buy Brand A or buy Brand B, or decide not to buy at all. If the item is important and claims only a slight proportion of the customer's budget, (which is in fact the case with many household products, including both food and non-food items), a purchase will almost certainly be made and a no-purchase decision will be merely a temporary postponement of the acquisition.

In the circumstances stated it will not be the absolute price of each brand that will govern the choice but the relative prices, and

---

[10] It is outlined in the Analytical Appendix, pp. 329–32.

these will decide the market shares of the brands rather than absolute sales. Total sales, however, will depend on absolute prices as well as on a number of other factors.

Very active competition between different brands may lead to the point where, to use the accepted term, a *commodity market* emerges. This means that the consumers fail to see any significant difference between the quality of the various brands and buy the one that is the cheapest at the time. If the prices happen to be equal, so will the market shares be. In a two-brand market the curve expressing the relationship between relative prices and market shares will then approximate the angular shape shown in Figure 13.5 (a). The price span indicated by $T_+ - T_-$ in the diagram, (assumed to be $\pm$ 2 per cent), is the range of indifference, meaning that as long as the difference between the two prices does not exceed 2 per cent, the market shares will tend to be equal, but as soon as the price difference exceeds this range, the market share of A will either drop to zero or rise to 100 per cent.

In Figures 13.5 (a) and (b) the percentage difference between the two prices, that is, $100 \times (P_a - P_b)/Pb$, is measured along the vertical axis, and the market share of Brand A, defined as:

$$100 \times S_a/(S_a + S_b)$$

where S_a and S_b are the sales of the two brands in each price situation, along the horizontal axis.

If the customers do perceive some significant difference between the two brands, and consider Brand A better than Brand B, the curve will be as displayed in Figure 13.5 (b).

This analysis enables us to give precise definition to *brand preference* and *brand loyalty*. The former is characterized by the market share of A when the two prices are equal, and also by the price ratio needed to make the market shares equal; thus in the case of Figure 13.5 (b) the market share concerned is about 60 per cent, and the price difference approximately 5 per cent. The reason why there is a band rather than a slender curve in the diagram is that the analysis will yield the result in this form.

Figure 13.6 shows the result of the investigation of a two-brand market. The product was a household cleaner, and it can be seen that the customers' preference leant towards Brand Y, since when the prices of the two brands were equal, Brand Y's share was around 62 per cent, and that of Brand X 38 per cent. In order to achieve equal market shares, the price of Brand X had to be roughly 8 per cent below that of Brand Y.

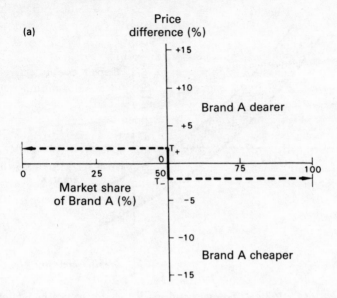

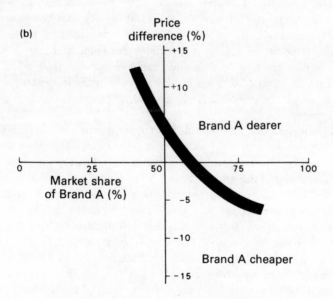

Figure 13.5 Price difference and market share: (a) in a commodity market; (b) where brand preference and loyalty are present

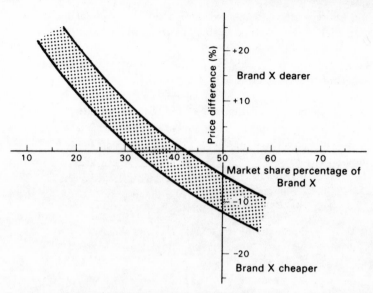

Figure 13.6 Price differences and market shares of two brands of a household cleaner

The measure of brand loyalty is its price. According to an American saying 'There ain't no brand loyalty that two cents off can't overcome', and while it should not be accepted at its face value, it points in the right direction: the value of brand loyalty which two cents price difference can overcome, is two cents. In Figures 13.5 and 13.6 brand loyalty appears in the form of the slope of the band: the steeper it is, the greater is the effect of a given price difference.

The outstanding merit of this form of analysis is that it enables the pricing executive to see the effect of a price change according to the behaviour of the competition. For example, if the prices are equal at the moment and the price of Brand X is reduced by something like 8 or 10 per cent, then, provided the price of Brand Y remains unchanged, the market shares will tend to equality, which means that the rate at which Brand X is sold will increase by about 25 per cent. If, however, the price cut is matched by Brand Y, the brand shares are most likely to remain unchanged. The extent to which combined sales may be expected to react when the price level is lowered, largely depends on the current extent of the penetration of the product.

The results of a series of systematic experiments of price variation in multi-brand markets carried out by Professor A. S. C. Ehrenberg and his research associates at the London Business School indicate that sales responses to price changes are immediate with no lags and independent of what went before; also that the effect is much the same for different grocery products, brands and variation in experimental conditions. In the circumstances of this study the percentage change in sales observed was about 2.6 times the percentage change in the price of the brand concerned.[11]

Blamires has proposed a refinement of the approach to the pricing of closely competitive products.[12] He suggests that the buy-response method can be made both more economical and more effective by disaggregating the potential customers, and that attitude tests make it possible to distinguish between four groups, the first two of which need not be faced with buy-response questions:

1 Those who will buy the test brand irrespective of relative prices.
2 Those who will buy a certain competitive brand irrespective of the price of the test brand.
3 Those who remain faithful to the test brand only as long as its price is not above that of a certain competitive brand.
4 Those who will remain faithful to a certain competitive brand only as long as its price is not above that of the test brand.

Blamires has demonstrated the applicability of his method by the exploration of the price sensitivity of the demand for Heinz Baked Beans, albeit with a sample that was far too small to yield statistically significant results: only 73 subjects, 36 of whom were eliminated as being price insensitive. However, the observed purchasing behaviour of consumers in several brand markets casts some doubt on the reliability of the attitude tests.

Apart from the behaviour of the competition, the effect of a price change will vary with the price awareness of the customers and on the stress put on pricing by the other marketing factors. Media advertising, special displays, etc. can both speed up and amplify the price effect.

As described in Chapter 10, price awareness can be measured by price recall, that is to say, by the proportion of the subjects who are

---

[11]See *A Tabular Report on the Winter Marketing Experiment, Vol. I*, prepared by Survey Research Associates Limited on behalf of the Centre for Marketing and Communication, London Business School, September 1986.

[12]Chris Blamires, 'Pricing research techniques: a review and a new approach', *Journal of the Market Research Society*, **23**, (3), July 1981, pp. 103–26.

able to name the price paid for their last purchase of the good, and the extent to which the prices named approximate those actually charged at the time in the shops. If the scatter of the prices named around the correct price is not symmetrical, this indicates that the *price image* tends to differ from the actual price.

Deviations of the price image from the current price have been observed in both directions. A low image implies some degree of sales resistance, whereas a high image means that the brand is considered cheap at the present price.

Finally, let us note that the results of the surveys here described might lead to decisions other than a price adjustment. The main alternatives are indicated in the decision tree, Figure 12.2, page 291.

The most drastic decision is to drop the product, a step which manufacturers are often reluctant to take, even though the elimination of undesirable products may lead both to increased total sales and to better profitability.[13] While it is hardly possible to generalize on this point, it seems appropriate to suggest that product abandonment decisions should be preceded by a period of 'milking',[14] especially if, by cutting out heavy advertising and other marketing expenditure, the price of the product could substantially be lowered.

Additional features of the questionnaires

Preceding the buy-response, the multiple choice and the price-last-paid questions, each subject should be asked to name the brand or brands normally bought and the size of pack preferred, since the answers to these questions will decide whether the interview should be continued at all, and if so, which part of the questionnaire is to be used. It might also be of interest to know in which type of retail outlet the subject buys the product.

In the same interview the subjects may also be asked to say whether they agree or disagree with certain statements, such as, for example, 'Brand X is good value for money', 'The container is very

---

[13] Cf. Paul W. Hamelman and Edward M. Mazze, 'Improving Product Abandonment Decisions', *Journal of Marketing*, **36**, (2), April 1972, pp. 20–26. It concerns a computer-aided model for product abandonment decisions, called PRESS (Product Review and Evaluation Subsystem), which deserves serious attention.

[14] Cf. the note** in Figure 12.2, page 291, for the definition of milking.

handy', and so on,[15] and questions could be put to find out which features of the brands with which the subject is familiar are particularly liked or disliked by him, whether or not a pack size different from those currently available would be preferred, and so on.

Fields of application

The survey methods here described are particularly useful for exploring the market for any frequently purchased convenience good, but can also be adopted to shopping and specialty goods, most of which fall into the category of consumer durables. In this case, however, the subjects must be persons who are either seriously contemplating a purchase or have recently bought one of the goods concerned.

Industrial markets generally need a different approach to a pricing problem. The main aspects were discussed in Chapters 6 and 7, but if the good in question is a recognizable component of the finished product of the buyer's firm, it is the final market that calls for exploration, and here the buy-response method may well be appropriate.

The buy-response method is also suitable for the solution of the pricing problems of such service establishments as, for example, dry cleaners, travel agencies, and so on.

Four case histories

The following examples of the application of buy-response analysis are taken from the files of Pricing Research Limited, London and have been communicated by Mr R. W. F. Eassie (now a director of MM Corporate Services Limited). They were first published in *Issues in Pricing Policy*, (edited by André Gabor), *European Journal of Marketing*, **13**, (4), 1979, pp. 173–181, and are reproduced here by permission.

---

[15] A three-point scale (agree – neither agree nor disagree – disagree) will be sufficient for most purposes, but some researchers prefer a five-point scale, adding 'strongly agree' and 'strongly disagree' to the list, which is then printed on a showcard.

Cast history 1: fresh food

A recent pricing research project is of some interest as it is a good illustration of the way the method works; this particular case not only provided data on the possibilities for premium pricing but also gave worthwhile confirmation of the precision of the technique and of the consumers' ability to answer buy-response questions with accuracy and consistency even during long complicated interviews.

The product to be researched was a fresh food. (It was necessary for reasons of confidentiality to disguise the exact nature of the product in this as in the other case histories here presented.) The problem was to determine the extent to which a pre-packed product of uniform quality could obtain a premium over standard products.

In this project a sample of 500 housewives were each shown four pairs of transparent packs containing the product. In each case one of the pairs was in conformity with the standard of the proposed premium line, while the other pair contained ordinary products suffering from some common blemish, e.g., wide variety of sizes in one instance, discolouration in another, cracked skins in third, and so on. It should be emphasized that the blemishes were comparatively trivial and were typical of those found in products normally on sale in the shops. The housewives were placed in their usual shopping situation of judging the products by their appearances.

So the position was that every respondent was looking at eight samples of the product, four of which were identical, though this last point was not revealed to the housewives. In each of the eight cases they were asked a buy-response question over the same range of prices.

The results for the four identical products are shown in Figure 13.7.[16] The buy-response curves for these products were extremely close to one another whereas the curves for the other four packs all gave significantly different results, but, for the sake of clarity, only one of the latter is shown in the figure. The conclusions that emerged from this piece of research were as follows:

- In this product field housewives were well able to distinguish even quite small variations in quality after a brief look at sample products.

---

[16]In order to safeguard commercial interests, the graduation of the price scale is not shown in Figures 13.7–11.

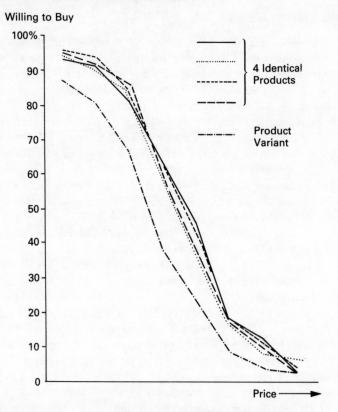

Figure 13.7 Buy-responses: five packs of food products

- Identical products resulted in virtually identical buy-response results, providing further evidence of the consistent nature of the buy-response methodology.
- Housewives were willing to pay a worthwhile premium for products of higher quality.

These findings were more important than the absolute price levels involved because, as with many fresh foods, the retail prices in the market concerned vary considerably through the course of the year.

The degree of precision achieved in this case is particularly worth noting because the fresh products used in various halls throughout the country could not in practice be quite as alike one another as samples of a manufactured product. The 'identical' packs were as far as possible of exactly the same standard but could hardly have been as closely matched as cans off a canning line.

Case history 2: packaging methods

The previous example was a case where the consumers showed a preference for one product over another, and were willing to pay a higher price for the product of their choice. One of the most important practical uses of the buy-response system is the way it puts consumers' preferences in perspective. In the business world the crux of the matter is not whether people feel some vague affection for a product but whether they will put their hands in their pockets and buy it at a price that makes sense to the manufacturer.

There are many research situations in which a respondent is asked to choose between two products in terms of colour, size, convenience, etc., or to rank each of several products on a number of five-point scales. Frequently the winner in this sort of contest is a new product incorporating some marginal advantage over the existing brands but which can only be marketed at a rather higher price. It seems reasonable enough to suppose that a better product can command a higher price, but acting on this assumption can lead to disaster because the consumer is often far from sure that the old cheap product is not still the best buy. This is where buy-response analysis comes into the picture. The technique enables one clearly to distinguish between superficial preferences and real life choices.

In one recent project a new form of packaging was tested. Initial qualitative research had shown that the new pack's good points easily outweighed any drawbacks among ABC1 housewives. Similarly the quantitative research among a sample of 250 housewives produced a lot of favourable comment for the new pack, for example:

	Agree	Disagree	Don't know
	%	%	%
New pack has better appearance than old one	88	11	1
New pack easier to open than old one	82	16	1

Some of the other features were not quite so much in the new pack's favour – but the general preference for the new type of packaging was quite strong. Then came the buy-response curve analysis which showed that for the 1 lb size of the product being researched the new pack could only command a premium of 1p, whereas the cost of the new pack would mean a retail price rise of 3p to maintain profit margins. Once one had looked at the pricing research results, the decision to abandon the new pack was obvious. But without the buy-response's down-to-earth examination of what people would pay, the consumers' superficial enthusiasm for the new packaging could have led to an expensive mistake.

Case history 3: snack product

The majority of projects involving pricing research is concerned with the advisability of altering specific prices, rather than the more broadly based problems described in the previous couple of case histories. In research of this kind the important point is to relate the results to the norms established over many years of work in this field. It cannot be emphasized too strongly that, despite its undoubtable practical relevance, the buy-response curve is not actually a demand curve. The interpretation of the slope of the curve, the relationship of the curve to a product's current price, the significance of breaking-points – the solutions to all such problems are heavily dependent on relating each new curve to the data bank of previous experience.

The value of this sort of investigation may be illustrated by means of work carried out on a snack product purchased both by adults and children and bought mainly in confectioners' or newsagents' shops. Two very similar pieces of research were carried out 18 months apart. Remarkably for these inflationary times, the prices of both the product and its main competitor did not rise over this period of a year and a half, which means that the results in this case history are exceptionally clear-cut. The product in question was more expensive than its competitor but, since it contained more per pack, the consumer was not making a straight comparison between two more or less identical products. The two rivals were also substantially different in texture and other characteristics, although the taste was similar.

Research was carried out using both children in the age range of 11–15 and adults. In Figures 13.8, 9 and 10 the buy-response curves for the product (*P*) and the main competitor (*C*) have been drawn so that their respective current prices at the time of the research coincide, though, as already mentioned, the retail price of *P* was actually higher than that of *C*.

Figure 13.8 gives the two buy-response curves for *P* (adult respondents only). They show a dangerously low acceptance of the current price at the time of the first research and a substantial improvement eighteen months later.

Figure 13.9 shows a high acceptance of the current price of *C* at the first research and a near 100 per cent level by the time of the second survey.

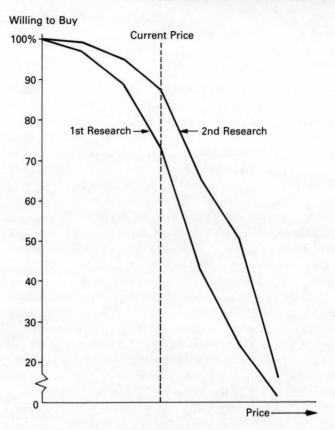

Figure 13.8   Buy-responses at two dates: snack product P

Figure 13.10 places the first research result for *C* on the same graph as the second research findings for *P* and shows that *P* is in very much the same position as *C* had been 18 months before. The results for the children were much the same as for adults.

An analysis of the figures together with comparisons with similar products and with other repeat purchase items of similar unit value showed clearly that there would be great risks attached to any attempt at raising *P*'s price at the time of the original research. By the time of the second research the buy-response results (together with those of multi-brand questions asked at the same time) indicated that a price increase of 1p per pack would cause a minor drop in volume but would be justified in terms of profits.

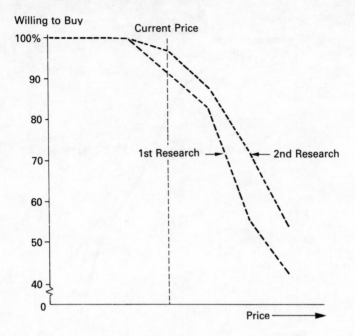

Figure 13.9   Buy-responses at two dates: snack product C

Another lesson to be drawn from this example concerns the competitive product *C*. At the time of the first research this brand could have put up its price with very little risk, and by the date of the second survey it was seriously underpriced. Because they had failed to research their price position, the manufacturers of product *C* were obtaining a much smaller profit than what was potentially available to them. They may well have been frightened to be the first to move their prices up but, if so, their fear was based on an ignorance that could easily have been dispelled.

Case history 4: sauce

The final case history here presented describes another practical application of the new methods of pricing research. The investigation concerned involved the testing of a sauce for use in cooking. Because of the novel nature of the product it was important to obtain initial reactions to the concept and then to leave the product for a period of in-home use before re-interviewing the respondents. In such cases, if the buy-response curve shows a greater willingness to

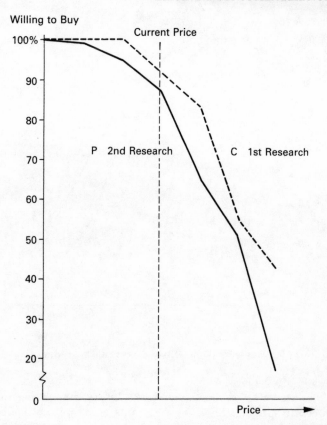

Figure 13.10   Buy-responses: products C and P at different dates

buy after trial than before, the data may well give an indication of the extent to which money-off offers will be necessary to stimulate initial purchases. On the other hand a severe drop in willingness to pay a reasonable price could well show that the concept has been over-sold by the advertising and that the product does not live up to its claims.

Of the total sample of 200 housewives, two-thirds were classified (as a result of other sections of the questionnaire) as being interested in the concept behind this new product. Buy-response questions were administered both before trial and afterwards at the recall stage. The results are shown in Figure 13.11.

A sharp fall-off occurs above 25p and this significant pricing point remains in both the pre- and post-trial research. In fact there is very

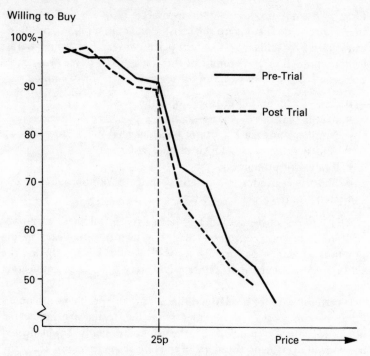

Figure 13.11 Pre-trial and post-trial buy-responses: sauce for cooking

little difference between the two curves, which shows that the product's performance was generally in line with the promise contained in the advertising.

The results of this research gave a firm indication of the maximum that could be charged for the product and also showed that there was very little sales volume to be gained by selling at any price below this level. Similarly there were no strong reasons for spending money on initial trial money-off promotions. The latter finding alone saved more than enough money to pay for the whole of the placement test.

Conclusions

Price is both an indicator and a reflection of value. People value what they have to pay for; they also have to pay for most of the possessions that they value. The willingness to pay a particular price for a particular product is the customer's ultimate verdict on the item concerned. It sums up the consumer's opinion of the product's attributes. From this it follows that pricing research is not a separate esoteric branch of marketing but the central part of many research projects. It may be of value in all sorts of ways, for example:

- Extent and timing of price adjustments.
- Merits of a price increase against a pack size decrease.
- Number and relative size of packs needed in a range.
- Added value of new forms of packaging.
- Testing of promotions.
- Shifts in attitudes to a product's price before and after trial.
- Retail outlet's pricing policy.

The buy-response method has been used in all these situations and in many other projects over the last twenty years giving practical guidance on pricing as well as providing help for the solution of problems that at first sight may have little connection with price.

It certainly cannot be claimed that all pricing problems are now a thing of the past. Improvements in the technique are being attempted all the time; for instance, increasingly sophisticated methods of measuring the slope of the buy-response curve are being developed so as to make it possible to produce more accurate forecasts of the effects of price changes and to compare the results obtained from research in widely different markets. Calculations of slope characteristics are now built into the pricing research computer program and enable a rapid comparison to be made with previous case histories.

In conclusion, the points to be emphasized are that pricing is an essential part of all marketing strategies and that market research techniques are now available to provide practical assistance in the solving of pricing problems.

Summary

Changes in the cost of production can be met by product variation, that is to say, by altering the quantity or quality of the standard pack, and by price adjustments. The former is the accepted practice with most count lines, but there are limits to its applicability, and in any protracted inflationary period the time will come when a further rise in costs must lead to a price increase which, in the case of count lines, is often coupled with the replacement of the standard pack by a somewhat larger size.

Where product variation is not a practical solution, even small changes in cost are likely to raise pricing problems, and the same applies when there is any change in the market of the product.

In approaching the problem of a price revision it is advisable to use a properly designed check list, an example of which is included.

Market research can be of substantial help in reaching a correct pricing decision by identifying the competition and revealing how price differences would affect sales.

One of the ways in which this can be done is the controlled shop experiment, which is, however, not at all easy to carry out properly. It also takes a long time to complete and is relatively expensive. A considerably quicker and less expensive method is the hypothetical shop situation survey. It has been proved that, if properly conducted, it will provide reliable results that are of considerable value in arriving at optimal pricing decisions. The main points to watch are the size and composition of the sample of subjects, the realistic character of the mock display and the inclusion of all the relevant brands in the enquiry.

The principal concept is that of the buy-response curve, with the questionnaire adapted to the problem in hand. The method is illustrated with several examples, including the case of a count line and the re-pricing of branded products.

Generally speaking, the steeper the buy-response curve is over the relevant price range, the greater is the price sensitivity of the customers. The measures obtained do, however, require interpretation in the light of experience, since the significance of the results is relative rather than absolute.

The method has also been extended to the study of multi-brand situations, the simplest case of which is the market dominated by two brands. The analysis will indicate the outcomes of price adjustments according to the behaviour of the competitor.

The extent of price awareness and the price image of the good, which is not invariably identical with its current price, can be explored at the same time. Further questions concerning the attitudes of the subjects may also be added which, together with the usual classification data, should help to recognize market segmentation.

The research methods described in this chapter are directly applicable to pricing studies concerned with any frequently purchased convenience good, but can also be adapted to help with the pricing of consumer durables, certain services and even some industrial products.

Four detailed case studies from the files of Pricing Research Limited, London, complete this chapter.

The theoretical foundations of the methods and the main statistical aspects of the surveys concerned are given in the Analytical Appendix by C. W. J. Granger; conjoint analysis is described in the Appendix by Trevor Watkins.

Appendix I to Part II
Analytical appendix

C. W. J. Granger

A.1 THEORY OF THE BUY-RESPONSE CURVE

Suppose that an individual consumer is asked to consider the purchase of a particular commodity. Appropriate questioning may produce a pair of prices, denoted by $\underline{R}$ and $\bar{R}$, with $\bar{R} > \underline{R}$, such that if the price of the commodity, denoted by P, falls into the region $(\underline{R}, \bar{R})$, then the consumer would buy it, but if P is outside the region, no purchase would be made. If $P > \bar{R}$, the price could be considered as being 'too high'. In economic terms, the price is too high if the utility the consumer expects to gain from having the commodity is less than the utility of the amount of money, P, that he would have to give up to make the purchase. If $P < \underline{R}$, the price is said to be 'too low'. Unless one is extremely familiar with the product, there will inevitably be some uncertainty about the amount of utility one will derive from having it. If the chance of getting an unsatisfactorily low utility becomes large enough, then no purchase will be made. This situation is known as one involving 'safety-first risk' in economics. As has been explained in Chapter 11, there are strong reasons to believe that a consumer's expectations about risk will increase as the price requested decreases. The price $\underline{R}$ represents that value where the expected utility of having the product and the expected risk just balance, so that a price below $\underline{R}$ leads to no purchase, because, in this situation, the perceived risk outweighs potential utility.

Let G be some reasonably homogeneous, large group of consumers. Suppose that, for each person in G, values of $\underline{R}$ and $\bar{R}$ are obtained for a given, completely specified commodity. Almost certainly, these values will vary from person to person so that $\underline{R}$ and $\bar{R}$ may be thought of as random variables. Define the functions $L_G(P)$, $H_G(P)$ as follows:

$L_G(P) = Prob\ (\underline{R} > P)$
   = Probability that a member of G, chosen at random, will find the article 'too cheap' if priced at P.
$H_G(P) = Prob\ (\bar{R} < P)$
   = Probability that a member of G, chosen at random, will find the article 'too expensive' if priced at P.

For ease of exposition, the subscript G will be dropped.

Clearly, $0 \leqslant L(P) \leqslant 1$, $0 \leqslant H(P) \leqslant 1$ as these quantities are probabilities. As G has been postulated to be homogeneous, it is reasonable to assume, as indicated in Figure AII.1, that $H(P)$ is monotonically increasing (that is, $H(P_1) > H(P_2)$, if $P_1 > P_2$ and

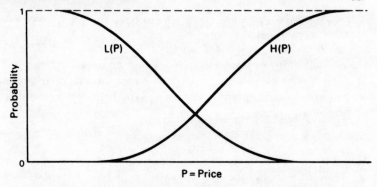

Figure AII.1   Curves of the L(P) and H(P) functions

$L(P)$ is monotonically decreasing. Thus, $H(P)$ and $1-L(P)$ have all the properties of distribution functions. From the definitions, it seems logical to expect that $H(0) = 0$, and as P becomes large $H(P) \rightarrow 1$ and $L(P) \rightarrow 0$.

Three further curves can be defined by

$$B(P) = 1-L(P)-H(P)$$
$$= \text{Probability that a member of } G, \text{ chosen at random will find the article, when priced at } P, \text{ belonging to his acceptable price range.}$$
$$l(P) = -dL(P)/dP$$
and
$$h(P) = dH(P)/dP.$$

$B(P)$ is the function of the buy-response curve and is clearly associated with the idea of a demand curve but has no quantity-of-purchase aspect, merely the plausibility of purchase. $l(P)$ and $h(P)$ are the frequency (or probability-density) functions of the quantities $\underline{R}$ and $\bar{R}$ respectively.

The theory so far outlined is completely general, but the most important aspect of the approach described in Chapter 11 is that it is specific and therefore of practical use. This arises because the following hypothesis has been tested and found to be acceptable:

Hypothesis A

$l(P)$ and $h(P)$ have a strong tendency to approximate log-normal frequency functions, so that if we denote $p = \log P$, then $l(p)$ and $h(p)$ approximate normal curves.

This hypothesis was tested specifically in Gabor and Granger (1966),[1] and also in later work, and found acceptable. Using the notation $X \sim N(m,\sigma)$ for the variable X having normal distribution with mean m and standard deviation σ, hypothesis A suggests that

$$\underline{r} = \log \underline{R} \sim N(m_1,\sigma_1)$$
$$\text{and } \overline{r} = \log \overline{\overline{R}} \sim N(m_2,\sigma_2)$$

However, it is easily shown that necessarily $\sigma_1 = \sigma_2 = \sigma$, as otherwise $B(p)$ could take negative values, which is impossible from its interpretation. Further, Gabor and Granger (1966) tested the hypothesis $\sigma_1 = \sigma_2$ and found it acceptable. It then follows that $B(p)$ has the expression

$$B(p) = 1 - L(p) - H(p)$$

$$= \frac{1}{\sigma\sqrt{2\pi}} \int_{-\infty}^{p} \left[\exp\left(-\frac{1}{2\sigma^2}(x - m_1)^2\right) - \exp\left(-\frac{1}{2\sigma^2}(x - m_2)^2\right) \right] dx$$

$$= \mathit{erf}(x + c) - \mathit{erf}(x - c)$$

where

$$x = \frac{p - a}{\sigma}, \quad a = \frac{1}{2}(m_1 + m_2)$$

$$c = \frac{b}{\sigma}, \quad b = \frac{1}{2}(m_1 - m_2)$$

and $\mathit{erf}(x)$ is the so-called 'error-function' or the cumulative distribution function of an $N(0,1)$ variable, given by

$$\mathit{erf}(x) = \frac{1}{\sqrt{2\pi}} \int_{-\infty}^{x} e^{-y^2 k} dy.$$

The advantage of this formulation is that tables of $\mathit{erf}(x)$ can be found in most standard statistical texts, so that $B(p)$ can easily be found for all p, once m_1, m_2 and σ are known. $B(p)$ is found to be symmetric about the point $a = \frac{1}{2}(m_1 + m_2)$ and to be bell-shaped.

---

[1] André Gabor & C. W. J. Granger, 'Price as an Indicator of Quality: Report on an Enquiry', *Economica*, 33, February 1966, pp. 43–70.

However, it is not strictly a probability-density function as the area underneath the curve is not equal to one.

It should be noted that the shape of $B(p)$ depends on just three parameters, a, b and σ. a can be interpreted as that price for which the largest number of the group G would purchase the article. σ and b are both measures of the range of acceptable prices and will depend both on the variability of the attitudes of the group to the article and, in practice, also on the closeness of substitutes available and the current prices of these substitutes.[2] It is reasonable to expect the existence of a relationship between b and σ. In an earlier study[3] this proposition was tested and evidence, based on several products, was found for a relationship of the form

$$\sigma = 0.78b.$$

If this were generally true, it would follow that the height of $B(p)$ at its maximum, at $p = a$, is $B(a) = 0.8$, that is, that the price at which the peak of the buy-response curve falls will be acceptable to 80 per cent of the purchasers of the commodity. However, since some exceptions to this tendency have also been observed, it could not be claimed to be of general validity.[4]

A.2 MODELS OF MULTI-BRAND MARKETS

Consider a consumer intent on making a purchase in a two-brand market or in a multi-brand market, provided only two of the brands are of interest to him, and that he is very familiar with both brands. Denote the brands by A and B, and let their 'too-high' prices be R_a and R_b. For the time being, it will be assumed that there are no 'too low' prices, or at least that the price-ranges that will be considered

---

[2] See the discussion relating to the buy-response curve and to the prices last paid in Chapter 11.

[3] Gabor, André and Granger, C. W. J., 'The Attitude of the Consumer to Prices', in *Pricing Strategy*, (B. Taylor and G. Wills, eds), Staples Press, London, 1969, pp. 147–9. It contains the theory without, however, quoting the value of σ.

[4] It should certainly not be expected to hold where inflation is rampant. Cf. Shamir, J., 'Consumers' Subjective Perception of Price in Time of Inflation', *Journal of Economic Psychology*, **6**, (4), 1985, pp. 383–98.

for the brands do not bring too low prices into operation to any noticeable extent. Denote by P_a and P_b the prices of the brands and, on using logarithms, denote $r = \log R$ and $p = \log P$.

Assume that the 'excess utility' of a commodity with 'too high' price R and sold at price P is proportional to

$$Eu = r - p$$

so that r is a measure of the expected utility of having the good, p is the utility of the amount of money one has to hand over to get the good, and Eu is the difference between two utilities. If Eu is negative, the consumer clearly will not buy the good, which is the purchasing rule that gives rise to the 'too high' curve described in Section A.1 of this Appendix.

For the two-brand market, a sensible decision rule for the consumer is:

1 Buy neither A nor B, if $r_a < p_a$ and $r_b < p_b$.
2 Buy A, if $(r_a - p_a) \geq (r_b - p_b)$ and $r_a \geq p_a$.
3 Buy B, if $(r_b - p_b) \geq (r_a - p_a)$ and $r_b \geq p_b$.

Thus, the consumer chooses the brand that provides the greater excess utility, provided this is positive. If neither brand provides a positive excess utility, then no purchase is made. If now a homogeneous group of consumers, G, is considered, the values for r_a, r_b will vary from one person to another and so these quantities can be considered to be random variables. As pointed out in A.1, these quantities individually appear to be distributed normally, and so it is not unreasonable to assume that the pair (r_a, r_b) are jointly normally distributed $N(m_a, m_b; \sigma_a, \sigma_b; \rho)$, where ρ is the correlation between r_a, r_b in the aggregate. It now follows from the decision rule that

Probability not buy $= \Phi^{(2)}(\bar{p}_a, \bar{p}_b; \rho)$

where

$$\bar{p}_a = \frac{p_a - m_a}{\sigma_a}, \quad \bar{p}_b = \frac{p_b - m_b}{\sigma_b}$$

and $\phi^{(2)}(x, y; \rho)$ is the bivariate distribution function of a random variable (X, Y) that is $N(0, 0; 1, 1; \rho)$, that is:

$$\text{Prob}(X \leq x, Y \leq y) = \Phi^{(2)}(x, y; \rho).$$

The values of this function are available in books of statistical tables; for example, in *Handbook of Statistical Tables*, by D. B. Owen, Addison-Wesley, 1962, Table 8.5.

The assumption that (r_a, r_b) are jointly normal also gives that $r_a - r_b$ will have a normal distribution with mean

$$m_{ab} = m_a - m_b$$

and variance

$$\sigma_{ab}^2 = \sigma_a^2 + \sigma_b^2 - 2\rho\sigma_a\sigma_b.$$

The decision rule now gives

$$\text{Probability buy } A = \{\text{Prob buy}\}. \left\{ 1 - \Phi\left(\frac{p_a - p_b - m_{ab}}{\sigma_{ab}}\right) \right\}$$

and

$$\text{Probability buy } B = \{\text{Prob. buy}\}. \left\{ \Phi\left(\frac{p_a - p_b - m_{ab}}{\sigma_{ab}}\right) \right\},$$

where Prob. buy $= 1 - $ Prob. not buy
$$= 1 - \Phi^{(2)}(p_a, p_b; \rho)$$
and, as before, $\Phi(x)$ is the distribution function of a univariate $N(0,1)$ random variable.

Consider now just those consumers in G who decide to buy one or other of the brands. Call this group G'. For a randomly selected number of the group G'

$$\text{Probability buys } A = 1 - \Phi\left(\frac{p_a - p_b - m_{ab}}{\sigma_{ab}}\right)$$

where it is important to note that this is a *conditional* probability, as it is assumed that the consumer will certainly buy either A or B. If it is further assumed that the *quantity* bought by members of G' does not depend on p_a, p_b, at least in realistic price regions, one has

$$\text{Brand share of } B = \frac{\text{Sales of } B}{\text{Sales of } A + \text{Sales of } B}$$

$$= \Phi\left(\frac{p_a - p_b - m_{ab}}{\sigma_{ab}}\right).$$

Thus, a plot of brand share against p_a/p_b on log-normal probability paper should produce a straight line, and hence estimates of m_{ab} and

σ_{ab}. Several large-scale experiments produced plots that agreed with this prediction.[5]

It is seen that brand shares can be predicted for any pair of prices p_a, p_b once the two parameters m_{ab} and σ_{ab} are known. It should be noted that the theory suggests that brand shares will remain unaltered if prices change but the ratio of prices P_a/P_b stays constant. This agrees with elementary economic theory in an inflationary period, provided incomes keep up with general price levels. The quantities m_{ab} and σ_{ab} have natural interpretations in a marketing context; m_{ab} measures the inherent preference for Brand A over Brand B, since if prices P_a and P_b are equal, then for given σ_{ab} the brand share of B is a function only of the constant m_{ab}. The extent to which consumers switch brands as the price ratio P_a/P_b, or the difference in log prices $p_a - p_b$, increases is considerably influenced by σ_{ab}, so this quantity is a natural measure of the degree of substitutability between A and B as perceived by consumers. A small value of σ_{ab} means that the brands are considered close substitutes. A high value would suggest that they are not so considered, so that price changes will have little little effect. Much of marketing practice, such as packaging, advertising and selection of brand characteristics, can be considered as attempts to change the values of m_{ab} and σ_{ab}, to give a higher relative perceived value to one brand and to reduce the extent to which consumers view brands as substitutes. One side-benefit from the two-brand price research discussed in Chapter 13 is that estimates of m_{ab} and σ_{ab} result. Changes through time in these quantities might be used to measure the success or otherwise of the firm's marketing effort.

There is no inherent difficulty in generalizing this theory to the multi-brand case or to reintroduce the too-cheap situation. However, the mathematics does become considerably more complicated and testing of the adequacy of the theory is much more difficult.

---

[5] Cf. A. Gabor, C. W. J. Granger and A. P. Sowter, 'Real and Hypothetical Shop Situations in Market Research', *Journal of Marketing Research*, **7**, August 1970, pp. 355–9; 'The Influence of Price Differences on Brand Shares and Switching', *British Journal of Marketing*, Winter 1969, pp. 223–30; 'The Effect of Price on Choice: A Theoretical and Empirical Investigation', *Applied Economics*, **3**, 1971, pp. 167–81; also A. P. Sowter and A. Billson, 'The Further Development and Testing of Theories of Choice', Nottingham University Consumer Study Group, December 1975, (unpublished research report).

A.3 GATHERING MARKETING DATA FROM THE PUBLIC

The techniques described in Part II of this volume have been tested and evaluated on information relating to the behaviour of actual consumers. The data have been collected in various ways, such as by conducting experiments in simulated shop situations in which consumers were asked to make hypothetical decisions between various alternatives, by observing changes in sales in supermarkets as prices or other marketing variables were altered, by questioning shoppers as they left a supermarket and by visiting potential consumers in their homes and performing doorstep interviews.

The same methods are also suitable for providing results that will be of help in the solution of pricing problems. Whichever method is used, great care has to be taken to ensure that the information is of good quality, not distorted by any important bias and generally reliable enough to be used in predicting the behaviour of a large group of consumers. There are many texts available that consider in detail the problems of obtaining good quality data from the public and of the subsequent analysis,[1] hence only the more relevant aspects of data collection will be discussed here.

First, consider a doorstep survey in which housewives are asked which of a pair of brands of some commodity they would buy at the stated prices if they met with the same situation in a supermarket. One of the first decisions concerns the choice of subjects to be interviewed. If there is a complete list of the households in the area, then one of the methods is to select a *random sample*. This is done by using a random procedure such that every household on the list has

---

[1] Cf. e.g. Robert Ferber and P. J. Verdoorn, *Research Methods in Economics and Business*, Macmillan, New York, 1962; Matilda White Riley, *Sociological Research, Vol. I: A Case Approach, Vol. II: Exercises and Manual*, Harcourt, Brace & World, New York, 1963; Leslie Kish, *Survey Sampling*, John Wiley & Sons, New York, 1965; C. A. Moser and G. Kalton, *Survey Methods in Social Investigations*, 2nd edn, Heinemann Educational Books, London, 1971; Des Raj, *The Design of Sample Surveys*, McGraw-Hill, New York, 1972; Ernest Krausz and S. H. Miller, *Social Research Design*, Longman, London, 1974; Jonathan Silvey, *Deciphering Data – The analysis of social surveys*, Longman, London, 1975; Peter Chambers, *Techniques of Data Collection*, Longman, London, 1976; Frank Yates, *Sampling Methods for Censuses and Surveys*, Macmillan, London, 1981; Arlene Fink and Jaqueline Kosecoff, *How to Conduct Surveys: A Step-by-Step Guide*, Sage Publications, Beverly Hills, CA, 1985; and Pamela L. Alreck and Robert B. Settle, *The Survey Research Handbook*, Dow Jones – Irwin, New York, 1985.

an equal chance of being selected. One way of doing this is by the use of a table of random numbers. Once the list is selected, every household on it should be visited and questioned.

As there may be considerable distances between some of the households on the list, the cost of using this technique may be too large in practice. A somewhat less expensive alternative is to select first a few sub-areas in the city to be investigated and apply random sampling to the households in these sub-areas only. The sub-areas should be carefully chosen so that between them they properly represent the whole city in respect of the socio-economic groups. If the areas are not properly balanced, it might be necessary to weight the results in order to make the sample more representative of the entire city.

Once the list is formed, it is important to keep to it. One of the highly reprehensible biases in survey work arises when a next-door neighbour is interviewed if the person originally selected is not in when the field worker first tries to make contact. Certain types of housewives are less likely to be found at home, such as those without children or where both spouses go out to work, compared to others, particularly those with very young children and old-age pensioners. Thus, replacing a household with no one in at the time of the intended interview by a neighbouring household will bias the sample away from certain groups and towards others. The correct procedure is to call back at least three times, if necessary, to find someone in, and to ask a neighbour what would be the best time for the next call. If all these efforts are unsuccessful or if the member of the household concerned refuses to co-operate, the address should be replaced by another selected at random. It is not an ideal solution but the best one can do.

For street interviews and simulated shop situation experiments it is not usually possible to use a random sampling technique. The nearest alternative is known as *quota sampling*. Provided that the relative sizes of the various socio-economic groups are known for the area, the field workers can be instructed to ensure that their own sets of interviews have approximately this same breakdown. This is not always readily achieved, but properly trained interviewers should be able to reduce the potential bias to negligible proportions, especially if their work is also effectively supervised.

It is very important that the interviewers should not lead the subjects into giving particular answers. In order to avoid this, it is advisable not to reveal the fundamental objective of the study to the interviewers, lest they might be tempted to obtain answers that they think will please the investigator and thus introduce a serious bias into the data.

In order to make sure that the interviews are genuine, the name and address of each subject should be recorded. If the interviewers are informed in advance that spot checks will be made, this will eliminate the risk of faked questionnaires.

Biases can also arise from the construction of the questionnaire. The greatest possible care should be taken to ensure that each of the questions is free from ambiguity, easily understood and not likely to lead to a particular answer. It is absolutely essential that a pilot study be conducted to discover possible problems with the questionnaire and with the instructions given to the interviewers. It is further important that a trial analysis of the replies obtained in the pilot study be undertaken. If this is not done, the possibility that some important questions are omitted occurs, and it is not unusual to find at this stage that the answers to some of the questions used cannot be sensibly or usefully analysed. If the pilot study reveals the presence of some important problem, it is vital that a second pilot be undertaken, to ensure that the problem previously recognized has been overcome and that its solution has not introduced any new problem.

A major decision that has to be made in the planning of any survey concerns the number of interviews to be conducted. The general answer is 'the more the better', but there is invariably both a budget constraint and a time limit to consider. Nevertheless, the investigator will still have some alternatives to choose from, as a larger number of interviews can usually be achieved by selecting fewer questions.

The answer to the question of how many interviews should be obtained turns on the extent of the accuracy of the estimates that is required by the investigator. Fortunately, there is a formula that can be used to help with the decision. Suppose that the investigator is interested in the *proportion* of people who hold a certain view, and let the true proportion be P. If out of n persons selected at random p_n are found to hold this view, then, with a probability of approximately 95 per cent, P will be in the region

$$p_n \pm 2 \sqrt{\frac{p_n (1 - p_n)}{n}} \; .$$

Thus, for example, if $n = 900$ and we find $p_n = 1/3$, then the true proportion will, with high probability, be in the region

$$0.33 \pm 2 \sqrt{\frac{0.33 \times 0.67}{900}},$$

that is between 0.299 and 0.361,

which are fairly close bounds. However, if a sample of $n = 100$ had been used, and observed p_n was again $\frac{1}{3}$, the bounds would be 0.236 and 0.424, which are less satisfactory.

To use this formula to decide on a value of n that should provide an estimate of P with sufficient accuracy, the investigator has to apply whatever knowledge is at his disposal in making a preliminary estimate of what p_n is likely to be, and then calculate the ranges for various values of n. The accuracy of the preliminary estimate is not crucial in this process; for example, a preliminary estimate of p_n at 0.40, say, would yield with $n = 900$ a range of $p_n \pm 0.031$, that is to say, a result that does not differ over the first three decimal places from the value found for $p_n = 0.33$.

If the data are to be obtained from a shop experiment, the variation of the prices should, as far as possible, follow the standard patterns described in textbooks of statistics as Randomized Blocks and Latin Squares.

Appendix II to Part II
Conjoint measurement in pricing research

Trevor Watkins

1 Introduction

Under modern conditions price has become that element of the marketing mix which is subject to more frequent changes than any of the others, and it is the strength of buy-response analysis that it can examine the effect of price variation of a given product against the background of the prices of competitive brands while taking all other characteristics of the products concerned as given. There are, however, situations in which it is necessary to treat also certain other elements of the marketing mix as simultaneous variates, as is the case when a functionally similar new product is to be developed or an existing product is to be re-vamped.

This appendix is devoted to the exposition of conjoint measurement, a relatively recent technique in marketing research which is particularly suited to dealing with such problems, and to the exploration of possible pricing research applications.

The underlying principle of conjoint measurement is that consumers 'trade off' features between brands in the choice process because no one brand represents an ideal combination of features (or attributes or characteristics) from their perspectives. The approach here taken is concentrated towards marketing practice rather than towards a mathematical exposition of the theoretical underpinnings of the technique, and realistic examples are given to illustrate practical applications.

2 What is conjoint measurement?

The method is based on a monotonic analysis of variance computer algorithm which essentially decomposes products into their attributes and measures the value of each of these component parts based on consumer judgemental input. As Johnson[1] notes,* 'The basic idea is that by providing consumers with stimuli from among which to choose, we can make inferences about their value systems based on behaviour rather than upon self reports. The word conjoint has to do with the fact that we measure relative values of things considered jointly which might be unmeasurable taken one at a time'. Thus, in deciding which model of car to buy a consumer may consider such attributes as seating capacity, price, top speed, rate of acceleration, name, and so on. Whilst the consumer may not put a

---

*See end of this appendix for references.

value of any one of these attributes in isolation, they are considered in combination as constituent parts of the total product offering. Because it is unlikely that the consumer will find an ideal combination of attribute levels in any one product offering, the technique is based on the assumption that a trade off between attribute levels will occur based on the consumer's value system for the attributes. Thus it is likely that no available alternative will appear to the consumer to be clearly better on every dimension of interest.

As with many multivariate techniques applied in marketing, conjoint measurement was developed in another social science discipline and transferred across. Thus early work by Debreu[2] in 1960 and by Luce and Tukey[3] in 1964 on psychological issues led to the publication by Kruskal[4] in 1965 of a technique for measurement based on a simple method of data collection and on the processing of the data by a computer programme known as MONANOVA. The first marketing application was published by Green and Rao[5] in 1971. Subsequently further advances were made leading to the development of other computer algorithms for conjoint measurement using either 'pair-wise' comparison of attributes or 'full-model' comparison (see below). Various approaches were compared by Jain et al.[6] in 1979. The major UK applications of the techniques of which there are few, feature in publications by Westwood et al.[7] in 1974 and by Blamires[8] in 1981.

3 How does the technique work?

Data are collected from the respondents in the form of ranking judgements about a range of possible attribute levels of products or services. For example, suppose a pricing decision has to be made for a new chocolate confectionery brand which could have one of two fillings (nut or caramel), one of two chocolate types (milk or dark) and one of three prices. This gives a rise of $2 \times 2 \times 3 = 12$ possibilities. The consumer is asked to rank these 12 possible products in order of preference, usually using a matrix structure of the type shown in Table AII.1.

Rankings are shown within the matrix with most preferred combination $= 12$, least preferred $= 1$. It follows that a milk chocolate bar with caramel filling offered at a retail price of 10p promises to be the most successful of the alternatives considered.

Table AII.1
Hypothetical preference price rankings for a new chocolate confectionery brand

	P_1	P_2	P_3	
Milk chocolate, nut filling	4	8	2	
Milk chocolate, caramel filling	10	12	7	e.g. $P_1 = 9\text{p}$
Dark chocolate, nut filling	3	6	1	$P_2 = 10\text{p}$
Dark chocolate, caramel filling	9	11	5	$P_3 = 11\text{p}$

It should be noted that this is a simplified example, in most cases more attributes and/or attribute levels would be necessary. In this case it is possible to use a pair-wise comparison[9] in which each possible pair of attributes is considered by consumers at each attribute level (i.e. in this example, chocolate type v filling, chocolate type v price, filling v price). The consumers' ranking task is simplified under conditions where the process could become absurdly complex. For example, in the above case, five names, six designs and four price levels would mean $5 \times 6 \times 4 = 120$ rankings in the full model which is clearly impractical in terms of realism and respondent fatigue. In the literature the term 'trade-off models' tends to be applied to the pair-wise comparison method. The full model can employ a fractional factorial design[10] to make the respondents' task easier.

Before the ranking data can be analysed, the basic form of the relationship between product attributes and preference rankings must be specified. In most applications the simplest approach, that of an additive relationship, is used although Johnson[11] describes an application in which a multiplicative model provided a better fit. The linear additive model assumes that total utility to the consumer is simply the sum of the utility of the parts, the attribute levels.

A computer-based algorithm, such as MONANOVA, is then used to attempt to place utility values of each attribute level so as to 'explain' the consumers' preference rankings. Thus ordinally scaled input is converted into interval scaled output. This forms a major attraction of the technique, as it is argued that the consumers' judgemental input is more realistic in that they are likely to decide only that one brand is preferred to another at a particular price rather than specifying by how much it is preferred.

Kruskal developed a 'goodness of fit' measure to assess the success of the data transformation. This he defined as:

$$\text{Stress} = S = \sqrt{\frac{\sum (Ri - \hat{R}i)^2}{\sum (\hat{R}i - R)^2}}$$

where Ri is the actual monotonic transformation of the rank of version i ($i = 1 \dots n$ versions, in this case 12) and $\hat{R}i$ is the predicted rank from the calculated scale values. R is the mean of the estimated rankings.

Thus the numerator is an expression of the closeness of fit of the predicted and the actual rankings and the denominator is a scale factor. The approach is not dissimilar to standard deviation calculations in simple statistics and is indeed close to Kruskal's measure of stress applied in the closely related technique of non-metric multi-dimensional scaling[12]. Clearly, a better fit is achieved when S is smaller because the numerator approaches 0 as the predicted and actual ranks are closer. Thus $S = 0$ is a perfect match between the predicted and actual values.

In general, the algorithm in MONANOVA will find a solution so as to maximize the goodness of fit (minimize S) between the two rank orders. A starting solution is generated and the algorithm then uses an iterative process to improve the solution (reduce the value of S) until a stop criterion is reached. This may be in terms of a maximum number of iterations or a minimum stated improvement in the value of S, for example.

Thus, although the goodness of fit (stress) measure concerns the two rank orders, the partial utility values associated with the predicted ranks can also be used in marketing planning. In the

Table AII.2
Derived utility scales in chocolate example

Attribute level	Estimated utility value
Milk chocolate	0.2
Dark chocolate	− 0.2
Nut filling	− 1.4
Caramel filling	1.2
Price level 1	0.1
Price level 2	1.3
Price level 3	− 1.3

simple example given in Table AII.1, the utility scales values calculated by the MONANOVA programmes were as in Table AII.2.

These data can be interpreted for marketing decision making. Thus for example, a switch from nut to caramel filling (gain of 2.6 units) of utility is equal for this consumer to a price increase from $P2$ to $P3$ (loss of 2.6 units of utility) and could be used to justify a higher price for this new product on this evidence. Using the additive model assumed, these utility values can be summed for each of the 12 versions which the hypothetical consumer ranked and the fit compared as in Table AII.3.

Table AII.3
Total utilities predicted and actual rankings in chocolate example

Product version	Predicted total utility	Predicted rank	Actual rank
MNP_1	− 1.1	4	4
MNP_2	0.1	7.5	8
MNP_3	− 2.5	2	2
DNP_1	− 1.5	3	3
DNP_2	− 0.3	5.5	6
DNP_3	− 2.9	1	1
MCP_1	1.5	10	10
MCP_2	2.7	12	12
MCP_3	0.1	7.5	7
DCP_1	1.1	9	9
DCP_2	2.3	11	11
DCP_3	− 0.3	5.5	5

Key: M = milk chocolate; D = plain chocolate; N = nut filling; C = caramel filling; P_1–P_3 = price levels. (In the case of a tie, the mean position is taken.)

In practical terms P_2 (10p) is the most preferred price (other things being equal) with P_1 (9p) being an alternative. P_3 (11p) has a strong negative effect and should not on this evidence be considered. The brand manager should use P_2 as the price on this evidence if it is at all possible.

Table AII.3 shows a very close fit which is almost exact apart from two tied rankings. Such ties are much more likely to occur in simple examples than they are in more complex attribute level combinations.

Applying the Kruskal Stress formula to these data:

$$S \sqrt{\frac{1}{140}} = 0.0845$$

which is a very low value illustrating a very close fit of the actual and predicted ranks. Because the data are ordinal it is not possible to apply the usual statistical significance tests such as t-tests which only apply to normally distributed data although some non-parametric tests have been applied (see below). Also, the estimated interval scale for the partial utilities is of arbitrary origin and unit and may be transformed for convenience by arithmetic operations.

Before examining practical pricing applications for the technique it is necessary to examine briefly the advantages and disadvantages of the process.

4 Advantages of conjoint measurement

The major advantage is the data collection method. A priori, it would appear to be more realistic for the respondent to consider a complete brand with specific attribute levels than to try directly to question the respondent on individual elements (such as price) of the brand. Moreover it is possible to use visual aids to enhance realism; dummy packs, advertisements or even product samples can be used in the data collection process. Ranking can also be argued to be more realistic and more akin to how consumers choose between alternative brands. They are likely to decide if one brand is better than another overall, not necessarily by *how much* it is better, that is, they make ordinal-scaled and not interval-scaled judgements in making purchasing decisions.

The output from the analysis offers a manager valuable insights into consumer choice. As Green and Wind[13] postulate, 'Being able to separate overall judgements into psychological components in this manner can provide a manager with valuable information about the relative importance of various attributes of a product. It can also provide information about the value of various levels of a single attribute'. Thus pricing decisions can be considered in the light of consumer utility judgements and compensating changes could be introduced for a price change.

If the conjoint analysis is repeated across a representative sample of a target market then, in conjunction with other data on consumer characteristics, the output can be used as a basis for market segmentation. The technique could identify the most (and the least) price-sensitive segments, which could then be used to guide marketing action. This will be illustrated by the examples which follow in Section 6.

Because the respondents' trade-offs between attributes are explicitly taken into account, the problems involved in asking questions about 'ideal' combinations of attributes, which are essentially unrealistic, are avoided. Bias in response, such as rationalizing, halo-effects and 'more is always better' thinking is avoided. For instance, in the above example price level 2 is most preferred rather than the cheapest price (P_1). The technique also means that both metric attributes (for example, price) and non-metric attributes (brand name, pack design) can be compared together even when they are considerably different.

5 Disadvantages of conjoint measurement

It is necessary to define the brand attributes and their particular levels before the data collection commences. Consumer responses are made to specific attribute combinations. If these attributes are not all the relevant ones for the consumer, then although the method will still operate, the obtained results will be misleading. It is thus necessary to undertake preliminary research with a pilot group of consumers to ensure that the criteria for the research are identified exactly and correctly.

As already noted, the complexity of the task for respondents increases rapidly as more attributes and/or levels are added. For a realistic assessment, an upper limit of perhaps 25–30 rankings by a single respondent seems feasible. This may involve a more complex design and/or an elimination of some of the interaction effects.

The model specification must also be identified at the outset of the research. In the above example an additive model is used; it would have been possible to multiply rather than add the calculated utility values, for example. Unfortunately, the wrong model specification is not necessarily signalled by a high value of S. An assumption of the technique is that the attributes are independent of each other. Thus there is no interaction between variables, that is, the degree of our hypothetical respondents' liking for nut filling does not vary according to price or type of chocolate. If such interaction does occur, it can be detected by using Kendall's tau statistic which can be used as an alternative to Kruskal's Stress measure.[15] As already noted, significance testing of the goodness of fit criterion is not possible and the results should be validated outside the method before use.

Finally, some attributes may have a threshold level below which there can be no trade-off for other attributes by consumers. Again, this should be identified by preliminary research so that all attribute levels included in the research are above this threshold level. An example might be a car which must be capable of at least 20 miles per gallon before a consumer would even consider buying it, whatever the price or other relevant attributes. Thus the levels of this attribute in the conjoint analysis must be greater than 20.

On balance, the technique has limitations which can be overcome and potential marketing applications which seem to offer a significant advance in practical pricing research. Fenwick[16] concludes his assessment of the technique with a word of warning:

> Despite ... dangers conjoint measurement promises to be a powerful analytical tool ... Nonetheless, conjoint analysis is no panacea and the pitfalls for the unwary are severe. In particular, the technique is such that goodness of fit provides little indication of the appropriateness of the underlying model, or of the trade-off scales obtained. Consequently analysis results should never be applied without substantial validation.

6 Applications of conjoint measurement in pricing research

A number of practical applications have been reported and these will be considered briefly from the pricing perspective.

(a) Colour TV choice Anttila, van den Hauvel and Möller[17] report an application of conjoint measurement in segmenting the market for colour TVs. They used four price levels, three brand names, three screen sizes, three levels of colour reproduction, two designs and no guarantee or one year's guarantee (determined in a pre-study). Using a fractional factorial design in which each of 200 respondents ranked 26 product compilations, data were collected in personal interviews. By carrying out an individual respondent conjoint analysis and then aggregating across respondents, they were able to isolate particular market segments on the basis of relative attribute

importance by using a cluster analysis.

These are shown in Table AII.4 on the basis of these aggregated data. Figure AII.2 shows the utility values of each attribute level included in the analysis.

Thus the price-sensitive segment were less concerned about colour reproduction than respondents as a whole, whereas the largest, quality prone segment were price-insensitive but highly influenced by colour reproduction, brand name and the availability of a one-year guarantee. The third segment shows above-average concern with screen size and design. As they report,

> ... the results were used for an evaluation of the competitiveness of the company's colour TV models within the segments. This evaluation showed a good coverage of the segments by the current product line except for the design-size conscious segment. After a follow-up research project designated to have a better estimate of the total size of this segment ... a new model specially designed for this segment was added to the product line.[18]

(b) Electronic calculator market: developing a new product Lunn and Blackston[19] report an application of pairwise conjoint measurement (trade-off analysis) in an attempt to model the market for electronic calculators. Nine product features were identified and 150 respondents in each of three countries were used. The results revealed the importance of the utility of each attribute level *relative* to other attribute levels. Thus a price rise of £3 from the basic price (loss of 7 units of utility) could be offset by adding an all function single memory in place of a constant open and only memory (gain of 7 units of utility) for the average respondent. This then led to more detailed development work which in turn led to a range of calculators optimally specified in price and function terms.

(c) Adhesive market modelling Lunn and Blackston[20] also report on the use of full model conjoint measurement analysis in the household adhesive market which was commissioned by a company when a competitive brand was introduced into a test market area which had an innovative container with a new type of applicator. The trade-off model was used to help determine the company's competitive reaction to the new test brand, by disaggregating both the test and the company's existing brand into major attributes and exploring consumers' priorities for these features. The relevant features are

Table AII.4

Relative attribute importances for three utility segments

Attribute	N = 200 Total response %	N = 59 Price-sensitive segment %	N = 71 Quality prone segment %	N = 35 Design-size conscious segment %
Price	17	44	9	5
Screen size	14	15	12	24
Brand name	22	14	24	12
Colour reproduction	31	20	38	25
Guarantee	11	5	16	4
Design	5	2	1	30

Source: adopted from Anttila *et al.*, (1980).

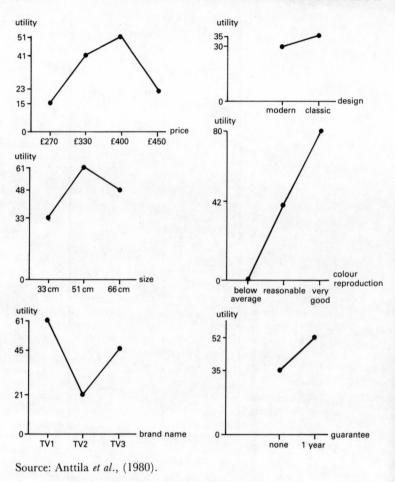

Source: Anttila *et al.*, (1980).

Figure AII.2   Utility values of six attributes of colour TVs

shown in Table AII.5. Respondents ranked the product offerings made up of combinations of these features. The sample involved two types of respondents:

(i) Those involved in testing the new product.
(ii) Those who had only the concept explained to them.

The results obtained from the conjoint analysis were compared for these two groups of respondents. Lunn and Blackston report the findings as follows:

Table AII.5
Adhesive market model: product attributes

Brand name	Brand leader	New brand
Container	Standard	Innovative
Bottle colour	Green	Red
Adhesive power	Greater than all the others Amongst the strongest Among the weaker ones	
Price	30p, 35p, 40p, 45p, 50p, 55p	

Source: Lunn and Blackston (1978).

- The relative appeal of the two types of container was about 3 to 2 in favour of the innovative one amongst the users who had only seen the concept. Amongst those who had tried it, the ratio was 4 to 1.
- Both groups shared similar priorities with regard to adhesive power.
- The strength of the brand leader's name was apparently related to the belief in its unique product superiority. Amongst the 'concept' group, the relative appeal of the brand names was 4 to 1 in favour of the brand leader's; amongst the 'product' group – bereft of its product superiority – it had no advantage at all.

The danger represented by the new brand was very clear, and the company set out to consider its optimal tactics. It was decided to attempt to slow down consumer trial of the new brand by cutting the price of their own brand in the test market area. The question was 'By how much?' The 'trade-off' results provided an answer. It is possible to make direct comparisons between different features – for example, is the gain in 'utility' represented by a price-cut from 35p to 30p greater than the loss in 'utility' entailed in having a standard container rather than an innovative one?

The results provided information in two other respects. They demonstrated that the new brand only required trial to gain consumer acceptance, so that the company's response should be one with immediate effect. They showed secondly, that the benefits of the new brand did not need the support of persuasive theme advertising, because they were self-evident to the user. This implied that, in the short term, the only way to combat the new brand was on price.[21]

These examples illustrate the practical value of the technique in pricing decisions, even though the pricing element is only one attribute which is considered in the analysis in conjunction with a realistic version.

7 Recent developments of the technique

Aspden and Gurd[22] have reported a model which they claim
develops the conjoint method in order to measure consumers' price
sensitivity. The essential difference is in the method of data
collection in which:

> ... each respondent is asked to make a series of choices between a range of
> options. The options are placed before the respondent and each has a
> price attached to it. Initially all prices are identical and at the bottom end
> of the range which pertains in the market under study. Each time an
> option is chosen, its price is raised by a fixed interval and the respondent
> chooses again.[23]

This approach involving repeated respondent choice making,
with price the only changing variable, seems less realistic than the
basic conjoint measurement and little evidence is presented on the
validity of the method.

Goldberg, Green and Wind[24] have recently expressed concern
about the independent attribute assumption of conjoint measurement specifically relating to price, which they claim is often highly
correlated with other product attribute levels which, if ignored,
could affect result validity. They also question the bundling issue:

> ... the question is whether one can predict a respondent's evaluation of a
> bundle of product attributes and price as a simple linear function of the
> summed part worths of the entities making up the bundle when each
> entity is presented with its actual price.[25]

This applies only in limited applications and Goldberg *et al.* explore
an example on the pricing of hotel amenities.

They apply a categorical conjoint analysis which unlike ordinal
methods such as MONANOVA has been very little used. Here the
basic idea is 'to find scale values associated with the independent
variables (expressed as dummies) such that additive combinations
of these scale values maximally correlate with similarly obtained
scale values for the response categories'.[26] They applied the
technique using a dummy variable canonical correlation programme
on data collected from 180 adults who were recent business users of
hotel facilities. Each respondent supplied one of three possible
answers to each hotel amenity-price combination. These three
possible answers were:

(a) Comes closest to describing your usual hotel/motel.

(b) Completely unacceptable.

(c) Represents what you want and are willing to pay for.

Respondents were then asked to distribute 100 points across six facets of hotel service being considered to reflect the relative importance of each attribute. Finally full description cards to describe a particular combination of hotel facilities were used and respondents were asked to indicate the likelihood that they would stay there.

The major findings were that:

- Simple functions of respondents' self explicated utilities for bundle components are not good predictors of their preferences for the total bundle of hotel amenities.
- The overall bundle price adds significantly to the accounted for variance in preference for hotel bundles.
- As expected, the price-preference function is a downward sloping demand curve.
- The hybrid categorical conjoint analysis model produced 'reasonable' results which, together with other information from the study, provided management with specific guidelines for the development of a new hotel chain.

Blamires[27] has criticized the conjoint analysis data collection approach because the alternatives presented to the respondent are not necessarily the ones which the respondent would consider in making a real purchasing decision. Also he argues that a high price may in practice make the respondent buy the same brand but at another store (that is, shop around for the lowest price of that preferred brand). This option, he argues, is not available (but presumably could be incorporated into the research design). Respondents may also wish to appear rational to the interviewer which may affect the rankings selected. This is a major problem for any form of pricing research.

Blamires suggests a hybrid model which he claims is a bridge between Gabor and Granger's buy-response method and trade-off analysis. However, the technique is retail-orientated and relates to fast moving consumer goods only. It disaggregates demand curves by price levels to assess price sensitivity by collecting data in a 'simulated store' testing procedure for added realism. It does not seem to be a new method, rather a special case of the buy-response method, individualizing the approach according to respondent's next most preferred brand or brand repertoire and by offering the choice to shop elsewhere.

8 Conclusions

This type of model applies in situations where products are sold as basic units with various add-on optional extras. It is a complex procedure. In the UK context, it is suggested that the development of applications of this technique is constrained by the rate of acceptance by marketing managers. Although there is evidence of a number of applications of the technique and of a number of market research agencies offering models based on conjoint analysis, these are relatively limited and credibility needs to be developed. This can only occur when managers are convinced that the technique can make a cost-effective contribution to their pricing decisions.

This should occur over time as and when a successful 'track record' for the application of the technique develops.

Future prospects for the use of conjoint measurement are bright if it is used with care and common sense. It has valuable diagnostic power and can give very useful indications of the likely effects of alternative strategies. It is flexible and versatile and, on balance, shows great promise in consumer pricing assessments which is a difficult research area.

References

1. Johnson, R. M. (1974), 'Trade Off Analysis of Consumer Values', *Journal of Marketing Research*, **11**, (May), p. 121.
2. Debreu, G. (1960), 'Topological Methods in Cardinal Utility Theory', in Arrow K. J., Karlins and Suppes P. (eds), *Mathematical Models in the Social Sciences*, Stanford, CA: Stanford University Press.
3. Luce, R. D. and Tukey, J. W., (1964), 'Simultaneous Conjoint Measurement: a New Type of Fundamental Measurement', *Journal of Mathematical Psychology*, **1**, (February), pp. 1–27.
4. Kruskal, J. B. (1965), 'Analysis of Factorial Experiments by Estimating Monotone Transformations of the Data', *Journal of the Royal Statistical Society*, Series B, **27**, (2), pp. 251–63.
5. Green, P. E. and Rao, V. R. (1971), 'Conjoint Measurement for Quantifying Judgemental Data', *Journal of Marketing Research*, **8**, (August), pp. 355–63.
6. Jain, J. K., Acito, F., Malhotra, N. K. and Mahajan, V. (1979), 'A Comparison of the Internal Validity of Alternative Parmeter Estimation Methods in Decompositional Multiattribute Preference Models', *Journal of Marketing Research*, **16**, (August), pp. 313–322.
7. Westwood, D., Lunn, J. A. and Beazley, D. (1974), 'The Trade Off Model and its Extensions', *Journal of the Market Research Society*, **16**, (3), pp. 227–241.

8. Blamires, C. (1981), 'Pricing Research Techniques: a Preview and a New Approach', *Journal of the Market Research Society*, **23**, (3), pp. 103–127.

9. Johnson *Op cit.*

10. Green, P. E., Carroll, J. D. and Carmore, F. J. (1978), 'Some New Types of Fractional Factorial Designs for Marketing Experiments', in Sheth, J. N. (ed.), *Research in Marketing*, Vol. 1, Greenwich CT: JAI Press, pp. 99–122.

11. Johnson *Op cit.*

12. Kruskal, J. B. (1964), 'Non metric multi-dimensional scaling: a numerical method', *Psychometrika*, **29**, pp. 115–129.

13. Green, P. E. and Wind, Y. (1975), 'New Ways to Measure Consumers' Judgements', *Harvard Business Review*, **53**, (July–August), p. 108.

14. Brown, G., Copeland, T. and Millward, M. (1973), 'Monadic Testing of New Products – an Old Problem and Some Partial Solutions', *Journal of the Market Research Society*, **15**, (2), pp. 112–131.

15. Johnson *Op cit*, p. 125.

16. Fenwick, I. (1978), 'A Users Guide to Conjoint Measurement in Marketing', *European Journal of Marketing* **12**, (2) p. 210–1.

17. Anttila, M., van den Heuval, R. R. and Möller, K. (1980), 'Conjoint Measurement for Marketing Management', *European Journal of Marketing*, **14**, (7), pp. 397–408.

18. Anttila *et al. Op cit*, p. 406.

19. Lunn, J. A. and Blackston, M. M. (1978), 'An Assessment of Micro-Behavioural Modelling and its Cost Effectiveness', *Bristol ESOMAR*, pp. 723–753.

20. Lunn and Blackston *Op cit.*

21. Lunn and Blackston *Op cit.*

22. Aspden, J. and Gurd, P. (1981), 'A tool of the Eighties – Pricing Sensitivity Model', *Proceedings of the Market Research Society* Conference, pp. 139–148.

23. Aspden and Gurd *Op cit*, p. 143.

24. Goldberg, S. M., Green, P. E. and Wind, Y. (1984), 'Conjoint Analysis of Price Premiums for Hotel Amenities', *Journal of Business*, **57**, (1), pt 2 pp. S111–S132.

25. Goldberg *et al. Op cit*, p. S111.

26. Goldberg *et al. Op cit*, p. S116.

27. Blamires *Op cit.*

Additional references

Akaah, I. P. and Korgaonkar, P. A. (1983), 'An Empirical Comparison of the Predictive Validity of Self-Explicated, Huber-Hybrid, Traditional Conjoint and Hybrid Conjoint Models', *Journal of Marketing Research*, **20**, (2), pp. 187–197.

Blackston, M. and van der Zanden, N. (1980), 'Validity of Conjoint Analysis: Some Real Market Results', *European Research*, **8**, (6), pp. 243–50.

Blamires, C. (1987), ' "Trade-off" Pricing Research', *Journal of the Market Research Society*, **29**, (2), pp. 133–52.

Bush, A. J. and Hair Jr, J. F. (1985), 'Improving the Predictive Power of Conjoint Analysis: The Use of Factor Analysis and Cluster Analysis', *Journal of Marketing Research*, **22**, (2), pp. 168–184.

Catlin, P. and Wittink, D. R. (1982), 'Commercial Use of Conjoint Analysis: A Survey', *Journal of Marketing*, **46**, (3), pp. 44–53.

Catlin, P., Gelfand, A. E. and Danes, J. (1983), 'A Simple Bayesian Procedure for Estimation in a Conjoint Model', *Journal of Marketing Research*, **20**, (1), pp. 29–35.

Christopher, M. (1982), 'Value-in-Use Pricing', *European Journal of Marketing*, **16**, (5), pp. 35–46.

Green, P. E. (1984), 'Hybrid Models for Conjoint Analysis: An Expository Review', *Journal of Marketing Research*, **21**, (2), pp. 155–169.

Green, P. E., Carroll, J. D. and Goldberg, S. M. (1981), 'A General Approach to Product Design Optimization via Conjoint Analysis', *Journal of Marketing*, **45**, (3), pp. 17–37.

Green, P. E. and Wind, Y. (1973), *Multiattribute Decisions in Marketing: A Measurement Approach*, Hinsdale, IL: Dryden Press.

Leigh, T. Wm., MacKay, D. B. and Summers, J. O. (1984), 'Reliability and Validity of Conjoint Analysis and Self-Explicated Weights: A Comparison', *Journal of Marketing Research*, **21**, (4), pp. 456–462.

Mahajan, V., Green, P. E. and Goldberg, S. M. (1982), 'A Conjoint Model for Measuring Self-and-Cross-Price/Demand Relationships', *Journal of Marketing Research*, **19**, (3), pp. 334–342.

Schiffman, S. S. *et al.* (1981), *Introduction to Multidimensional Scaling*, New York, Academic Press.

Segal, M. N. (1982), 'Reliability of Conjoint Analysis: Contrasting Data Collection Procedures', *Journal of Marketing Research*, **19**, (1), pp. 139–143.

Shrinivasan, V., Jain, A. K. and Malhotra, N. K. (1983), 'Improving Predictive Power of Conjoint Analysis by Constrained Parameter Estimation', *Journal of Marketing Research*, **20**, (4), pp. 433–438.

Wittink, D. R. and Cattin, P. 'Alternative Estimation Methods for Conjoint Analysis: A Monté Carlo Study', *Journal of Marketing Research*, **18**, (1), pp. 101–106.

Software:

Adaptive Conjoint Analysis System (ACA), Ketchum, ID: Sawtooth Software, Inc., 1985.

Conjoint Designer, New York: Bretton-Clark, 1985.

Nottingham papers on pricing

The publications are listed in chronological order

André Gabor, 'A Note on Block Tariffs', *Review of Economic Studies*, **XXIII**, (1), 1955, pp. 32–41.

I. F. Pearce, 'A Study in Price Policy', *Economica*, **23**, May 1956, pp. 114–27.

I. F. Pearce and Lloyd R. Amey, 'Price Policy with a Branded Product', *Review of Economic Studies*, **XXIV**, (1), 1956, pp. 49–60.

André Gabor and C. W. J. Granger, 'On the Price Consciousness of Consumers', *Applied Statistics*, **X**, (3), 1961, pp. 170–88.

André Gabor and C. W. J. Granger, 'Price Sensitivity of the Consumer', *Journal of Advertising Research*, **4**, (4), December 1964, pp. 40–44.

André Gabor and C. W. J. Granger, 'The Pricing of New Products', *Scientific Business*, August, 1965, pp. 3–12.

André Gabor and C. W. J. Granger, 'Price as an Indicator of Quality: Report on an Enquiry', *Economica*, **33**, February 1966, pp. 43–70.

André Gabor, 'Comment on Peak Loads and Efficient Pricing', *Quarterly Journal of Economics*, **LXXX**, (3), August 1966, pp. 472–80.

André Gabor, 'Pricing Policies for Successful Marketing', *Business*, October 1966.

André Gabor, 'Pricing in Theory and Practice', *Management Decision*, Summer 1967, pp. 28–33.

André Gabor, 'Determining your Price Structure at Home and Abroad', *PERA Conference Proceedings*, 1968, pp. 4:1–8.

André Gabor and C. W. J. Granger, 'The Attitude of the Consumer to Prices', in *Pricing Strategy*, (B. Taylor and G. Wills, eds), Staples Press, London, 1969, pp. 132–51.

A. P. Sowter, André Gabor and C. W. J. Granger, 'The Influence of Price Differences on Brand Shares and Switching', *British Journal of Marketing*, Winter 1969, pp. 223–30.

André Gabor, 'What Price Will Consumers Pay?' *Marketing*, April 1970, pp. 28–31.

André Gabor, C. W. J. Granger and A. P. Sowter, 'Real and Hypothetical Shop Situations in Market Research', *Journal of Marketing Research*, **VII**, August 1970, pp. 355–59.

André Gabor, 'Marketing's Role in Investment Decisions', *Marketing*, September 1970, pp. 44–47.

André Gabor and Anthony P. Sowter, 'The Customers' Views', *Co-operative Management and Marketing*, December, 1970, pp. 46–50.

Anthony P. Sowter, 'How Competitive is the Co-op?', *Co-operative Management and Marketing*, January 1971.

André Gabor, 'New Product Pricing', *Marketing*, February 1971, pp. 46–49.

A. P. Sowter, André Gabor and C. W. J. Granger, 'The Effect of Price on Choice: A Theoretical and Empirical Investigation', *Applied Economics*, **2**, (3), 1971 pp. 167–81.

André Gabor, C. W. J. Granger and A. P. Sowter, 'Comments on Psychophysics of Prices', *Journal of Marketing Research*, **VIII**, May 1971, pp. 251–52.

C. W. J. Granger and A. Billson, 'Consumers' Attitudes Toward Package Size and Price', *Journal of Marketing Research*, **IX**, August 1972, pp. 239–48.

A. Billson, A. Gabor, C. W. J. Granger and A. P. Sowter, *Decimalisation and the Consumer*, SSRC, London and Nottingham University Consumer Study Group, October 1972.

André Gabor and C. W. J. Granger, 'Ownership and Acquisition of Consumer Durables', *European Journal of Marketing*, **6**, (4), Winter 1972/73, pp. 234–48.

André Gabor, 'Price and Consumer Behaviour – A Review', *OMEGA*, **1**, (3), 1973, pp. 279–96.

André Gabor, 'How to Compete', *Management Today*, May 1973, pp. 119–27.

André Gabor, 'Pricing in the Retail Business', *Marketing*, June 1973, pp. 33–35.

André Gabor and C. W. J. Granger, 'A Systematic Approach to Effective Pricing', in *Marketing Concepts and Strategies in the Next Decade*, (L. W. Rodger, ed.), Cassell/Associated Business Programmes, London, 1973 pp. 171–94.

A. P. Sowter, 'Pricing Models', *Bulletin of the Institute of Mathematics and its Applications*, **9**, (11), November 1973, pp. 345–47.

André Gabor and J. M. Bates, 'Comment on Jaguar's Pricing Policy', *European Journal of Marketing*, **8**, (2), 1974, pp. 180–82.

André Gabor, 'Customer Oriented Pricing', in *Research into Retailing and Distribution*, (D. Thorpe, ed.), Saxon House and Lexington Books, Farnborough, 1974, pp. 43–54.

André Gabor, 'The Theory of Constant Arc Elasticity Functions', *Bulletin of Economic Research*, **26**, (2), November 1974, pp. 114–27.

André Gabor, 'Price and Consumer Protection', in *Proceedings of Workshop II*, International Institute of Management, Berlin, 1975, pp. G:1–15.

André Gabor, 'A Further Note on Arc Elasticity', *Bulletin of Economic Research*, **27**, (2), November 1976, p. 127.

André Gabor, 'Pricing for Profit', in *The Director's Handbook*, (G. Bull, ed.), McGraw-Hill, London, 1977.

André Gabor, David Morris and David Reason, 'Price Distributions, Price Comparison Surveys and Price Competition', *Journal of Consumer Policy*, **2**, 1978, pp. 349–356.

André Gabor, 'Praktijproblemen bij Prijsbepaling', *NIVE News*, The Hague, **3**, (10), October 1978, p. 3.

André Gabor, 'How to Price', *Management Today*, January 1979, pp. 54–7.
André Gabor, 'Cost-based and Market-oriented Pricing', *The Director*, **31**, (9), March 1979, pp. 29–30.
André Gabor (Guest Editor), *Issues in Pricing Policy* – European Journal of Marketing, **13**, (4), 1979.
André Gabor, *Collected Economics Papers*, MCB Publications, Bradford, published as a special issue of the *International Journal of Social Economics*, **6**, (5), 1979.
André Gabor, *Collected Pricing Papers*, MCB Publications, Bradford, published as a special issue of *Management Decision*, **17**, (8), 1979.
André Gabor, 'Pricing Gets Market Oriented', *Marketing*, November 1979, pp. 75–8.
André Gabor, 'Price and Consumer Protection' and 'Decimalisation and the Consumer', Chapters 3 and 6 of *Economics of Consumer Protection*, (David Morris, ed.), Heinemann Educational Books, London, 1980.
André Gabor, 'Pricing a Convenience Food', *Economics*, **XVI**, (1), Spring 1980, pp. 16–19.
André Gabor, 'Pricing Strategies for Established Brands', *Marketing Trends*, A. C. Nielsen Co., Oxford, 1980, 1, pp. 8–10.
André Gabor, 'On the Theory and Practice of Transfer Pricing', Chapter 9 in *Demand, Equilibrium and Trade*, (Λ. Ingham and Λ. M. Ulph, eds), The Macmillan Press, London, 1984, pp. 149–170.
John M. Bates and André Gabor, 'Price Perception in Creeping Inflation: Report on an Enquiry', *Journal of Economic Psychology*, **7**, (3), 1986, pp. 291–314.
John M. Bates and André Gabor, 'Changes in Subjective Welfare and Purchasing Behaviour', *Journal of the Market Research Society*, **29**, (2), 1987, pp. 183–207.

Several of the above papers have been reprinted in books of readings, including: *Price Policies and Practices*, (D. F. Mulvihill and S. Paranka, eds), John Wiley & Sons, New York, 1967; *Readings in Market Research*, (K. K. Cox, ed.), Appleton-Century-Crofts, New York, 1967; *Readings in Marketing*, (C. J. Dirksen, A. Kroeger & L. C. Lockley, eds), Richard D. Irwin, Homewood, Ill., 1968; *Progress of Management Research*, (N. Farrow, ed.), Penguin Books, Harmondsworth, 1969; *The Environment of Marketing Behavior*, (J. Holloway and R. S. Hancock, eds), John Wiley & Sons, New York, 1969; *Modern Marketing Management*, (R. J. Lawrence and M. J. Thomas, eds), Penguin Books, Harmondsworth, 1971; *Creating and Marketing New Products*, (G. Wills, R. Hayhurst and D. Midgley, eds), Crosby Lockwood Staples, London, 1973; *Analytical Marketing Management*, (P. Doyle, P. Law, C. Weinberg and K. Simmonds, eds), Harper & Row, London, 1974.

Unpublished research reports:

A. P. Sowter and Λ. Billson, 'Practical Problems in Buy-response', Department of Economics, The University of Nottingham, 1975.

A. P. Sowter and Λ. Billson, 'The Further Development and Testing of Theories of Choice', Department of Economics, The University of Nottingham, 1975.

Author Index

Subject Index